Constructing a Chinese School of International Relations

This edited volume provides a critical assessment of current theoretical contestations in the Chinese International Relations (IR) epistemic community and imaginative and innovative production of IR scholarship in the context of China's rapid rise to a global power status. The Chinese IR epistemic community has become one of the most dynamic and fastest growing national branches of global IR community, both in terms of the number of researchers, and increasingly, in terms of the output of publications.

There has been a conscious move from simple efforts aimed at the acquisition of knowledge about IR from the West to purposeful and coordinated efforts intended for the production and creation of knowledge of IR in China. The contributors to this volume examine and debate the possibility and prospect of constructing a (contested) Chinese School of IR as a conscious effort to produce alternative IR knowledge and as an assertion against IR theorization exclusively based on Western experience. It considers the implications of such intellectual creativity, drawing upon local concerns and indigenous sources for the global production of knowledge of IR beyond the West.

Reflecting the varied perspectives of both active participants in the debates within China and observers and critics outside China, this work will be of great interest to students and scholars of IR theory, Non-Western IR and Chinese Studies.

Yongjin Zhang is Professor of International Politics at the University of Bristol. His research interest and publications cut across the disciplinary boundaries of International Relations theory and Chinese history, politics, economic transformation and International Relations.

Teng-chi Chang is an associate Professor at the Department of Political Science, National Taiwan University, Taiwan. He specializes in: China's foreign policy and history, theories of International Relations, Chinese Communist ideology and politics, cross-straits relations and classical theories of sociology.

Worlding Beyond the West

Series editors: Arlene B. Tickner,
Universidad de los Andes, Bogotá
Ole Wæver
University of Copenhagen, Denmark
David Blaney
Macalester College, USA
and
Inanna Hamati-Ataya
Aberystwyth University, UK

Historically, the International Relations (IR) discipline has established its boundaries, issues, and theories based upon Western experience and traditions of thought. This series explores the role of geocultural factors, institutions and academic practices in creating the concepts, epistemologies and methodologies through which IR knowledge is produced. This entails identifying alternatives for thinking about the 'international' that are more in tune with local concerns and traditions outside the West. But it also implies provincializing Western IR and empirically studying the practice of producing IR knowledge at multiple sites within the so-called 'West'.

1 **International Relations Scholarship Around the World**
  Edited by Arlene B. Tickner and Ole Wæver

2 **Thinking the International Differently**
  Edited by Arlene B. Tickner and David L. Blaney

3 **International Relations in France**
  Writing between discipline and state
  Henrik Breitenbauch

4 **Claiming the International**
  Edited by Arlene B. Tickner and David L. Blaney

5 **Border Thinking on the Edges of the West**
  Crossing over the Hellespont
  Andrew Davison

6 **Worlding Brazil**
  Intellectuals, identity and security
  Laura Lima

7 **International Relations and American Dominance**
  A diverse discipline
  Helen Turton

8 **Global Indigenous Politics**
  A subtle revolution
  Sheryl Lightfoot

9 **Constructing a Chinese School of International Relations**
  Ongoing debates and sociological realities
  Edited by Yongjin Zhang and Teng-chi Chang

10 **The International in Security, Security in the International**
  Pinar Bilgin

Constructing a Chinese School of International Relations

Ongoing debates and sociological realities

Edited by Yongjin Zhang and
Teng-chi Chang

LONDON AND NEW YORK

First published 2016
by Routledge
2 Park Square, Milton Park, Abingdon, Oxon OX14 4RN

and by Routledge
711 Third Avenue, New York, NY 10017

Routledge is an imprint of the Taylor & Francis Group, an informa business

© 2016 selection and editorial matter, Yongjin Zhang and Teng-chi Chang; individual chapters, the contributors

The right of Yongjin Zhang and Teng-chi Chang to be identified as author of the editorial material, and of the individual authors as authors of their contributions, has been asserted by them in accordance with sections 77 and 78 of the Copyright, Designs and Patents Act 1988.

All rights reserved. No part of this book may be reprinted or reproduced or utilised in any form or by any electronic, mechanical, or other means, now known or hereafter invented, including photocopying and recording, or in any information storage or retrieval system, without permission in writing from the publishers.

Trademark notice: Product or corporate names may be trademarks or registered trademarks, and are used only for identification and explanation without intent to infringe.

British Library Cataloguing in Publication Data
A catalogue record for this book is available from the British Library

Library of Congress Cataloging in Publication Data
Names: Zhang, Yongjin, author. | Chang, Teng-Chi.
Title: Constructing a Chinese school of IR : ongoing debates and sociological realities / Yongjin Zhang and Teng-Chi Chang (editors).
Other titles: Constructing a Chinese school of international relations
Description: Abingdon, Oxon ; New York, NY : Routledge, 2016. | Series: Worlding beyond the West ; 9 | Includes bibliographical references and index.
Identifiers: LCCN 2016003343| ISBN 9781138910195 (hardback) | ISBN 9781315692432 (ebook)
Subjects: LCSH: China–Foreign relations–Philosophy. | International relations–Philosophy.
Classification: LCC JZ1734 .C66 2016 | DDC 327.51001–dc23
LC record available at https://lccn.loc.gov/2016003343

ISBN: 978-1-138-91019-5 (hbk)
ISBN: 978-1-315-69243-2 (ebk)

Typeset in Times New Roman
by Wearset Ltd, Boldon, Tyne and Wear

Contents

List of contributors vii
Acknowledgements ix

Introduction: the making of Chinese international theory? 1
YONGJIN ZHANG AND TENG-CHI CHANG

PART I
Ongoing debates 15

1 What's in a name? A critical interrogation of the
   "*Chinese School* of *IR*" 17
   L.H.M. LING

2 The "Chinese School" debate: personal reflections 35
   REN XIAO

3 Why is there no Chinese IR theory? A cultural perspective 52
   WANG YIWEI AND HAN XUEQING

4 The rise of China and Chinese IR theories: practice and
   theory-building 68
   WEIXING HU

5 Debating the Chinese School of IR: a reflective review from
   Taiwan 81
   TENG-CHI CHANG

6 Mapping the world from a Chinese perspective? The debate
   on constructing an IR theory with Chinese characteristics 98
   NELE NOESSELT

PART II
Towards sociological realities 113

7 The English and Chinese Schools of International Relations: comparisons and lessons 115
   WANG JIANGLI AND BARRY BUZAN

8 Navigating the core-periphery structures of "global" IR: dialogues and audiences for the Chinese School as traveling theory 143
   PETER MARCUS KRISTENSEN

9 The Tsinghua Approach and the future direction of Chinese International Relations research 162
   XU JIN AND SUN XUEFENG

10 Balance of relationship and the Chinese School of IR: being simultaneously Confucian, post-Western and post-hegemonic 177
   CHIH-YU SHIH AND CHIUNG-CHIU HUANG

11 Constructing a Chinese School of IR as sociological reality: intellectual engagement and knowledge production 192
   YONGJIN ZHANG

   Conclusion: the Chinese School of IR as an intellectual project – a critical assessment 210
   HUN JOON KIM AND YONGJIN ZHANG

   Bibliography 224
   Index 259

Contributors

Barry Buzan is Fellow of the British Academy and an Emeritus Professor of London School of Economics, London, United Kingdom.

Teng-chi Chang is Associate Professor in the Department of Political Science, National Taiwan University, Taipei, Taiwan.

Han Xueqing is Assistant Professor of School of Law and Politics, Shanghai Normal University, Shanghai, China.

Weixing Hu is Professor at the Department of Politics and Public Administration, the University of Hong Kong, Hong Kong, China.

Chiung-chiu Huang is Assistant Professor at National Cheng-Chi University, Taipei, Taiwan.

Hun Joon Kim is Assistant Professor at Korea University, Seoul, Korea.

Peter Marcus Kristensen is Post-doctoral Fellow at the University of Copenhagen, Copenhagen, Denmark.

L.H.M. Ling is Professor of International Affairs at the New School, New York, United States.

Nele Noesselt is Professor of Chinese Politics in the Department of Political Science, University of Duisburg-Essen, Germany.

Ren Xiao is Professor at Fudan University, Shanghai, China.

Chih-yu Shih is Professor in the Department of Political Science, National Taiwan University, Taipei, Taiwan.

Sun Xuefeng is Professor of International Politics at the Institute of International Studies, Tsinghua University, Beijing, China.

Wang Jiangli is Associate Professor of International Politics in the Department of Political Science, Zhejiang University, Hangzhou, China.

Wang Yiwei is Professor at Renmin University, Beijing, China.

Xu Jin is Senior Fellow at the Institute of World Economics and Politics, Chinese Academy of Social Sciences, Beijing, China.

Yongjin Zhang is Professor of International Politics at the School of Sociology, Politics and International Studies, University of Bristol, Bristol, United Kingdom.

Acknowledgements

This volume presents a collection of essays originated from an international conference held in Beijing on *The Chinese School of IR and Its Critics* in July 2013. As a collaborative project involving contributors from around the world, it is indebted to many individuals and institutions. As editors, we would like to extend our most sincere thanks to all those who have made the completion of this project possible. Our gratitude goes first and foremost to authors of this volume for their good will and cooperation in the preparation for this collection. A number of participants in the Beijing conference, whose papers do not appear in the volume, have made important contribution to shaping the project. We owe a note of thanks in this regard to Chang Chishen, Chen Yudan, Linsay Cunningham-Cross, Ginger Hwang, Song Xinning, Yuan Yi and Zhang Xiaoming, among others. We are grateful to Hun-Joon Kim, who did not participate in the Beijing conference, for co-authoring the concluding chapter.

The Chiang Ching-Kuo Foundation (CCKF) in Taiwan provided generous financial support (Project Number: CS019-U-12) for the project, which enabled us to hold a successful conference in Beijing. We would also like to acknowledge the assistance provided by the Institute of International Studies of Tsinghua University, through the good office of Sun Xuefeng, in supporting the organization of the Beijing conference. We would like to register our deep appreciation of that support.

Arlene Tickner and other series editors have been very supportive of the project and are instrumental in obtaining anonymous reviews of earlier drafts, which prove valuable in configuring the volume and in improving analytical quality of individual chapters.

Finally, we would be seriously remiss not to mention the active support for this project we have received from our respective home institutions, the School of Sociology, Politics and International Studies of the University of Bristol and the Department of Political Science of the National University of Taiwan, which makes possible the successful completion of this project.

Introduction
The making of Chinese international theory?

Yongjin Zhang and Teng-chi Chang

The spectre of the rise of China that has triggered the putative global power shift has fuelled intense speculations about the future of global order. It has spawned more than a cottage industry in the studies of China rising, with competing visions and claims about its implications for the systemic transformation of global politics in the twenty-first century. Is a rising China a status quo or a revisionist power? How is this awakened lion, 'peaceful, amicable and civilized' (Xi 2014), going to use its rising power, and for what purpose? What does China want? Will a China rising in a world not of its own making bring a completely new script to global politics? These are among searching questions that have been grappled with in the existing literature. Anxieties about the rise of China, which is 'historically outside of the golden circle of influentials in the modern era' (Agnew 2010: 570), are palpable. Yet, we seem to have at best only very fragmented knowledge, if at all, of the hidden world of intellectual debate within China that shapes Chinese understanding of its changing position and responsibility in the global power hierarchy and informs China's distinctive visions and imagination of the future global order. In *What Does China Think?*, Mark Leonard (2008) stated rather provocatively that 'we know everything and nothing about China' and proceeded to ask rhetorically

> But how many people know about the debates raging within China? What do we really know about the kind of society China wants to become? What ideas are motivating its citizens? We can name America's neo-cons and the religious right, but cannot name Chinese writers, thinkers, or journalists – what is the future they dream of for their country, or for the world?

There is clearly a high political stake in exploring the hidden intellectual world of Chinese International Relations (IR) for understanding what particular sensibility of its own China might bring to the construction of future global order, as China becomes the second among equals of all great powers.

The disciplinary IR is guilty, too, of being oblivious to the changes of the intellectual world of Chinese IR and its knowledge production and theoretical ambition. Recent pioneering efforts to address such oblivion include three volumes in this series (Tickner and Wæver 2009; Tickner and Blaney, 2012,

2013) in addition to two works by Acharya and Buzan (2007, 2010b) as well as Kristensen and Nielsen (2013a, 2013b). There is also *Ancient Chinese Thought, Modern Chinese Power* edited by Daniel Bell at Tsinghua University in Beijing and published by Princeton University Press in 2011. But these are rare examples.

That disciplinary IR is oblivious to, and autistic about, non-Western IR is perhaps best exemplified in the instance of three panels at the 2012 ISA Annual Convention in San Diego organized by the *European Journal of International Relations* to address the question of 'The End of International Relations Theory'. In all panel presentations, there was a conspicuous absence of any critical reflection on the European-modern episteme upon which the proliferation of IR theories has been invariably and exclusively based. There was no purposive engagement with non-Western IR in evaluating the progress or stasis of theoretical development, as panel presentations were fixated on narratives of the 'paradigm wars', post-positivist critiques and beyond. The local production of theoretical knowledge and attempts at theoretical innovation beyond the West were simply unregistered and unrecognized in the panel discussions of theoretical proliferation and pluralism. No attempts were made to evaluate from the marginalized voices and perspectives in the non-Western world the putative theoretical progress and crises as well as opportunities for theoretical renewal central to the claim of the end of IR theory.

In the instance of Chinese scholars' search for an IR theory with Chinese characteristics and their efforts to construct a Chinese School of IR, however, it is the rise of Chinese international theory rather than its demise that is in contention. If disciplinary IR does aspire to be a truly global and inclusive discipline, it has a great stake in exploring exciting and productive theoretical debates in the Chinese IR epistemic community in search of Chinese international theory, and in starting a conversation with alternative approaches in order to understand how Chinese scholars talk about IR theory and what innovative intellectual products they may offer to the global discipline.

This book project is an attempt to explore the intellectual world of Chinese IR hidden largely from Western IR. It took its present shape at a workshop on *The Chinese School of IR and Its Critics* organized by two editors of this volume, which took place on 8–9 July 2013. It was at a quiet setting at the Xijiao Hotel in Beijing in the vicinity of Tsinghua University that lively debates and intellectual engagement were conducted among invited contributors from around the world over two days. All contributing chapters in this volume, with the notable exception of the concluding chapter, are revised versions of selected papers presented at this workshop in Beijing.

Collectively, this book scrutinizes critically debates about and contestations to the construction of a Chinese School of IR as sociological realities. It speaks to and is informed by current theoretical contestations in the Chinese IR epistemic community and imaginative and innovative IR scholarship produced in the context of China's rapid rise to global power status. It examines how Chinese scholars speak theory to the discipline. It debates the possibility and prospect of constructing a (contested) Chinese School (or perhaps Chinese Schools) of IR as a conscious effort to produce alternative knowledge of IR and as an assertion against IR theorization exclusively based on Western experience. It considers disciplinary stakes in and global implications of such intellectual creativity, drawing upon local traditions and concerns, knowledge claims and indigenous sources for the production of knowledge of IR beyond the West. In so doing, it introduces some important thinkers in Chinese IR and seeks to tease out the intellectual rationale behind and theoretical underpinning of a rising China's distinctive script of world politics from peaceful rise, harmonious world, to *tianxia*. In so doing, it promotes mutual engagement between a Chinese School of IR as an alternative approach to theorizing and the existing theoretical scholarship in the discipline.

Contextualizing the rise of Chinese international theory

International studies as academic pursuit are relatively new lines of intellectual activity and creativity in China. At the beginning of China's opening and reform in 1979, disciplinary IR as we understand today was virtually non-existent in China, although the 'international' undoubtedly weighed heavily on Chinese foreign policy concerns and appeared as a subject, together with other social science subjects, in the teaching curriculums of some universities that started to recover from the devastation of the Cultural Revolution, more on which later. After nearly 40 years' enduring and increasingly intensified intellectual engagement with the global IR epistemic community, however, IR is now a well-established and thriving discipline in China. With the proliferation of university departments on international studies as well as vibrant development of research agenda and teaching curriculums (Qin 2007; Shambaugh 2011), there has been a population explosion of professors and students of IR in China. There has also been dramatic growth of research institutes and think tanks for international studies and foreign policy matters, both at the national and provincial levels and in numerous universities, in addition to those under the umbrella of the Chinese Academy of Social Sciences. The *2013 Global Go To Think Tanks Index Report* released by the Think Tanks and Civil Societies Program of the University of Pennsylvania counted 426 Chinese think tanks out of the 6,826 think tanks in the world, the second-largest number of think tanks in the world, only after the United States (Xu 2014; MaGann 2014). The scholarly community of Chinese IR has become arguably among the most dynamic, and certainly the fastest growing national branch of the global IR epistemic community, both in terms of the number of researchers, and increasingly, in terms of the output of publications. The rise of China proves momentous in further stimulating intellectual creativity and the production of imaginative and innovative IR scholarship in China. The quantitative growth is now increasingly complemented by the qualitative change (Yang 2012). There has been a conscious move from simple efforts aimed at the acquisition of knowledge about IR from the West to purposeful and coordinated efforts intended for the production and creation of knowledge of IR in China. ISA's 2015 Annual Best Book Award to Tang Shiping of Fudan University for his book *The Social Evolution of International Politics*, published by Oxford University Press, is a powerful testimony. With the emergence of a self-conscious epistemic community of IR and the growing regional and global networks of IR scholars working in China, the intellectual world of Chinese IR has changed dramatically in this social process.

Intellectually, Chinese debates on whether the distinctive national social experience of China should be taken into consideration in pursuit of constructing China's own international theory can be traced back to the 1980s. It was at the first national conference on IR theory in Shanghai in 1987 that the question of developing an IR theory 'with Chinese characteristics' was first raised. The call was arguably intuitive, mimicking 'socialism with Chinese characteristics' and it is mainly the politics of legitimation of the subject that is behind this call. More than 20 years later, similar calls – whether it is for developing an IR theory 'with Chinese characteristics', or for 'indigenizing IR in China', or for constructing 'a Chinese School of IR' – are no longer a reflection of solely concerns for political legitimation. They are also backed up by intellectual justifications. They are consciously reflective of and driven by growing epistemic scepticism about the existing theoretical claims and the intellectual discontent with their inability to explain the specific problems China is confronted with as it rises. At a national conference on IR theories held in Shanghai in 2004, an explicit call was issued for theoretical innovation, which would 'embody the Chinese characteristics, incorporate both Marxist international thought and the scientific core of Western IR theories, and cultivate the Chinese cultural heritage' (Shi 2006).

Politically, the rapid rise of China and China's changing role in global politics have provided stimulus for the indigenous production of knowledge in IR in three distinct ways. It accentuates Chinese scholars' awareness of the deficiency of the explanatory power of existing (Western) IR theories. It makes it imperative to have a theoretical construct and research agenda that cater to a rising China's strategic challenges and policy needs. It provides central empirical problems and analytical puzzles to theorize IR from a distinctive Chinese perspective, among which are China's changing identity in global politics, its integration into international society, and the prospect of its peaceful rise. There is also the question of the legitimacy of rising Chinese power and its challenges to the long-term viability of the existing liberal global order dominated by the United States (Zhang 2015b).

The convergence of a long intellectual ferment and a new political logic in the first decade of the twenty-first century has therefore facilitated a purposive debate within China's IR academia on constructing Chinese international theory. This debate has not only evolved as a counter-discourse in theorizing China's peaceful rise/development to refute the prevalent 'China threat' claims based on allegedly deficient Western IR theories. It has also a distinctive thrust that seeks to bring China's own national experience and cultural heritage to bear on the creative production of indigenous and local knowledge about the 'international'. It is in this context that questions have been raised and debated such as 'Why is there no Chinese international theory?' (Qin 2007), and 'Why is there no Chinese School of IR theory?' (Yan 2009, 2011d). It is also against this background that Chinese scholars' diligent search for theoretical innovation discussed and contested in the contributing chapters of this volume should be appreciated. If these attempts at theoretical innovation and contestations by Chinese scholars have led to a number of claims and hypes heralding the arrival a Chinese School of IR, assertions about the feasibility, inevitability or desirability of constructing such a school have also been heavily contested, as the raging debates elaborated in this volume demonstrate (see also Callahan 2004b; Qin 2004, 2007, 2011b; Shi 2006; Wang 2009; Noesselt 2012). That said, it is these ongoing theoretical contestations among Chinese scholars and their critics and the innovative production of IR scholarship centred around the construction of a Chinese School of IR as sociological realities that constitute one of the most contentious, and arguably the most productive and perhaps also the most promising, site of IR knowledge production beyond the trans-Atlantic West.

This rigorous and dramatic disciplinary growth of IR in China and attempts at the local production of theoretical knowledge would have perhaps remained politically and intellectually unremarkable at the global level and would have had less interesting global implications but for the combination of historically contingent circumstances out of which it has grown. The first of which is the changing political circumstances in post-Mao China, particularly the opening and reform launched in December 1978 dubbed as China's 'second revolution' (Harding 1987). It is the burying of Mao (Baum 1994), metaphorically, that proved decisive in creating intellectual space and securing institutional opportunities for disciplinary IR to take roots, arguably for the first time, in China. The growth of disciplinary IR, however, still has to battle with often repressive political and intellectual conditions, (self-)censorship and political control under an authoritarian government for example, which are not always conducive to the production of knowledge. It has also been deeply entangled with complex policy needs and national interests of a rising China (See Chang Chapter 5 this volume; Noesselt Chapter 6 this volume).

Second, as mentioned before, IR as an academic subject had at best only a precarious existence in Chinese universities' teaching curricula at the end of the 1970s. As did other social science subjects more generally. Disciplinary IR was virtually non-existent. This cannot be accounted for only by the devastation of the Cultural Revolution, when, for a decade, all Chinese universities and research institutes were either closed down, or stopped operating at their full capacity. Equally devastating is the near-total intellectual insulation of Chinese scholars from disciplinary development in, and dialogue with, the West in almost all social science disciplines between 1949 and 1979, when no meaningful intellectual conversation took place, largely as a consequence of China's alienation from international society, when revolutionary China lived in 'angry isolation' (Nixon 1967; Zhang 1998). For all intents and purposes, when the 'paradigm wars' started with the publication of Kenneth Waltz's *Theory of International Politics* in 1979 in the United States, there was virtually no direct 'professional communication' between Chinese and Western scholars in political science and IR. The intellectual world of Chinese IR, if any, was a *terra incognita* of disciplinary IR flourishing in the West.

In hindsight, 1979 opened great opportunities for Western IR to expand into and claim the disciplinary world of Chinese IR as a *terra incognita* and for the construction of IR as an academic discipline in China. This is the third historically contingent circumstance. IR disciplinary growth in China has therefore in its own way made indispensable contribution to the global distribution of IR as an academic subject to study, thus rendering IR the globalized discipline we know today. The growth of disciplinary IR in China started understandably from an active learning process focused on knowledge acquisition from the existing scholarship produced mostly in the West. The sharp learning curve of Chinese IR, perhaps unsurprisingly, has been overwhelmingly influenced by IR scholarship from the United States. This was a period when 'a romantic view of the West dominated, and scholars copied Western scholarship without much regard for Chinese perspectives and ideas' (Wang 2009: 105). Qin (2007) listed 85 key theoretical works in English that had been translated into Chinese and published by five major presses in China by March 2007. More than 90 per cent are American. Like other national IR scholarly communities around the world, scholars in the emerging Chinese IR epistemic community 'follow the American debates, and teach American theories' (Wæver 1998: 723). The internalization of the American IR theoretical discourse in China was often celebrated as the 'progress' in Chinese scholars' theoretical understanding of IR. The colonization of Chinese IR's intellectual terrain can perhaps best be illustrated by the fact that even Chinese academic debates on the prospect of China's peaceful rise was originally 'structured around the three mainstream IRTs' (Qin 2011b: 246). Self-identified Chinese realists, Chinese liberals and Chinese constructivists grappled among themselves with the question whether China's peaceful rise is possible, largely reproducing the same debate in the United States.

In actively appropriating American IR wholesale into China as a purposive intellectual engagement, many Chinese scholars once regarded American IR, rather mistakenly, as 'the (global) discipline'. The bitter-sweet irony of this engagement is that while it has helped this 'not so international' discipline (Wæver 1998) go global, it has produced no global IR that is in any manner inclusive of Chinese voices, experiences and knowledge claims. Rather, it has produced and reproduced an asymmetric core and periphery structure of communication in this highly stratified discipline (See Kristensen Chapter 8 this volume). In so doing, the growth of disciplinary IR in China has conceded to the American intellectual hegemony and self-marginalized, perhaps unwittingly, Chinese voices, knowledge claims and ambition for theoretical innovation. Yet, it is from the margins of the globalized discipline that Chinese IR scholars have launched fierce contestations to, if not a revolt against, the intellectual hegemony of Western IR theories. Such assertions from the margins are undoubtedly aimed at seeking the recognition of knowledge claims made by Chinese scholars in the globalized discipline still dominated by the West. However, in making conscious efforts to find their own voices and to bring Chinese tradition to bear on the understanding and theorization of IR, Chinese scholars, through these contestations, have already begun to address a number of concerns on Amitav Acharya's 'new agenda of international studies', contributing to facilitating the emergence of a 'Global IR' as 'a truly inclusive discipline, recognizing its multiple and diverse foundations' (Acharya 2014: 647).

Chinese IR before 1979

The analytical focus of this volume is squarely on the disciplinary growth of IR and knowledge production in China after 1979. The contributors aim to capture dramatic changes in the intellectual world of Chinese IR, in particular the key debates, contentions and contestations in the construction of a Chinese School of IR and in the making of Chinese international theory. This is, of course, not to suggest that Chinese IR as either an academic pursuit or policy concerns started to rise only in 1979. The rich lineage of contemporary Chinese IR in both theory and practice can be traced back to that epic clash of the British and the Chinese empires in the mid-nineteenth century, if not earlier, when the worldviews embodied in the Westphalian international and Chinese *tianxia* came into violent conflict. Even before the outbreak of the Opium War, Imperial Commissioner Lin Zexu went out of his way to get paragraphs of Vattel's *Le Droit des gens* (The Law of Nations) translated for his reference and 'followed international law to the letter in proclaiming opium contraband and demanding its destruction in 1839' (Liu 2004: 119). The political and trans-lingual negotiations in the treaty making after the second Opium War of 1858–1860 on banning the use of Chinese word *yi* (non-Chinese/barbarians) in all official communication between the Qing and the British governments, and in translating Henry Wheaton's *Elements of International Law*, both of which are captured brilliantly by Lydia Liu (2004), are two examples of contestations between the Westphalian international and Chinese *tianxia* in the transformation of Imperial China into a Westphalian state. The international certainly exercised profound influence on late Qing thinkers in their understanding of the nature of the great transformation of China's relations with the expanding West, ranging from Wei Yuan, Yan Fu, Kang Youwei, to Liang Qichao. The most consequential ideational influence exerted by the international for the transformation of modern China, however, proves to be that on Dr Sun Yat-Sen, in particular his proclaimed *Sanmin Zhuyi* (Three Principles of the People), i.e. *minzhu zhuyi* (nationalism/national self-determination), *minquan zhuyi* (people's rights/democracy) and *minsheng zhuyi* (people's livelihood/socialism) (Wells 2001).

International studies as an academic subject appeared in the teaching curricula and syllabi in Chinese universities in the Republican period (1912–1949). A painstaking research recently completed shows clearly that numerous courses on international studies are found in undergraduate programmes of three Chinese universities in the 1920s and the 1930s, namely, Tsinghua University and Peking University in Beijing and St John's University in Shanghai. A total of 14 international studies courses were taught, for example, at Tsinghua University in the 1929–1930 academic year, which include the League of Nations, International Organization, IR, International Law, Diplomacy and Japanese Politics (Lu 2014). What is particularly interesting to our current discussion that is revealed by this study, but not discussed in any detail, is the fact that these international studies courses were mostly taught either by Chinese scholars trained in and returned from the United States, or American lecturers resident in China. One of them was no other than Quincy Wright, president of the American Association of Political Science in 1948–1949, and president of the American Society of International Law in 1955–1956. Viewed from this perspective, the post-1979 growth of international studies is but the appropriation of American IR redux.

Whether post-1949 Chinese IR as an academic field of inquiry existed or not remains contentious. If there was a disruption of international studies discussed above in the higher education institutions on the mainland after 1949, across the Taiwan Strait there was more continuity, i.e. IR continued to be taught in universities there. Even on the mainland, the China Institute of International Studies (CIIS), now ranked as one of top 100 most influential think tanks by *2013 Global Go To Think Tank Index Report*, was founded in 1956 under the auspices of the Chinese Ministry of Foreign Affairs. The China Foreign Affairs University was likewise first established in 1955, with close affiliation with the Chinese Ministry of Foreign Affairs. One could also point to the formal establishment of three international politics departments in 1963–1964 in Peking University, Renmin University and Fudan University respectively; and the founding of the China Institutes of Contemporary International Relations (CICIR) in 1965, all with directives from the central government, as evidential of the existence of Chinese IR before 1979.

This volume chooses to focus on the IR disciplinary construction and knowledge acquisition and dissemination in mainland China after 1979, not because it is oblivious to the rich history of international studies in China, which in fact informs discussions and analysis conducted in a number of chapters in this volume. We do maintain, however, that it is only after 1979 that IR began to emerge in mainland China 'as a self-conscious academic discipline attempting to understand and theorize about the dynamics of world politics' (Acharya and Buzan 2007: 293); that the transformation of the intellectual world of Chinese IR after 1979 with a self-identified IR epistemic community is historically unprecedented, that the growth of IR as a self-conscious discipline integral to political science is qualitatively different from previous periods, and that the intensive interactive learning and engagement between the Chinese IR epistemic community and the global one is unparalleled. Also unprecedented is the recent articulation of its theoretical ambition to assert Chinese voices and experience as alternative foundations in producing new theoretical knowledge that promotes a truly global IR. Debates about constructing a Chinese School of IR since 1979 and attempts at making Chinese international theory are, therefore, worth investigating as a topic of its own standing.

Introduction 9

There is an added reason for this focus. In so far as we are aware, there has been no single volume published in English that offers a critical assessment of the Chinese School project that represents a collective effort and reflects the varied perspectives of both active participants in the debates within China and observers and critics outside China. It is time to reveal, through a collaborative endeavour, the hidden intellectual world of Chinese IR and to bring these largely internal debates among Chinese scholars to the attention of the global IR epistemic community.

Chinese School of IR as ongoing debates

For this purpose, this volume has intentionally brought together a broad range of divergent perspectives about and critical assessments of the intellectual enterprise of constructing a Chinese School of IR as sociological realities. Given the contested nature of the Chinese School of IR project, it is debates, contentions and disagreements among contributing chapters rather than consensus, agreed understanding and a convergence in judgment on a number of critical questions that readers are likely to encounter. Why should there be a search for Chinese international theory? Is constructing a Chinese School of IR a viable intellectual project, or is it made to serve certain political purposes? Is it possible, and indeed desirable, to have a national (or geographically-based) approach to theorizing IR, and what are the perils of such a pursuit? What are after all political and disciplinary stakes, nationally and internationally, in the Chinese School of IR project?

Instead of providing a summary of each chapter, the rest of this introduction will try to foreground some key contentious points and claims made and discussed in different chapters in this volume that are constitutive of the construction of a Chinese School of IR as sociological realities. The volume is divided into two parts. Part I of this volume has six chapters, organized under the generic title of *Ongoing Debates*, which attempt to flesh out lively contentions and sharp disagreements about the hotly contested concept/idea of a Chinese School of IR and the possibility and desirability of its construction. It opens up with L.H.M. Ling's interrogation into the name of a *Chinese* School of *IR* with a certainly iconoclastic, and some may say outrageous, claim that 'what is *Chinese* is not *IR*, and what is *IR* is not *Chinese*'. She warns that unless the Hobbesian conception of the state and associated understanding of IR are fundamentally subverted, a Chinese School of IR is likely to be 'domesticated into another variant of Westphalianism'. 'To declare a Chinese School of IR', in her words, 'would negate its original intent' (Ling, Chapter 1 this volume).

'Naming' is indeed central to the debates among Chinese scholars on the construction of a Chinese School of IR, as reflected by Ren Xiao (Chapter 2 this volume), who is its strong advocate and is credited to be one of the first to use the 'label' Chinese School and to call for its construction. As discussed in his chapter as well as the chapter of Wang and Buzan, behind enduring contentions in 'naming' a 'Chinese School of IR' in preference to 'IR theory with Chinese characteristics' lie Chinese scholars' attempts to seek autonomy from political influence and constraints and to dilute ideological content in their endeavour. The call for constructing a Chinese School of IR is also an articulation of discontent about the hegemonic status of existing Western, mainly American, IR theories and an attempt to mount challenges to the claim of universality of those theories. This is not just a voice of protest. Inspired by the English School, it is also an assertion of a particular identity of Chinese IR in search for global recognition vis-à-vis IR as the American social science. In spite of considerable misgivings and ongoing debates about the possibility of national and geographically-based approaches to theorizing IR, a broad consensus has emerged out of these contentions, that is 'that IR theory should be developed within China, and that this should be independent from government ideology and related to the wider pursuit of theory in IR globally' (Wang and Buzan Chapter 7 this volume).

One claim that Ren (Chapter 2 this volume) has made about the Chinese-ness of a Chinese School of IR proves to be particularly controversial. The 'Chinese' who carry out innovative theoretical work that contributes to the construction of a Chinese School of IR, in his words, 'mainly refer to researchers living and working in the People's Republic of China'. This is contrary to Ling's call to transcend 'Westphalia's territorially-fixed, nationally defined notions of what qualifies as "Chinese"'. It is contested by what Chang (Chapter 5 this volume) calls 'evolving Chinese identities un-owned by any national projects' and 'cultural Chinese-ness'. Further, such an understanding of Chinese-ness would foreclose many opportunities for non-Chinese scholars (including a number of contributors to this volume) and those ethnic Chinese living outside the People's Republic to contribute to the construction of a Chinese School of IR and a search for Chinese international theory.

The Chinese-ness is understood in a different manner in Wang and Han's chapter, where a number of polemical claims are made provocatively in explaining why there is no Chinese IR theory. Claims such as 'Traditional Chinese culture does not favour universalism', 'Chinese culture is so developed, leaving hardly any room for highly abstract IR theory', and 'traditional Chinese thinking favours pragmatic moderation and prefers harmony to fundamentalism' are likely to be seen as expressions of China exceptionalism. So is the explicit claim that 'the unique characteristic of Chinese culture prevents China from developing Western-paradigm IR theories' (Wang and Han Chapter 3 this volume).

To the extent that the relationship between power and knowledge in the construction of a Chinese School of IR have been explored and debated in the contributing chapters, three dimensions are worth noting. First, in what sense is the construction of a Chinese School of IR, or more broadly the search for Chinese international theory, a political project? How has knowledge been hijacked to serve power? This has been investigated by Nele Noesselt (Chapter 6 this volume). Her investigation leads to two key arguments, highlighting the political nature of the Chinese School project. One is that 'the search for a "Chinese" paradigm of International Relations theory is part of China's quest for national identity and global power status'; and the other is '"Chinese" theories of international politics are expected to fulfil two general functions – to safeguard China's national interests and to legitimize the one-party system'.

The second power–knowledge dimension that has been explored is rather paradoxical. While Western IR remains undoubtedly dominant and proves to be integral to, and indispensable of an account, IR disciplinary growth in China and Chinese knowledge repertoire of IR, existing IR theories have been increasingly seen in Chinese scholarly debates as inadequate in explaining and understanding foreign policy challenges a rising China has to confront, and more broadly, in meeting the needs distinctive to Chinese IR. Robert Cox's claim that 'Theory is always for someone and for some purpose' is conveniently used to delegitimize the claim of universality of existing IR theories, to provincialize Western IR, and to justify the assertions of Chinese voices and knowledge claims (Hu, Chapter 4 this volume and Chang, Chapter 5 this volume). From the Coxian perspective, and to the extent that IR theory constructs the world that it purports to describe and is constitutive of the reality that it addresses, Chinese scholars have their own interest in being part of the game.

The third dimension concerns the rise of China and its implications for the rise of Chinese IR theory. It is simply too facile to assume that the construction of a Chinese School of IR is a natural product of the rise of China. In a more straightforward sense, the peaceful rise of China, as both Hu (Chapter 4 this volume) and Chang (Chapter 5 this volume) argue, does provide Chinese scholars with a core problematique for the construction of Chinese international theory. It is true that global disparities in material power between China and the United States – and more broadly the West – are narrowing significantly and changing rapidly. Nevertheless, whether China's ascendancy of power helps recover China's subjectivity in IR as discussed by Wang and Han (Chapter 3 this volume), and how, if it does, remain open-ended questions that need to be explored, not simply assumed. If the growth of the discipline in the United States 'cannot be separated from the American role in world affairs after 1945' (Hoffmann 1977: 47), the position of power in the international system does matter. How would China's changing role in global politics then facilitate and promote both 'action-oriented IR theory' and 'knowledge-oriented IR theory' (Hu, Chapter 4 this volume), i.e. 'the development of theoretical IR thinking in China about systemic IR theory and foreign policy theory in China' (Wang and Buzan, Chapter 7 this volume)?

These ongoing debates and contestations outlined above are important in understanding the social processes that have led to the articulation of a theoretical ambition and the production of innovative theoretical knowledge in Chinese IR. They are, equally importantly, constitutive of the emergence of a Chinese School of IR as constructed sociological realities, as they embody the battle cries, the moods and all-too-human interests of both advocates and opponents alike, and because, as Joseph Schumpeter (1994: 783) argued, 'their antagonisms come within the general sociology of group antagonisms and of party warfare. Victory and conquest, defeat and loss of ground, are in themselves values for such schools and part of their very existence'.

In Part II, *Towards Sociological Realities*, five chapters, therefore, turn to examine the extent to which the construction of a Chinese School has become genuine sociological realities. Wang and Buzan (Chapter 7 this volume) look into academic histories of both the emerging Chinese School and the relatively mature English School. In so doing, it offers a rather methodical comparison between the two in six dimensions, namely, origin/founders/organization; naming; context; aims/intentions; theoretical sources; and historical projects. One of the purposes of such a comparison is to tease out what lessons the emerging Chinese School can draw from the experience of the English School. Two valuable lessons outlined are particularly challenging to those advocating the construction of a Chinese School of IR. One is that 'the English School has avoided falling into any narrow orthodoxy that would straightjacket its conversation. It has cultivated an open conversation with several different and sometimes contending strands'. The other is that 'the English School does not make the case for national approaches to IR theory'. It follows that 'a good part of the explanation for its success is precisely that it eschewed parochial concerns and aimed to construct theory at the global level'.

Peter Kristensen does not contest the idea of national or geographically-based approaches to theorizing IR, as he argues that 'there is not one IR discipline but several national disciplines of which the American core dominates most syllabi, textbooks, journals and conferences'. His starting point is to take the Chinese School as a constructed sociological reality and to put it side by side with other non-American regional and national approaches, European, Indian and Brazilian in this instance, in 'a stratified space of IR with asymmetric core-periphery structures of communication'. Kristensen is critical of the lack of deep engagement of dialogues between the Chinese School and other European Schools on the semi-periphery and the IR theorizing in other rising powers such as India and Brazil on the periphery. He argues in particular that the prospect for recognition of a Chinese School depends on its navigation of these centre-periphery structures. In this sense, the Chinese School needs to travel to engage audiences not only at the American core, but at the semi-periphery and periphery of the stratified IR space, as the production of knowledge 'is never made exclusively in one place and consumed in its original version in another place, it is made as it travels' (Kristensen, Chapter 8 this volume).

Xu and Sun (Chapter 9 this volume) provide an insightful discussion of the evolution of the so-called Tsinghua Approach to IR, arguably one of the most promising sites of innovative local knowledge production in Chinese IR that has attracted considerable international attention, particularly with the publication by Princeton University Press of *Ancient Chinese Thought, Modern Chinese Power* by Yan Xuetong *et al.*, edited by Daniel A. Bell and Sun Zhe in 2011. As members of the Tsinghua Team, Xu and Sun provide insiders' view of the achievements made by the Tsinghua Team in conducting research on pre-Qin Chinese international thought in the decade between 2005 and 2015. They also closely engage with the critics of the Tsinghua Approach, and outline the future challenges to the Approach's theoretical ambition, i.e. enriching existing IR theories and drawing policy lessons by exploring ancient Chinese international thought as well as practice in inter-state relations.

Theoretical innovation in Chinese IR is the focus of the discussions conducted in the other three chapters in Part II. Shih and Huang (Chapter 10 this volume) cultivate with diligence valuable local knowledge sources for theoretical innovation. They boldly draw on Confucianism 'to map the route to the discovery of a general theory of balance of relationship' and present the balance of relationship as geoculturally distinctive and contending explanatory theory parallel to more familiar theoretical constructs of balance of power and balance of threat. Balance of relationship, they assert, can be construed as central to a Chinese School of IR that is simultaneously Confucian, post-Western and post-hegemonic. In this fashion, what comprises the Chinese-ness of a Chinese School of IR is again thrown into question in a particular manner, as both authors are ethnically and culturally Chinese but write on the Chinese School of IR from sites outside the current jurisdiction of the People's Republic of China.

Zhang (Chapter 11 this volume) takes Chinese intellectual engagement with trans-Atlantic IR as a central analytical focus and emphasizes the constitutive role of the diffusion of Western IR in the disciplinary growth of Chinese IR and in the making of Chinese international theory. The chapter examines the long march to theoretical innovation in Chinese IR as complex social processes of change of the intellectual world of Chinese IR. It highlights three epistemic turns, namely, epistemic optimism, epistemic scepticism and epistemic reflexivity, in these long social processes. It is the latest epistemic turn to purposive reflexivity, it is argued, that has led to promising indigenous production of knowledge in China, as international studies in China have moved decisively from simply knowledge acquisition to knowledge production/creation. The chapter illustrates Chinese scholars' attempts at producing new theoretical knowledge by examining respectively three projects conducted by Yan Xuetong, Qin Yaqing and Zhao Tingyang, which are also touched upon in a number of other chapters.

The concluding chapter jointly authored by Hun Joon Kim and Yongjin Zhang offers a critical assessment of the Chinese School of IR as an intellectual project in a summary fashion as a continuation of the conversation and debate. By way of articulating their intellectual discontents with the Chinese School project, the chapter identifies four specific obstacles to overcome for the Chinese School of IR as an intellectual project to move forward. These are exceptionalism, dualism, the romanticization of Chinese tradition, culture, history and thought, and great power conceit.

It undertakes certain intellectual as well as political risk for the Chinese School project to call for, to embark on, and to persist in constructing theoretical knowledge that is more sensitive to Chinese historical experience, philosophical tradition and political context. It may prove perilous to insist on the 'Chineseness' of this distinctive approach, as it is likely to foreclose other more productive and fruitful pursuit of new knowledge. It is precisely for this reason that the construction of a Chinese School of IR, as an intellectual project, should seek to open up more opportunities and channels of conversation with its audiences and critics alike in the global IR epistemic community. It should invite global scrutiny. This invitation is also a challenge to those who are anxious about the end of IR theory to engage critically with the approaches to alternative theoretical knowledge production in non-Western epistemic space or to ignore them at their own peril. It is our hope that this volume provides some openings and creates opportunities for such mutual engagement.

Part I
Ongoing debates

1 What's in a name?

A critical interrogation of the "*Chinese School* of *IR*"

L.H.M. Ling

"What's in a name?" this chapter asks.[1] In the case of International Relations (IR), I propose, a lot. Unlike Shakespeare's claim that a rose by any other name "would smell just as sweet,"[2] this chapter argues that the act of naming not only defines an object of inquiry but also how we study it. In identifying a "Chinese" school of IR, I submit, whatever *difference* Chinese theorists may offer is crammed into the *sameness* that constitutes the mainstream – that is, Westphalian/Western IR. Hence, the "Chinese School of IR" would not represent anything new or different. Rather, it becomes domesticated into another variant of Westphalianism. In other words, what is "Chinese" is not "IR," and what is "IR" is not "Chinese."

I begin with the term "IR." Given its conceptual history, IR necessarily centers on the state, which comes primarily from Hobbes. A state, he theorized, emerges from a social contract decided between self-interested individuals (really, men) who willingly submit to an absolute, impervious judge – the Leviathan – in exchange for security from murderous anarchy. Governance in the Chinese context contrasts strikingly. Its dominant tradition, Confucianism, regards the state as a loving but disciplining parent. Historically, agents of the dynasty (regardless of royal house) retained the title of "mother–father officials" (*fumu guan*). Their mission: to "love the people as a child" (*ai min ru zi*).

Equally, I question the term, "Chinese." What does this designation indicate: geography or ideas? If the former, then does it refer only to those IR theorists who work at institutions in and publish from the Chinese mainland, thereby claiming to represent a "Chinese" voice? If so, a double paradox emerges. It simultaneously includes those writing from China on China but who are neither ethnically nor culturally Chinese (Bell 2008)[3] *and* excludes all those who are ethnically-culturally Chinese but who work and write on Chinese politics and philosophy from sites outside the Chinese mainland (Pan 2013, 2014).[4] Or, does the designation of "Chineseness" refer to ideas only? If so, then distinctive traditions like Confucianism and Daoism qualify as worldviews in their own right (Ling 2014). These transcend Westphalia's territorially-fixed, nationally-defined notions of what qualifies as "Chinese." Wherein lies the "Chineseness," then, in the "Chinese School of IR"?

One aspect, however, binds IR and the "Chinese" school: patriarchy. Both make assumptions about power derived from the patriarchal household. As this chapter will show, part of the modernization (Westernization) of the Confucian state means patriarchy exiling its traditional power-sharing role with matriarchy. Hence, proponents of the "Chinese School" may have more in common with their Westphalian brethren than both would care to admit.

To demonstrate, I compare two iconic texts: *The Leviathan* and *Sanguo Yanyi* (*Romance of the Three Kingdoms*). Thomas Hobbes (1588–1679) completed *Leviathan* in 1651, when threats to the English state finally ended. It was also three years after the Treaty of Westphalia, concluding the Thirty Years' War for some and the Hundred Years' War for others. The treaty also established contemporary IR's two signature features: national sovereignty demarcated by fixed borders reinforced with commerce and trade as the venue of peace. Luo Guanzhong (*c.*1330–1400) wrote *Sanguo* in the fourteenth-century, at a time of dynastic transition from the Yuan to the Ming. But he centered the novel on an era of even greater political instability eleven centuries before: that is, when the Han dynasty declined around 200 CE, loosening central control for the first time in 400 years. The three kingdoms of Shu, Wu and Wei battled for hegemony in the ensuing vacuum.

Some may object to this comparison. After all, *Leviathan* is a political treatise, whereas *Sanguo* entertains as a novel only. I would remind the skeptical reader that *Leviathan* proceeds from a conjecture – the State of Nature – that is as fanciful as any found in a novel. At the same time, *Sanguo* imparts as much about politics, both in action and philosophy, as does *Leviathan*.[5] Others may ask: Why *Sanguo*? Why not draw on the mainspring of Chinese political thought like the *Analects* (*c.*5 BCE) or the *Huainanzi* (*Master of Huainan*, 139 BCE)? *Sanguo*, I propose, animates the concepts and principles of Chinese political thought. We see them in action in a specific context rather than as maxims offered for perpetuity, albeit illustrated with parables. For this reason, *Sanguo* offers a more precise comparison to the *Leviathan*. Both demonstrate *worldmaking*. (More on this below.)

Let us now turn to Hobbes and his Leviathan.

The Leviathan in IR

Life in the State of Nature, Hobbes (1988 [1651]: 65) famously declared, is "solitary, poor, nasty, brutish, and short." It amounts to a condition of "warre of every man against every man," given the lack of justice or right, law and order (Hobbes 1988 [1651]: 66). A radical equality prevails. Even "the weakest has strength enough to kill the strongest, either by secret machination, or by confederacy with others, that are in the same danger with himselfe" (Hobbes 1988 [1651]: 63).

This conjecture reflects what Europeans believed at the time about the New World. Note Hobbes' (1642) description of it in *De Cive* (*On the Citizen*):

> They of America are Examples hereof, even in this present Age: Other Nations have been in former Ages, which now indeed are become Civill,

and Flourishing, but were then few, fierce, short-lived, poor, nasty, and destroy'd of all that Pleasure, and Beauty of life, which Peace and Society are wont to bring with them.

In contrast, Hobbes set up the Leviathan as a mirror to European Man: rational, objective, and advanced – but even more perfect. The Leviathan is an "artificial man," a machine whose "*heart* [is] but a *spring*; and the *nerves*, but so many *strings*; and the *joints*, but so many *wheels*, giving motion to the whole body" (Hobbes 1988 [1651]: 1, original emphases). Because the State-as-Leviathan functions like a machine, while retaining the rationality and reason of European Man, it is able to distinguish between reality and fantasy. "Imagination," Hobbes derided, "is nothing but *decaying sense*" (Hobbes 1988 [1651]: 4–5, original emphasis).

Herein lies Hobbes' "doctrine of method" (Weinberger 1975). Not only is it scientific and materialist, but also Hobbes' method is explicitly anti-metaphysical. Man's inherent rationality, Hobbes asserted, accounts for this science of politics. It explains why man left the State of Nature, despite its "absolute freedom," to enter into a social contract of "relative freedom." Society buffers man from the radical equality of murder so he can sleep soundly at night with all his possessions in tow. Should disputes arise, the State-as-Leviathan will adjudicate in the courts, evenly and without prejudice. Anything else would mean constant war (Hobbes 1988 [1651]: 80).

Westphalians extend this Hobbesian framework to world politics. Since no Global Leviathan exists, they reason, world politics must operate in a situation akin to the State of Nature. A presumption thus takes hold: world politics concerns that space *between* states (Prozorov 2014). Realists (Waltz 1979) fill it with "nothing" (anarchy and chaos); Liberals (Jahn 2013) and members of the English School (Suganami 2010), with "something" (regimes and institutions); and constructivists (Onuf 2013), like Marxists/neo-Marxists (Gill 1993), with "everything" (norms and identities; capitalism and class struggle). Nonetheless, all agree that power defines world politics. And the state serves as its greatest instrument as well as constituent.

Realists put it most bluntly. They routinely cite Thucydides' singular line from the *History of the Peloponnesian War* (431 BCE): "The strong do what they can, the weak suffer what they must." It comes from a chapter misleadingly titled, "The Melian Dialogue," since no real dialogue ever takes place. Athens' generals come to the island of Melos and present an ultimatum to its inhabitants: join us against Sparta or die. The Melians insist upon neutrality; thereupon, the Athenians kill all the men and enslave their women and children. Athens would look weak, otherwise, the generals surmise. Such is the "tragedy" of great power politics (Mearsheimer 2001).

Kenneth Waltz (1979) updates Hobbes for IR through Neorealism.

Neorealist IR

Waltz finds an overarching structure or system for world politics. It encompasses states as identical "units," much like individuals in the State of Nature, since both are competitive, self-enclosed, and self-interested. (Individuals in the State of Nature, according to Hobbes, are like mushrooms after a rain: they pop up atomistically and automatically if the conditions are right.[6]) Change occurs when a unit's structural position changes. Since military capability makes the biggest difference in this "self-help" system, only "great powers" matter. Waltz (1979: 72) explains:

> It would be as ridiculous to construct a theory of international politics based on Malaysia and Costa Rica as it would be to construct an economic theory of oligopolistic competition based on the minor firms in a sector of an economy.

Hegemony marks the norm in inter-state relations. States seek *hegemonic* power despite their inability to control the world "reliably." Waltz (1979: 194–195) gives four reasons why:

> First, power provides the means of maintaining one's autonomy in the face of force that others wield. Second, greater power permits wider ranges of action, while leaving the outcomes of action uncertain ... Third, the more powerful enjoy wider margins of safety in dealing with the less powerful and have more to say about which games will be played and how ... Fourth, great power gives its possessors a big stake in their system and the ability to act for its sake. For them management becomes both worthwhile and possible.

"Weak states," in contrast, operate on "narrow margins": "Inopportune acts, flawed policies, and mistimed moves may have fatal results. In contrast, strong states can be inattentive; they can afford not to learn; they can do the same dumb things over again" (Waltz 1979: 195).

Still, Waltz stays with the systemic approach. "To explain outcomes, we have to look at a system's dynamics and not just at the characteristics and strategies of the units" (Waltz 1979: 342). He turns to micro-economic theory for the perfect analogy. Like firms, "units" (states) in the inter-state system operate in an environment of law-like regularities. Just as firms must respond to a market dictated by the laws of supply and demand, so too must states respond to an international environment dictated by the laws of power politics (e.g. balance of power).[7] In this way, world politics can have "order without an orderer" (Waltz 1979: 79).[8]

From this basis come three Westphalian visions for world order: "hegemonic stability theory" (Gilpin 1981; Kindleberger 1981; Keohane 2005 [1984]), "democratic peace theory" (Risse 2000), and a "liberal world order" (Ikenberry and Slaughter 2006). Each proposes that the United States can maintain an "open, rules-based" system for all *despite* its hegemonic status (otherwise known as "global leadership") (Clinton 2011; Ikenberry 2011). Hegemonic stability theory claims the world needs a hegemon to maintain peace and prosperity for all. Democratic peace theory and a liberal world order share a premise that extends this logic: liberal democratic values and institutions, rather than outright hegemonic rule, ensure global peace and prosperity; accordingly, all states should, in essence, convert to the West (Fukuyama 1992).

Indeed, Wendt (1999) finds a progression here. World order can advance from Hobbesian enmity to Lockean rivalry to Kantian friendship. Hobbesian enmity's "warre of all against all" could give way to Lockean rivalry's governing norms and institutions that, in turn, facilitate Kantian friendship. It takes place when (collective) norms subsume (individual) self-interest. States would resolve disputes without resort to violence, knowing that cooperation benefits all. Under Kantian friendship, Wendt predicts, "external norms [will] become a voice in our heads telling us that we *want* to follow them" (Wendt 1999: 299, original emphasis).

In sum, mainstream IR reflects and perpetuates a Hobbesian–Westphalian legacy updated by Neorealism. The machine-like Leviathan ensures law and order internally; conversely, it exposes an anarchical, murderous State of Nature externally. Neorealism reconciles this apparent contradiction by drawing on Hobbes' scientific method. It posits that the inter-state system, as in oligopolistic competition, imposes a set of rational rules such that order can prevail without an orderer. Military capability is key but it affects the positioning *among* individual "units" (states) rather than the system itself. For this reason, IR focuses on "great powers" since these wield the greatest impact on international hierarchy.

Sanguo defines the world and its politics quite differently. Let us see how.

Sanguo Yanyi and *tianxia*

Seven centuries after its first appearance, *Sanguo Yanyi* (*Romance of the Three Kingdoms*) still rocks.[9] Its influence ranges from the vast Chinese mainland to Korea–Japan in the Northeast and Hong Kong–Taiwan–Singapore–Vietnam in the Southeast to even parts of Los Angeles and Vancouver in the Western Pacific. Besides various versions of the book, *Sanguo* resurrects constantly through films,[10] TV dramas,[11] *manga*,[12] *anime*,[13] computer games,[14] and Internet discussions.[15] Even in locations far from the Chinese heartland like Vietnam, for example, conversations frequently include sayings from the epic,[16] and numerous temples worship Guan Yu, *Sanguo*'s ideal of the noble warrior.

More pointedly, *Sanguo* remains relevant to politics in Asia. Ma Ying-jeou, current president of Taiwan, has cast the island's relations with China in terms of the novel's opening line: "Long divided, the world will unite; long united, it will fall apart" (*tianxia da shi, fen jiou bi he, he jiou bi fen*) (Chen 2014). Mao certainly invoked *Sanguo* (Lai 2011). And South Korea's president, Park Geun Hye, notes her love of the epic in her autobiography (Park 2007).

The novel exemplifies rivalry in world politics – and more. The leaders of one kingdom constantly seek to defeat the other two so as to establish a new, unifying dynasty. For this reason, social scientists often take "three kingdoms" as a metaphor for a multi-polar world politics (Niou and Ordeshook 1987). But the plots and schemes in *Sanguo* do not simply reflect rule-bound self-interest or possessiveness, as Wendt ascribes to Lockean rivalry.[17] Rather, decisions to ally or fight tend to reflect contending psychologies such as greed, ambition, fear, lust, jealousy, vanity and brotherly love – sometimes in the same person. Still at other times, alliances reflect singular, uncompromising norms of honor, duty and righteousness.

Indeed, emotional complexity pivots *Sanguo*. A brief review of its main characters suffices:

1. Cao Cao: Self-Aggrandizing Power Politics. Cao Cao (AD 155–220) seems to personify Hobbesian Man in the State of Nature. A low-level official from a family associated with eunuchs,[18] Cao rises to become chancellor of the Han dynasty in its dying years. To deflect charges of unseemly ambition, Cao never proclaims himself emperor – despite acting like one and holding the actual emperor hostage. *Sanguo* depicts Cao as ruthless, conniving and self-serving. For instance, Cao kills his kindly godfather, who had given him safe haven, for fear the old man would inadvertently reveal the secret. But the epic also notes Cao's utmost competence, savvy and – contrary to the times – emotional honesty. "I'd rather owe the world," Cao famously declares, "than have the world owe me" (*ning yuan wo fu tianxiaren, bu yuan tianxiaren fu wo*). Cao represents a kind of self-aggrandizing power politics – and yet he is more than that. Cao often decides on friend or foe depending on person, circumstance and talent. He imprisons then releases the noble warrior, Guan Yu, precisely because of the latter's talents in warfare and his unswerving dedication to Liu Bei (AD 161–223), his "elder brother" (*da ge*). When Guan Yu dies, Cao mourns grievously.

2. Liu Bei: Brotherly Love. The epic celebrates, above all else, brotherly love. It finds iconic expression in the relationship between Liu Bei ("first brother"), Guan Yu ("second brother") and Zhang Fei ("third brother"), so ordered according to age. Each supports, comforts and protects the other, always. Even when Cao Cao captures Guan Yu, hoping to recruit him, the latter returns to Liu's side at the first opportunity despite countless hazards along the way. The three men's "oath of loyalty in a cherry orchard" (*taoyuan san jieyi*) is legendary:

> We ask not to be born in the same year, same month, same day (*bu qiou tong nian, tong yue, tong ri sheng*), but hope to die in the same year, same month, and same day (*dan yuan tong nian, tong yue, tong ri si*).

Cao commands in lonely isolation, in contrast, perhaps accounting for his frequent migraines. Advisors and ministers abound but they perform mainly as lackeys. Cao does not inspire the kind of brotherly love that Liu enjoys. For example, Liu values the brilliance of a minor character (Pang Tong) despite his ugly face and body. Here, the epic makes a subtle point: all the plotting and scheming, warring and fighting may thrill but it pales next to the succor and devotion of one's brothers-in-arms. Even conjugal love cannot compare. Liu jokes "Wives are like clothes (*qizi ru yishang*), whereas brothers are like the palm of one's hand (*xiongdi ru shouzhang*)."

3. Zhuge Liang: Strategic Genius. Sanguo's third key figure is Zhuge Liang. Always elegantly attired in silk robes and waving a fan made of crane feathers (even in battle), Zhuge is Liu's master strategist and, later, his prime minister. Chinese history memorializes Zhuge as an overall genius. Two examples suffice. In the critical Battle of Red Cliff (*chi bi*), along the southern bank of the Yangzi River, Liu finds himself outnumbered by Cao in men and ammunition. Defeat seems imminent, but Zhuge finds an extraordinary solution. He has several small, straw boats made to send in the thick fog of night towards the enemy's fleet. Thinking Liu is attempting a sneak attack, Cao's admirals order thousands of arrows shot at the boats. Zhuge's men later retrieve the boats – and the arrows – to use against the enemy the next day. A second example comes from an episode titled, "Empty City Scheme Retards the Enemy" (*kong cheng ji tui di*). Sima Yi, great commander under Cao's son, Cao Pi, advances towards Zhuge who has encamped within a small city. Zhuge is caught off guard, without adequate forces, yet he cannot run. He knows Sima's army can easily capture his few men. Instead, Zhuge leaves the city gate slightly ajar. He orders some soldiers to impersonate servants, casually sweeping leaves outside. Zhuge stations himself atop the city gate, plucking the *guqin*, a zither-like instrument. The master strategist plays calmly, melodiously. *He must have lots of men armed to the teeth to play so well*, Sima guesses with his troops just beyond the city gate. He retreats and Zhuge is saved for another battle, another day.

4. Sima Yi: Trickster Genius. Sima Yi represents another kind of genius. A devious trickster, he waits patiently – almost a lifetime! – before making his move. Initially appointed as one of several advisors to Cao Pi, Sima lays low until his seventies, even feigning illness on the brink of death before seizing power. Sima's grandson eventually rises to become the founding emperor of the Jin dynasty, thereby ending the era of Three Kingdoms. Sima's political and cultural symbolism lies in its *immanence*. That is, not all is what it seems – especially when it comes to power.

5. Narrator. We cannot discount the role of the ubiquitous narrator in *Sanguo*. Not only does it relate all the events and characters that transpire over a century, but the narrator also provides a philosophical framework to understand them. The novel's opening line, for instance, about how time and power invariably turn division into unity, *and back again*, reflects a distinctly reflexive worldview. That Sima Yi ends up the dynastic winner, when he was not even in contention in the first place, underscores the novel's recognition of irony in history, if not the need for philosophical detachment to understand it. Nothing stays the same, the novel alerts us, yet everything remains eternal given this essential truth.

Sanguo's longstanding cultural appeal thus surpasses mere power politics. Certainly, power matters (and entertains greatly). But the epic also stresses a larger sense of what it means to go to war, sacrifice one's life, persevere despite repeated failures, and make the most of triumph which is, ultimately, momentary. The novel asks: What is it all *for*?

Another kind of world-making

Sanguo suggests another kind of world-making. It departs significantly from Hobbes' mechanistic logic or Westphalia's systemic one. Instead, *Sanguo* relates a world that values the intuitive, the spiritual, and the highly dialectical.

Note this episode titled, "Seven Times Caught, Seven Times Released" (*qiqin qizong*).[19] It involves, again, that master strategist Zhuge Liang. This time, he is prime minister of Shu, sent to conquer a southern territory (in what is today's Yunnan province). Seven times Zhuge manages to capture – and release – the local "barbarian king," Meng Huo.[20] Why? Meng would not accept Shu rule "in his heart" (*xin fu*). Until he does, Zhuge vows, he would free him after each capture. Zhuge would not accept Meng as a defeated enemy only.

Upon the seventh capture, Meng is led into the prime minister's tent in chains. To his surprise, a table of fine meats and wine greets him. A soldier unshackles Meng while Zhuge's trusted general announces to Meng: "The Prime Minister feels ashamed to meet you in person.[21] He commands me to let you to return home, to battle us another day. You may leave as soon as you like." Meng is moved deeply and tears begin to flow. "I may be a person outside of Chinese culture (*huawai zhi ren*)," he weeps, "but I still know what's right and proper (*liyi*). How could I [alone] be [so] shameless (*xiouchi*)?" And, as legend has it, Meng Huo finally accepts Shu rule.

The skeptical reader could scoff: a clever tactic, that's all. Moreover, it's *Sanguo*'s rendition. How do we *know* Meng willingly "converted" and matters followed the way the novel describes?

Zhuge's world-making does not end with "subjugating" Meng. Zhuge retains Meng to stay in charge and, in time, he becomes a high-ranking official in the Shu court (Li 2009). No simple act of co-opting the enemy, Zhuge aims for "harmonious governance" (*wei he*). The master strategist withdraws his troops even as he reinstalls Meng. But before departing, Zhuge orders a transfer of important technical knowledge regarding agriculture and construction, salt and metals to the local people. Zhuge thus improves their material lives while leaving alone their customs and traditions, lifestyles and religions. Meng Huo's people are able to prosper on their own terms rather than those of the conquerors. To this day, the descendants of Meng Huo revere Zhuge Liang (Li 2009).

Yin/yang dialectics account for Zhuge's reasoning:

> It would not be easy (*yi*) [to stay] for three reasons. Stationing outsiders would require a military occupation [*yang*-occupation], but there is no way the troops could sustain/feed themselves [no *yin* counterpart], that's one difficulty. The barbaric peoples have suffered much [*yin*-emptiness], losing fathers and brothers [on the battlefield]. If I were to station outsiders here

without troops [another *yin*-emptiness], it would be a disaster in the making. That's a second difficulty. The barbaric peoples have murdered and killed [*yang*-aggressiveness], naturally they harbor suspicions, especially of outsiders [more *yang*-aggressiveness]; that's a third difficulty. [For these reasons], I don't leave anyone behind [*yin*-withdrawal] and I don't transport away any supplies [*yang*-advance], thereby allowing us to remain in mutual peace [*yin/yang* balance] and without incident (*wushi*).

(Author's translation)

Confucian governance as ontology frames this epistemology of *yin/yang* dialectics. The state, the *Lunyu* (*Analects*, c.5 BCE) instructs, should behave towards the people "as if you were watching over an infant" (De Grazia 1973: 205). The *Mengzi* (*Book of Mencius*, c.2 BCE) reinforces this familial connection in state governance: "no benevolent man ever abandons his parents, and no dutiful man puts his prince last" (de Grazia 1973: 131). Here, Confucian governance reflects an even older legacy. *Liji* (*Ritual Records*, 12 BCE) notes, "the happy and gracious sovereign is the father and mother of the people"; the *Shujing* (Book of Documents, 12 BCE) accords universal, almost divine, authority to both parent and state: "Heaven and earth are parents of all creatures. Sincerity and wisdom become the sovereign; for he is the parent of the people" (*Shujing* quoted in Thomas 1927: 42, 163–283). Even Laozi (c.6 BCE), the advocate of Daoist *wuwei* (non-coercive action), urges the state to regard the people as "a child" (Laozi quoted in Thomas 1927: 163). Why?

Tianxia

Tianxia (All-under-Heaven) centers this worldview (Zhang 2014). A relational ontology, *tianxia* conveys a grand sense of *world-ness*: that is, a universe composed of many worlds. It bears three, inter-related meanings: (1) the "universe" or the "world," (2) the "hearts of all peoples" (*minxin*) or the "general will of the people," and (3) a "world institution, or a universal system for the world, a utopia of the world-as-one-family" (Zhao 2006: 30). Sun Yatsen rallied his republican revolution in 1911 with the slogan: "*tianxia wei gong*" ("Justice for All-under-Heaven"). More recently, China's President Xi Jinping invoked the phrase "*tianxia an*" ("peace under heaven") when discussing central–local party relations.[22]

More than a cosmos, *tianxia* imparts a universal dynamic. It relates vertically, between heaven, man and earth, with the Emperor ("Son of Heaven") mediating across all three. (For this reason, traditional Chinese medicine connects human and political health with environmental and astronomical health (Ling 2016).) *Tianxia* also radiates horizontally, from a moral–ethical center to the peripheries, as stipulated in the *Zhongyong* (Doctrine of the Mean). Seeing itself as the center of Confucian morality and ethics, the Chinese dynasties took on the title of *Zhongguo* (Middle Kingdom).

More specifically, *tianxia* insists on an intimacy between the individual and the universe. One of the Confucian canons, *Daxue* (The Great Learning), details this sense of reverberative inter-relationality. It bears quoting at length:

The ancients who wished to illustrate illustrious virtue [*ming ming de*] throughout the [universe],[23] first ordered well their own states [*zhi guo*]. Wishing to order well their states, they first regulated their families [*qi jia*]. Wishing to regulate their families, they first cultivated their persons [*xiu shen*]. Wishing to cultivate their persons, they first rectified their hearts [*zheng xin*]. Wishing to rectify their hearts, they first sought to be sincere in their thoughts [*cheng yi*]. Wishing to be sincere in their thoughts, they first extended to the utmost their knowledge [*zhi zhi*]. Such extension of knowledge lay in the investigation of things [*ge wu*]. [And the process repeats in reverse from the individual's investigation of things] to tranquility and happiness in the [universe] (*tianxia ping*).[24]

In sum, *Sanguo* reflects and perpetuates a Confucian–Daoist legacy.[25] The state is not a self-enclosed, self-interested institution whose domestic law and order tempers the murderous anarchy of world politics. Instead, the state features as one component within a worldly world order, ranging from the individual to the family to the state to *tianxia*, and back again. Accordingly, the *nature* of the state (whether "virtuous" or "villainous") depends on how well or badly the other components are faring. *Yin/yang* dialectical reasoning helps to attain peace and happiness within oneself as well as in *tianxia*; it enables an "investigation of things" (*ge wu*) in a way that resonates harmoniously with the larger environment. Military capability matters – why else would *Sanguo*'s three kingdoms war with one another so often? – but it does not and cannot replace proper governance, defined as parental love and discipline. "Love your people as a child" (*ai min ru zi*), the canons instruct.[26] And, as conveyed by *Sanguo*'s narrator, we must always keep in mind that certainty eludes. Triumph in the long-run cannot be confused with success in the short-term. No matter how many battles Cao Cao of Wei or Liu Bei of Shu or Sun Quan of Wu wins in the moment, ultimately it is Sima Yi's descendant who unifies All-under-Heaven and declares a new dynasty, Jin.

Comparisons

A comparison between *Leviathan* and *Sanguo* reveals differences as well as similarities. The differences glare; the similarities, less so.

Differences

Leviathan and *Sanguo* show two radically different ways of world-making:

1 *Leviathan*'s Machine vs *Sanguo*'s Heroes/Villains. Whereas Hobbes's State-as-Leviathan approximates a more perfect union of (European) Man with Machine, *Sanguo* conveys a world politics filled with psychologically and emotionally complex characters: e.g. conniving yet effective Cao Cao (no matter how many battles he loses, he always end up "on top"),

Table 1.1 Differences between *Leviathan* and *Sanguo*

	Leviathan	*Sanguo*
Context for inter-state relations	State of Nature: "warre of all against all"	The principle of the *Dao*: "What is long united must separate. What is long separated must unite." (*he jiu bi fen, fen jiu bi he*)
Nature of the state	Absolute, impartial judge	Parental love and discipline
Analytical method	Scientific rationality, systemic logic	Yin/Yang dialectics, *tianxia*'s reverberative inter-relationality
Strategies	Military power balancing, hegemonic stability	Self-aggrandizing power politics (Cao Cao) Brotherly love (Liu Bei) Strategic genius (Zhuge Liang) Trickster genius (Sima Yi)

honorable yet disappointing Liu Bei (he exemplifies virtue but fails to establish a new dynasty), brilliant yet unfulfilled Zhuge Liang (he labored devotedly for a losing cause, Liu Bei), trickster yet ultimately successful Sima Yi (his grandson becomes emperor of the new Jin dynasty). The skeptical reader might protest: Of course, the two texts would differ. *Leviathan* is a political treatise; *Sanguo*, a novel! However, I would point out that political texts do not necessarily evade emotional complexity. Note, for example, Thucydides' *History*. The entire book shows a complexity underappreciated by Realists who tend to restrict it to one line from one chapter. Two consecutive chapters, in particular, warrant attention. In "Pericles' Funeral Oration," Athens' best and brightest leader comforts mourners by giving them *meaning* to the loss of sons and brothers, fathers and husbands on the battlefield. It is a sacrifice worthy of the ages, he tells them. This is the solid prize with which, as with a garland, Athens crowns her sons living and dead, after a struggle like theirs. For where the rewards of virtue are greatest, there the noblest citizens are enlisted in the service of the state.[27]

Yet the very next chapter "The Plague," details the city's horrifying descent into rats and disease, ignominy and corruption. Wherefore Athens' glory and meaning, then? Another classic IR text, Machiavelli's *The Prince* (1513), merits no less for its emotional complexity. It advises the Prince to switch, at will, from the charismatic Lion to the calculating Fox. The Prince needs both to stay in power. In the *History* and the *Prince*, emotions range far and wide, obviously and with nuance. Hobbes' *Leviathan*, I submit, rejects emotional complexity not due to the nature of its text but for what it considers necessary for its method: scientific rationality.

2   *Leviathan*'s Scientific Method vs *Sanguo*'s Brotherly Love. There is little sense of identity in *Leviathan*, only interests. Even Wendt (1999),

who seeks to define the "state as a person," attributes to it a "pre-social" nature. In contrast, *Sanguo* lushly portrays politics as the very vortex of sociality, as demonstrated by the loyalty oath sworn by Liu, Guan and Zhang on that beautiful, blooming day in the cherry orchard. And characters like Zhuge Liang belie Hobbes' derision of imagination as a "decaying sense"; they constantly draw on this intuitive resource to win wars and gain tactical advantage. Daoism (especially the *Zhuangzi*) teaches that the enlightened life must *feel* right in addition to knowing and doing right (Ames 1998).

Morality in politics accounts for this poetic sense in life *and* governance:

Descending from Zhou times (eleventh–third centuries BC), there prevailed *liyue lun* (discourse on rituals and music), the vision of a feudal society (in the most general sense) in which political rule was supposed to be conducted mainly through "rituals and music," as the governing principles of an organic and stable moral order. Here "rituals and music" should not be understood literally. They are the name for institutions with a direct moral purpose, including the systems for fief and tribute, land, education, etc. Since morality was intrinsic to these institutions, the norms of the external order could serve as criteria of ethical evaluation. In the horizon of *liyue lun*, textual study or *jingxue* – scrutiny of a series of Confucian classics – came to be the major branch of learning (Zhang 2010: 57).

3 *Leviathan*'s European Man vs *Sanguo*'s Genius/Trickster. Postcolonial theorists have long noted how Neorealism's "structural logic" echoes a former era's "colonial logic." Both divide and rule, beguile and betray, use and abuse, rendering violence a structural and logical imperative (Krishna 1999, 2008). And like colonial logic, Neorealism revolves world politics around the West: only Europe's Enlightenment norms and institutions (e.g. liberal tolerance, free-market values, rule of law, "universal" human rights) can govern the globe. Neorealist IR cannot recognize that the Other has anything to offer – despite hard evidence to the contrary (Behnke 2008; Hobson 2012). Far from a lawless, cut-throat State of Nature, as depicted by Hobbes, the "New World" managed to sustain a non-violent pact, the Iroquois League (1450–1777), among six nations for over three centuries (Crawford 1994). We can forgive Hobbes for not getting the facts right, but generations of IR theorists after him cannot enjoy the same. Such intellectual blinkeredness stems from Hobbesian certainty; it cannot tolerate trickster genius – or any kind of not knowing (Chan 2009). *Sanguo*, on the other hand, excels on the exploits of the strange and the unknown, especially if these come from genius, trickster or no.

4 "Warre of All against All" vs *Tianxia*. Most of all, *Leviathan* and *Sanguo* reflect different ontologies. Extended to IR, *Leviathan* transposes law and order internally to anarchy and chaos externally. Only power politics can fill the void. *Tianxia*, on the other hand, posits a worldly world order filled with an intimate network of individuals–families–states–universe, constantly

interacting back and forth, both vertically and horizontally. *Tianxia* also forwards the possibility of a virtuous, sustainable world order. It depends, foremost, on proper governance at home "inside" and in the world "out there." Both require parental love and discipline. For this reason, Zhuge releases Meng Huo seven times until the latter has a change of heart; only then does Zhuge consider his mission complete. This episode contrasts sharply with the Athenian annihilation of the Melians, simply because the latter sought neutrality.

Similarities

And yet some similarities also apply. These include an acceptance of hierarchy, Self-centeredness and patriarchy. Hierarchy results from the impervious, absolutist state in *Leviathan* and, by Neorealism's extension, the power politics of the inter-state system. For Waltz, Malaysia and Costa Rica "naturally" matter less in world politics than the United States or any other "great power." Hierarchy defines *Sanguo* given its fixation on kings and lords, generals and warriors. Never does the epic concern itself with the ordinary soldier or common folk. Since both qualify as a "child," as urged by the classics, they remain passively and mutely in the background; all action comes from their "superiors" above. Likewise, action in *Leviathan* proceeds in one direction only: from Self to Other. Already mentioned is Westphalianism's – and, by extension, IR's – Eurocentrism. *Sanguo* shares a similar centrism. Tender though it was, the episode between Zhuge Liang and Meng Huo still tells of the latter's conversion to the former, with no instance of a reverse. Indeed, *tianxia*'s horizontal axis radiates outwards only. Dynastic politics always sought to "transform" (*zhuan hua*) the Other to the Confucian center; never the other way around (Hevia 1995).

Patriarchy combines both hierarchy and self-centeredness. Pateman (1988: 50) showed how Hobbes' social contract cannot include Woman: she remains part of Man's possessions, lumped together with "chattel."

Table 1.2 Similarities among *Leviathan* and *Sanguo*

	Leviathan	Sanguo
Hierarchy	Only great powers matter	Only lords and kings, generals and warriors matter
Self-centeredness	The West knows best; the other must convert	The Confucian center knows best; the other must transform
Patriarchy	The sexual contract within the social contract; "great powers" are like men, "weak states" are like women	From "mother–father officials" to the Confucian Father-State; the people must be filial

In civil society, Leviathan's sword upholds the civil laws that give individuals protection from forcible subjection, but individuals of their own volition can enter into contracts that constitute "masters" and "servants." Or, more accurately, male individuals can [because in] the natural state all women become servants, and all women are excluded from the original pact.

Paternalism underwrites Neorealist IR (Chowdhry and Ling 2010). Feminists (Peterson 1992; Tickner 1992) note, for example, the hypermasculine traits that Waltz attributes to "great powers": i.e. they have "autonomy" without considering who and what makes such privilege possible; impunity ("wider margins of safety") for actions taken regardless of result ("uncertain outcomes"), yet still entitled to managerial status and authority ("have more say about which games will be played and how"), no matter the havoc left behind ("inattentive," "afford not to learn," "do the same dumb things over again") (Waltz 1979: 195). Conversely, "weak states" evoke the cosseted, corseted hyperfeminized female: they are confined to "narrow margins" where a single misstep could cause "fatal results" (Waltz 1979: 195). Yet, as both feminists and postcolonialists point out, "great powers" cannot be so great or powerful without the labor and resources of "weak states" (Escobar 2011; Seth 2013) not to mention all the subalterns within and across states, e.g. women, immigrants and other feminized subjects (Chowdhry and Nair 2002; Marchand and Runyan 2011).

Sanguo, in turn, brims with patriarchal storytelling. Women appear either as love interests or objects of statecraft or both. In the episode titled, "Beauty's Scheme" (*meiren ji*), one man uses a beautiful woman to bait and destroy two other men. Alternatively, *Sanguo* shows some "remarkable" women characters whose worthiness lies primarily in their ability to approximate men. Here, we briefly return to the "barbarian king," Meng Huo. His queen, Madame Zhu Rong (*zhurong furen*), earns praise in the epic for her leadership and martial arts. Three times she leads her troops to fight Zhuge's men. Three times the latter feign defeat (*zhabai*). She prudently refrains from chasing after them – until the third time. Seeing them retreat again, she cannot resist and orders pursuit, only to find herself trapped. Zhuge's men bring her to the prime minister. But he orders her release in exchange for two generals whom Meng Huo has captured. The "barbarian king" cannot refuse and the two men, the real focus of the story, honor each other by battling another day.

Since the spread of the modern state, Westphalian patriarchy has colluded with local patriarchies all over the globe. Asia is no exception. Korea's rapid economic development in the 1960s–1970s under Park Chung Hee, for example, demonstrates the corrosion of the traditional balance between "father" and "mother" authority in Confucian governance. Park Chung Hee rallied society to vindicate the state's subjugation in a Hobbesian world of economic competition through militaristic rhetoric: "Let's Fight and Construct!" (*ssaumyu geonseolhaja!*), "Export is the Only Way to Survive!" (*soochoolmani salgilida!*), "Exports as Total War!" (*soochool chongryukjeon!*), and "Trade as War!" (*mooyukjeonjaeng!*) (Han and Ling 1998: 64). From this basis, he shifted society easily from an infant requiring care to the Confucian wife/mother/daughter who must sacrifice daily (e.g. low wages, long hours, no unions, high taxes) for the family-nation under the all-knowing, patriarchal protection of the Father-State.

But there is a limit to the Confucian Father-State. Student protestors discovered it at Tiananmen Square on 4 June 1989 (Ling 1994). After the massacre, Deng Xiaoping groused like an embittered father: the student protestors were "dregs of society"; they had no purpose other than to "subvert our country and subvert our Party" (Deng quoted in Han 1990: 370).

Conclusion

Understandably, Chinese theorists seek a "Chinese School" of IR. Whether culturally, historically, philosophically, or simply in terms of problem-solving, IR as we know it simply ill-suits contexts outside the West. (Indeed, many who have nothing to do with a "Chinese" school also seek a more globally-cognizant IR.[28]) The differences between theory and understanding, not just practice, gape too widely to sustain continued adherence to mainstream IR. And yet, precisely for this reason, a "Chinese School of IR" does not make sense. The categories of "Chinese" and "IR" reflect the field's Hobbesian–Westphalian legacy. To declare a "Chinese School of IR," then, would negate its original intent.

"What if we were to switch *Leviathan* with *Sanguo*," some might query. "What kind of world politics would we have?" As mentioned at the beginning of this chapter, I believe non-Western traditions like Daoist dialectics have much to contribute if we seek a more open, democratic and "global IR" (Ling 2014). However, simply switching one canonical text for another, no matter where it originates, does not offer an alternative to current Western/Westphalian hegemony. Rather, Daoist dialectics would focus on how each affects the other, from within and out, that makes the difference. Hence, the question needs to be changed: "Where are the private connections, complicities, and complementarities between *Leviathan* and *Sanguo* despite their public contrasts, conflicts, and contradictions?"

One such connection is patriarchy. The Leviathan not only acts as a machine but it is also racialized (white) and gendered (hypermasculine). In *Sanguo*, Liu Bei jokes that women are like clothes, one wears them or sheds them at will; whereas, brothers are like the palm of one's hand, an indispensable part of one's body. This hypermasculine/patriarchal connection between *Leviathan* and *Sanguo* could lead theorists to speculate that neither text serves us well. This chapter's comparison has highlighted how different ontologies and epistemologies are at play when looking at "IR" in different parts of the globe. It does not suggest, however, that we stay with traditional interpretations or uses of them. Certainly, we are capable of greater creativity.

But I may presume too much. Perhaps advocates of a "Chinese School of IR" are willing to pay for the price of admission into the Club of IR by embracing familiar resorts to hierarchy, self-centeredness and patriarchy, as demonstrated by successful strategies in Asian capitalism. Acceptance would signal that "Chinese IR" has finally arrived. In that sense, the "Chinese School of IR" does live up to its name.

Notes

1 I am deeply grateful to Shirin Rai and Laust Schouenborg for their insightful comments. Any errors, however, redound to me alone. Many thanks, also, to Ebby Abramson for his research assistance.
2 This line comes from Shakespeare's *Romeo and Juliet* (1594): "What's in a name? That which we call a rose/by any other name would smell as sweet" (II.2).
3 Bell's webpage gives this brief autobiography:

> Daniel A. Bell is Chair Professor of the Schwarzman Scholar Program at Tsinghua University in Beijing and director of the Berggruen Institute of Philosophy and Culture. He was born in Montreal, educated at McGill and Oxford, has taught in Singapore and Hong Kong, and has held research fellowships at Princeton's University Center for Human Values and Stanford's Center for Advanced Study in the Behavioral Sciences.
> (Online, available at: http://danielabell.com/ accessed 14 July 2015)

4 I myself am an example. I was born and partly raised in Taiwan but educated in both the Western and Eastern hemispheres. Today, I conduct and publish research on IR with Asia as a geocultural–philosophical focus and teach at a university in the United States. There are others who were born, raised and educated through to university level in the Chinese mainland but now write and teach from elsewhere. Are their insights into Chinese politics and intellectual thought any *less* "Chinese" than those scholars who work at institutions on the Chinese mainland?
5 As D'Souza (2014: 6) notes, one of the outcomes of colonial knowledge production in and from the West is an analytical separation between science and art, philosophy and poetry:

> Consequently, ontological knowledge, immanence and transcendence, become intellectualized as analytical categories distanced from the storms that engulf everyday life. Ontology is reduced to a problem for epistemological reflection and as such ceases to *Be* the self-awareness that informs our ways of *being* in the world [original emphases].

6 However, Waltz (1986: 339) recognizes that states are "not unitary and purposive actors." Their pursuits are rarely concisely and consistently formulated. Nonetheless, he writes, "I assumed it to be such only for the purpose of constructing a theory."
7 Balance of power theory stipulates that if one state becomes too strong, it will motivate others to ally with one another in the system to check or "balance" any claim to hegemony.
8 Hardt and Negri (2000) later adapted this concept to global capitalism. They dubbed it "empire" to highlight global capitalism's seeming omnipresence and universal impact.
9 Here, I draw on the novel both in its original, written form and its depiction through a recent, highly popular TV series, "Sanguo," first aired on Chinese television in 2010.
10 The film, "*Chi bi*" ("Red Cliff," 2008), for example, was based on an episode of *Sanguo*. Directed by John Woo, the film had an international cast but was performed in Mandarin. The 2010 TV series, "*Sanguo*," enjoyed high ratings in Taiwan. Online, available at: http://news.sina.com.tw/article/20120712/7312574.html; http://dailynews.sina.com/bg/ent/tv/sinacn/file/20120802/02003629939.html; http://big5.chinanews.com:89/yl/2012/07-25/4058001.shtml (accessed 14 July 2015).
11 Chinese Central Television (CCTV) aired its first dramatic series on the epic in 1994. Titled, "*Sanguo Yanyi*," it was extremely popular. Many claim the 1994 version was "truer" to the novel than the 2010 one.

What's in a name? 33

12 In Japanese, online, available at: http://mangafox.me/manga/sangokushi/; in Vietnamese, online, available at: www.sachbaovn.vn/doc-truc-tuyen/sach/tam-quoc-dien-nghia-tap-1-(truyen-tranh)-MUQwQTQ2MkI) (accessed 14 July 2015).
13 In Japanese, see *Kōtetsu Sangokushi* (2007), online, available at: www.viki.com/tv/2594c-koutetsu-sangokushi-completed (accessed 7 March 2016).
14 In Korean, online, available at: http://samleague.no3games.com/nmain.php; http://cafe.naver.com/scsamguk; https://itunes.apple.com/kr/app/id431552463; http://cafe.naver.com/samtactic; in Japanese, see *Sangokushi Taisen* (2005, 2006), online, available at: www.youtube.com/watch?v=kMM8fKRs5-c (accessed 7 March 2016); in Vietnamese, online, available at: http://3d.3qc.vn/teaser/xich-bich.htm, http://luyengame.com/games/tamquocchi.html (accessed 14 July 2015).
15 In Chinese, see: "*Xin sanguo yanyi: zhong, e, mei*" ("New Romance of the Three Kingdoms: China, Russia, US"), *tianya shequ* (one of the biggest bulletin boards in China), 30 September 2010.
16 For example: "*Vợ chồng như quần áo, anh em như tay chân*" ("wives are like clothing; brothers are like the palm of one's hand"); "*Nhắc Tào Tháo, Tào Tháo đến*" ("speak of the devil [Cao Cao] and he appears"); "*Ba ông thợ may bằng một Gia Cát Lượng*" ("three stinky leather tanners can triumph over one genius Zhuge Liang").
17 "[The] neoliberal or rationalist explanation holds [that] states comply with sovereignty norms because they think it will advance some exogenously given interest, like security or trade" (Wendt 1999: 287).
18 Cao's father was the foster son of a favored eunuch in the Han dynasty court.
19 This episode comes from Chapter 89 of *Sanguo Yanyi*. The full text in Chinese is online, available at: http://cls.hs.yzu.edu.tw/san/bin/body.asp?CHNO=089. Author's translation, accessed 14 July 2015.
20 The Chinese designation of "barbarian" (*man*) entails an internal dialectic. The term does not have the same fixity in role or meaning as it has in the West. As with Meng Huo, *man* indicates geographical and cultural distance from the Confucian center; it is not an objectified condition but subject to change, depending on circumstance. For greater elaboration on the Chinese concept of "barbarian" and its appropriation by the West, see Liu (2004). For elaboration on the Western concept of "barbarian," see Beckwith (2009).
21 Zhuge's shame refers to Meng's shame. Zhuge does not want to aggravate Meng's humiliation at being captured a seventh time by having his captor witness it in person.
22 See, CCTV broadcast on 12 January 2015. Online, available at: http://video.sina.com.cn/p/news/c/v/2015-01-13/204264505273.html (accessed 14 July 2015).
23 Here, I change Legge's original translation of "*tianxia zhe*," literally "those under heaven," from "kingdom" to "universe." I believe the latter better conveys the sense intended by the *Daoxue*.
24 *Daxue*, Chinese Text Project. Online, available at: http://ctext.org/liji/da-xu (accessed 14 July 2015). Translation by James Legge except for where I insert a square bracket.
25 Historically, Daoism's emancipatory, water-like ideals have critiqued and subverted Confucianism's order-centered, rites-bound approach to governance. But over the millennia, the two traditions have borrowed substantially from each other, especially regarding the art of statecraft. See, for example, a Daoist treatise like *Huainanzi* (*Master of Huainan*, 139 BCE) that reflects many Confucian, even some legalist, notions. The same applies to the *Analects*. It draws key insights from Daoist concepts and methods. Indeed, individuals routinely integrated both in their daily lives. See, for example, Egan (1994) and Major *et al.* (2010).
26 Monarchy in the West, in contrast, transitioned from this parental–paternal relationship with its subjects, as propounded by Sir Robert Filmer in *Patriarcha* (1680), to a Hobbesian–Lockean compromise that emphasized property as the basis to contractual relations. In the latter, the state contracts with an individual who, in Locke's (1991 [1689]: 142) words, is "a man at his own free disposal."

27 "Pericles' Funeral Oration," Human Rights Library, University of Minnesota. Online, available at: www1.umn.edu/humanrts/education/thucydides.html (accessed 14 July 2015).
28 Note, for example, the Presidential Theme of the 2015 International Studies Association meeting in New Orleans was "Global IR and Regional Worlds." Online, available at: www.isanet.org/ (accessed 14 July 2015).

2 The "Chinese School" debate
Personal reflections

Ren Xiao

The invitation extended to me for contributing a chapter to this volume gives me an opportunity to reflect on the process of development of the "Chinese School" as an intellectual enterprise. As an "insider" in the sense of being a member of the Chinese International Relations (IR) community and a participant in the "Chinese School" debate, I will try to elaborate on the process as faithfully as I can. This may be useful for people outside of China to understand what this intellectual enterprise is all about. This chapter will first lay out how the aspiration for a "Chinese School" came into being. This is followed by a discussion of the methodological debate as an integral process in the emergence of a Chinese School. The third section provides a brief examination of contentions and skepticisms both in and outside of China about the construction of a Chinese School of IR. Accordingly, my discussions focus on three of the most contentious debates in the evolution of a Chinese School, i.e. naming (and why naming is important), methodological debate, and possibility and desirability debate. These debates are central to IR disciplinary growth in China and for knowledge creation and innovation by Chinese IR scholars, and thus they should be attached importance to. I will conclude the chapter by a discussion of why the emergence of a "Chinese School" is inevitable.

Labelling and naming a "Chinese School"

In retrospect, there were two main reasons for coining the term "Chinese School". The first arose from the dissatisfaction with and questioning of the status quo of Chinese IR as a field. In 1998, I wrote a short essay "Fragmented Thought on International Studies in China", in which I criticized the phenomenon that "even questions [in Chinese IR debates] are imported from abroad". To me, all the major topics debated in Chinese IR at that time, such as the "rise and fall of great powers" and the related topics such as "is the United States in decline", "the end of history" and "clash of civilizations" were invented outside of China and followed by the Chinese IR community. This phenomenon stimulated me to logically ask, "Why do we [Chinese IR scholars] always address theoretical questions others have raised?" My own answer was that Chinese IR lacked its own theoretical considerations. I urged that this situation be changed (Ren 1998).

The second reason arose from a sense of dissatisfaction. Before the term "Chinese School" was coined, in the Chinese IR community there was the call for constructing an "IR with Chinese characteristics". For example, Liang Shoude of Peking University stated, "the purpose of emphasizing the Chinese characteristics is to comprehensively and accurately reveal the nature of international politics, and fully construct our own IR as a discipline". The "Chinese characteristics" require self-esteem, self-confidence, self-accomplishment in the disciplinary construction of IR, and to give it a Chinese imprint. Of course, this shall not be an average Chinese imprint but rather distinguished and innovative contributions (Liang and Hong 2000: 33–34). However, there are two problems with this proposal. One is that in spite of his efforts, Liang is not successful in defining what he means by "Chinese characteristics" and how such characteristics can be embedded in Chinese IR theory. The other is that "IR with Chinese characteristics" is more or less a replica of the political discourse of "socialism with Chinese characteristics". This political baggage is problematic.

Sometime in 1999, I began to edit a volume (in Chinese) titled *New Perspectives on International Relations Theory*, which was to be a collection of IR theoretical essays written by scholars at Fudan University. As the editor, I needed to write an introduction for the volume. I took it seriously and later submitted the main part of the introduction to a Beijing-based journal *Ou Zhou* (*Journal of European Studies*). At that time, the journal, published by the Institute of European Studies at the Chinese Academy of Social Sciences (CASS), attached much importance to publishing articles in theoretical studies. My article, entitled "Theory and IR Theory: Some Thoughts", appeared in issue 4 of *Ou Zhou* in 2000. I was generally critical of the development of Chinese international studies at the time. More specifically, I made the following points. First, I was not in favor of the term "IR with Chinese characteristics". Second, I urged that Chinese IR scholars should have an aspiration for theoretical innovation, and should strive to articulate their own theoretical propositions with a view to constructing more systemic theories. Third, I proposed to form a "Chinese School of IR theory", but cautioned that to construct a Chinese School of IR theory is a long-term goal. There emerged some favorable conditions, objective or subjective, for such an aspiration to be realized, and we can be cautiously optimistic about such a prospect. Fourth, the purpose of constructing Chinese IR theories is not to counter Western theories. Nor does it seek a difference for difference's sake. Rather it means that Chinese IR scholars, instead of just absorbing and transplanting Western IR theories, should have the spirit of thinking independently and should not always follow others. In brief, the Chinese IR scholars should seek to make their own theoretical contributions (Ren 2000).

Earlier in the same year, Mei Ran, a young scholar at Peking University, wrote an article for *Guoji zhengzhi yanjiu* (*Studies of International Politics*) published by the School of International Studies at Peking University. Mei Ran argued that "students of IR theory in China should strive for creative and independent theoretical research in IR in order to construct a 'Chinese School of international politics'". In his words,

To display a "China brand" is to expose the unreasonable circumstances of the current global IR community and to stress the significance of changing this situation, as well as to demonstrate the courage of Chinese scholars to participate in this change.

(Mei 2000: 65)

For Mei, one country's (i.e. the United States') domination of a discipline was an abnormal phenomenon and was not favorable to healthy disciplinary development of IR. Knowledge of IR must be produced on multiple sites.

The reality was that at the turn of the twenty-first century, American IR enjoyed a nearly dominant position in the global IR community, so much so that it might be said to be overly influential and is even called "an American social science" (Hoffmann 1977). This has led to an unhealthy general situation. Since the end of World War II, American IR, with the backing of US hegemonic power and its own academic productivity, exerted great impact on global IR. The impact was so great that it has frustrated many non-American scholars, given that IR literature was full of "isms" and terms "imported" from the United States. The United States has a distinct academic culture of cherishing novelty and making difference. Over the past years, American theories using all kinds of labels often contend and stimulate one another. Various new or fashionable viewpoints and research techniques emerged one after another and often attracted attention from scholars in other countries. However, "one flower blossoming is not spring". If voices in IR knowledge production are from one country only, this is not a healthy situation. Moreover, there are limitations to American IR, including its perspective, way of thinking, and conscious or unconscious ideological idiosyncrasy. This needs to be balanced or redressed. Broadly speaking, the intellectual world of IR needs alternative ideas or approaches from other regions and countries.

Further reinforcing American dominance in IR is another phenomenon. The American IR community constitutes a "whole" or "society" to itself. American IR scholars often cite each other's work and are rather uninterested in IR scholarship produced in other countries: deep-seated within the American IR community there may be a psyche of arrogance. The character of American IR has much to do with the American character and, intentionally or unintentionally, American IR is designed for hegemonic maintenance (Qin 1999). Though not always the case, this observation indeed captures something deep-seated in American IR. Nonetheless, only resenting the US intellectual "hegemony" is not very useful. The key to the issue lies in non-American IR communities producing innovative and meaningful scholarship and providing the world with alternative ways of thinking about IR (see Ling 2014 as an example) and of solving the world's pressing problems.

To my best knowledge, the term "Chinese School" was originally adopted and proposed by Mei Ran and myself in the two above-mentioned articles. This explicit call for constructing a Chinese School of IR was boldly made out of the dissatisfaction with Chinese IR at the time and as a conscious move to counter the intellectual hegemony of the US-dominated scholarship in the discipline.

To some extent, the initiative was also enlightened by the English School, which was the "reference point" in my mind at the time, and the idea of learning from the English School emerged. To me, scholars of the English School did not chase the fashion and follow the footsteps of the mainstream American IR scholarship. Rather, they steadfastly took their own path and successfully founded a road of inventing a new academic school (Dunne 1998). Today, both the distinctive approach and contribution of the English School have been widely recognized by the global IR community, including the American IR community. An examination of the development experience of the English School reveals that some lessons can be generalized and learned. They include the following: (1) taking one's own path and not following the new fashion; (2) networking with academic researchers with similar interest and developing scholarly theories step by step; (3) stressing academic inheritance – from Martin Wight to Hedley Bull to John Vincent is a lineage widely recognized, while the British Committee on the Theory of International Politics was the organizational anchor; (4) publishing their writings in the form of research article, which is often more useful than that in the book form of meager quality; and (5) long-term persistence (Ren 2003; see also Wang and Buzan this volume).

My article proposing a "Chinese School of IR", when published, triggered both direct and indirect responses. One criticism asserted that no school like that comes into being because there is a call for it to be established. This is certainly correct. A "Chinese School of IR" does not come into being when the name is given. It can only emerge and become established when it has a distinct theory that is recognized in the IR community. This being true, the criticism misunderstands the purpose of my call for constructing a "Chinese School of IR". The purpose of my appeal was to caution Chinese IR scholars against simply blindly following Western theories and to call for Chinese IR scholars to seek to produce innovative scholarship in theorizing IR. A "Chinese School" was proposed not to refer to the reality, but rather to articulate an aspiration.

A second criticism was that this initiative "does not help" with any disciplinary development. Su Changhe and Peng Zhaochang (1999: 15–19), for example, argue that

> in the primary stage of disciplinary development, overly stressing the opposite side by referring to nationhood does not help with the emergence of the so-called "school". Rather, it is likely to sink their own research into unnecessary and emotional struggle between "factions", and thus unfavorable to the healthy development of IR as a discipline in China.

This criticism does not hold because real debates between academic groups are a good thing, which only discuss academic questions and do not involve others. Of concern rather is the lack of meaningful and vigorous debates. Genuine debates are increasing these days, and this is a positive development in Chinese IR.

A third criticism contended that the English School is not a national school but is only limited to England, a part of the United Kingdom. Thus it is inappropriate to derive the term "Chinese School" (Zhang 2008). This criticism is far-fetched and unpersuasive. Let us now assume that there is no such a thing as the "English School" at all in the world, is the term "a Chinese School of IR" entirely meaningless? My answer is "no". On the contrary, the term "a Chinese School of IR" is still meaningful. To me, what matters is that Chinese IR scholars carry out sufficiently creative research work and therefore substantiate the name of "a Chinese School of IR". Still there are others who claim that using the name of a country in the nomenclature of an academic school has not been done before. This is not true either. For example, in economics there is an "Austrian School" represented by Ludwig von Mises and others. Just as nobody would believe the Austrian School included all the Austrian economists, nobody would think all British IR scholars can be lumped together under the umbrella of the "English School". On the contrary, usually such a name loosely refers to a group of academics who live and work in a specific country, share the same academic interests and similar academic views, and have published creative academic scholarship and thus exerted a wide-spread influence.

A fourth criticism is from Shi Bin of Nanjing University. In his view, although "Chinese characteristics" is not an academic term and comes with certain political baggage, it is acceptable for it to be used generally. "A Chinese School of IR" is not necessarily that accurate, either. However, naming does not matter and the key is the content scholars insert into the theoretical exploration. Shi himself would like to adopt "Chinese exploration" (*zhongguo shi tansuo*) (Shi 2006).

"Chinese exploration" as defined by Shi Bin shares a similar aspiration and appeal with what I call "a Chinese School". However, "Chinese exploration" is not as clear-cut or inspiring as "a Chinese School". Still there is a comment by Zhang Ruizhuang of Nankai University that in a challenging way says "show me". Yet a comment like this is unfair, since the call for "a Chinese School" primarily appealed to what was desired when that call was made. And for the proponents of the Chinese School, they indeed aspire to produce something original to establish themselves in the global IR community. In a nutshell, all these debates and discussions are useful and they are favorable to the deepening of the relevant explorations.

The methodological debate

In addition to the naming debate, there is also a methodological debate in Chinese international studies. This debate has much to do with the issue of constructing "a Chinese School of IR". In 2003, two leading Chinese journals, one in social sciences in general and the other in IR, *Zhongguo shehui kexue* (*Social Sciences in China*) and *Shijie jingji yu zhengzhi* (*World Economics and Politics*), jointly organized a small-scale yet well-represented conference on "Research Methods in IR". I was invited. The conference took place on 20 September 2003 at the place of the *Zhongguo shehui kexue* editorial office in

Beijing. The participants included Wang Yizhou, editor of *World Economics and Politics*, Qin Yaqing of China Foreign Affairs University, Yan Xuetong of Tsinghua University, Zhang Ruizhuang of Nankai University, myself and others. The list was an impressive one, representative of different institutions nationwide. At that time, Yan Xuetong was enthusiastically advocating "scientific method" in international studies. He asserted that in Chinese IR "traditionalism is still the mainstream, while scholars committed to scientism are the minority. People who are capable of engaging in quantitative analysis are few, and those capable of quantitative forecasting are even fewer". He believes that the future development of China's IR will be similar to that in the United States, and that the scientization of IR research is inevitable and scientism will eventually become the mainstream. The capability of forecasting is a key testing criterion if a field is "scientific". The lack of predicative capabilities of an IR theory is indicative of its lack of scientific methodology (Yan and Lu 2005).

I had reservations about Yan's view and disagreed with him strongly, for I believed that he overestimated and exaggerated the importance of the so-called "scientific method" in IR research. Thus, I decided to use "Taking methods seriously without being constrained by methods" (重视方法, 不惟方法) as the title of my presentation. This view was clearly different from what Yan was strongly advocating. Unsurprisingly, I heard Yan's criticisms even before I spoke. For Yan, Chinese IR should become more akin to American IR by conscious employment of a "scientific method", thus denying the possibility of a Chinese School, whereas for me, IR methodology has to be pluralistic, and a distinct Chinese School has to be built to highlight Chinese contributions to IR.

I spoke after Yan had presented. My main argument was that the usefulness of "science" in social science research and IR should not be overemphasized. Different research methods have different roles to play and they also have their respective limitations. Scientific methods are no exceptions. A "scientific method" can be applied to certain studies. For example, a "scientific method" can play an important role in the comparative studies of comprehensive national power. However, a conclusion like "anarchy is what states make of it" can hardly be reached by employing a "scientific method". This is not to deny the usefulness of scientific methods in IR research. The choice of methodological approaches in research has much to do with the topic a researcher has chosen to study. There is no "best" method in social science research. We needed multiple methods and should be open-minded in terms of methodological choices. Methodological pluralism would not hinder the development of IR research. Rather, it would promote and enhance innovative scholarship of IR in China (Ren 2004). The "scientific method" accusing other methods of being "unscientific" can be compared to Western medicine criticizing Chinese medicine for being unscientific. In fact, Western and Chinese medicines have their respective principles. Western medicine directly goes to disease, while Chinese medicine puts emphasis on the general balance of the human body, namely, a wholistic approach to health. To combine Western and Chinese medicines in a dialectical way may be the most effective way to combat diseases.

The presentations at this national conference on IR research methods appeared later in a special issue of *World Economics and Politics*. It is an important cluster of short articles. Yan wrote in his piece that

> The procedures of a scientific research method include finding a question, putting forward hypothesis, operationalizing concepts, empirical testing, and reaching a conclusion. If a research method does not include conceptual operationalization and empirical testing, it is not a scientific method in its strict sense. To ensure that research process and conclusion can both be openly tested, scientific method requires common rules to set criteria, without which no test can be carried out.
>
> (Yan 2004)

This is a strictly positivist understanding of theory. But Yan is unclear about what "common rules" and "criteria" mean. In my view, Yan's understanding of social science is mistaken since his understanding is actually that of natural science. Consequently, he adopts natural scientific ideas of "testing" and "forecasting" to refer to and handle social scientific issues, and sees other methods as unscientific. This goes to the extreme and is wrong. Furthermore, whether the "scientific method" Yan advocated strongly is really useful is questionable. This can be illustrated by an anecdote involving Yan himself. It was widely reported in the Chinese media on 11 June 2008 that Yan Xuetong, director of the Institute of International Studies at Tsinghua University, published an essay in the *Global Times* and publicly apologized to the readers for wrongly predicting that "a military conflict across the Taiwan Strait will take place no later than 2008". In Yan's own words,

> When Chen Shuibian came to power in 2000, I have kept predicting that a military conflict across the Taiwan Strait will take place no later than 2008. However, the 'UN membership referendum' and the 2008 leader election in Taiwan did not trigger any military conflict but rather were accompanied by a more stable and peaceful prospect.
>
> (*Global Times* 10 June 2008)

This apology reveals serious limitations of the so-called scientific method in IR research.

Qin Yaqing made some comments during the above-mentioned method conference. For him, there were many debates in Western IR surrounding two methods: what he calls positivism and heuristics. "Now the same debate is also appearing in China, and this is a good thing". He himself proposed a third way by calling it "the third culture", obviously borrowed and deduced from C.P. Snow's "two cultures" (Snow 1998). Qin argued that scientific method needed to be reinforced in China's IR studies, but a scientific myth should not arise. Other methods, including the heuristics method, should not be excluded in IR. For Chinese IR, integrating scientific and humanistic methods is a more meaningful middle way. Humanistic spirit should be integrated into social science research (Qin 2004).

When the conference was over, I had a brief exchange with Yan. I said that it would be great if there emerged a Tsinghua School under his leadership. In the later years, Yan and his Tsinghua associates set up a major research project and they meticulously studied pre-Qin Chinese thinkers and their thoughts. Their work yielded innovative scholarship, which is clearly not achieved through employing a "scientific method" (see Xu and Sun this volume). This again shows the merit of methodological pluralism.

To me, the behavioralist movement in American social sciences harvested significant achievements. As a component of the movement, quite a few research methods and techniques have become institutionalized and are widely used today. Meanwhile, it ought to be recognized that there are serious shortcomings in behavioralism. Because of their pursuit of "pure" science, many studies have become ahistorical. History is disappearing! The tremendously rich linguistic, cultural, religious and social phenomena have diminished under the slogan of scientization. Colorful and complex human acts are reduced to a few game theoretical laws. However, all human and social sciences are, in the final analysis, the study of human beings. In the social sciences, without human care, history disappears and meaning diminishes. A negative result of the behavioralist movement is that some studies are increasingly becoming meaningless. What they lack are indeed the human elements and care.

In China, some IR scholars are adamantly advocating "scientific" IR research, or the "scientization" of IR studies. This is not entirely wrong since Chinese IR indeed needs to extract some useful things, such as the quantitative research method, from "scientific behavioralism". But, I argue, in terms of research approaches or methods, there is no such thing as the single best method. We should advocate multiple methods or the coexistence of different approaches, in IR and other research areas. It is unnecessary and undesirable to unify research methods out of the conviction that there is one single best method. Also, I have reservations about the "scientization" proposal. To me, this proposal is greatly influenced by American behavioralism, the dominant aspect of which believes IR should be "scientific". The chief meaning of that is there exist universally applicable methods and only through employing these methods can IR become "scientific". Though not totally groundless, this proposal has a big problem because it neglects humanistic significance, and as a result, would turn IR into an "ahistorical" field (Ren 2005).

In fact, the kind of debate is not limited to the IR community. In China's economics community, for example, there have also emerged similar debates. Some economists question whether there is such thing as "Chinese economics", just as there are no Chinese physics, chemistry, and biology. The opponents point out that economics can never become a science like physics, chemistry, or biology. Economics' propensity as a social science can never change. The fundamental reason for this is that what is studied in economics is human activities and behavior. Human beings have multiple purposes or collective acts, and thus different institutions, organizations and political parties as well as ideas, values and ideologies. All these elements complicate human activities. In this sense, to establish economics with Chinese characteristics is both necessary and important (Wang and Ma 2015). This debate in economics is much like the one in Chinese IR, and essentially reflects the different views on the nature of social science. "Scientism" (*kexue zhuyi*) is questioned.

Debates at home and abroad

The debate on a "Chinese School of IR" drew attention from both Chinese and international IR communities and had a visible impact. Within China, one example of this is the 2004 national conference on IR theory held at Shanghai Jiaotong University, which calls explicitly for "Constructing Chinese Theory, Establishing a Chinese School". The organizers pointed out that constructing Chinese IR theory is by no means to create a unified or single IR theory. The development and growth of Chinese IR theory lies in the formation of, and contention between, different academic schools and theoretical approaches. Exchanges and contentions are the best, and probably the only, way for theoretical development and innovation, and there is no exception at home or abroad. The longstanding lack of theoretical innovation has greatly delayed the steps of theoretical development in China. Thus there is an urgent need for Chinese IR to construct Chinese IR theories and schools (Yu 2005). This debate has also aroused some interest and captured attention abroad.

In November 2005, an IR graduate student forum was held at Tsinghua University in Beijing and the issue of establishing China's IR theory once again became the focus. Yan Xuetong argued that IR theory itself had no nationhood and thus there is no way for the objective of creating China's IR theory to be realized (Yan 2006). In his opinion, the term "English School" in IR theory, like the "Chicago School", "Copenhagen School" and "Florida School", refers to a theory or school of thought that is not yet that systemic, and such terms do not mean they bear statehood or nationhood. Isaac Newton was one of the founders of classical physics but he did not see his theory as an English theory (Yan 2006). Again, in my opinion, Yan risked two pitfalls here. First, he sees social science in the same light as natural science and therefore mixes the fundamentally different nature of the two. Natural science is the same throughout the world and highly consistent. Researchers in different countries can easily understand each other through using formulas. Experiments in natural science can be repeated and there are common criteria. In contrast, social science is about the social or human world, and it is impossible for social science to have precise criterion or standards like those in natural science. Second, Yan's view disregards a fact – namely, which country a founder of social science theory comes from has an important impact on theory-building. Social science researchers are human beings who grew up and live in a specific social environment. Their background, cultural inheritance and individual concerns all affect the process of their theoretical thinking and activities, and so does their nationality. Therefore, the situation of "Chinese", "American", "English" and "French" theories exists, so do Brazilian and Indian ones (Kristensen in this volume). Nonetheless, this does not deny that theories built by those theorists possess universality one way or another, and this is a different question. Hence, a theory's place of origin is not unimportant, and this originates from the nature of social science.

This "Chinese School" debate also caught some attention internationally. Victoria Hui of the University of Notre Dame, a Hong Kong native, came up with the idea to organize a panel on "Should there be national schools of IR?" at the 2008 American Political Science Association (APSA) annual meeting in Boston. The proposal was accepted without problem and included in the annual meeting program. Hui intended to bring the debate to the "mainstream" arena of the international academic community. The effort was an admirable one. Both Yan Xuetong and I were invited as representatives of different views. The panel also included Jack Snyder and Yuan-Kang Wang, with Hui as the chair. There were views of both "yes" and "no" in the panel, and in the audience too. I obtained an impression that there were more "no" answers among the participants, and the main reason behind these "no" answers seemed to be that proposing a "national school" sounded somewhat "nationalistic" while advocating theoretical universality looked more "cosmopolitan" and thus had more supporters. Nevertheless, one senior scholar in the audience commented that "a Chinese School is inevitable", which made me feel that somehow I was not alone. Earlier on, during the March 2008 International Studies Association (ISA) annual meeting in San Francisco, the participating Chinese IR scholars and Chinese PhD candidates studying in the United States together held an informal discussion, and they used "From knowledge consumers to producers: the theorization of Chinese IR" as the theme. Attendees included Qin Yaqing, Su Changhe, Wang Zhengyi, Sun Xuefeng and myself, as well as Pu Xiaoyu, Chen Dingding and others who were pursuing their PhDs in American universities. The participants exchanged views and placed emphasis on difficulties in theory-building, for instance, the importance and difficulty of conceptualization, with which I agreed.

Around that time, it was Qin Yaqing of China Foreign Affairs University who developed more fully the idea of "a Chinese School of IR". In 2005, Qin published an important article entitled "The Core Question of IR Theory and the Formation of a Chinese School", which had a wide-ranging impact. For Qin, although Chinese IR scholars had a desire for a Chinese School of IR, they usually thought about the intellectual origins and pattern of thinking for international politics, and they were rarely aware of the significance of the core theoretical question. As a result, a solid theoretical core could not emerge, and neither did a Chinese School. What should be the core theoretical question for China's IR research then? Qin argues that China's peaceful integration into the international society can be such a core question, within which concrete research questions can be generated and research agendas set up. "With the self-consciousness of the core question, we can then have the purposeful self-consciousness of theory-building. And this is the necessary precondition of establishing a Chinese School" (Qin 2005: 175–176). Later Qin published another article arguing that the emergence of a Chinese School is not only possible but also inevitable. For him, China's rapid development, significant social transformation and deep-seated ideational change, together, prompt Chinese elites to begin to solve China's identity problem vis-à-vis international society. The fundamental debate over China's relations with the international system and the related practices will inevitably lead to the formation of the Chinese School (Qin 2006).

In April 2013, during the ISA annual meeting held in San Francisco, Wang Yiwei and Zhang Yongjin organized a panel, "Diffusion of IR Theory: the End of the Western and the rise of Chinese IR Theory", a somewhat sensational title. The panel was actually about the contentions for constructing "a Chinese School of IR". An apparent underestimation, ISA assigned a room with a capacity to seat between 50 and 60 people. It proved too small for the number of people who turned up for the panel (estimated around 100). Consequently, the room was so jammed that the latecomers could not even enter it, let alone join the discussion. This incident revealed an enormous international interest in the issue of constructing "a Chinese School of IR".

As one Chinese scholar argued in 2007, "The IR theoretical research in China, after a few generations' efforts, has undergone the phases of understanding and digesting the Western IR theories and begun to shift to the phase of substantially building China's own IR theory" (Zhang 2007: 14). No matter how accurate this statement is, to produce innovative theoretical scholarship is an objective the Chinese IR community is pursuing today. The degree of difficulty for this endeavor is appreciated. To use an analogy, building a theory is like building a mansion, which needs numerous bricks or stones. A foundation has to be laid first and then a mansion can be gradually built. Although how a systemic theory is understood is subject to debate, there should be no question that a Chinese School is emerging today.

The prospect

Discussing this issue in 2008, I argued that the debate on the issue of "a Chinese School of IR" was meaningful and was revealing of the growing self-consciousness of China's IR community in making an original theoretical contribution. Fermenting in it was the vibrant growth of Chinese IR theoretical discourse (Ren 2009). What I stressed then was the possibility rather than necessity of "a Chinese School of IR". I was cautious about "inevitability" because the emergence of a Chinese School of IR needed a process of creation and conversion. Assuming that there is no Chinese IR theory at present, which may be contentious, whether a Chinese IR theory will emerge is up to the efforts made by the Chinese IR community – and how successful these efforts will be. Meanwhile, I concur with the viewpoint that there need to be multiple academic schools in Chinese IR. The more that different schools of thought interact with and stimulate each other, the more likely it is that academic research is advanced. In fact, rather than too many, there are too few serious academic debates on the subject of Chinese IR. Moreover, there are no winners and losers in any academic debate; rather, scholarship is advanced and knowledge is produced because of mutual stimulation and inspiration. Accepting multiple schools does not mean that the term "a Chinese School of IR" does not hold or is meaningless. To me, the call for a "Chinese School of IR" will at least play a role in promoting theoretical innovation and will reinforce the level of consciousness and sense of autonomy in China's IR community (Ren 2009). These views are still valid today and need to be further developed.

A few years ago, a question was asked "why there is no non-Western International Relations theory" (Acharya and Buzan 2010a). This is a flawed question. First, the assertion at least is not entirely true. According to this argument, it is as if only the Western, especially American, generalizations are theories. Second, if people accept this assertion, they would easily hold an attitude of making a fetish of Western theories. In fact, the right way is not "looking up at" or "looking down at" but looking at non-Western theories on an equal footing. It is incorrect to assume what the Westerners call theory is a theory and there is no IR theory in the non-Western parts of the world. If there is a theory in Thucydides' *History of the Peloponnesian War*, isn't there a theory in Sun Tzu's *The Art of War*? Contemporarily, if John Mearsheimer's *Tragedy of Great Power Politics* (Mearsheimer 2001) is a theory, is not Qin Yaqing's *Guanxi yu guocheng* (Relationality and Process) (Qin 2012b) a theory? Earlier on, Shi Yinhong of Renmin University argued that "IR theory must be defined sufficiently broadly. All theoretical considerations about International Relations are IR theories" (Shi 2004). It is necessary and important to make this kind of emphasis, which is conducive to being liberated from fascination with and blind faith in Western theories. Disenchantment is needed here.

The questions that should be raised are: Should the Chinese IR community contribute to global IR? If so, what contributions can it make? And how? These questions are probably what drive the "Chinese School" as an intellectual enterprise. They are also questions that the Chinese IR community cannot escape and must think about. It is completely natural and normal that the academics have different opinions on the issue of "a Chinese School of IR". This is an embodiment of a healthy scholarly debate. When I used the term "a Chinese School of IR", I often added quotation marks, implying that it is a goal rather than an existing matter. Without doubt, serious debates between different views can only enhance, not obstruct, the promotion of academic studies.

In my view, the key word for the exploration of the "Chinese School" question is "Chinese-ness". The products of social science are just like literature, film and other forms of art: the more national, the more cosmopolitan. The intellectual and theoretical products that arise from one's own society and experience would only attract more attention and exert more influence transcending the boundaries. On the contrary, simply following the scholarship of other countries by introducing and imitating is not meaningful and cannot be a constructive enterprise. This kind of work would not win international respect and occupy a place in global IR. Furthermore, the existing theories need to be redressed, balanced or further developed. I believe this is without any dispute.

What is "Chinese-ness" then? It includes the following elements. First, innovative research work carried out by the Chinese. "The Chinese" is an inclusive term and could be the Chinese scholars working or studying abroad. Yet here "the Chinese" mainly refer to researchers living and working in the People's Republic of China. When T.D. Lee and Chen-Ning Yang won the Nobel Prize in Physics, both of them were Chinese Americans and they completed their research work in the United States. Thus it was American scientists who won the prize, and this is commonly recognized. Second, it refers to the Chinese style and character, including the Chinese way of seeing IR and the world and involving the experience, thought, feelings and expectations gained from its interactions with the outside world. Third, it refers to the inherent content and "code" of the Chinese culture. The "Chinese contribution" should spring from Chinese thought and culture, without which the efforts that Chinese academics make to theorize IR would likely become "water without the spring". In this regard, some useful work has been carried out, including research into the Chinese concept of "harmony" (*he*). To some extent this is inspired by the ideas of building a harmonious society and harmonious world. Another example is the research work on pre-Qin Chinese thinkers carried out by Tsinghua University scholars. This admirable effort has yielded penetrating and thought-provoking products.

Regardless of the formation of Chinese-ness in the construction of IR theory, theory-building is an incremental and long-term process. It is the real life efforts and diligent work of Chinese IR scholars that matter in theoretical innovation and knowledge production in constructing a Chinese School of IR. Likewise, it will be a long process for the theoretical achievements of Chinese scholars to be recognized by the global IR community. With the passage of time, I am becoming more optimistic; today I tend to believe that the emergence of a Chinese School is inevitable. For this confidence I have five reasons.

First, there is a difference between big and small countries. In a great power, usually there is a greater degree of intellectual and theoretical autonomy. In this sense, China is different from other places such as South Korea, Taiwan and even Japan. In South Korea, for example, most IR scholars working at major academic institutions obtained their advanced degrees from American universities. They usually embrace American theories and take them for granted. At most they employ American theories and combine with the reality of their own country or the Northeast Asian region, and rarely is an endeavor made to construct an innovative theory. Often there is a lack of a spirit of enquiry, especially about American theories. But theoretical development exactly needs to query the existing theories and, building on this, put forward a new proposition or theory.

Seeing it this way, it is arguably favourable for scholars and theorists to have grown up in their native country. What matters is probably a combination of the following two elements. On the one hand, they have international experiences and know about international scholarly development. On the other, they are solidly based in their native country and are nurtured by it. By combining the two and through creative efforts, they are more likely to carry out distinct research work. The intellectual autonomy allows them to fulfill innovative work.

There is, for example, an attempt at "indigenizing" (*bentuhua*) social science in Taiwan, and this has yielded some high-quality products.

Second, self-consciousness is on the rise in almost all the fields in Chinese humanities and social sciences disciplines today. Chinese philosopher, Li Zehou, has elaborated on "now is the time for Chinese philosophy to step onto the stage" (Li and Liu 2011, 2012). Another Chinese philosopher, Wu Xiaoming, argued that Chinese academic research must shift away from "apprenticeship" and enter into its own claim and assertion (Wu 2014). In economics, Justin Lin of Peking University, former chief economist of the World Bank, has put out the banner of "new structural economics", which is becoming the third wave of development economics. The first and second wave of development economics respectively put emphasis on the role of the state or the role of the market. As a development and innovation, the new structural economics Lin espouses aims to establish a new systematized theory to help people better understand and restructure the economic world. This new theoretical enterprise strives to address the question as to why successful economies all adopted the export-oriented strategy and all possessed effective market and capable government simultaneously (Lin 2012, 2013).

In sociology, according to Zhai Xuewei of Nanjing University, Chinese sociologists have realized that, throughout the process of learning from the Western scholarship,

> Our perspectives are certainly stipulated by the Westerners. Our research approach and method, through their training, have become procedures, whereas skillfully applying these procedures means we obtain a certificate to engage in the disciplinary studies. But there is a tough follow-up question. On the one hand, this kind of formalized research has empowered the researchers to possess scientific (objective) or disciplinary characteristics when studying Chinese society, culture, history, human psychology and behavior. On the other, despite this transformation, studies in the structure, features and approaches of the Chinese and Chinese society have not become clearer and more persuasive. Very often, they have become unclear and inconsistent with the fact. A society, in many study reports, is becoming something without its own history and culture. Men, in many investigations and experiments, have become human beings without social background and situation.
>
> (Zhai 2013: 5–7)

Exactly under these circumstances, sociologists and psychologists put forward proposals for the "indigenization of human, social and behavioral sciences" and "native aptness". For Jin Yaoji, a leading sociologist, the character of sociology is affected by a sociologist's "cognitive orientation" and by the social structure around him/her. Thus, although sociology in China does not necessarily lead to a "Chinese sociology", the sociological studies carried out by Chinese sociologists will inevitably reflect on the character of Chinese culture and society more or less. In this sense, the "Sinicization of sociology" is likely and also inevitable (Jin 2013). Overall, developments in different social science disciplines in China are impacting on and stimulating each other. Indigenization or Sinicization is the shared goal of these efforts, and this is an extremely positive trend.

Third, historically speaking, the rise of theory and the rise of power were closely related and this implies something. During the first half of the twentieth century, Great Britain was the world's power center and also the center of international politics. In this same period, the center of IR was also Britain. In economics, British economics represented by Alfred Marshall and John Maynard Keynes enjoyed a dominant status as well. After World War II, the world's power centers decisively shifted to the United States and the Soviet Union. The United States rose prominently as the hegemonic power and became the unquestionable center of gravity of IR theory and IR as a discipline. Into the twenty-first century, China is rising rapidly in the world, and this is a major development in world economics and politics. The changes in China's relations with the outside world have raised numerous questions and also pose a huge demand for and stimulus to IR theory-building. Consequently, the transformation has boosted the self-confidence of Chinese IR community as well as its self-consciousness and identity. Against this backdrop, the Chinese School of IR theory will likely rise together with the rise of China, and this is emerging as an unavoidable trend.

Fourth, IR theory is indeed emerging in China today. In addition to the work done by Qin Yaqing, Yan Xuetong and their associates (See Xu and Sun, and Zhang in this volume), I would like to mention theoretical explorations of a group of Shanghai-based scholars and their research into the "*gong sheng*" (symbiosis) theory. Their work makes me more confident in the "inevitability" of the emergence of the Chinese School. In recent years, this group of Shanghai-based social scientists conducted active studies in symbiosis theory. The sociologists, especially Fudan University professor Hu Shoujun, pioneered this endeavor. In 2006, Hu published a seminal book *Shehui gongsheng lun* (*A Theory of Social Symbiosis*) (Hu 2006), and also founded a research center on social symbiosis at Fudan. The work of such sociologists triggered an interest from the Chinese IR community, especially that of Jin Yingzhong, secretary general of the Shanghai Society of IR. Later Jin published three articles in Shanghai-based journals applying the concept of *gong sheng* to IR. In July 2012, the Shanghai Society of IR convened a symposium to commemorate the twenty-fifth anniversary of China's first nationwide conference on IR theory. Some non-IR scholars including Hu Shoujun also attended.

A year later, two Fudan professors, Su Changhe and myself, respectively published their articles on *gong sheng* (symbiosis) in the influential journal *Shijie jingji yu zhengzhi* (World Economics and Politics) and attracted much attention. Two Beijing-based young IR scholars, Xiong Lili and Chen Xuefei, wrote review articles questioning the validity and usefulness of the *gong sheng* concept. Su and myself then published response essays in November 2014, further elaborating on the related historical and theoretical issues. Earlier on in

June 2014, three scholarly societies of philosophy, sociology and IR in Shanghai, jointly convened a seminar on *gong sheng*. All these academic activities and the products they have yielded indicate the growth of a burgeoning Shanghai School, which uses "symbiosis" as the key concept (Ren 2015).

In Beijing, the research team at Tsinghua University has also yielded distinct and important products, "the Tsinghua Approach" characterized by the following three features. First, its motivation originates in a desire to enrich modern IR theory and, no less importantly, to draw policy lessons for China's rise today. Second, it seeks to do so by drawing on China's political thought from the golden age of Chinese philosophy in the Spring and Autumn and Warring States period (770–222 BC). This is the most distinctive feature of the Tsinghua Approach and where a Chinese consciousness is in full display (Zhang 2012: 75, see also Xu and Sun this volume). "From the global perspective of Chinese IR, its significance lies in having rendered the question 'why is there no non-Western International Relations theory?' somewhat obsolete" (Zhang 2012).

Finally, China's experience is providing IR theory with a new empirical foundation. No matter whether a theory is a summation or interpretation of laws, there is a question of the empirical foundation on which it builds. Today's "mainstream" IR theories have an apparent tendency toward Euro-centrism and their empirical foundation is limited to the Western experience since the Peace of Westphalia, while non-Western practices in IR are largely neglected. These empirical limitations raise a question about the universal validity of Western theories. Intellectually, the Chinese are good at thinking about the world's universal issues and concerns, including those disharmonies and relations between North and South and among religions and civilizations. Those are not new questions at all but have eternal ramifications. Thinking about those questions thoroughly can lead to a Chinese contribution to IR and therefore the growth of a Chinese School of IR.

Conclusion

The above five reasons convince me that the emergence of a Chinese School of IR is simply a matter of time, and to me, it is actually an on-going process. That is also why to say there is or is not a non-Western IR theory proves a simplistic way to make an argument. Initiatives to construct "a Chinese School of IR" since the turn of the twenty-first century are the most meaningful and autonomous initiative in Chinese IR and are likely to yield innovative products in future years. It marks the beginning of a new stage of the development of IR as a field in China. With multiple efforts by Chinese scholars at theoretical innovation, there may emerge a few distinct schools of thought in different parts of the country, mainly Beijing and Shanghai, the two major intellectual centers. Serious debates have been going on over the past decade or so and have inspired Chinese IR scholars to think hard and conduct original research work. The growth of a Chinese School will occur along with the rise of China in the world, and throughout this process Chinese IR theory will gain momentum.

The biggest challenge the emerging Chinese School of IR faces is always the "what is it" question, which has never been an easy one and may usefully force the Chinese School to distinguish itself from other IR scholarship or schools of thought. This too requires Chinese IR scholars to make continuous efforts and yield products to "prove" their distinctness. Of course this means enormously hard work and productive research. This also means further informed debates within the Chinese IR community to stimulate relevant scholarly thinking. To date, Chinese IR academics have accomplished some preliminary achievements or successes. If they can continue to be successful in future years, the emerging Chinese IR theory will have an increasingly greater voice in the global IR community. I previously held a cautious attitude toward this prospect but I am more optimistic now.

3 Why is there no Chinese IR theory?

A cultural perspective

Wang Yiwei and Han Xueqing

Introduction

Some 50 years ago, Martin Wight (1966: 37–38) asked 'why is there no international theory' in his thought-provoking essay, attributing the 'scattered, unsystematic, and mostly inaccessible of IR theory' to 'the intellectual prejudice imposed by the sovereign State, and the belief in progress'. More recently, Amitav Acharya and Barry Buzan (2007: 292, 297), clearly inspired by Wight, considered a more specific question 'why is there no non-Western IR theory?', claiming that IR theory has to be either a 'systematic attempt to abstract or generalize about the subject matter of IR' or 'self-identified by its creators or widely acknowledged by the mainstreams in the IR academic community'. They also asserted that the most significant reason for non-Western IR theory's absence was that Western IR theories have followed the 'right route' to an understanding of IR issues, while the non-Western ones are still constrained by local conditions, unable to enter the IR discourse realm constructed by the West, leading to the awkward situation that 'non-Western IR theories do exist, but are hidden'. Later, Acharya (2011: 619–637) placed further emphasis on voices and experiences beyond the West that have long been neglected, suggesting that scholars should pay more attention to the genealogy of the international system, the diversity of regionalism and regional worlds. Inspired by Wight, Acharya and Buzan, this chapter asks 'why is there no Chinese IR theory?'.

The chapter starts with the premise that there is not yet a single theory or a series of theories that deserve the title a 'Chinese School of IR'. The analytical discussion proceeds as follows: The existing debates and claims regarding the question 'why is there no Chinese IR theory?' are summarized in the chapter's first section. In the second section, five explanations are put forward to answer the question from a cultural perspective. The third section identifies how Chinese culture could offer something that goes beyond Western IR theory. Finally, the chapter tries to demonstrate that there is great potential for a Chinese IR theory to emerge and evolve, and the 'Chinese dream' of IR theory is in shaping.

Constructing IR theory with Chinese characteristics: three debates

Although China was fully involved in international affairs only in the late 1970s, as early as in 1987, the need for distinctively Chinese IR theory was emphasized at China's first national conference on IR theory in Shanghai. Since then, many Chinese IR scholars have devoted themselves to distinguishing Chinese IR from Western discourses. Constructing 'IR theory with Chinese characteristics' or a 'Chinese School of IR theory' has since become a contentious issue, triggering three waves of academic debate.

The first debate concerns the necessity to construct 'IR theory with Chinese characteristics'. Liang Shoude (1997a: 2) from Peking University insisted that, as a latecomer in international affairs, China should get rid of Western theoretical discourse and construct her own IR theory system. Sceptics argued that as a high abstraction of complicated real-world IR, IR theory should go beyond any 'national experiences' or 'national characteristics' and become universal. For example, Song Xinning (2001: 61–74) from Renmin University indicated that the quest for 'IR theory with Chinese characteristics' was more or less an 'ideology-driven' concept. This debate took place at the turn of the century. Several years later, a second debate came when a more 'neutral' name was given to the pursuit of 'Chinese IR theory '.

At the beginning of this century, many Chinese scholars preferred the phrase 'a Chinese School of IR theory'. Mei Ran and Ren Xiao first proposed the idea of constructing 'a Chinese School of IR theory', arguing that the US-dominated IR was full of prejudice, and China should construct her own theoretical school as the British did (Mei 2000: 63–65; Ren 2003: 70–71). Proponents further depicted a quest for the Chinese School as a pillar of China's rise in an era of globalization. To the extent that 'theory is always for someone and some purpose' (Cox 1981), 'every IR theory is provincial in cultural terms' (Zhang 2011: 785). By the same token, IR was still effectively an art of the states, and 'the absence of Chinese IR theory' was a stigma imposed on China by the great powers, or an inevitable tragedy of globalization (Wang 2005). The reactivation of ancient Chinese culture and social tradition may symbolically underline her hope for a theoretical framework distinctive from that of the mainstream Western approaches (Wang 2009; Kristensen and Nielsen 2013a). However, opponents of the 'Chinese School' project came from the 'scientistic camp', believing that IR theory, or, definitely, any international theory, should cast away local flavour, and be 'scientific, universal, and generally acknowledged' (Yan 2006), thus making the 'Chinese School' unnecessary. The real dispute of the second debate was about the claims of universality of IR theories. One of the central questions debated is 'Is IR theory science or art?' (Wang 2002; Sun 2003).

In 2006, Qin Yaqing published an essay 'A Chinese School of International Relations Theory: Possibility and Inevitability' in a prestigious Chinese journal '*Social Sciences in China*', stating that although Chinese international studies have been heavily influenced by Western scholarship, an indigenous framework was already growing, making the construction of Chinese IR theory not only possible, but also natural (Qin 2006). With most IR scholars convinced that building 'a Chinese IR theory' was necessary and urgent, a third debate later emerged, which focused on how to construct it.

The third debate was on the ways and methods to build a Chinese IR theory. Chinese scholars have generally followed two routes. The first can be called 'historical'. Following this route, Zhao Tingyang (2011) and Gan Chunsong (2012) advocated revitalizing theoretical elements from ancient Chinese '*Tian Xia*' system and '*Wang Dao*' thought; and Yan Xuetong (2011a) reinterpreted the pre-Qin political thoughts, trying to find inspiration for contemporary Chinese IR theory. The other route can be labelled as 'dualistic', of which Qin Yaqing is a strong advocate. Qin Yaqing (2012) believes that Chinese and Western theories are philosophically, thus fundamentally different and strives for a distinctive Chinese IR theory by analysing and utilizing Western theories. This debate continues today with an emerging consensus among Chinese IR scholars about the necessity of constructing a distinctively Chinese IR theory. They are either busy examining the poverty of Chinese IR theory, or looking for more effective ways to theorize Chinese IR. As a promising achievement, Tang Shiping (2013) has developed a social evolution theory of IR.

In the three debates discussed above, 'why is there no Chinese IR theory' has already been explored by a number of Chinese scholars. Su Changhe (2005: 26–30) took the small size of career academics circle, the neglect of scientific and positivist approaches, and lack of problem awareness as the main obstacles in development of Chinese IR research, suggesting that China should have 'IR theory with Chinese characteristics' or 'a Chinese School of IR theory' when conditions were ripe. Qing Yaqing (2007: 322–329) attributed the paucity of Chinese IR theory to the general unconsciousness of 'internationalness', the dominance of Western IR discourse, and absence of a hard theoretical core in Chinese IR research. Yan Xuetong (2011: 256) argued that 'three lacks', i.e. the lack of basic methodological training, of education in traditional Chinese political thoughts, and of theoretical debate, rendered Chinese scholars unable to develop systematic explanations of IR. On 'why is there no Chinese IR theory?', these essays found reasons in multiple aspects, as the issue is influenced by not only contemporary factors human and academic like China's IR academic circle and their research but also elements geographically and chronologically beyond, like the country's rich heritage and Western dominance in many ways. While these efforts would no doubt help people understand practical predicaments in constructing a Chinese IR theory, they have difficulties in explaining what fundamentally underlies the dilemma that constructing a Chinese IR theory is confronted with. In other words, some historical, ideological and cultural factors have been neglected, or deemed to be less important in these researches. At the very core, IR is about human knowledge production, and human beings are found in the cultural structure of their society. Culture as a new and special perspective offers a better way to understand the limits of IR theorization, thus contributing to explaining why there is no Chinese IR theory.

Why is there no Chinese IR theory? Cultural explanations

China is an ancient civilization of brilliant cultural traditions, and has long been a major international player. But why is there not yet Chinese IR theory? To uncover the underlying explanations for this, five reasons could be found in Chinese ways of thinking, production and living.

1 Traditional Chinese culture does not favour universalism, unlike the West and her IR theory

Universalism, as part of the Western tradition, is a derivative from Christian monotheism. In the West, entrenched universalism has two forms: 'cultural superiority' and 'manifest destiny'. *Cultural superiority* means that Western civilization is the universal template, while *manifest destiny* deems Western civilization as a whole the preference of God. Influenced by Christian theology, western theories were regarded as universal. 'Theory' is defined as 'a formal set of ideas' (Oxford English Dictionary sixth edition 1830). Based on this definition, Western theorists complicated social science in their all-out effort to understand a complicated society in approaches that were highly abstractive and complicated. Thus, a universal theory has remained the Holy Grail in the Western IR community. A typical example is Kenneth Waltz, an influential realist, who simply divided the world into numerous so-called 'like units' and took the current state of the international system as perpetual (Waltz 1979). In the West, IR theory means the systematic efforts to provide solutions to international affairs, creating new ideas in the process.

By contrast, making polytheism and atheism compatible, traditional Chinese culture is pluralistic and non-universalist. The Chinese people trace themselves and the world back to '*Pan Gu*' and '*Nü Wa*' in the remote past. They also worship '*Buddha*' and '*Avalokiteshvara*', but never have had an established religion. In China, gods are created by men, and often walk among men to guide them, through worldly power, and gods that do not serve will not be served. In this sense, most Chinese are atheists. Through the ages, kings in China believed 'the sages, in accordance with spirit-like way, laid down their instructions and All-under-Heaven yield submission to them' (Yao 2009: 388). In China, worshipping is but a way to edify the masses. Influenced by the non-universalist tradition, Chinese IR theory highlights secular matters. Not surprisingly, 'when the first IR professorship was set up in the University of Wales at Aberystwyth immediately after World War I, most Chinese still believed that half of the Analects is enough to govern the whole world' (Qin 2007: 324).

Moreover, Chinese culture does not breed missionary spirit, though China has a long history of navigation and experienced sailors. Zheng He sailed the Indian Ocean seven times to show off the graciousness of the Chinese emperor, rather than to expand Chinese culture and territory. In essence, Chinese culture can be classified as a 'learning culture'. China places much emphasis on 'extensive browsing' and 'solid accumulation' rather than going against nature for 'wide dissemination' and 'vigorous promotion'. In the *Analects*, the master said, 'When I walk along with two others, they may serve me as my teachers. I will select their good qualities and follow them, their bad qualities and avoid them' (Jin 2010: 116).

In conclusion, Chinese people like to learn from others, rather than setting examples for others. Non-universalist without missionary spirit, Chinese culture naturally disfavours the construction of a Chinese IR theory in any Western style.

2 Chinese culture is greatly developed, leaving hardly any room for highly abstractive IR theory

Unlike Western Christianity, Chinese culture shows great diversity. Chinese culture has prospered long since very ancient times. Generally speaking, there have been three main ancient schools of thought in China, among which Confucianism is considered the dominant one. Confucianism highlights the principle of 'self-cultivation, family harmony, state governing and world peace'. It emphasizes that a well-cultivated and virtuous person and happy family are prerequisites for good statesmanship and a harmonious world. Daoism ranks after Confucianism, which insists that 'the Dao that can be trodden is not the enduring and unchanging Dao; the name that can be named is not the enduring and unchanging name' (Cui 2003: 3). In Daoist eyes, Dao is the fundamental law and inherent logic of the world, with profound implications that cannot be described simply by words. Buddhism places much emphasis on the virtue of forgiveness and holds that 'too much persistence makes no insight'. That is to say, once too much emphasis is placed on one side, one will lose the insight for the whole situation. Likewise, once too much effort is put to building a Chinese-paradigm theory, i.e. too much desire for an indigenous theory, people will lose the patience to find other approaches. Fei Xiaotong, a well-known Chinese sociologist and anthropologist, once made a classical comment on China's cultural diversity when he asserted that Chinese culture is too developed for religion. By the same token, Chinese culture and philosophy are so diversified that they cannot be summarized into any single system of thinking.

In addition, Chinese culture is not based on alphabetic writing. Chinese words carry meaning, not sound. The connotation of Chinese characters is definitely rich and Western alphabets can hardly catch their diversified meanings. In this sense, Chinese scholars cannot construct Western-paradigm IR theories, which are characterized by abstractive assumptions and logical simplicity. Sometimes, even the same words have different interpretations in China and the West. For example, while the Chinese people highlight 'peaceful' in 'peaceful rise', the Westerns focus more on 'rise'. For 'scientific development', Chinese understanding is 'good and sustainable development', while its translation turns out to be 'development by science and technology'. Lacking recognition by the West in a Western-dominated world, Chinese ideas and theoretical discourse are difficult to 'go abroad' (Wang 2012).

To summarize, the diversity of Chinese culture and the nature of Chinese language make it impossible for any single theory or school of theories to cover all Chinese experience. The title 'a Chinese School of IR theory' seems so heavy that no school can bear its weight so far.

3 China's identity is still taking shape, struggling between 'Traditional China' and 'Modern China', and 'Global China'. Chinese IR theory lacks unified identity

Liang Qichao, a renowned polymath in the late Qing dynasty, classified Chinese history into three stages – 'China's China', 'Asia's China', and 'the world's China', reflecting China's triple identities in her long history. Following Liang Qichao's logic, China today also has triple identities of Traditional China, Modern China, and Global China. Traditional China is cultural China, of continental and agricultural culture based on Confucianism, Daoism, Buddhism and more. Modern China is political China forged by her revolution. Global China describes economic China shaped by reform and globalization. In practice, traditional and agricultural China based on self-sufficient small peasantry is no doubt an anathema for Western theoretical universalism. When finally forced into the international system, China followed the Western path and finally lost the aspiration for her own theoretical discourse. Globalizing now, China has vigorously adopted an all-round opening policy, and begun to adjust her role in the world. China today is experiencing vertigo in transition between her identities. Struggling between Tradition and Modernity, and not fully Global yet, China is not yet ready to decide a path for constructing a distinctive IR theory of her own. In other words, China is still struggling between Westernization and tradition.

In history, 'Westernization or not' has been a controversial issue in China since the First and Second Opium Wars (1840–1842, 1856–1860) and the first Sino-Japanese War (1894–1895). Some Chinese scholars in fact argue that 'The cultural consequences of the Opium War (1840–42) … were much greater and deeper than the defeat in the battlefields' (Qin 2007). There have been three contentious debates about 'Westernization' in China. The first debate happened in the 'Westernization movement' in the late Qing dynasty, when China came to realize the power of modern industry and technology. There emerged a group of advocates for Westernization. Zhang Zhidong, a cabinet minister level official, for example, put forward the idea of 'Chinese Mind, Western Techs' to mediate this debate. The second debate took place during the May 4th Movement, when people realized that China fell behind the West not only because of technological backwardness, but also because of her own deep-seated socio-economic problems. At the end of this debate, Marxism was introduced and gained popularity. China moved on to find herself a suitable mode of development. In this sense, the May 4th Movement was regarded as a great enlightenment, a conscious examination by the Chinese people of themselves and their own tradition in China's modern history (Ge 2001; Li 1987). The third debate took place in the 1980s, when the reform and opening-up policy was underway and the Chinese people were exposed to unrestrained Westernization, or rather, Americanization.

These three debates ran through China's modern history, a time of distorted relations between China and the West, and interrupted the flow of Chinese thinking, which left the core of Chinese IR theory vacant.

4 Path dependence development makes China lose its subjectivity in the IR community

In economics, 'path-dependence' means that under certain conditions, further input can bring not only increased output, but a greater output rate, which, once this mechanism is institutionalized, would self-reinforce and breed into a cycle, virtuous or vicious, that will not be able to terminate itself (Arthur 1989; Keohane 2005).

In the West, procedural rationality prevails in that democracy and human rights are believed to be the way to order and legitimacy. Yet this is but a self-fulfilling prophecy. For China, the very concept of IR theory is a complete import from the West, introduced into China when most Chinese scholars were eager to imitate the West at the early stage of opening and reform. At that time, many Chinese IR scholars succumbed to their longing for quick fame and brought in theories good or bad from the West by the truckload, to make themselves closer to Western concepts, methodology, and in the terminal stage, thinking. For a long while, Chinese scholars preferred to borrow from Western social sciences over building her own theoretical framework, out of habit or other reasons. Even some who advocated for a Chinese IR theory were doing so not for academic or practical necessity but for gaining the attention of the Western IR community. Now China's increased capacity and involvement in expanding globalization has given the matter a positive push, kindling theoretical awareness for independent Chinese IR studies in many, who are trying to find information in the country's ancient wisdom for her current IR need. But heritage alone would not suffice in the quest for a Chinese School of IR, and the cult of Westernization, once rampaging in China's IR circle, had left in our minds marks of its path-dependence that are hard to remove. It would be some time before China's IR community could be innovative, and a typical manifestation of the above-mentioned path-dependence is the Americanization of Chinese IR.

Today's world remains one of great power politics, with IR theories serving as its justification and endorsement. Even non-Western theories are rarely free from the off-the-shelf American paradigm, while barbed wire fences were built by the big three of realism, liberalism and constructivism. Their descendants such as democratic peace, hegemonic stability, and clash of civilizations are no less American. Chinese IR clearly did not escape this. In the late 1980s, the Ford Foundation sponsored the first translation of American IR classics into Chinese. Later, many Chinese IR scholars studied IR methodologies in the United States, making the Americanization of Chinese IR studies inescapable. The Americanization of Chinese IR has, however, dire consequences. It steers Chinese IR heavily towards great power politics, and make it indifferent to small powers, and uninterested in Chinese cultural heritage. It also fosters a fetish of the three mainstream IR theories and uncritical acceptance of their claims of universality. However, IR theories are the end product from American experience, and are certainly inconsistent with Chinese reality. The cult of American IR will ruin Chinese minds.

5 Traditional Chinese thinking favouring pragmatic moderation prefers harmony to fundamentalism

Pragmatism is part of Chinese culture. Confucianism showed a pragmatic attitude towards life. Wang Yangming, a great philosopher in the Ming dynasty, once proposed the principle of '*zhi xing he yi*' (unity of knowledge and practice), which is essentially a pragmatic attitude that well summarizes the Chinese wisdom of '*xue yi zhi yong*' (to learn in order to apply knowledge to practice). Generally speaking, Chinese pragmatism stresses a good life in this world rather than happiness in the afterlife. It highlights 'how to get the job done' more than 'seeking the truth from facts', and emphasizes daily life over pure thinking.

Influenced by Marxism, Chinese pragmatism is totally different from Western apriorism and philosophical idealism. Mao Zedong, the greatest Marxist in China, wrote a famous monograph, *On Practice*, fusing Marxist theory with China's reality. Deng Xiaoping also focused on the effectiveness of policies, and put forward the 'three favourable standards' to testify whether his theory is in accordance with the actual situation of China's development. On Chinese practical philosophy, Engels once made the following comment: 'in everything practical, and war is eminently practical, the Chinese far surpass all the Orientals' (Engels 1960: 190–191). So Chinese practical rationality, when bearing fruit in international affairs, offers practical policy rather than highly abstract IR theories.

The other factor in Chinese thinking that hinders a Chinese School of IR theory is a preference for moderation. For a long time, the Western way of thinking has dominated the IR community. In the West, all things and concepts in the world can be reliably labelled self and other, and must have an antithesis: advanced and backward, angel and devil, democracy and despotism, market and government, freedom and oppression are all examples. Dominated by such dichotomous thinking, the West often defines herself as 'civilized people civilizing barbarous others'. The core hypotheses of all three major Western IR theories are based more or less on hypothetical, artificial and extreme situations. Realism is based on the assumption of the evil nature of man and international anarchy, liberalism is for rational man so rarely seen, and constructivism is based on assumptions determined primarily by shared ideas rather than material forces.

In contrast to Western thinking, in Chinese culture, the world is conceptualized not as two-dimensional, but as three-dimensional; everything can be divided into three parts. Dao De Jing said, 'Dao gives birth to One; One gives birth to Two; Two gives birth to Three; Three gives birth to All' (Gu 1997: 58). That is to say, there are three paths to handle daily affairs at both extremes and in the middle, and the middle path could often make the two others better by meshing them. This is the so-called Doctrine of the Mean. This preference is deeply rooted in Chinese thinking, not of mere compromise, but for harmony that serves the situation best without bias, known as *zhi zhonghe*. The philosophical base for this is that Chinese people always view things as a process. In Chinese culture, there are no absolute good or sheer evil, pure happiness and mere misery, as they could transform to each other when conditions are met. As Master Lao Tzu said: '*Huo xi, Fu zhi suo Yi; Fu xi, Huo zhi suo Fu*' (Misery! – Happiness is to be found by its side! Happiness! – Misery lurks beneath it!) (Sun 2010: 85). Therefore, Chinese people believe that international affairs are so complicated that theoretical assumptions simply cannot cover all eventualities.

Beyond Western IR theories: what can Chinese culture offer?

The unique characteristics of Chinese culture prevent Chinese scholars from constructing Western-paradigm IR theories. This same momentum can, however, contribute to constructing a culture-based Chinese-paradigm IR theory. Though Chinese IR has not yet built up its own theoretical frameworks, there have been elements rooted in Chinese culture that can take us beyond Western IR theories.

Chinese cosmopolitanism

Cosmopolitanism has a tradition in Western political thought, which has developed through three stages of ancient, modern and post-modern. Ancient cosmopolitanism can be traced back to Greek and Roman antiquity. Ancient Greece focused on human rationality and the ethical concerns towards world-scale city-state; while in Rome, cosmopolitanism was not a mere philosophy, but rather a strategy of world domination. Characterized by the ethical ideals of stoic and cynic philosophers, cosmopolitanism was finally universalized and entered worldly affairs. Modern cosmopolitanism had German sources, of which Kant, Kelsen and Habermas were the most distinguished, who viewed the world as an 'interdependent community'. In the post-modern stage, seeing the utopian side of Kant's perpetual peace and Kelsen's 'just war', Habermas and the other scholars updated Kant's idea of cosmopolitanism (Douzinas 2007).

In linguistics, 'cosmos' and 'politan' refers to universe and citizen of cities, cosmopolitanism means 'citizens of the world'. Western IR theories are largely made possible by modern cosmopolitanism, represented by Immanuel Kant, who provided ideological incentives for the formation of IR theory.[1] Believing in the power of human's rationality, Kant proposed perpetual peace and argued that it can only be achieved when international law is guaranteed by 'unanimous consent' for a universal and effective world alliance that establishes rights and obligations between states and guarantees universal citizenship over nation states. Moreover, Kant (Reiss 1970: 116–125) prophesied the arrival of an unprecedented 'nation-state community' and the realization of 'rights of world citizenship'. In Kant's mind, there were three definitive factors for 'perpetual peace': (i) the civil constitution of each state shall be republican; (ii) the law of nations shall be founded on a federation of free states; (iii) the rights of world citizens shall be presupposed by universal hospitality. For Kant, cosmopolitanism is metaphysical and 'pure concept'. Generally speaking, Kant made great achievements in bringing universal elements into Western IR theories. However, the ultimate concern of individualism in Kant's cosmopolitanism lacks universal care for the whole world. It falls therefore into hypocrisy. As Carl Schmitt (2007: 27–37) argued in *The Concept of the Political*, 'Kant's cosmopolitanism is definitely a feeble attempt that imposes virtue elements on IR studies'.

Compared with Western cosmopolitanism, Chinese cosmopolitanism has a different root and content. Chinese cosmopolitanism emerged first in the Zhou dynasty (1046–256 BC) more than a millennium before the unification of the first Chinese empire. It helped the Chinese get out of the great chaos at the end of Shang dynasty (early seventeenth–eleventh century BC) and managed successfully the peaceful interactions among numerous tribal states of different sizes, which retained a high degree of autonomy. In the Zhou dynasty, the emperor constructed a '*tianxia*' system (All-under-Heaven system), an open network or a 'world-home' consisting a world government and states (Qin 2012b). The framework of '*tianxia*' was the 'tributary system'. The tributary system operated at three levels: (i) China served as the centre, neighbouring states should acknowledge and respect China's legitimacy and authority, at least in a symbolic way; (ii) to demonstrate subservience, neighbouring states should pay tribute regularly to the Chinese emperor, and in return, neighbouring states would receive gifts exceeding their tributes; (iii) the emissaries of neighbouring states should perform ritual obeisance when the Chinese emperor delegates an imperial letter of patent, or a seal of rank, as the signs of local power. After coronation, the neighbouring states became China's 'tributary' (Zhang 2015); whenever these states were invaded, the central empire would help them. Properly speaking, the '*tianxia* system' in its broad sense implies a world order in which the emperor of China ruled directly in the name of *tian zi* (the Son of Heaven) while the rulers of neighbouring states governed indirectly as they channel rights from the heaven through *tian zi* (Chang 2011). The *tianxia* system was not only a hierarchy, but also a universally-accepted world system ruled by voluntary involvement rather than coercion. In this system, every state enjoyed a high level of autonomy, precious gifts and security guarantees from the central empire with minimum exertion. Therefore, the concept of '*tianxia*' was not merely geographic and political, but with rich historical and cultural implications (Liu and Wang 2011).

Using a traditional Chinese worldview to understand IR is an innovative approach. To this endeavour, Zhao Tingyang has made notable contributions. For Zhao, Chinese cosmopolitanism has three cultural implications: (i) The world is a universal interest-sharing system, whose fundamental belief is '*yi tianxia Guan tianxia*' (describing the world for the world's sake). Therefore, '*tianxia wu Wai*' (there is nothing foreign or alien in the world); (ii) the *tianxia* system can guarantee maximum possible power and interest for all states, so that every state would like to join and stay; (iii) the *tianxia* system can form a network of mutual benefit, in which the interests of the imperial centre and all other states enhance and supplement each other, promoting world prosperity and peace (Zhao 2005, 2009d, 2010). In Chinese culture, there is neither the concept of 'nation state' nor 'boundaries', but a '*tianxia* system' (All-under-Heaven) as a holistic world.

If modern Western cosmopolitanism is an important ideological source of Western IR, traditional Chinese cosmopolitanism embodied in the *tianxia* system is a vital force shaping the way Chinese people think about IR. The comparison of the two kinds of cosmopolitanism will help understand why China cannot produce Western-paradigm IR theory. Modern Western cosmopolitanism is based on simple and abstract assumptions. This so-called theoretical grace conceals selfish national interests under the slogan of 'universal good' (Carr 1946). Traditional Chinese cosmopolitanism, however, takes '*tianxia*' (the whole world) as an indivisible public domain and considers the world's problems in context of the whole world, enabling Chinese thinking to go past national interests for the interest, value and responsibilities of this world as a whole in the long-term (Zhao 2005), taking us beyond the paradox of universality and particularity. In sum, Chinese cosmopolitanism is inclusive, and favours culture over force, and free-choice over coercion. Ruling by cultural appeal and uniting '*tianxia*' together is the ultimate ideal of Chinese cosmopolitanism (Ren 2014: 30).

Ethical idealism

Western ethical tradition dates back to ancient Greece. Deeply influenced by independent city-states and a coastal environment, ancient Greeks were born to prefer public life over private family. In terms of public issues, the Greeks showed great originality and liked to make philosophical contemplations on questions like justice and democracy. Plato viewed the world in this manner, and with great effort and genius chartered a republic ruled by a 'philosopher-king'. At the end of antiquity, Christianity, to a large extent, embodied of Western civilization, attempted to surpass human reasoning distributed in man with an omnipotent God above. Therefore, two different ethical logics lie in Western social science. One is the theoretical framework built on the human ability of reasoning through the maximum abstraction of things, and the other is the worship of God, the ultimate exaggeration and wish of human capacity. Unlike the West, Chinese ethical tradition takes root in Chinese culture. Take the two most influential philosophical schools, Confucianism and Daoism in ancient China, for example. According to the Confucians, the Masters (Confucius and Mencius) took prevailing *Li* (rites and norms) in the Zhou dynasty as the sign of an ideal society and added ethical content to it – *Ren* (benevolence) proposed by Mencius. For Mencius, '*Ren*' (benevolence) is not merely a moralist slogan, but a part of daily life for all – *Xiu Shen* (self-cultivation), *Qi Jia* (family-management), *zhi guo* (state-governing) and *ping tianxia* (world-peace). For self-cultivation, *Ren* means controlling oneself when no one is watching. For family-management, *Ren* means love, fidelity, and piety. For statesmanship, *Ren* refers to loving the people. Towards the world-peace, *Ren* is loving people of the world. If the ruler of a nation can *xian tianxia zhi You er You, hou tianxia zhi Le er Le* (be the first to be aware and the last to relax), his governance can be called *Ren Zheng* (benevolent governance), which would be a hopeful outlook. A classic of Confucianism, the *Li Ji*, or *Book of Rites*, expresses a vivid imagination of this nice outlook:

> When the Grand course was pursued, a public and common spirit ruled all under the sky; they chose men of talents, virtue, and ability; their words were sincere, and what they cultivated was harmony. Thus men did not love their parents only, nor treat as children only their own sons. A competent provision was secured for the aged till their death, employment for the able-bodied, and the means of growing up to the young. They showed kindness and compassion to widows, orphans, childless men, and those who were disabled by disease, so that they were all sufficiently maintained. Males had their proper work, and females had their homes. (They accumulated) articles (of value), disliking that they should be thrown away upon the ground, but not wishing to keep them for their own gratification. (They laboured) with their strength, disliking that it should not be exerted, but not exerting it (only) with a view to their own advantage. In this way (selfish) schemings were repressed and found no development. Robbers, filchers, and rebellious traitors did not show themselves, and hence the outer doors remained open, and were not shut. This was (the period of) what we call the Grand Union.
> (Zhang and Dong 1995)

In the above outlook, all people – male and female, old and young – have their proper places, live a decent life and build their families; the earth should be made to yield all its resources and all things are made to contribute their utility, the circulation of commodities should be extended to full development; and finally sincerity and courtesy will result, selfishness will disappear and peace and harmony will prevail (Li 1986). This is so called 'Confucian idealism'.

As for Daoism, Dao is an important mark of social development, which means 'natural'. To be specific, Dao refers to the ideal state that all things are returning to their good nature. Daoism criticizes any artificial institution or regulation set up by the secular society, while desiring a fair, quiet, peaceful and simple life in nature. In Daoism, Dao is the fundamental law and inherent logic of nature. As long as it exists, all things in the world would proceed following its own logic. The ideal results of the 'Dao' can be called '*Wu Wei er Zhi*', or governance in non-interference. A classic of Daoism, the *Dao De Jing*, gives detailed depiction of human life and Daoist ethics in the following words:

> In a little state with a small population, I would so order it that though there were individuals with the abilities of ten or a hundred men, there should be

no employment of them; I would make the people, while looking on death as a grievous thing, yet not remove elsewhere (to avoid it). Though they had boats and carriages, they should have no occasion to ride in them; though they had buff coats and sharp weapons, they should have no occasion to don or use them. ...There should be a neighbouring state within sight, and the voices of the fowls and dogs should be heard all the way from it to us, but I would make the people to old age, even to death, not have any intercourse with it.

(Gu 1997)

In general, Western idealism has a metaphysical or Christian origin that is indifferent to daily life and keen on the omnipotence of God. As there is but one heaven and one path thereto, the purpose of human reasoning should be to find it, and competition and hostility would naturally grow, for *Deus Vult*. Chinese secular culture has long been prosperous and non-religious, and society is the byword of cultural space. No pagans, no others, and nothing is impossible (Zhao 2010). Therefore, Chinese ethical idealism is far closer to workaday life, or in other words, Reality. It can imbue IR theory with emotions seemingly unscientific, which nevertheless make us human. In Chinese ethical idealism, there was, is, and will always be a gentleness that contributes to making IR theory 'nicer' in text and action, than what we have today.

Harmony

'Harmony' is an important concept for the survival and development of human society. Dating back to ancient Greece, the Western concept of 'harmony' came from natural science and music, and the earliest users such as Pythagoras and Heraclitus. Taking numbers as basic elements of the universe, Pythagoras concluded that the reasonable, or 'right' relationship among numbers can be called 'harmonious'. In Pythagoras' perspective, the most harmonious figure in geometry is the circle, and in society the most harmonious is virtue. Slightly different to Pythagoras, Heraclitus holds that there was no absolute harmony in the world, all harmonies were made visible differences. Harmony can be defined in musicology as the way in which different notes are played or sung together to make a pleasing sound. In addition, Hegel also had an important point on 'harmony'. In Hegel's mind, 'harmony' was the highest level of 'abstract beauty' (Hegel 1983a). To sum up, the Western idea on Harmony places much emphasis on rearranging and judging different things in accordance with universal truth and power.

'Harmony' is also a core concept of Chinese traditional culture. It is a strong tradition from the dawn of Chinese culture. In Chinese classics, *He* and *Xie* are two words of similar meaning, of making a variety of things co-exist with each other. There are three different views on harmony in Chinese tradition. To coexist, Confucianism proposes the concept of *ZhongHe* (moderation), which is the wisdom to allow and allow for differences. The Master advocates *Li zhi suo*

Yong, He wei Gui (harmony is an essential purpose of ritual applications) and urges to achieve harmony through cultural rituals and norms. Mencius emphasizes particularly the importance of harmony among people, as expressed in his axiom *TianShi BuRu DiLi, DiLi BuRu RenHe* (Opportunities of time vouchsafed by Heaven are not equal to the advantages of the situation afforded by the Earth, and the advantages of the situation afforded by the Earth are not equal to the union arising from the accord of Men) (Wang 2010: 56). It is worth noting that harmony is not equal to uniformity. Confucianism respects differences. The Master says that *JunZi He er Bu Tong* (The superior man is affable, but not adulatory). In the Confucian view, there is an obvious difference between *He* (harmony) and *Tong* (uniformity), as *He* acknowledges the presence of differences and aims at accepting others, while *Tong* neglects diversity and tries to assimilate others. Second, to balance the interaction of Yin and Yang, Daoism highlights *Tian Ren He Yi* (harmony of human and nature). The core principle of Daoism is the dialectics of circulation, as Man takes his law from the Earth, the Earth takes its law from Heaven, Heaven takes its law from the Dao, and Dao take its law from Nature. In essence, Daoism pursues harmony among *Tian* (heaven), *Di* (earth) and *Ren* (people). Towards a higher state of consciousness, Buddhism looks for its own state of harmony, of *Yuan* among all things. In Buddhism, ultimate beauty is peace after all competitions settle themselves. In this sense, *Pu Du Zhong Sheng* (giving relief and help to all mortal beings) becomes an inseparable part of Buddhist life. So in China, harmony has become an inherent part of society, and the way and philosophy of daily life.

In sum, the Western concept of harmony comes from research on music, art and natural sciences, and tends to label others as aliens, others, inferiors and test subjects for conquest and conversion. The Chinese view on harmony draws on the country's agricultural heritage and the awe of nature, and takes harmony as an ideal for peace and coexistence. In the Chinese mind, the best way to defeat enemies is to end hostility with the enemy by mutual understanding and friendship. Even standing conflicts are best concluded without bloodshed. This ethic of harmony over conquest is important for an inclusive IR theory. In this way Chinese harmony could offer what the Western tradition cannot.

The Chinese dream of IR theory

IR theory cannot escape Western discourse hegemony anywhere in our time. China has not produced her own IR theory within the Western-paradigm, as this secular country has no missionary sprit and has little interest for the theoretical tool of preaching. In addition, few dare to shed chains of path dependence put around them by Western paradigms and stereotypes in China's struggle with Westernization. Even for those who can and dare, they are too busy with the complexity of culture and identities in this continent-sized land.

In modern times, Western civilization and her claim of universal values have made the Chinese dream in IR theory impossible. But crises in recent years have shaken this Western arrogance, rendering theories once claimed as universal feeble, fallible and regional in a diversifying world (Wang 2007). The once grand theories are becoming busted myths. To better adapt to the call for a new and good Chinese IR theory, Chinese scholars could take universality claims from West and all world into an inclusive value system by, for, and of all Mankind, just as the teachings of Buddha from India blend with the Chinese heart into Zen. As a consequence, the Chinese dream of IR theory will turn into reality with the full shaping of global China. To be specific, the Chinese dream of IR theory has triple implications.

It is certainly possible to build Chinese IR theory on Chinese culture. For IR theory, the Chinese dream begins from a willingness to carry on the Chinese heritage and to deal with the issues that China is facing today instead of blind Westernization. American IR theories is part of US discourse hegemony, which distort the reality of the world through abstraction to serve US interests under universalist slogans. The inception of Chinese IR theory marks a new confidence in an independent Chinese theoretical framework to emerge, and a new awareness of what US-dominated international IR discourse really is. Chinese IR researchers should seek, with Chinese eyes and in a Chinese way, a path towards not only rationality, legitimacy and purposiveness of Chinese IR theory, but also long-term interest of both China and all mankind. China can only really contribute most when China is both Chinese and independent.

The Chinese dream for IR theory is also compatible with Western civilization. It is time to emerge from the cult of so-called universal values and path dependence on Western IR theory. Chinese IR needs some serious de-Americanization and de-Westernization. This does not mean, however, hostility towards American or European ideas. China's IR theory informed by a civilization of millennia could not but be inclusive and free from vicious nationalism plaguing the whole age of nation states, in the service of progressive global governance. Chinese IR theory must do good for China, and equally certainly all others, when the Chinese dream, Western dream and World dream converge. But this has to be done among a different kind of civilizations, of the civilizations ours are to become, and for this China will provide her momentum and public goods in a theoretical sense.

Chinese IR is innovating IR theory to share with the world. The time when Western IR theories try to force all into universalist uniformity is ending as a bad dream, while a new Chinese IR theory brings a dream of harmony, whose realization will not only add something good to the treasure house of IR theories, but will also bring equality, respect and coexistence there among different schools of IR theories. Even with a renewed confidence in her own theoretical capacity, Chinese IR will not seek to repeat the tragedy of Western universalism in theory and practice, but will seek to share the very theory of cultural inclusiveness, of recognition, respect and coexistence among theories and civilizations, something never done or within American, European, or Western theories.

Note

1 For more about Kant's cosmopolitanism see H. Reiss (ed.) *Kant's Political Writings*. Cambridge: Cambridge University Press, 1986.

4 The rise of China and Chinese IR theories

Practice and theory-building

Weixing Hu

The rise of China has inspired great interest in the study of International Relations (IR) and IR theories in China. Many Chinese scholars argue there should be a Chinese School of IR theories as China rises up to become a great power in world affairs (Liang 1997a; Ren 2000; Mei 2001; see also Ren this volume). Will the rise of China lead to the emergence of a Chinese School of IR theories? Should China construct a national approach to IR studies? These questions are heatedly debated in China. To me, one of interesting implications of the debate is whether the rise of China contributes to Chinese IR theory-building. Putting it differently, is there any inherent linkage between a country's international practice and IR theory-building? Some Chinese scholars use the English School of IR theories as an example to argue for a Chinese School of IR theories. In their understanding, the English School is a specific line of thought and framework in understanding and explaining IR from English perspectives and experiences. If the English School is a theory deeply grounded in the normative classics of Western political theory, international law and European IR practice, a Chinese School of IR could also emerge from the Chinese IR practice and cultural traditions (Ren 2003; Tang 2005; see also Wang and Buzan in this volume). Others argue that the prevalent IR theories today are all developed by American scholars in the postwar era and this has a great deal to do with the US' hegemonic power position and its international practice in world affairs (Meng 2005; Wang and Buzan in this volume).

As China rises up to be a great power in world affairs, Chinese scholars have climbed a steep learning curve on IR studies and theory building since the 1980s. China's IR studies and theoretical debates have flourished in recent years, as the rising power faces all kinds of challenges, practical and theoretical. China needs to find practical solutions to various IR problems and it also faces epistemological questions of IR. The new practice and reality that China faces as it rises up to be a great power in world affairs have prompted great efforts by Chinese scholars to explore and construct new theoretical discourses for China's emerging role in world affairs. As Zheng Yongnian (2011) argues, a rising great power needs IR theories to guide its international practice as well as to make other countries understand its international behaviour. Without basic understanding among nations in IR, there would be no mutual trust and ground rules for international interactions. But where do IR theories come from? Are they "discovered" or developed by "scientific research" and theory-building exercise alone or are they also inspired by practice?

IR theory-building is a knowledge construction exercise. As such, it is not necessarily driven by international practice or the experience of a country acquiring great power status. So the rise of China does not necessitate, or lead to, the "rise" of Chinese IR theories. Nevertheless, we should not entrap ourselves by the question of whether the rise of China would lead to a Chinese School of IR theories. We should ask ourselves what are the sources and dynamics of IR theory-building and whether there is any cogent connection between international practice and IR theory-building.

To answer this question, we need to answer what is IR theory first and what is its relationship with international practice. As Qin Yaqing (2011b) contends, IR theories can be classified into "action oriented theory" and "knowledge oriented theory". An action-oriented theory serves as guidelines for action and provides basic principles for decision-making and policy implementation, such as the "leaning toward one side" strategy and the "three world" theory by Mao Zedong. A knowledge-oriented theory is a perspective to understand the world and an achievement of knowledge production or reproduction, such as Kenneth Waltz's structural realism and Hedley Bull's international society theory. Following the logic of Qin's typology, it is clear that these two types of IR theories are inseparable rather than independent from each other. Although they serve different purposes, knowledge oriented theory is an abstraction or theorization of IR actions that explains causes and patterns of social phenomenon. Academic research that leads to knowledge building is always prompted by practical needs, reflection of experiences and observations of actions and practice. As Qin argues, if problems do not arise, research has nowhere to begin. Theory building and knowledge production have to go through questioning, debating, testing and revision. Without actions, academic research would stay at the superficial level and hardly lead to theory building and knowledge production (Qin 2011a: 430–431). So to a large extent, theory building is an epistemological issue. As Chinese axioms say, theory comes from practice and is applied to guide practice (理论源于实践, 但又指导实践) and we should "seek truth from the fact" (实践是检验真理的唯一标准).

But that is more about action oriented theory and its development follows the logic of "practical sense". How about knowledge oriented theory? When it comes to IR theories, most people refer to knowledge oriented theory or academic theories, which are more abstract and analytic. Can they be developed by academic research and deductive reasoning alone without the guide of "practical sense"? What role does practice play in this type of IR theory building? The present mainstream IR theories, as Vincent Pouliot (2008: 257–288) argues, primarily derive from instrumental rationality (logic of consequences), norm-following (logic of appropriateness), or communicative action (logic of arguing). These logics of social action, however, suffer from a representational bias in that they focus on what agents think about, instead of what they think from.

Knowledge oriented theory is inspired by social actions. To build a theory, we have a notion of "truth" in our thinking. We use that notion of "truth" as a benchmark to assess what and why something is relevant in theory-building. Yet our notion of "truth" is to a large extent informed by our prior practice. So knowledge oriented theory cannot be developed without following the logic of practicality.

This chapter makes three arguments concerning practice and theory building in Chinese international studies. First, new Chinese foreign policy practice has enabled Chinese scholars to develop an array of action oriented theories such as regional cooperation, big power strategy and cooperative security. Second, since the rise of China has become a central problematique for Chinese IR theoretical discourse, the Chinese scholarly community has increasingly learned from and incorporated Western IR theories and approaches into its research agenda and theory-building enterprise. They have tried hard to make sense of how great powers like China can rise peacefully in world affairs and how China's practice can be transformed into theoretical discourse and be guided by IR theories. Third, the practice and reality that a rising China faces have also empowered an epistemological process in which Chinese scholars have rediscovered the value of such traditional Chinese IR concepts as "*tianxia*" and started to reconceptualize the organizational principle of world politics. They have been making every effort to contribute to the knowledge oriented theory-building through theoretical projects such as a new normative world order and relation-based IR theories.

Theory and practice of IR: the Chinese story

Whether there is a Chinese School of IR theories depends on, first, what we mean by IR theories. This is related to the ongoing and endless debate about the essence and the nature of scientific knowledge. IR now claims a diverse range of theories, ranging from positivist, materialist and rationalist, to reflective and constructivist theories. They could also be labelled modern, post-modern, structural, post-structural, critical, normative, qualitative or quantitative. To Amitav Acharya and Barry Buzan (2010: 3), there is different understanding of what is IR theory even between Americans and the Europeans,

> [Because] of the dichotomy between the hard positivist understanding of theory, which dominates in the US, and the softer reflectivist understanding of theory found more widely in Europe. Many Europeans use the term theory for anything that organizes a field systematically, structures questions and establishes a coherent and rigorous set of interrelated concepts and categories. The dominant American tradition, however, usually demands that theory be defined in positivist terms: that is defines terms in operational form, and then sets out and explains the relations between causes and effects. This type of theory should contain or be able to generate testable hypotheses of a causal nature.

The Chinese notion of IR theory is on the "soft" side of the Acharya–Buzan dichotomy. According to Qin Yaqing (2007: 315–316), theory is defined as a system of ideas or a system of generalizations that accounts for facts and is associated with practice. In this definition, he emphasizes that a theory is a system of generalizations that explain practice as well as a system of ideas and concepts that organizes thoughts in a field. Qin's notion of theory underscores some relations between theoretical generalization and practice. By this logic, as China rises up, it will build up its system of ideas and knowledge of world affairs and that will lead to generalizations of world affairs.

To use Qin's classification of action oriented theory and knowledge oriented theory, we also know that linkages between theory and practice cannot be severed. On a spectrum of theory vs practice, theory and practice are not separable and they are dialectally related. We often mistake that the theory is often taught in the ideal of a vacuum and the practical is learned through the reality of life. Yet theory cannot be developed in vacuum. Theory-building is inspired and guided by practice. Theoretical knowledge is dry and abstract. It is essential for our reasoning and reflections. Action oriented knowledge can guide policy making and provide specific advice to actions. Both types of theory are actually important for a country's relations with the outside world and to improve international interactions. A state in the world is like a person in a community. It needs all kinds of experiences and learns from its actions. China has acquired both action oriented and knowledge oriented theory as it increasingly integrates itself into world affairs.

The theory-building process is an epistemological process as well. If the world is the reality we want to learn, our theory-building process is how we learn and how we arrive at the "truth" in learning and understanding. To build an IR theory, we have a notion of "truth" inherently grounded in our reasoning and we use it to judge the "truth" and "non-truth". This epistemological process helps us to attain correct knowledge of the world. Practice and theory-building are inseparable. Theory guides reasoning and action while action inspires theory and tests theory. Man is full of subjective initiatives. Man's practice is a process of learning by doing. Practical knowledge can often lead to a deeper understanding of a concept through the act of doing and personal experience. The Chinese epistemology is influenced by its practical and realistic attitudes towards learning about the world (实践论). Knowledge and wisdom are largely learned and derived from action and practice. They believe that theory building is like a process of "practice – cognition/theoretical understanding – practice again – further cognition/theoretical understanding" (实践, 认识, 再实践, 再认识).

If this epistemological process explains action oriented theory building, is it applicable to knowledge oriented theory? To what extent does practice influence knowledge oriented theory building? I think they are inherently related and we should not treat them in isolation. The present mainstream IR theories, from structural realism and liberal institutionalism to constructivism, are all developed on the basis of rationality and contextualized reasoning. Realist and liberal theories assume that nation-states are rational, "selfish", utility maximizing and constrained by "material forces". While constructivist theorists challenge the "material structure" of IR and the logic of consequences, their theoretical propositions make a "cultural turn" toward a more socially oriented theory that emphasizes norm-following and the logic of appropriateness. For Alexander Wendt (1992: 391–425), material forces still matter in interest-constructing but people are intentional actors. State identities and interests are in important part, constructed by social structures. "Anarchy is what states make of it". But whether they are realist, liberal or constructivist IR theories, they are all rationality based theories. They put the study of state or individual behaviour in a bounded causal-relational framework with a set of operationalized variables. This type of narrowly defined generalizations, built on a set of testable hypotheses, explains causal relations between "causes" and "effects" to a limited degree. This "bounded reasoning" neglects a larger and more dynamic picture of social actions and human behaviour. That is why we need to bring the logic of practicality back into theory-building.

Social actions and practice are conducted with background knowledge or prior knowledge of action and consequences. The prior knowledge guides actions and provides conceptual framework for understanding. Social actors are dynamic and so are nation-states in IR. They learn by doing and change after learning, which constitutes background knowledge of future actions (Pouliot 2010). Our knowledge of social actions must incorporate this dynamic learning background into theory-building. We must consider the role of practice in understanding social actions and human behaviour. To understand the role of practice in social actions, we must first comprehend the background knowledge, not just representational knowledge, of states. Otherwise we would suffer what Pouliot calls "representational bias" in IR theory-building. Pouliot (2008: 276) distinguishes practical knowledge from representational knowledge in IR theory-building. In his view, representational knowledge is rational and abstract, while practical knowledge is reasonable and contextual. The logic of practicality is ontologically prior to other logics of social action. In IR, it is actors' "practical sense" that guides their instrumental rationality, norm compliance, or communicative action (see also Zhu and Nie 2010).

In search for theoretical innovation, Chinese scholars are also inspired by changing practice in IR, such as China's rise and great power rivalry, regionalism, globalization, and non-traditional security, to name a few. Social actions and practice are sources of ideas and theoretical research, but how to interpret social actions and practice is also important. Pouliot's (2008, 2010) call for a "practice turn" in IR theory-building has stimulated intensive interest among the Chinese IR scholars as well as in the Western scholarly community. In their research, Chinese scholars have become keen to challenge the biased representations of Chinese international practice by Western scholars. Qin Yaqing (2014) recently wrote to challenge the emerging discourse of "assertive China" in Western IR studies and international media. In his view, the discourse is a wrong or biased representation of China's international strategy and foreign policy practice. Due to a lack of understanding of the Chinese *Zhongyong* (中庸)

culture, the "assertive China" discourse wrongly portrays a "revolutionary turn in China's international strategy" because it could "turn a constructed narrative into a conventional wisdom" in IR studies (Qin 2014: 313).

Practice and the search for Chinese IR theories

IR theoretical research activities in China involve three types of activities, as summarized by Qin Yaqing. The first is on building original theory, which is new theory incommensurable to the existing theories (Type I). The second is introductory and critical analysis of an original theory (Type II), and the third is application and testing of a theory (Type III). As he argues,

> when we say that there is no Chinese IR theory, we use the knowledge-oriented meaning of theory and the first type of theory as the defining standard, or we mean that Type I theory is yet to emerge from the IR community in China.
>
> (Qin 2007: 314)

Many Chinese scholars have turned their attention to constructing what Qin calls knowledge oriented theory, not just action oriented theories. Knowledge oriented or "original IR theory" began to emerge in China in recent years.

Since the opening and reform in the late 1970s, China's new international practice began to move Chinese IR scholarship away from the Marxist-only theoretical research. Chinese scholars have benefited from international exchanges and the engagement with the international IR community. Western IR theories and textbooks were introduced into China, and many Western IR classics were translated into Chinese. Some general IR textbooks were first translated and introduced to Chinese readers, and then some IR classic works from the United States and Europe were translated. These include *Contending Theories of International Relations* by James Dougherty and Robert Pfaltzgraff, which was translated into Chinese and published in the late 1980s. Among contemporary IR classics that were first translated into Chinese and published in the early 1990s are *Politics Among Nations* by Hans Morgenthau (1990); *Man, The State and War* by Kenneth Waltz (1991); *Power and Interdependence: World Politics in Transition* by Robert O. Keohane and Joseph S. Nye (1992); Robert Gilpin, *War and Change in World Politics* (1994).

Since then, Chinese scholars began to incorporate more Western concepts into their studies of IR. Benefiting from professional exchanges with Western IR communities, a new generation of Chinese scholars was able to study in the West and conduct more in-depth studies of Western IR theories and scientific social sciences methodology abroad. A growing number of Chinese IR and foreign policy studies began to seek to make sense of IR by adopting Western IR theoretical frameworks and concepts. Debates on adopting appropriate theoretical models for analysing Chinese IR are a good indication of the call for more rigorous input from a wide array of theories including Western IR theories.

Although their research outputs and influence so far are not very satisfactory, a great number of Chinese scholars have used the concepts and theories introduced from abroad in their works, and efforts to theorize Chinese IR have intensified. Some concepts, theories and analytical methods applied by these scholars also find their way in to the speeches and reports prepared by policy makers for their leaders (see Noesselt this volume). With China's recent and continuing ascendency, Chinese intellectuals are becoming more confident about the Chinese development model, so too have Chinese IR scholars become more confident in developing their own IR theories. They are no longer satisfied with simple application and adaptation of Western IR theories to the Chinese practice. They want to use Chinese concepts (or culture and ideas) to tell the Chinese story and explain the Chinese view of world affairs.

In retrospect, the first 10–15 years were a time when Chinese scholars mainly introduced and absorbed the Western IR scholarship and played "catch-up" in learning. If the first 10–15 years were "learning through translation", the next 10–15 years (from the late 1990s to the present) are what Qin Yaqing (2010: 31) calls "from the theory-learning phase to theory-building phase". During this period, many Chinese scholars began to question and even challenge Western theory, and became more rigorous in developing IR theory from the Chinese perspective. They began to develop their own research programmes in IR studies that are quite distinct from the classic Western IR theories. Actually, the first group of Chinese scholars who challenged the dominance of Western IR theories and approaches are some "old-generation" IR scholars in China. Because they were upset by the wholesale importation of Western IR theories into the university classroom and academic studies, they waged a countervailing attack by calling for building a "Chinese IR theory" or an "IR theory with the Chinese characteristics". Copying Deng Xiaoping's notion of a "socialist road with the Chinese characteristics", they used the term "IR theory with the Chinese characteristics" to showcase the uniqueness of China, not just in its development road but also in its social sciences development (Liang 1997a; Song 2001). Yet, what comprises "Chinese characteristics" is confusing, which stirred up a great deal of debate within the Chinese IR academic community (Ren in this volume). Putting aside the semantic meaning of the label, a number of essential questions are raised: Does IR theory have "national characteristics"? Does IR theory serve only Chinese national interests or should it be universally applicable? Is China's IR behaviour exceptional in comparison to that of other countries? If China is exceptional, does every exceptional country have its own IR theory (Chan 1999; Hu *et al.* 2000)?

There is an argument that IR theories are produced by scholars from great powers and that the practice of great powers enables scholars to produce IR theories. There is some truth to this claim, but it is also misleading. It is misleading on what comprises a theory and how it is produced. Theory guides practice and practice informs theoretical research in return. Good IR theories serve nations' foreign policy practice and they also benefit and are further developed from practice and experience. Many argue that China's IR theorization should be based on its international experiences, such as PRC's relations with socialist countries in the early 1950s, the "fight with two fists" policy toward the Soviet Union and United States in the 1960s, and the late twentieth century perspectives on war, peace and non-alignment (Lin 1994; Gu 2005). To develop China's foreign policy and IR theories, as Yang Jiemian (2013) argues, China's rise as a great power will contribute to its diplomatic and IR theories. In his view,

> China's rich diplomatic practice and arduous theoretic exploration, a distinctive diplomatic theory system has emerged consisting mainly of the overarching thought, strategic thinking and policy principles. The diplomatic theory with Chinese characteristics at present and in the future will undertake three historic missions, namely, underscoring of the Chinese characteristics, the guiding role of the diplomatic theory, and its worldwide significance. Therefore, China has to strengthen awareness of diplomatic theory, self-confidence of the theory, and the guiding role of the diplomatic theory. At the same time, Chinese diplomatic theory should draw on what is good in foreign theories, and vice versa, for the sake of becoming more compatible with the theories of the world, identifying "Chinese characteristics" with "the worldwide significance", and providing the mainstream international diplomatic theories with more pluralism, diversity and fairness.

Since the 1990s China has been rapidly rising up in world politics. As China rises, its domestic agendas and foreign policy goals are becoming more interactive. The new patterns of domestic–international linkages have reshaped Beijing's attitude toward prevailing international norms and regimes. China's rapid social changes and economic development have gradually redefined its domestic and foreign policy agendas. There is evidence that growing economic interdependence with the outside world creates constraints on Chinese foreign policy behaviour as well as incentives to adapt to the prevailing norms in contemporary IR. In order to bring fast economic development to bear on its foreign relations, Beijing has consciously changed its foreign policy behaviour and made it compatible to some liberal international norms. China has increasingly conformed to the international norms of regional integration, multilateralism, globalism and international legal order (Johnston 2007).

Yet China's perception and conceptualization of IR is influenced by its values, culture and self-image of its role in world politics, as well as domestic agenda. As its national power rises, China's self-image of being "Asia's Sickman" and the memory of China's 'century of humiliation' has been replaced by rising nationalism, pride and self-esteem. The Chinese people have become more confident in world affairs. In dealing with other states, China has learned to be more self-assured to defend its national interest. China now could more forcefully oppose an interventionist policy of Western powers that could compromise China's "core national interests". China has also learnt to change its behaviour by observing international norms and standards and to contribute to international dialogues and discourse with its own ideas and concepts. China is spending more resources in building up its national image and soft power.

It is clear that Western liberal values are expanding their space in China's IR discourse. On the other hand, Beijing is more confident and straightforward in championing for international institutional reforms and power sharing in world politics. Beijing's attitude toward the existing international economic institutions is "remaking, but not breaking". China has also taken initiatives to form new regional institutions like the Shanghai Cooperation Organization, BRICS and its New Development Bank, and Asian Infrastructure Investment Bank to extend its influence to regional economic governance. To some extent, China continues to contend with Western states over human rights, sovereignty and principles of IR. China's international behaviour is consequential of its interactions with other states, especially major powers in the world. Chinese elites have become more receptive of modern norms in IR but, at the same time, they still firmly uphold some traditional norms and values in foreign policy making, such as sovereignty, territorial integrity and national interests.

In developing Chinese IR theories, Chinese scholars have demonstrated an increasing self-awareness of constructing a distinctive Chinese IR theory to challenge the dominance of Western IR theories while China's rise as a great power brings more confidence to Chinese scholars' search for a distinctive Chinese IR theory. Beginning with the debate on building an "IR theory with Chinese characteristics", there has been rising self-consciousness and self-identity based on China's cultural traditions, foreign policy practices and post-1949 international experiences. The economic reforms and opening-up since 1978, especially the China rising up experience in recent years, as well as the learning from Western theories and Marxist perspectives on international politics, have provided rich nutrition for thought for IR theory development in China.

Why do many Chinese scholars believe there should be a Chinese School of IR theory? Robert Cox's argument that "theory is always for someone and for some purpose" (Cox 1981: 128) is music to the Chinese ear. Western IR theory has been developed as an academic discipline by Western scholars' self-conscious efforts to understand and explain how the world works and how nations interact with each other from their own experience and practice. To many Chinese scholars, Western IR theory is not value-free or completely neutral. Although some concepts and approaches can be good analytical tools, mainstream IR theories (predominantly developed by Western scholars), such as realism, liberalism, and national security theory, are Western views of IR based on Western experiences (Wang 2004; Ye 2005). As Wang Yiwei and Ni Shixiong argue, the current IR theorizing work is predominately occidental, and as China is rising as a great power the occidental dominance will be replaced by a discourse based on global equality and comprehensive dialogues between the East and West as well as the North and South, and against this backdrop a Chinese School of IR theory is emerging (Wang and Ni 2002).

However, rich international experiences and ideational learning alone cannot lead to the construction of a Chinese School of IR. As Qin Yaqing (2007: 334) correctly argues, "a Chinese IR theory is likely to develop around the core problematic of China's identity vis-à-vis international society, a century-long puzzle for the Chinese and the world alike". Developing a knowledge-based IR theory requires some key framing questions for such a theory. What is the core problematique for Chinese IR theory?

Towards knowledge oriented IR theories in China

As discussed above, one major difference between the present Chinese IR theories and the Anglo-Saxon IR theories (considering the British and American IR scholarship share similar basic assumptions and theoretical tenets) is that between action-oriented theory and knowledge-based theory. To develop a knowledge-based IR theory, what Chinese scholarly community lacks is what Qin Yaqing (2005) calls "the core problematique" of IR theory. In his view, the core problematique for American IR theory is its concern of the post-war world order and its hegemonic management of the world order, while the central concern of the English School of IR theory is on the international society and how to maintain the British role in the society. In discussing Japan's IR theory, Takashi Inoguchi (2010: 55) identifies three key framing questions for the development of the IR discipline in Japan since 1945. These three questions are: (1) What went wrong with Japan's IR? (2) What kind of international arrangements best secure peace? And (3) Why is it that so much remains to be desired in our diplomacy?

What is then the core problematique for Chinese IR theory, if there is one? The core problematique comprises both the key material concern and the core metaphysical source for the theory construction. The problematique must be big-picture questions and have long-term historical impact on the country's development. In recent years some Chinese IR scholars have expressed a strong interest in revitalizing the past experience toward a new diplomatic and IR theory for the present world and to use that to challenge the Western power politics. The discussions and debate on the *tianxia* (All-under-Heaven) concept is such an example. However, like the concept of harmonious society, it is neither realistic nor operational in today's IR reality. If *tianxia* and harmonious society do not work, what else can be the core framing question(s) for the Chinese theoretical view of world politics? Can China's peaceful rise, rising as a responsible great power, building a harmonious international society, or its integration into international society serve as such a core problematique? Some Chinese scholars have given positive answers. There are ongoing debates on this (Su 2003; Yan 2008; Yan *et al.* 2011; Qin 2007).

China rising is an epic historic event in world history. China's ascending to great power status is fundamentally changing the post-Cold War world order and will inevitably lead to other countries' responses, regionally and world-wide, and to structural changes in the international system. Others have natural concerns about China's potentiality to become a hegemonic power. The Chinese government and IR scholars are motivated to respond and reassure others about China's intention to rise peacefully on the international stage. Chinese scholars have written extensively about China's resolution for a peaceful rise and why China's rise will be peaceful, not a threat to others' security.

However, China rising is a long historical process and the practice of a China rising so far has yet to create a knowledge oriented Chinese IR theory. China's rise helps to generate some key framing questions for theory, i.e. how the rise of China transforms world order and builds a new international system. The rise and fall of great powers is a recurring theme in world history, and it is not a new problematique for IR theories. But as many Chinese scholars claim, China is a unique country and its exceptionality generates a new set of core problematiques for IR theories. The exceptionality lies in its peaceful rise, though China's practice and behaviour is consequential of how others react to China's rise in world politics and there are frictions and even conflicts when China comes to defend its national interest and territorial integrity. Therefore, the practice of a China rising has created and will continue to create important issues for Chinese IR theoretical research. These issues include China's perspective on sovereignty and national interest, the relationship between a rising power and existing dominant powers in the international system, China's human rights practice, its opposition to hegemony in world politics, and ongoing influence of the China development model under the conditions of globalization, etc. All these are important issues and can contribute to Chinese IR theoretical development, but they have yet to become the core problematiques for Chinese IR theories (Qin 2007).

Despite scepticism about and criticism of the call for a Chinese School of IR, Chinese scholars have made some solid steps in constructing more knowledge oriented IR theories in recent years. In the last 20 years we have seen an emerging effort to construct Chinese IR theories or use the Chinese perspective to explain IR. In the 1990s, a group of Chinese scholars began to apply Chinese cultural concepts and traditional approach to IR studies. Scholars in this school of thought pay more attention to ancient Chinese philosophical thoughts and attempt to locate their contemporary applications in Chinese foreign policy practice and IR theorization. In this endeavour, three exemplar projects stand out. These research projects are: (1) Zhao Tingyang's conceptualization of international society based on the traditional Chinese notion of "*tianxia*"; (2) Yan Xuetong's "moral realism" and his introduction of traditional Chinese philosophical concepts of humane kingship and hegemony into the modern IR analytical framework; and (3) Qin Yaqing's "relational theory of International Relations" based on processual relationalism and Chinese dialectical logics (see Xu and Sun, Wang and Buzan, and Zhang in this volume).

The Chinese used to have a Sino-centric view of the world in history. Under the *tianxia* system (All under Heaven), the Chinese emperor derived his power to rule the world from the mandate of heaven. The Chinese empire and the emperor, through invested titles and authority over vassals (分封制), had established and operationalized a hierarchical tributary system to rule the country. Over time this system was extended to the relations between China and non-Chinese states in the region. This system, based on the Chinese suzerainty, not sovereignty, established and maintained regional order in East Asia for a long time (Fairbank 1968). Zhao Tingyang (2005, 2009a, 2009b) has reinvented this ancient *tianxia* concept to provide an alternative way to contemporary world order and global governance. Zhao's reinvented *tianxia* concept views the world in three different senses: the physical earth under the sky; a common choice or universe made by all peoples on earth (in the "hearts" of all people) and a political institution to ensure universal order on earth. Zhao's reconceptualised "world" is an idealized supreme political system. The system sets itself apart from the Western notion of world order and governance based on national sovereignty, balance of power, or international institutions. The *tianxia* system is in a better position to take care of the interests of the whole world and achieve global governance through a more harmonic way. Although Zhao's research is exceedingly idealistic and remains incomplete, it provides an interesting glimpse into the rising efforts of knowledge oriented theory building among Chinese scholars and their thinking on a rising power's role in future IR.

Yan Xuetong's work is representative of the rising Chinese intellectual tide to reactivate traditional Chinese thinking in modern IR studies. Yan is a ground breaker among those Chinese scholars who attempt to rediscover the value of traditional Chinese culture and philosophical thinking in modern IR and use it as the primary source of inspiration for constructing Chinese IR theories. They go back as far as to the Zhou dynasty to find IR concepts that are similar to expressions of "national interest" or an "international system" in the Western IR literature. Yan's research has mapped out how traditional Chinese philosophers viewed the concepts of international order, legitimate rule, the nature of the state and the source of leadership in IR. International leadership, based on the research of the Warring States inter-state relations, requires moral authority. International order based on hegemonic rule is less stable than the political rule built on "moral kingship" (Sun 2007; Yan 2008; Yan *et al.* 2011). Yan's works in some sense validate the view that the Chinese experience and thinking can make valuable contributions to IR theory-building.

Qin Yaqing's effort in constructing knowledge oriented theory is close to the existing mainstream Western approaches to IR studies, as he tries to develop his theory in parallel with mainstream Western IR theories. Different from the historical and cultural approaches, Qin's theory is developed on the basis of "processual relationalism". He argues that the Western mainstream IR theories have all missed an important dimension in the models, i.e. the study of processes in the international system and of relational complexity in IR. He tries to close the gap by focusing on "process" and "relationality" in IR studies. Bringing in Chinese philosophical thinking on inter-personal relations and *Zhongyong* dialect (the doctrine of the mean), he argues that the core of IR process consists in relations. International process is made of on-going interactions in practice, and through these interactions actors define and redefine their interests in process. So by replacing the Western concept of "society" with the Chinese notion of "relationality", Qin's model of processual constructivism attempts to make sense of state identities, interests and international power from the perspective of inter-subjective reasoning, relational networking, nurturing collective emotion and forming norms. In his model, state identities are relational identities and international power is relational power (Qin 2005, 2013). Qin's work is inspirational in terms of an independent ontology of the social process and relationality. But he still has a long way to travel before his theory becomes more complete and operationalized.

Conclusion

Some Chinese scholars strongly believe that IR theories are all "national theories" and Western IR theories reflect, for example, the Western identity, interest and worldviews through theoretical prisms. This is because the Western discourse derives from Western stories and experiences and Western IR theories reflect their values and worldviews. Western knowledge oriented theories, in their view, are often disguised as neutral and objective so that they can be seen as universally relevant to all. This reasoning provides a powerful incentive for Chinese scholars to seek Chinese IR theories or IR theories with Chinese characteristics. In my view, IR theories should not and cannot be "Sinicized" or just made relevant to the Chinese practice. IR theories as knowledge construction should not have any imprint of "nationality". China needs IR theories to engage in a dialogue with other countries as it quickly rises to great power status in world affairs. If a theory is for someone and for some purpose, Chinese IR theories are for the purpose of understanding and explaining China's rise in world politics and how world order should be transformed with the influence of a rising China.

IR theories are developed from actions and experiences. Theory-building is a dynamic process in which practice inspires further theorization and knowledge guides future actions. By the logic of practicality, "practical sense" is important for building knowledge oriented theory as well as action oriented theory. In building knowledge oriented IR theory, "practical sense" is indispensable to guide instrumental rationality, norm compliance, or communicative action, no matter it is realist, liberal institutionalist or constructivist IR theory. Practice or practical knowledge derived from past experience and historical and cultural traditions is imperative in the theory-building exercise. In this sense, the practice of a China rising is and will continue to be important for Chinese IR theory-construction. It can generate some key framing questions for the development of Chinese IR theories as the rise of China creates significant problematiques for world order and global governance. The rise and fall of great powers is a recurring theme in world history. It is not a new problematique for IR theories. But as many Chinese scholars would argue, China is a unique country and its exceptionality would generate a new set of the core problematiques for IR theory-building.

5 Debating the Chinese School of IR

A reflective review from Taiwan[1]

Teng-chi Chang

> A conventional cutting up of reality is at best a convenience of the mind ... Subdivisions of social knowledge thus may roughly correspond to the ways in which human affairs are organized in particular time and space. They may accordingly appear to be increasingly arbitrary when practices change.
> (Robert W. Cox 1986: 204–207)

Introduction

China Studies in Taiwan have played an important part in the whole international China Studies field due to Taiwan's geographical and cultural proximity to the mainland. Its extraordinary sensitivity to the patterns and changes of the PRC's elite politics and foreign policy was once a precious asset for Taipei's Western partners. In addition to the familiarity gained by the shared culture and experiences during a seven-decade-long conflict, another advantage of Taiwan is its China expertise, which can be divided into two major approaches. The first approach, the so-called "traditional approach", features a deep comprehension of Chinese history and the internal politics of the Communist Party of China (CPC). A few veteran members of this approach were in fact defected Communists from the CPC. The research findings by this approach were internationally influential as they correctly predicted major events like the Sino-Soviet conflict and the downfall of the Gang of Four. The second approach, the so-called "scientific approach", started in the late 1980s as a natural result of returning social scientists educated in the West, mainly in Taipei's top ally the United States. Equipped with American social sciences theories, scholars of this approach have produced quality books and papers recognized by their Western colleagues (Chiu and Chang 2013: 439–440). Taiwan's unique political and cultural status and its intellectual endowments empowered by these two approaches mean that a Taiwanese perspective on the debates and emergence of a Chinese School of IR can provide some added value in critically evaluating this intellectual endeavor across the Taiwan Strait.

Meanwhile, considering the context of time and space, a Taiwanese perspective on the Chinese School also stands out by having an edge in both mainstream IRT's scientific training and familiarity with Chinese history and culture.[2]

To paraphrase Robert Cox (1986, 1996), the conventional IR knowledge on China's IR should correspond to such a context of time and space. However, as Peter M. Kristensen puts it in his chapter of this volume, Chinese IR was virtually "imported" from the United States, which dominates conventional IR. The rapid change of China's position and identity nowadays have made conventional knowledge, of mainstream IRT in particular, increasingly debatable, if not arbitrary. In this regard, three chapters in this volume contributed by scholars from Taiwan have demonstrated Taiwan's intellectual competitiveness. I maintain that such a unique intellectual position will continue to contribute to reflective interpretations of Chinese history, culture and international politics.

One other compelling reason to offer a Taiwanese perspective refers to Taiwan's identity. Taiwan embraces both an identity force of estrangement and a relational opportunity of reconnection in regard to China. A growing "post-Chinese identity" in Taiwan may facilitate the agency of Taiwanese authors for critical reflections and innovations with historical sympathy to the construction of a Chinese School. For example, Shih Chih-yu's distinction between "ethnic Chineseness" of Southeast Asian intellectuals to sensitize difference and hybridity and "cultural Chineseness" of Northeast Asian intellectuals to pursue cultural centrality is a good initiative in studying how the evolving Chinese identity globally will facilitate scholarly debates (Shih 2005, 2015). A post-Chinese identity, registered in the intellectual capacity to creatively tap into shared cultural and historical resources, enables reconnection among Chinese or China scholars each in accordance with their strategic decisions. When reviewing the Chinese School as an intellectual endeavor, a Taiwanese perspective hence promotes dialogues between evolving Chinese identities un-owned by any national projects, and will be readily accessible to Chinese and China scholars anywhere.

The rest of this chapter provides a reflective review of the debates integral in the evolution and emergence of a Chinese School of IR. Analytically, it focuses on three issues of debate. It starts with a critical review of the search for central problematiques in constructing a putative Chinese School of IR. This is followed by a review of methodological and ontological debates among Chinese scholars in this endeavor. The third section moves to discuss intellectual and physical resources and constraints in the construction of a Chinese School of IR. The final and concluding section offers my evaluation of the prospect of constructing a Chinese School of IR as an intellectual project, with my suggestions for moving this project forward.

The analysis of this chapter is in part based on my ongoing project, launched in 2009 with support of the "Database of Journal Articles of Chinese IRT (1996–2014)". Another supporting source are my in-depth interviews conducted with senior Chinese IR scholars between 2010 and 2012. In addition, insightful Taiwanese studies directly or indirectly referring to Chinese IRT have been indispensable building blocks of my study. I will include my reflections on their scholarship, where appropriate.

The search for central problematiques

William Robinson (2005: 26) famously contended that knowledge is never neutral or divorced from the historic context of its production. Neither is the Chinese School. The early appeal for constructing a Chinese School of IR originated from the debate about an IR with Chinese characteristics. In the late 1990s, this appeal was an intuitive echo of the official party demand: "Constructing Socialism with Chinese characteristics". Ostensibly, the problematique of this appeal was of political concern: how could Chinese IR best serve the ruling party's line? After a period of theoretical learning from the West and a wave of reflections, the "Chinese characteristics" appeal faded away. Zi Zhongyun's 1998 edition of *The Exploration of International Political Theories in China* was a landmark. The "Chinese School" concept itself first appeared in 2000 in Ren (2009a: 70) and Mei (2000: 65–66). As it gradually replaced the official appeal for constructing IR with Chinese characteristics, a growing independent interest in the knowledge of Chinese international history and foreign policy became salient (Ren 2009a: 15). If well developed, a Chinese School of IR is also expected to be better able to define and serve China's national interests (Wang Yizhou 2009: 103–120; Zhu 2009: 1–14).

However, Chinese learning by importing mainstream IRT did not fit the Chinese context well, neither could it better serve China's national interests. Further challenged by its rising power and its uncertain role on the international stage, it became clear that China's real problem was the lack of its own knowledge system to express and explain itself to the outside world. The same difficulties can be found in the answer to the Acharya–Buzan thesis: "Why there is no non-Western International Relational Theories" (Acharya and Buzan 2007: 287–312). Western IRT, American IRT in particular, has acquired hegemonic status in a Gramscian sense. It defined the general backdrop and problematiques for IR study elsewhere through economic and intellectual expansion. Researchers outside the so-called "center" seem to have no choice but to adopt mainstream's core concepts and problematiques. Such awareness of the need of theories to reflect local experiences and concerns has accordingly been growing (Wang 2006a: 45). As Su Changhe (2003: 19) made it clear: "theories always grow out of questions". This view in some way paralleled the traditional ideas of senior diplomat Huan Xiang (1991), who stated that IRT's purpose is to serve the foreign policy needs of the host nation. Nations around the world are always challenged by various specific questions. This trend is further inspired by the approach and achievements of the English School (Pang 2003: 20–25; Ren 2003: 70–71; Wang 2005: 56–60). Nonetheless, as Wang and Buzan's chapter in this volume correctly identifies, naming debates of the Chinese IRT still went ahead of its substantive content. This means that the "Chinese voice" itself has continued to be one of the central problematiques of the Chinese School, a finding similar with my interview-based study on China's struggling identity as a "great power" (Chang 2004), which underlines "representation of China" as a central problematique.

"Representation" is a legitimate problematique that helps unearth specific contexts ignored by the established theories. New approaches and tools may be required to explore the ignored reality. For example, a significant number of Japanese scholars contributed to exciting philosophical and historical studies investigating mutual historical imaginations and knowledge constructions in and between Japan, China and East Asian countries. Motivating these Japanese efforts is a desire to recover Japan's representation of its subjectivity. Meanwhile, other East Asian countries may share this need for representation, due to similar historical experiences on the road to modernity (Shih 2008, 2011b). The lack of corresponding local theories by mainstream IR facilitates the need for re-theorization of the ignored experiences now and then. Ronald Toby's rediscovery of a Japanese style world order based on China's Hua-Yi order is a good example of this (Toby 1998; Yasunori 1987, 1988).

Clearly, the tension between China's rise and the post-war peace steered by the West has been another widely shared problematique, which is something that should certainly be addressed by a feasible Chinese School. Numerous mainstream studies have engaged with this issue; in the process of which they have drawn on theories of hegemonic stability and power transition, etc. The main focus of mainstream IRTs is generally whether China is a revisionist power or a status quo power (Glasser 2011; Shambaugh 2005; Abramowitz and Bosworth 2003; Johnston 2003; Wang Yuan-Kang 2010), and how the established hegemon can defend its primacy (Haas 2008; Zakaria 2009; Beckley 2011; Kissinger 2012; Tellis 2014). Mainstream literature rarely seeks support from the English School, not to speak of other "local" knowledge. This trend further turned normative after criticisms by Western journalists on China's "neo-colonialism" when China embarked on its "charm offensive" in South Asia, Southeast Asia and Africa (Kurlantzick 2007; US Senate Committee on Foreign Relations 2008: 127). Normative or ethical factors are considered by European scholars when deterministic and materialist views of the mainstream IRT are cautiously avoided (Buzan 2010: 7). For scholars in mainland China, the question is often reformulated as "how a rising power can join the international society peacefully?" (Qin 2005; Jia 2005), or "how China, based on its central role in regional history of thoughts and politics, could rise into a cooperative great power"?[3]

To engage the problematique of "how China will rise", theoretical efforts to overcome the Cold War structuralist theorization and its consequent "inevitable tragedy" (Mearsheimer 2001) have invited serious attention. Among them, scholarly studies on East Asian philosophy and historical experiences are growing both in quality and in number. Because of the principal role that ancient China once played in the relatively stable region, the Chinese School, if eligible, may lead to a major breakthrough in both IRT and modern IR. China's unique role and experience in ancient East Asia has been stressed by scholars like Fairbank (1969) and Mancall (1984) during the Cold War period. Back then, neither Fairbank nor his fellow scholars' efforts were able to draw enough attention beyond area studies. Therefore, none of their research was regarded as theory-oriented. Only recently, efforts of re-theorizing East Asia re-emerged, not from mainstream IRT or American political science, but from interdisciplinary studies stressing historical contexts and/or non-material factors. Behind this re-theorization, the problematique could be upgraded to a more sophisticated one: "how did different cultures and peoples manage and conceptualize their international orders?" (Zhang and Buzan 2012: 3–4; Suzuki *et al.* 2015) Along with this exploration there has already been a debate on how likely it is that contemporary Asia may repeat its Pax Sinica history (Acharya 2003; Kang 2010).

Above I have discussed three core problematiques that may drive a possible Chinese School forward. What kind of problematiques or research questions would meet the requirements of a feasible Chinese School, then? Shi Bin (2004: 8–13) highlights "the consciousness of methodology and problematiques extracted from [China's] own concerns, values and discursive platform to facilitate the 'Chinese exploration' of theorization". I have to contend that such consciousness is neither sufficient nor sustainable. IR scholars from Taiwan suspect that these Chinese concerns and values could only be used to decorate official narratives like "harmonious world" and such, which are designed to dilute the "China threat" concept (Huang and Chen 2010: 74–75). In contrast, Qin (2005: 165–176) proposes sounder criteria of credible problematiques that draw on Wæver's analysis (1998: 687–727) and include three requirements. First, the problematiques need to be extracted from specific historical stages and international events in China. Second, the problematiques are applicable beyond local concerns and illuminate a wider generalization of theory. Third, the research results should address important issues of development and human progress in general. That means that theorization should also be able to take care of common issues and puzzles shared by the world beyond China.

Of greater importance are the relations between the problematiques of a feasible Chinese School and its methodological preferences. Qin (2008b: 75–80) claims that problematiques for the Chinese School of IR do not need to reject the epistemological or methodological approaches of mainstream IRT. As an example, he provides the famous Chinese musical work "the Butterfly Lovers Violin Concerto", which is often compared to Tchaikovsky's "Romeo and Juliet Overture". This violin concerto is considered a masterpiece that tells a Chinese legend with a universal concern for humanity. The remarkable thing is that the work is entirely composed by means of Western musical theory. Therefore, the key is not to reject methodology different to one's own, but to ask the right questions from multiple perspectives.

In my view, Qin's position is agreeable. Still, there have been fierce methodological debates in how to advance the Chinese IRT. The shape of the debates resembles the contention between the traditional and the scientific approaches in Taiwan's China studies. Insisting on the universal nature of social science, some advocates that promote studies on ancient Chinese political theory and history reject the name of the Chinese School, while others are more skeptical of the positivist methodology. In this way, the naming debate becomes a methodological debate.

The question of methodology/ontology

Early Chinese School sceptics in China who criticized "Chinese characteristics" as a "nationalist formula" somehow share ideas with the scientific approach in Taiwan. For example, considering Chinese international thought and the history of the Spring and Autumn period valuable for IR, Yan Xuetong and members of the Tsinghua Approach prefer mainstream positivist methods as opposed to other more traditional methods. Yan once told me in a 1999 interview at Tsinghua University that his role in the development of Chinese IRT would be like Waltz's in American IRT. Not surprisingly, this scientific preference may be regarded Eurocentric, even though Yan and his colleagues may not be aware of it (Yang 2012: 83; Zhang 2012: 74–75). What matters most for them is the reality of what is going on, rather than what school name you stick on it. It is therefore unnecessary to worry about providing a certain school with an abstract title (Yan and Xu 2009; Wang and Buzan 2014: 8–12). For them, the contributions made by Chinese scholars are local applications of IRT, which cannot be confused with the establishment of a Chinese School.[4] Reflecting this way of thinking, Ren (2009b: 24–25) recalled that Yan initially proposed the name "*Science of International Politics*" for launching an English journal as a way to celebrate Tsinghua's scientific approach. This was not, however, accepted by the publisher Oxford University Press. Instead, it became *The Chinese Journal of International Politics*.

Regardless of the naming debate, I argue that the rigid scientific methodological stance is inadequate to successfully engage the three proposed Chinese problematiques discussed earlier. In the Acharya–Buzan thesis mentioned above, the advantage of Western IRT was supposed to be that it had discovered the "right" path to understanding IR, which would mean that the Westphalian straightjacket would be universal and, just like mathematics, devoid of cultural differences. Therefore, the research methods examining the Westphalian system should be universally applicable to historical data around the world. As an IRT student from Taiwan where IR scholarship has been overwhelmed by mainstream IRT, I am not going to switch to arguing the opposite and conclude that the Westphalian order is historically contingent (Zhang and Buzan 2012: 4). However, I do maintain that the current mainstream IRT has overemphasized anarchy as being divorced from time and space, hence hindering a real global IR agenda (Hobson 2002: 12). Meanwhile, I find the inter-paradigm debate and the so-called Neo-Neo synthesis (Baldwin 1993) not a fortification of mainstream IRT, but rather an erosion of its orthodoxy.

A number of other theories derived from the mainstream rationalist or realist paradigm, such as rational choice, bandwagoning, soft balancing and socialization, have somewhat engaged with the problematique of how China could peacefully join the world. Nevertheless, all three problematiques that China's case has evoked are far from having been well addressed and tested. For me, the shortcomings that mainstream IRT shares are rooted in the areas of methodology and ontology. This observation is shared by reflections from both Taiwan and China on mainstream IRT's individualistic ontology and its conception of a static anarchy (Huang 1992; He 1998: 30–44; Qin 2008a: 9–17; Shih et al. 2008: 29–38). This finding was enlightened by the different ontological and epistemological positions that IR scholars respectively adopted. The American side has a tendency to rely on monist methodology and materialist ontology, while the European side prefers a pluralist methodology and an ideational ontology enriched by historical studies (Qin 2005: 165; Hurrell 2001; Wæver 1998). In light of this bifurcation, the debates on the Chinese School extend to methodology and ontology in the quest for new approaches to address the Chinese problematiques.

To come to the point, if the central problematique still is whether the US hegemony will prevail or not, the methodology/ontology of mainstream IR will continue to perform well. If the problematiques of the Chinese School are considered, we need to be cautious about mainstream IR's ahistorical theorization and its intellectual narrow-mindedness. These are not simply abstract, theoretical puzzles. On the contrary, they have practical as well as policy-oriented consequences. Simple "copying from" and "socialization with" such narrow-mindedness, I argue, is the origin of the tragic offensive stance both Washington and Beijing now adopt toward each other.[5]

Some IRT scholars in Taiwan have argued that it is essential to extend the debate of possible Chinese School innovations to the meta-theoretical levels (Shih and Chang 2010; Chen 2011). In the space of meta-theoretical exploration, mainstream's materialist ontology no longer monopolizes the landscape of the debate. Differing from Wendtian constructivism, they believe that innovations may bear a note of Asian epistemology and ontology (Shih and Chang 2011: 280–297). To illustrate this breakthrough, the sociological and historical turn for the studies of Chinese IR and Chinese IRT are worth addressing.

With methodological consciousness taking root in developing Chinese IRT in the last decade or so, various efforts have been pooled together to make theoretical innovation. One such effort echoes the "sociological turn" that surged in Western IRT in the late 1980s (Ruggie 1986: 131–157). This "Chinese turn" resembles the English School's criticisms of mainstream IRT for its under-socialized and egoist assumptions (Buzan 1993: 327–352). To correct the mainstream's bias, two separate but related and ambitious theoretical adventures are particularly notable: the Relational (*Guanxi*) Theory advanced by Qin Yaqing in Beijing, and the Balance of Relations Theory (BoR) proposed by Shih Chih-yu in Taipei.

The Relational Theory highlights the traditional Chinese concept of *Guanxi*, usually translated as *relations*, as an independent ontological element in all social interactions. The ontological implication of this position is that "all in the universe are related and correlated", a proposition with cosmological appeal that is ostensibly at odds with the mainstream's individualist perspective. Further inspired by the structuration theory of Anthony Giddens and the constructivist's focus on "process" and "constitutiveness", the Relational Theory emphasizes the mutual transformation of material and ideational factors (Fang and Jin 2009:

56–61). Based on earlier explorations by Qin, Gao argues that "being" always co-exists with relations (Qin 2009b; Gao 2010). In this way, because relations can both be material and ideational, the dichotomy between materialist and ideational worldviews is relaxed. Nevertheless, in accordance with Qin's views on the Chinese School's problematiques, his relational theory is as universally applicable as the rationalist theories. As a result, his theory seems to constitute a combination of Western theory with Chinese tradition (Wang and Buzan 2014: 18).[6]

Qin's theorization of relationality in IR is paralleled by the attempts of Shih Chih-yu and Huang Chiungchiu from Taiwan, who theorize BoR in unpacking the logic of Chinese foreign policy/history in contrast to Balance of Power (BoP) (Shih 2013; Shih and Huang this volume). Ontological as well as methodological implications of the BoR theory are clear. Complying with the metaphor of kinship, BoR theory presupposes the spontaneity of mutual benevolence between national states. Kinship is defined here as a universal social relations framework featuring bilateral interactions. It is also the fundamental ethical base for many Asian societies. The process of these interactions is through the Confucian concept of role-adapting and identity-building. In my understanding, the expanded bilateral kinship relations and processes lead to specific international orders that resemble ancient Sino-centric East Asia. In contrast, multilateral relations based on atomized individualistic relations and processes lead to international orders resembling the Westphalian world. These orders could coexist in a hybrid form, or clash with each other. Actors living within them could switch between BoR and BoP options depending on the changing sociopsychological context, which requires decision makers' rational or relational estimation. So could the mainstream's "balance of threat", in a sense, be better categorized by a BoR theory than by BoP? For instance, Xi Jinping's appeal for a "new model of great power relations" could also be examined as pursuing relational security in a Chinese context. By the same token, exploring the specific social settings of a given international order with ontological and methodological pluralism in mind will be more productive for the Chinese School when engaging with its problematiques. After all, social actions would be impossible without some underlying social ontology (Wight 2006). To push forward such a different school of IRT, it is necessary to go beyond the positivist "iron cage" forged by the Cold War ontology, and give way to ontological and methodological pluralism.

Since knowledge of specific social and historical contexts is crucial not only for data-mining, but also for the field of IRT as a whole, the historical turn in IR theorizing is not a simple issue of research tools or methodology. As Chinese history enters Chinese IRT, ontological and methodological pluralism can mutually reinforce one another. The historical turn is accordingly connected to the problematiques of the Chinese School. Questions on how China is represented, how China will rise, and how different orders could be managed and conceptualized in the past and future can be properly tackled only by a critical review and reflection of the records of Chinese foreign history.

One thing that all China IRT scholars agree on is that many historical cases in China (and in East Asia in general) are under-interpreted and under-explained by the mainstream theories. Deeper understanding of these cases will surely deliver a powerful input into constructing a Chinese School. However, finding better concepts and theories for engaging Chinese and East Asian history cannot simply be achieved by copying and learning from the West. There have already been a few attempts by cultural and sociological researchers theorizing the historical experiences of China and East Asia. For example, Chen Kuan-hsing from Taiwan emphasizes the rupture and continuity between a pre-modern Asia that operated within the tributary system and a post-modern Asia that operates within a system of equal nation-states (Baik *et al.* 2004: 35–36). The problematique of East Asia is caused by the ontological gap between these two systems. The *Analysis of Chinese Imperial Governance of Rite* by Huang Chi-lian (1992) is widely recognized as one of the most systematic studies on the Chinese tributary system. This kind of exploration has been largely ignored by mainstream IRT, and when it was noticed, it was deemed as being part of a field of exceptionalist or particularist area studies.

It is encouraging to see growing scholarly interests in bringing back historical East Asian and Chinese experience into IR theorization. This augurs well for the future development of a Chinese School of IR.

Historical studies on Chinese and East Asian IR can be helpful in transcending the mainstream presentist bias. Victoria Hui, for instance, highlights the unique political economic features of the dominant unit in the ancient Chinese system, which differs from the Westphalian context. Meanwhile, she disagrees with Yan Xuetong and the Tsinghua Approach's attempts to use classical Chinese political theory to construct a new IR theory (Hui 2010: 124–140; 2012a). In contrast, Wang Yuan-kang offers path-breaking studies, which uphold his universal offensive realist stance and dismisses the ideational effects that the Confucian ideology might have exerted over imperial China's war and peace decision (Wang 2010). Also within a positivist analytical framework, Zhou Fangyin employs a quantitative method to build an equilibrium model of the tributary system that explains the self-deteriorating tendency of China in three historical cases. The three cases he has pointed out indicate the system's dynamic and evolutionary nature (Zhou 2011b). Nevertheless, as Zhang and Buzan's criticisms of Zhou indicate, his positivist presumption that treats states as "rational" actors may ignore institutional innovations based on a particular historical and social context (Zhang and Buzan 2012: 7). By bringing back the historical social context, Brantly Womack's work on ancient China's outstanding management of asymmetric relations with neighbors and David Kang's historical exploration series on Asia's international order support the pacifist inclinations of the tributary system (Womack 2010; Kang 2007, 2010, 2013).

There are also studies that categorize historical contexts and indigenous worldviews of the regional order in ancient East Asia and China and demonstrate how they have empowered the agency of local actors (Zhao 2005: 40–48; Chen and Zhou 2008). In this respect, Qin (2009a: 306–343) notices a surge of what he calls the "traditional approach", which grounds IRT on the traditional East Asian order and classical Chinese philosophy, especially Confucianism. An example of this trend are the *Tian-Xia* or 'All-under-Heaven' related studies and debates initiated by Zhao Tingyang (Zhao 2005; Qin 2010: 26–50). To my knowledge, Zhao's All-under-Heaven system is an ideal-type concept extracted from ancient Chinese order and ideas that is universal not because it insists on free trade and modern individualist civil rights, but because it tolerates various polities autonomously operating and freely trading in peace under a loosely regulated overarching authority. Undoubtedly, Zhao's ideal-type conception is enlightened by China's tributary system, but it is not a copy of a historical reality. Unlike Zhao's ideal type, Zhang and Buzan's conceptualization of the tributary system as international society draws on the English School. Similarly but theoretically more sophisticatedly, their *Pax Sinica* stresses the institutional arrangements based on intersubjectively accepted norms manifested in discursive and ceremonial practices. The participants of this society retained autonomy even when they acknowledged the legitimacy of this rank-ordered hierarchy (Zhang and Buzan 2012: 15).

It is also worth noting that historians in Taiwan have offered in-depth studies on the historical Chinese order and its tributary system. Reputed historian Chang Chi-hsiung proposes the concept of the *Chinese World Order* that differs from Zhao's All-under-Heaven system in at least two aspects. First, Chang's *Chinese World Order* is not only an ideal type extended from kinship, it is also an international law governing what he called the system of suzerainty. Chang categorizes the Westphalian system before the twentieth century as a system of colonization, as both the systems of suzerainty and colonization are hierarchal. Chang's case studies on the diplomacy of the late Qing empire and the Republic of China (ROC) show that both the Qing and the ROC were heavily affected by ideas of the system of suzerainty (Chang 2007; 2010: 106–146; 2011). In contrast, Kan Huai-chen's reservations on the concept of the modern nation-state leads him to bring forward the approach he calls "East Asia as method".[7] He argues that many historical events that happened in the Chinese space did not happen within the present PRC borders, neither were they based on China as a nation-state. Therefore, when important events in Chinese history are reviewed, the modern political boundary of China should be bracketed. They need to be re-evaluated with a broader perspective. As a historian informed by both Japanese and Chinese studies, Kan contends that the ancient East Asian order was a rite-based order that symbolized and legitimized the subjectivity of its participants (Kan 2004: 507–531; 2007: 3).

My reflection on the historical turn in Chinese IR is that the Chinese School, if feasible, should be a society-based and history-informed enterprise in which ideational factors and material forces are carefully conceptualized and examined. My own studies also suggest the indispensable importance of ideational and discursive forces featuring in Tang–Tibetan and Qin–Mongolian relations. The Tang dynasty's Heavenly Khan system and the Qing dynasty's tributary system can be adequately comprehended only when Chinese norms and beliefs are taken into account. The contemporary relevance of this analysis can be found in the relations between China and her neighboring countries (Chang 2010: 34–49; Chang and Chen 2012: 89–123).

Intellectual resources and constraints

One key argument made by Acharya and Buzan (2010) in *Why Is There No Non-Western International Relational Theory* is that both intellectual as well as physical resources are indispensable for the construction of an IRT theory. Well-informed problematiques and a well-organized methodological foundation are the essential intellectual resources. By and large, the debates on the core problematiques and methodology of the Chinese School demonstrate a self-consciousness of the fact that no innovative theoretical results could emerge by simply copying imported mainstream IRT or repeating official Marxist-Leninist teachings (Wang 2009a). It remains important, though, for Chinese scholars to monitor closely the progress in the theorization of IR in the global IR community and to engage in the debates concerned.

In examining the changing intellectual resources of the Chinese School, I propose a historical division of the evolution of Chinese IRT in four stages: (1) The period before 1980, which is characterized by policy demands; (2) the period from 1980 to 1990, in which IR as a modern discipline started taking shape; (3) the period from 1990 to 2000, in which Western IRT was widely studied through translations and assimilation with Chinese thinking. In this period "poverty" and "imitation" were seen as Chinese IRT weaknesses by a few key researchers, which led to a situation in which leading figures suggested taking bold steps for constructing a Chinese School (Peng and Su 1999: 18; Wang 1995: 11–12; Wang and Buzan 2014: 11); and, (4) the current period, started in 2000, which is characterized by critical reflections on mainstream IR theories and a series of innovative attempts at indigenous theorization of IR, providing fertile ground for the embryo of the Chinese School to grow.

Besides, the potential of the Marxist influence in Chinese IR can never be underestimated, especially in this globalizing era in which there is a growing wealth gap between the North and the South. My own analysis over the typology of China's "great power diplomacy" strongly suggests that China's identity as the leading Third World nation has been and will continue to be active in Beijing's three interchangeable great power identities (see Table 5.1). The image of China as a leading Third World nation is deep-rooted in the PRC's Marxist intellectual legacy.[8]

Nevertheless, as Wang (2011: 94–95) suggests, Marxist international studies in mainland China are facing severe challenges: aging faculty members, a shrinking amount of them, and outdated research methods, just to name a few. For Wang, their "Chinese characteristics" are degenerating into vain political requests. In this regard, if the construction of a Chinese School continues, the intellectual challenge of engaging the Marxist legacy and modern Western Marxist IR scholarship will be a serious one (Wang and Buzan this volume).

Table 5.1 Three interchangeable great-power (GP) identities of China

	China as a pragmatic GP following the logic of BoP	China as a GP thst is also a "responsible stakeholder"	China as a GP challenging the status quo
Perceptions of the status quo	Bipolar or multipolar systems that allow China to maximize interests by BoP.	An institutionalized international society in which China should assume "responsibilities" and provide public goods.	An unjust world in which "hegemonism" and "power politics" help exploit the weak by force and biased rules.
Causal beliefs of international relations	Distribution of power provides both constraints and opportunities for state units.	Legitimate institutions and regimes enhance the feasibility and credibility of Chinese foreign policy.	International structure and institutions are human creatures and subject to human agency to revise.
Foreign policy guidelines	Non-interventionism; peaceful co-existence; "hiding light and biding time".	China being "a responsible great power".	To build "a fair and rational new international political and economic order".
Intellectual resources	The Legalist School of ancient China; classical realism; Marxist-Leninism.	Confucianism; Institutionalism.	Rebellious heroes of Chinese folk novels; prototype Marxism; Maoism.
Policy practitioners in modern China	Deng Xiaoping	Chiang Kai-shek Zhou Enlai Jiang Zemin Xi Jinping	Mao Zedong

Sources: Chang 2004, 2013.

Regarding the intellectual resources for the construction of a Chinese School, Qin (2006, 2010: 40–45) suggests three potential propositions on Chinese ideas and practice. The first is the All-under-Heaven worldview (Chang's *Chinese World Order*) and various other ancient East Asian tributary systems. The second is modernization thoughts and Chinese revolutions.[9] The last is China's reformist thinking and the experiences of China's integration into the international system. There are also people who disagree with the above propositions. For example a renowned Beijing scholar that I interviewed contends that the late Qin diplomacy of Li Hongzhang, the Northern government during the early Republican period, the War of Resistance, and the ROC's changing role and practice in mainland and Taiwan, should also be indispensable building blocks for a future possible Chinese School.[10]

This suggests that Qin's view on the intellectual sources of the ongoing Chinese School needs expansion and clarification. To date I have only found a very limited amount of studies included and examined by the main body of Chinese School literature, but their contribution could be significant. The first has been advocated by Buzan and Little's studies on international systems in world history (Buzan and Little 2000). Erik Ringmar's comparison of the Sinocentric, the Tokugawa and the Westphalian systems is an outstanding demonstration of how comparative studies of international orders and systems can result in progress for the Chinese School (Ringmar 2012). The Taiwanese scholar Tang Hsin-wei's (2010) studies on bilateral relations between two greatest powers from the seventeenth to the twentieth century is another illustration of how China's behavior as a great power in historically bipolar systems can be unique or universal.

Meanwhile, Zhao and Chang's rediscovery of Chinese philosophical heritage of *All-under-Heaven* or the *Chinese World Order* notion should not be limited to ideal types or imagination. Lin Hsiao-tin, a Taiwanese expert of China's frontier history, has examined the status evolution of Kanjut from the late Qing to the Republican eras and demonstrated how the tributary protectorate became imagined as a "lost territory". Peter Katzenstein (2006: 10–20; 2012: 3–7, 235–237) also highlights the philosophical heritage of civilizations and accordingly points out the differences between the ancient East Asian order and the modern European order. He defines the former as a combination of formal hierarchy and informal reciprocal equality, and the latter as a combination of formal equality and informal hierarchy. He further argues that China, as a civilization, is in essence an open empire. This makes China resemble more the United States than it does the German or Japanese empires. The logic behind Katzenstein's thesis is that the concept of civilization is gradually replacing the idea of the nation-state as the new bearer in international politics. Within this new civilizational order, philosophy plays a central part in order and peace.[11] Studies of Lin and Katzenstein suggest that the organizing principles found in the history of Chinese international orders and systems should be carefully investigated as a valuable intellectual source for the construction of a Chinese School of IR.

The last but not the least intellectual resource of the Chinese School concerns the ethical appeals of international studies. I strongly contend that treating ethical appeals as Nye's soft-power concept, as the Tsinghua Approach intends to, is seriously misleading (Zhang Feng 2012: 90–102; Yan 2014). As Qin's proposal of the problematiques for the Chinese School makes clear, development and progress of humans in general should be a sincere and scholarly concern. The resources should consist of shared values then and now, no matter whether they are socialist or Confucian. Shi Yinhong (2009: 32–29) agrees that the shared values should include economic growth, liberty, social justice and environmental preservation. He argues that the current global transition does not merely constitute a change in the balance of power, but is more fundamentally a transition in terms of ideas. Uneasy about what exactly the content of the change will encompass, American scholars like Ikenberry are optimistic about the future of the West just because of the ideological narrowness of what the Chinese regime embraces (Ikenberry 2008).

In this regard, Wang Jisi (2006: 19–20) concedes that the ruling Communist Party traditionally exerts a tight grip over social sciences in China. The correctness of a theory could be determined by how well it suits the political missions and doctrines. Such a political environment, Wang observes, has impeded the real appreciation of the problematique of "Chinese characteristics", and led to its demise. Fortunately, compared to their colleagues from other social sciences, it seems that political obstacles in China's IR scholarship have gradually been eased. As Tang Shiping (2010) suggests, widespread slogans are no longer the major weakness of the Chinese School now. Instead of the political slogans, he now blames the abundant publications lacking specific research awareness.

Regarding the physical resources of the Chinese School in mainland China, such as libraries, IT infrastructures, funding, institutional resources like career structures, quality journals, better training, a talented young generation of researchers and intellectual ethos, all have significantly improved. What I consider as particularly invaluable assets for the Chinese School are the human resources from the transitional generation and their contribution to Chinese IRT. According to a careful study by Wang Yizhou, most of the current Chinese IR scholars in and from the mainland experienced the Cultural Revolution. Some of them went to the West for degrees or as visiting scholars. A common trait of these scholars is that they are talented in comprehending both Western theoretical analyses as well as possessing a deep understanding of Communist Party guidelines on discourse. Most of them were born in the late 1950s and 1960s. Another common feature is that in their studies all bring to light an open diversity in theoretical preferences and an identity crisis regarding China's status and role in a changing world (Qin 2006: 13).[12] It is clear that such diversity combined with an identity crisis and the relaxation of political control facilitated the Chinese IRT's breakthrough in the mainland (Wang 2006a: 44–59; 2006b: 7–12). Given the long-time marginalization of China in the international (academic) society, it seems likely that the Chinese School efforts are so far somewhat like a soul-searching business for the transitional generation and their young successors. Beneath the tension in the peaceful rise argument, the debate is more about defining what or where China actually is, rather than about preaching the "China Model" or the "Beijing Consensus".

Prospects and suggestions

Social science is bound to be "social", which means that it is impossible to stand alone in a vacuum stripped of time and space. The late founder of modern mainstream IRT Kenneth N. Waltz (1979: 8) once claimed that theory is an artistic creation "shaped by the taste and style of a single hand". The "taste and style" here are by definition socially and historically bound, but this should not decrease their wider applicability. It follows that the "Chinese School of IR" will be marked by Chinese taste and Chinese style. In order to avoid the trap caused by mainstream's presentist bias, "Chinese" here should not just be referring to a specific nation-state or a static official Chinese identity in the present day. The prospect of the future Chinese School should be judged by how well the "taste and style" of the Chinese School engage with its problematiques, respond to its methodological requirements, and are supported by its resources.

Debating the Chinese School of IR 95

These questions lead to the criteria for evaluating the achievements of a future Chinese School. In this regard, Qin's proposal of a set of criteria is worth noting. First Qin believes that the problematiques of the Chinese School must be extracted from Chinese history and experiences. Second, the locally extracted theses must be universal in potential, and applicable beyond its origins. Finally he insists that the core hypotheses of the school must be fundamentally different from other existing IRT. Following his criteria, Qin proposes to divide the development of Chinese IRT in three phases – a pre-theory phase, a theory-learning phase, and a theory-building phase – that are all based on different degrees of theoretical consciousness. His research shows that the Chinese IRT field has been on the "deep-learning" track since 2001, but is yet far from the construction of paradigms that are required by a specific IR School (Qin 2005, 2010: 32–33).[13]

Based on my reflections on the debates examined, I would like to modify Qin's formula by adding two amendments. First of all, my previous investigation has indicated that Asia, East Asia in particular, provides the valuable bedrock and background to extract good Chinese School problematiques (Zhang and Buzan 2012: 7). This is particularly true because the territory of the contemporary PRC is ontologically and geographically not exactly the same as that of historical China. This is to say that a future Chinese School should not become a national IR theory only intending to deliver a "China voice". The second amendment of the criteria emphasizes more the methodology and ontology, rather than the "hypotheses". I argue that the same hypotheses may have been explored by mainstream IRT, but that a Chinese School should be capable of reengaging them through different methodological approaches and ontological assumptions in its research designs. Accordingly, the mainstream criteria of what exactly defines a theory or a school can also be re-examined.[14]

Although it is still too early to proclaim a Chinese School, a growing interest in constructing a Chinese School of IR with its own core problematiques is evident. Even though Western IRT has had a big head start, the period of catching up by Chinese IR scholars is underway. Therefore, I believe that the full development of a Chinese School is only a question of time and resources. As for the essence of a future Chinese School, I do not expect that a specific core concept like the one of "international society" will emerge soon. Pang Zhongying (2003: 25) once foretold that if a Chinese School is possible, it should be like an umbrella covering theories with compatible problematiques and theoretical features. There could be two or more branches existing under the same hood. Yu Zhengliang (2005) and Wang and Buzan (2014: 3) similarly believe that a possible Chinese School would not be a monolithic, unified theoretical system, but that it would be constantly enriched by two or three lines of internal debates. The name of the Chinese School would at most be a title that refers to studies and scholars sharing similar problematiques, ways of reasoning and other intellectual resources.[15]

In summary, the current state of the Chinese School of IRT can be understood as a knowledge community sharing broadly similar theoretical interests. I am cautiously optimistic about its future. Beneath its problematiques about the tension between rise and peace is China's identity and its role in the international system or society. Equally important is the question of the uniqueness of cases in China and Asia. The puzzle must be addressed in a pluralist way using interdisciplinary methods. Among them I suggest that a synthesis of sociological and historical studies that emphasizes both explanatory and interpretive analyses should take the lead. My bold advice for one key step forward that constructing a Chinese School should take is that it must enlarge its scopes and domains in time and space. It should bring East Asia back in. I am by no means trying to pursue a purely Sinocentric, de-Westernized IR research agenda. On the contrary, I believe any re-theorization of East Asia will constitute a dynamic dialogue "in the East" as well as "between the East and the non-East". In the process of this dialogue, as I have demonstrated many times in this reflective review, other historical actors in ancient or modern East Asia should have an active presence in the debates: e.g. Vietnam, Japan, Korea, Mongolia and even Ryukyu and Tibet. Moreover, while the intellectual disconnection between past and present is more extreme in the mainland (Wang and Buzan 2014: 27), Taiwan's intellectual sources of the Chinese historical and cultural legacy can offer vigorous and constructive input into the fulfilment of a better grounded Chinese School. In this way, the Chinese School enterprise should engage with its East Asian colleagues and improve the shared problematiques, in order to eventually better contribute to the world IRT family as a whole.

Notes

1 The author would like to sincerely thank the National Science Council of Taiwan for granting support to his projects "An Evaluation of the 'Chinese School' in International Relations Studies: A Dialogue of Theories and Cases" (NSC100-2410-H-002-072) and "Foreign Relations of Ancient China: a Historical and Theoretical Review" (NSC 101-2410-H-002-120).
2 By "mainstream IRT" this chapter means the three major International Relations theories dominating IR in America: realism/neorealism, liberalism/neoliberalism and constructivism. When "Western IRT" are mentioned, American mainstream theories and the English School are both included.
3 According to Ren (2009a: 71), the latter approach was first raised by Jack Snyder in 2009.
4 Interview of C, 2010/7/14.
5 On the offensive approach the United States and China adopted in recent years, see Chang (2013). On the "inevitable" tragedy mainstream theorists foretold, see Mearsheimer (2001) and Kaplan (2005). A "defensive" prediction of this sort is "Why the Sunnylands Summit won't stop Sino-American Rivalry", by Stephen Walt (2013).
6 In March 2015 Qin officially announced the name of his approach: "The Relational Theory of International Politics". Online, available at: http://nanhai.nju.edu.cn/show.asp?id=680, 2015/5/20.
7 The idea of Kan's "East Asia as method" is inspired by "China as method", proposed by Japanese philosopher Yuzo Mizoguchi (1999).
8 A senior scholar interviewed directly claims that, according to their historical background, scholars of IR at Peking University were mainly assigned to the studies of the Soviet bloc, those at Renmin University mainly to the "Third World", and those at

Fudan University mainly to the developed world. The CASS (Chinese Academy of Social Science) took charge of the studies of specific countries and issues. Interviewee C, 2010/7/14.
9 One interviewee insisted that the Marxist theories belong to the Western IRT as large, it should not be singled out from the Western theories. Interview of A, 2010/7/23.
10 Interview of E, 2010/7/7.
11 By reviewing the latest literature, Shih Chih-yu (2011: 331–334) further enriched this "civilizational approach".
12 A senior interviewee put it very simply: "who is China?" (Interviewee E 2010/7/7).
13 In Wang Yiwei's word, it is now in a stage between "copying" and "construction" (Wang 2009: 103–120).
14 Interviews of B and E, 2010/7/7; 2010/7/15.
15 For example, Li Yihu (2004) believes the Chinese concept of "Geju" resembles the "structure" of the mainstream IRT, but its discursive implications are richer than "structure". A more rigor exploration of "Geju" theory could be a branch of the Chinese IRT.

6 Mapping the world from a Chinese perspective?

The debate on constructing an IR theory with Chinese characteristics*

Nele Noesselt

China's rise to global power status has triggered a debate about the interests and orientations of the People's Republic of China (PRC) in world politics. International China watchers examine continuities and shifts in China's foreign policy to make predictions about China's future international positioning strategy. Whereas one school of thought assumes that conflict between the United States, the old power centre, and the currently rising PRC is inevitable, others argue that, owing to increasing global interdependencies, an open conflict is rather unlikely to occur. The most recent research puzzle concerns the impact on China's foreign policy behaviour of the power transfer to the next generation in 2012–2013. Some analysts predict a turn to more assertive behaviour and expect confrontations between China and the West to rise.

Almost unnoticed in the Western research literature, Chinese political scientists are concerned with the same research puzzles. On the one hand, they try to define China's new identity as an international player and its strategic role in global politics. On the other hand, under the label of "constructing a theory with Chinese characteristics" (or even a "Chinese School"), they conceptualize and interpret the international system from a Chinese perspective and develop visionary interpretations of a future world order.

Chinese foreign policy think tanks not only analyse recent changes and development trends in the global system, but they also include perceptions and images of the "self" and the "other" as well as the roles attributed to China by the outside world in their strategic calculations. The debate on developing a "Chinese School" of International Relations (IR) thus should not be misread as an abstract theory discussion, but rather as a reflection of current constellations and shifts in global politics and their impact on the PRC. While the IR debate takes place in the socio-philosophical context of "Chinese" social science, it simultaneously mirrors the international China debate and theories of IR that guide the behaviour of other states vis-à-vis the PRC. In fact, there is not only one but a multitude of debates somehow associated with the "Chinese" paradigm. The following analysis of these inner-Chinese IR discourses sheds light on their epistemological and ontological foundations and proposes a sub-categorization of the different discourse elements according to their functional dimension(s) and/or policy relatedness.

Inquiries into the philosophy of science and research traditions

Two cognitive sources can be said to underlie the current attempts to develop a "Chinese" theory of IR: Sinicized Marxism (Cheng and Guo 2012; Wang, Cungang 2009, 2011) and (reinvented) Confucianism (Wang, Rihua 2011). At first glance, this (re)turn to the past – to the early twentieth century, when Marxism-Leninism was reformulated into Mao Zedong Thought (Schram 1989), or, respectively, to the times of the Hundred Schools in the pre-Qin era, which is seen as the breeding ground for Chinese thinking about "inter-national" relations (Chan 1999a; Ye 2003; Xu, Jielin 2004) – appears quite paradoxical given the iconoclasm of the early Maoist period and Chinese scholars' current attempts to establish innovative and independent indigenous research approaches and theories. While Confucianism belongs to the old order that Chinese communism claimed to overcome, Marxism, being imported from the "West", can certainly not be considered as a distinct "Chinese" research tradition.

However, these two "traditions" of knowledge have guided theory as well as policy formulation in China over the last few decades. They have been merged into the concepts of a "(socialist) harmonious society" and a "(socialist) peaceful rise", put forward by the Hu–Wen administration (Yu, Jianrong 2006). Nonetheless, incompatibilities between the materialist legacy of Marxism and the more philosophical legacy of pre-Qin state philosophy still persist – as the twists and turns in Chinese foreign policy illustrate. It goes without saying that any analysis of the "Chinese School" debate must begin by considering the ideational backbones of the current debates among China's political and academic elites.

Re-Marx: theory innovation for the twenty-first century

Even today, "Marxist" terminology and philosophy is still omnipresent in Chinese IR debates. Following the modernization of IR research in China during the 1980s – when decisions on the reform of the education system were implemented, milestones of Anglo-American IR studies were translated into Chinese and the Chinese IR community generally took "Western" (mainly US-born) methods and theories as their universal standard (Yu and Chen 1999; Ni and Xu 1997) – Marxist IR approaches were reduced to a side phenomenon in modern IR research, but they never completely vanished from the scene. Official diplomatic and political discourse continues to use foreign policy terminology inherited from Maoist times, which is deeply inspired by Marxist epistemology. Consequently, academic papers investigating recent developments and the main orientations of Chinese politics integrate these official terms of Chinese-style Marxism – such as "contradictions" (*maodun* 矛盾) or the "characteristics of the era" (*shidai tezheng* 时代特征) – into their analyses (Chen 2012: 136–138).

Furthermore, as the majority of people working in universities or think tanks in the 1980s and 1990s had been socialized in Maoist times and were trained along the lines of Marxist philosophy, the reception of "Western" IR research did not immediately result in a substitution of the general research frames used for the analysis of world politics.[1] Even though the younger generation of Chinese IR scholars now often looks at the world through neo-realist glasses, their research is at the same time deeply influenced by the remnants of Maoist-Marxist concepts. Apart from terminology, Marxist IR approaches provide a certain view of world politics that engages in the critique of hegemony and inequalities of global power contributions, which explains the overall tendency of Chinese articles to condemn US hegemony and to vote for a "democratization of International Relations" (Li, Bin 2005).

Bearing this in mind, the fact that a subject search for "Marxist IR" (*Makesizhuyi guoji guanxi lilun* 马克思主义国际关系理论) on the China Academic Journals database[2] in May 2014 led to only 80 articles should not be interpreted as a victory for "Western" IR frames over Marxist-Maoist ones. Articles on world politics and Chinese foreign relations are quite often just descriptive assessments that do not mention theory at all.

Moreover, even in the twenty-first century, Marxism-Leninism, together with Mao Zedong Thought, Deng Xiaoping Theory, the theory of the "three representations" and the concept of scientific development, continues to be a pillar of the Chinese party-state; all of these concepts have been written into the Party's official constitution. Marxism functions as an official state doctrine and as a formative element of the system's identity as a socialist (one-party) state. A document on the future of social sciences in China issued by the Central Committee of the Communist Party of China in 2004 defines Marxism as an indispensable element of any innovative reformulation of IR theory by Chinese academia (Central Committee 2004). In 2004, in order to support the reactivation of Marxism and to use it as the starting point for a distinct "Chinese" theory formulation, Hu Jintao launched a huge Marx project that sponsors research on Marxist theory for the twenty-first century (Chen 2012: 136). Chinese scholars involved in this project are currently working on historiographical assessments of the evolution of Marxism abroad and in China and have to fulfil the challenging task of coining a Marxist theory that is based on China's past and more recent experiences. Along this line, the "China model", i.e. the hybrid mixture of plan and market under one-party rule, is identified as part of "Marxist" research (Su 2012).

Marxism as such is definitely not a "Chinese" theory, but if it is adapted to the constellations in China (as done by Mao Zedong), it can at least be seen as an amalgam of different ontological and epistemological traditions that can move beyond the existing IR theory frames and could thus provide the starting point for a "Chinese School" (Wang, Cungang 2009: 8). However, as Marxism itself falls under the category of "Western" theories, the argument that China's theory innovation presents an alternative to the "West" obviously lacks solid causal foundations.

Archaeological excavations

In addition to Maoist-Marxist epistemology and the research agenda derived therefrom (the focus on the objective laws of world development, historical and dialectical materialism, as well as the unity of opposites), in 2005, Qin Yaqing, one of the key proponents of the Chinese discourse to construct a "Chinese School", postulated that China's IR contribution should consist in theorizing the "peaceful rise" of a socialist country to global power (Qin 2005). The theoretical assumptions derived from China's "socialist" experiences could, so the argument goes, then serve as an orientation for other (non-democratic/non-capitalist) emerging powers. Qin's reflections are written as a counter-story to neo-realist scenarios of an inevitable conflict between old and new power centres as well as between different civilizations.[3]

In recent post-colonial assessments of IR theorizing beyond the West, the "harmonious world" and the "peaceful rise" have been presented as potential "Chinese" contributions to IR theory. The theoretical validity of these concepts, however, is widely contested in, as well as outside, China. Both notions were first introduced by China's political leaders and subsequently developed by academic society – only selected advisors from universities and think tanks were involved in the shaping of these concepts.[4] As a consequence, in order to step out of the assumed political predominance of politics over political research, some scholars involved in the "Chinese" IR debate(s) have turned from policy-linked Maoist-Marxist frames towards ancient Chinese philosophy instead. Their main points of reference are the Spring and Autumn period (770–476 BC) and the Warring States period (475–221 BC), during which several small Chinese kingdoms contended for leadership and hegemony. The interactions between those kingdoms (which were unified under the victorious Qin emperor in 221 BC) and the related writings of the political advisors and state philosophers of the time are seen as a historic example of "inter-national" relations in a regional context far from the West (Chan 1999; Ye 2003; Xu, Jielin 2004).

While the majority of related analyses are limited to a historical reconstruction of structures and principles of interaction in ancient times, the "Tsinghua group" headed by Yan Xuetong looks at ancient Chinese philosophical texts to excavate guiding strategies for political action. What they find, however, is not a theory of international politics but rather a catalogue of "correct" ways of governing the country (and the world). Yan Xuetong has developed a threefold typology of political rule: "true kingship" (*wang* 王 or *wangdao* 王道) leads to a stable international order; "hegemony" (*ba* 霸) establishes hierarchies and asymmetries, and the international order oscillates between stability (relations between the hegemon and its allies) and chaos (confrontation between the hegemon and its opponents); while "tyranny" (*qiang* 强) will inevitably lead to disaster and decline (Yan 2008: 137). "True kingship", also labelled "humane authority", is the only way to maintain a long-lasting and stable order. This resonates with the PRC's symbolic commitment to benevolence, peace and cooperation, as summarized under the label of "great power" (*daguo* 大国),

which is held up as a Chinese alternative to the old-style idea of expansion-based empire (*diguo* 帝国).

The claim that China's international engagement does not follow the path of military struggle for hegemony and zero-sum power competition also underlies the current reinvention of the *tianxia*. The meanings ascribed to *tianxia* exemplify the Chinese imagination of what an "empire" should be about. *Tianxia* stands for: "the whole country", which, from a Western perspective, could be labelled "China" or "Chinese empire"; "the whole world", which did not represent the world in the geographical sense, but illustrated the geocultural construction of the world as the sum of territories and regions that had symbolically accepted the authority of the Chinese emperor; or "Chinese civilization", as opposed to the illiterate "barbarian" tribes across the four oceans that, in Chinese imaginations, surrounded Chinese territory.[5]

Translated into modern IR terminology, the notion of *tianxia* combines ideas about the identities and roles of the main actors in the international system with those of an idealized world order. While reflections on *tianxia* have occupied Chinese historians and philosophers over the past centuries, its current reinvention and adaptation to the constellations of the twenty-first century have been inspired by the writings of Zhao Tingyang. Contributing to the general bashing of the discursive hegemony of "Western" IR, Zhao identifies the Westphalian system as a degenerated order linked with negative attributes: the international system is anarchic; nation states compete against each other in zero-sum games; and wars and conflicts result from the absence of an ethical code of conduct (Zhao, Tingyang 2005). In contrast to this dark scenario, he depicts *tianxia* as a hierarchical but stable alternative blueprint for the twenty-first century (Zhao, Tingyang 2003).[6] And even though, in political practice, the Westphalian concept of the sovereign nation state has had a lasting effect on China's positioning in international politics, that China views itself as a "civilizational state", displaying the legacy of China's self-image as the centre of *tianxia*, is still discernible in contemporary Chinese writings on Chinese foreign affairs and international politics. According to Zhang Weiwei, a "civilizational state", in contrast to a nation state, does not rely on military-based expansion. It does not copy any other state's or empire's development model, and the guidelines of its strategic behaviour are derived from its own – and distinct – cultural traditions and historical patterns (Zhang, Weiwei 2012).

This utopian construction of the world and China from a Chinese culture-based perspective is not just a phenomenon of the twenty-first century, but has its historic roots in the late nineteenth and early twentieth centuries, when China's intellectual elites struggled to rebuild China's territorial integrity and its national sovereignty. Among these literati scholars was Kang Youwei, who, in his *Datongshu* 大同书 (*Book of Great Unity*), lay down the draft for a utopian world community without any frontiers or territories – a global community beyond the nation state, similar to a reformulation of *tianxia*, this time not as a local, but as a global order.[7]

Taking into account the historical circumstances under which Kang Youwei, Zhao Tingyang and Zhang Weiwei propagate(d) their visionary models of a

Mapping the world from a Chinese perspective? 103

world order derived from Chinese philosophy, it is more than obvious that, in all these cases, these utopian models are part of an ongoing and unfinished state-building process. The *Datongshu* was written in the shadow of the national humiliation by external forces and the growing internal dispute over which was the right path to modernize China. Only after the abolition of the "unequal treaties", forced upon the Chinese empire during the Opium Wars, did China regain its status as a sovereign state. But, the quest to regain its old position of power continues and determines China's politics to date. The debate about a "Chinese" IR theory thus finally reveals itself as a continuation of the late imperial intellectual debates on self-strengthening and reform.[8] Furthermore, it is at the same time also a variation of the "China model" debate (Wang, Yukai 2008; Yu, Keping 2008). The "China model" illustrates the PRC's claim to pursue an autochthonous development path in domestic politics – and as such corresponds with the debate on constructing a "Chinese" paradigm for IR and world politics.

The functional dimensions of theory building

The above-sketched reflections on the functions of IR theorizing in China lead one to the question of how the term "theory" (*lilun* 理论) itself is understood among China's epistemic communities. Furthermore, one has to clearly differentiate between the meanings ascribed to IR theory in general and the particular ones attributed to Chinese IR by outside observers, as well as those developed and used in the inner-Chinese debates.

Quite recently, Chinese IR debates have caught the attention of international scholars engaged in a post-modern, post-colonial deconstruction and reconstruction of IR theory building. The assumption is that theory in general serves to analyse past events, to anticipate trends or, in a normative way, to guide or justify political action. However, with regard to "Chinese IR", Acharya and Buzan introduce a wider definition of IR theory that integrates "the harder, positivist, rationalist, materialist and quantitative understandings ... and the more reflective, social, constructivist, and postmodern [understandings of the theory spectrum]" (Acharya and Buzan 2007: 291). They also concede that IR might include normative assumptions; even pre-theoretical concepts are viewed as elements of an emerging IR theory framework in Asia. As a working definition, Acharya and Buzan propose labelling any IR concept that is either recognized as a theory by the international academic community or identified as such by its progenitors or, regardless of academic acknowledgement, represents a systematic and abstract approach to IR as a contribution to IR theory (Acharya and Buzan 2007: 291). While China's historical theory and practice of IR has, with only a few exceptions, generally been ignored by the international English-speaking IR community,[9] the recent post-modern/post-structuralist trend in international IR theory seems to follow the other extreme and takes concepts as theory that, from a critical point of view, do not fulfil the basic requirements to be grouped under the label of "theory" as defined in "general" IR.[10]

In contrast to this all-encompassing definition, Alagappa reduces theory in the Asian context to a normative-constitutive function, which is directly linked to the policy level (Alagappa 2011: 222). According to this understanding, theory does not function as a framework for analysis, but is rather a tool for exerting power in international politics. Alagappa assumes that "theory" in the Asian context "has a predominantly practical orientation with emphasis on understanding and interpreting the world to forge suitable national responses" (Alagappa 2011: 222).

If one takes a closer look at Chinese writings on "theory", one soon discovers that there is no unified definition. Generally, a Marxist understanding of theory, which was imported during the early stages of Sino-Soviet cooperation and ideological proximity, is still discernible in quite a few IR publications. The "official" Chinese (Marxist) understanding of the meaning and function of (IR) theory is as follows: It is a system of concepts and principles that reflects the objective laws of (political) processes. Its main function is to guide political action (Wang, Jisi 1994: 482). This definition has its roots in the Maoist era. In his essays, "On practice" and "On contradiction", Mao Zedong proposed a recursive interrelation between theory and practice based on dialectical materialism. Any theory has to be deduced from political practice and verified by political practice (Mao 1937a). "Theory", according to Mao, was not something to be produced by the academic community; rather, it should be formulated by the political leaders. The main aim of these political "theories" was not to explain the world but to realize the socialist world revolution (Chan 1997: 59).

In the reform period, IR theories in the Chinese context have continued to serve the dual function of guiding and legitimating political action. Obviously, this understanding of "theory" is different from the definitions commonly agreed upon in the general IR literature. If theory in China has to guide political practice, its main focus has to be on foreign policy, and not on international or global politics in general. Only frameworks applicable in the bi- and multilateral context of international politics are regarded as being worth studying (Ren 2000: 20). Contrary to this practical, Marxist-inspired definition of "theory", the more liberal school of Chinese IR scholars affiliated with Fudan University in Shanghai argues that "theory should serve to promote the forward-looking awareness or predictive power of international affairs and to serve to accumulate knowledge" (Chan 1998: 16). The field of IR theory research in post-Maoist China has become more fragmented and pluralized, reflecting the educational background of the different groups or networks of scholars. Those educated at US or European universities often tend to rely on the theory frameworks used at their foreign alma mater, while those engaged in theory innovation are noticeably inspired by post-modern, critical IR approaches.

Geeraerts and Men postulate that, in the Chinese political context, the validity of a "theory" is not measured in terms of its explanatory power but rather according to its ideological soundness and its ability to guide political action (Geeraerts and Men 2001: 252). With regard to Chinese IR theory during the 1990s, Wang Jisi argued that "ideology" was an essential element of any theory, whereas in the "Western" discourse, ideological attributes were taken as evidence that non-"Western" IR lacks a scientific foundation and should instead be classified as strategy (Wang, Jisi 1994).

While the majority of Chinese IR publications are rather descriptive and seldom operate with an abstract theory framework, articles belonging to the "theory" category are often overview articles of theory debates in the "West". Only 5 per cent of the articles published in Chinese IR journals deal with the formulation of a "Chinese" IR theory, whatever this term might stand for (Qin 2009).

In Chinese analyses of IR theory, narratives such as the "end of history" (Fukuyama 1992) and the inevitable breakdown of communism, the "clash of civilizations" (Huntington 1996) and the paradigm of "democratic peace" are all identified as elements of foreign strategy that help to cement and stabilize the predominant position of the United States on the global stage (Hu 2003). This clearly shows that "theories", according to the "Chinese" understanding, bear a strategic connotation. If the assumptions were correct that the theory-formulating state generally tends to present its concepts as universally applicable frames and not as part of its national strategic calculations, Chinese publications could thus be expected to group the "Chinese School" debate under the rubric of "theory".

However, a closer look at Chinese academic publications reveals that concepts such as the "peaceful rise" or the "harmonious world" are simultaneously classified both as strategy (*zhanlüe* 战略) and theory (*lilun*) and that these two categories are often used interchangeably. Moreover, quite a few studies by Chinese IR scholars deal with the thoughts (*sixiang* 思想) on international politics of China's political leaders, which they regard as the main sources of "Chinese" IR – although these studies do not develop a systemic set of hypotheses and theoretical assumptions.[11] Some Chinese articles, however, operate with the logical differentiation between diplomatic strategy and IR theory, thus linking strategy to states' foreign relations and not to world politics, which is conceived as a more abstract category (Yang 2004).

The reference to "strategy" illustrates that this stream of IR research is still focused on the operational dimension of "theory" – understood as a tool for measuring and predicting developments in China's external environment and for configuring appropriate positioning measures. The mentioning of IR "thought", by contrast, stresses the ideational dimensions of IR theory building in China. The collected writings of China's political leaders on world politics operate with constructions and interpretations of the world that do not necessarily reflect political "reality", but are compatible with the system's ideological underpinnings and justify certain political actions.

Given the plurality of views and methodological approaches prevailing among China's epistemic communities, it would obviously not make sense to reduce the notion of "theory" to one single definition. There are definitely scholars who seek to overcome the perceived parochialism and hegemony of concepts derived from European history by adding frames derived from Chinese history to the ongoing global debate on the reformulation of IR in the post-Cold

War period. It remains, however, questionable whether this approach might lead to the creation of a novel and universal IR theory, or will just broaden the historical-empirical repository of IR theorizing.

The main innovative potential of the Chinese IR debate is presumably not the formulation of any completely new analytical understanding or normative construction of world politics. Chinese scholars who specialize in pre-modern China's history and philosophy of IR identify many parallels and equivalents to "Western" IR. The greatest point of divergence between "Western" and "Chinese" theory-based IR research is to be found in calculations and projections of China's current and future posture in the global realm. These "theories", however, should not be misread as analytical frames. They develop an idealized image of the world that is favourable to national development interests. In order to avoid being misled by the term "theory", one should consider referring to IR debates in China not as systematic frameworks of analysis, but rather as "world views" that "do not reflect the world ... [but] represent it, not only constraining our vision but also enabling us to develop a language of concepts and terms that in turn make it possible to talk intelligibly about IR" (Griffith 2007: 1). A "Chinese" theory of IR would thus look at the world from a "Chinese" perspective and include strategic calculations. As such, it would not only consist of visionary interpretations of how the world should be organized, but also comprise reflections on the "self" and the "other". Given that the emergence of the search for a "Chinese" IR theory is linked to the launching of the reform programme, one could expect that this debate, rather than formulate an abstract blueprint for international and global interactions, primarily reflects national and domestic concerns.

Chinese IR theory and political action

The remaining tantalizing question is whether the formulation of "Chinese" IR theories can be expected to have any impact on China's foreign behaviour.[12] Analysts of China's strategic culture have argued that China's external actions are inspired by elements of Confucian-Mencian as well as legalist-realist "parabellum" calculations (Johnston 1995). While Johnston's category of "cultural realism" acknowledges the existence of both traditions in China's security thinking, he identifies parabellum elements as the operational code, and classifies elements of Confucian-Mencian culture as part of the autocommunication among China's political and intellectual elites. Responding to these statements, Feng Huiyun argues that strategic culture is not a static, unchangeable frame, but is highly context-dependent (Feng 2007). Feng states that Johnston's selection of Chinese texts (the *Seven Military Classics*) and the time frame chosen (Ming dynasty) lead to results that could not be taken as universal patterns of Chinese strategic culture. According to Feng, Confucian ideas of benevolence, justice and righteousness are still the key determinants of China's foreign politics, although they do not imply that the political elites will accept actions directed against China that could harm its national sovereignty or territorial integrity

Mapping the world from a Chinese perspective? 107

(Feng 2007). Again, China's rather pragmatic conduct of foreign relations in the post-Maoist period has led many scholars to assume a predominance of "realpolitik" frames in Chinese IR thinking (Christensen 1996).

The overall question under which this controversy over the identification of the operational code of Chinese foreign policy falls is, once more, whether China possesses a unique political (and strategic) culture *sui generis* or whether it emulates elements of strategic traditions similar to the ones practised (and reflected) by the "Western" world. Chinese scholars engaged in the archaeological excavation of Chinese IR traditions do not care too much about the similarities and dissimilarities between "Chinese" and "Western" political philosophy in general; they are more concerned with ascertaining the predominance of harmony over belligerence in China's tradition-based IR thinking.[13] Partly opposing this approach, Victoria Hui stresses that history, not abstract philosophy, should guide the search for a "Chinese School" (Hui 2010, 2012b). This statement, composed as a response to "Chinese" criticism of her comparative monograph on world order in the Chinese and the European historical context (Hui 2005), highlights an often overlooked aspect: not all of the texts and research approaches grouped under the label of a "Chinese School" operate on the same level. Studies on the ideational, philosophical traditions of the *tianxia* system or the interactions between the ruler and the ruled do not necessarily depict political reality. Following this line, literature on historical political philosophy might be seen as corresponding to "Western" research on Kant or Rousseau – who are not regarded as architects of any kind of systematic IR theory formulation but instead are seen as representatives of certain philosophical streams that inspired theory building. The reflection on political ideas and philosophy is often rather disjointed from "real" political practice. Theories as analytical frames and strategies, by contrast, are generally derived from concrete historical events (often critical junctures in world politics).

Furthermore, one should distinguish between the theoretical-philosophical narrative of China's foreign relations and the ideational patterns of foreign behaviour and practices of interactions deduced therefrom, and those frames used to calculate the strategic responses of other players in the international system. Foreign policy discourses often stick to ideational paradigms and present a country's foreign policy as legitimate interests. Likewise, studies on China's participation in world affairs present its engagement as standing in line with its general moral and ethical foundations. The actions and moves of other players, by contrast, are often described by applying neo-realist frameworks that identify power maximization and national security interests as determinants of the behaviour of other powers in the international system.

If the ideational dimension of the Chinese IR debate is first of all a discursive, legitimating element, one might be tempted to assume a general incompatibility between the country's nomothetic-ethical ideas and its foreign policy conduct. However, as various scholars have pointed out before, China's reluctance to resort to military means could be taken as an indicator, although not final proof, of the predominance of "harmony" over "use of force".[14] Shih Chih-yu and

Huang Chiung-chiu, who look at China's foreign policy through the analytical glasses of Confucianism, argue that China's external behaviour tends to achieve a "balance of relationships", and not a "balance of power" as realist theories would predict (Shih and Huang 2012). As they correctly highlight, China's (re)turn to Confucianism should not be misread as a general negation of the use of force, including the right of self-defence. One should not forget that Confucianism is only one of the various ideational streams that shape China's foreign policy in theory and practice. The combination of legalist and Confucian-Mencian ideas enhanced by elements taken from "Western" social science and political philosophy, which function as mind maps for China's elites, results in political practices that, despite their Confucian-Mencian ingredients, can be quite rational and strategic. At the same time, however, this rationalist dimension of Chinese politics should not be misunderstood as leading to a neo-realist practice of power politics (Shih and Huang 2012). What Shih and Huang label the "power of relationships" stands in line with earlier culture-based psychological explanations of Chinese politics (Pye 1968; Shih 1990). The balance of relationship approach is based on the hypothesis that states' behaviour in bilateral interactions is not about maximizing power and pursuing national interests. Instead, it assumes that states will agree to make concessions to protect relational security and to reduce uncertainty – observable not only in Chinese foreign policy but likewise applicable, as the authors argue, to the United States (whose foreign policy is identified as a combination of balance of power and balance of relationships) (Shih and Huang 2012: 2).

To grasp the different functional dimensions of the "Chinese School" debate, one has to differentiate clearly between the level of foreign policy and world politics. With regard to the former, the "Chinese" debate materializes as ex-post discussion, often including justificatory elements, about foreign-policy decision making. If one conceives of IR theory as analytical lenses that help to select data and to reduce the complexity of world politics, one could argue that Chinese scholars have already successfully developed their own analytical frames to make sense of the world from a "Chinese" perspective. Whereas neo-realist theories interpret the PRC's border disputes with the Soviet Union, India or Vietnam as an expression of hard-core power politics, Chinese scholars stress the overall focus on harmony and argue that all these actions were undertaken to restore order. The Chinese side argues that Chinese foreign policy remains determined by the Five Principles of Peaceful Coexistence and relies on harmony and stability. The maritime expeditions of Ming dynasty China, in contrast to Western colonial powers, did not end up with a military conquest of overseas territories. Again, if one looks at PRC history, the so-called "punitive mission" against Vietnam ended with the withdrawal of Chinese troops behind the old border lines.[15]

With regard to world politics, Chinese scholars have outlined normative incompatibilities between "Chinese" and "Western" views on world order (Pan 2012). Given these ideational gaps, these Chinese publications assume that states, even in similar situations, do not act in a similar way. Although most

Chinese IR scholars agree that no systematic "Chinese" IR theory has been developed so far, abstract ideas and concepts that have been derived from China's political culture and philosophy more or less directly influence China's behaviour – and so define the way in which Chinese scholars (and the political elites) view the world and perceive the other players involved. The actions taken, however, certainly do not rely on "Confucian-Mencian" ideals but mirror rational strategic cost–benefit calculations.

Conclusion

This chapter has shown that, in order to make sense of the "Chinese School" debate, one has to differentiate between two functional dimensions of theory/strategy formulation. The academic debate still sticks to meta-theoretical reflections on the possibility of producing a distinct "Chinese" IR theory and discusses its conceptual sources. Even though there is no single unified understanding of theory, many researchers engage in rather abstract research on the history and philosophy of Chinese "international" politics and seek to identify potential add-ons or alternatives to the established "Western" theory frames. The foreign policy debate, also grouped under the "Chinese School" approach, by contrast, has produced a range of "new" IR concepts – which are presented as elements of Chinese ancient thought on order and principles of interactions.

Given that leading scholars and think tank researchers serve as advisors to the Chinese government on issues of international politics, there are direct linkages between the academic debate(s) and the official political strategy discourse. Theoretical reflections on power distributions and principles of interactions are merged into policy recommendations. Chinese scholars calculate the impact of existing theories on the strategic decisions of China's regional and global neighbours. The "peaceful rise" and the "harmonious world" are coined as "new" frames to present an alternative labelling and interpretation of China's foreign policy that does not subscribe to the current neo-realist "new assertiveness" debate. Furthermore, Chinese scholars contributing to this stream of research reject any theory that would contradict the PRC's claim to pursue an independent development strategy that is different from the "West"[16] – as this would imply a transition towards democracy – and also draw a clear line between the theory and practice of the Chinese "model" and the development strategies of other (failed) socialist systems. By introducing an "independent" IR terminology such as *daguo* and *wangdao*, rooted in the Chinese classics, Chinese scholars implicitly deny the applicability of "Western" concepts (hegemony) and related scenarios (power competition, imperial expansionism) to the Chinese case. These narratives target two audiences: with regard to the Chinese society, they consolidate the image of an independent Chinese approach to politics and justify China's development strategy by presenting it as a history- and tradition-based approach. Addressing the international community of states, and especially China's regional neighbours, Chinese IR concepts seek to defuse threat perceptions. Accordingly, these concepts function as elements of soft power building and public diplomacy (on soft power: Li, Jie 2007; Yu, Xintian 2008). However, it remains questionable how far this reference to a Confucian heritage of Chinese politics determines and constrains China's foreign behaviour.

One way to decipher the multiple coexisting "Chinese" strategy and theory approaches is to apply Johnston's distinction between ideational and operational dimensions of Chinese (foreign) strategy. Along this line, the reinvention of Chinese traditions and references to philosophical notions in China's official policy discourse serves domestic purposes. It contributes to national identity building and symbolically stabilizes political rule. The conduct of Chinese foreign policy, however, mainly relies on rational cost–benefit calculations and often operates with assumptions drawn from "Western" IR.

Apart from foreign relations, the "Chinese" IR debate also covers the world order dimension. This includes ideas on ordering principles, power distribution and the overall structure of the world system. The current international system is seen as unfair and unilaterally dominated by the United States and its allies – the search for a "Chinese" paradigm of IR theory thus finally reveals itself as part of China's global positioning ambitions.

While the overall "Chinese" theory debate has remained rather abstract – the 2013 conferences on IR theory research in China stressed the need to develop a "Chinese theory" that might start from China's Confucian-Mencian culture, but failed to come up with systematic theory assumptions (Song 2013) – the field of international political economy is where "new" theory (or rather strategy) elements become manifest. Taking the global financial crisis of 2007–2008 as a starting point, Chinese IR scholars, especially those who follow a Marxist IR approach, have recently referred to the crisis as empirical evidence of the failures of capitalism and the "Western" approach to global financial governance (Wang, Xiangsui 2011: 21). China is the most active advocate of a reform of international institutions and global financial governance. Since 2008, China has continuously reiterated its demands through the BRICS joint declarations, G20 meetings and Davos summits. In March 2009, the head of the National Bank of China, Zhou Xiaochuan, presented a proposal for replacing the US dollar with a new supranational currency unit (Zhou, Xiaochuan 2009). Behind these public statements hides a huge controversial debate on theories of international political economy (as a subfield of IR) and their Sinification as conducted by China's epistemic communities.

The various workshops and conferences on "Chinese" IR held over the last few years have had to fulfil the challenging task of elaborating add-ons that are compatible with China's official foreign strategy but that also pay tribute to China's new status as the world's second largest economy, the number one creditor of the United States and a central player in the reform of the architecture of the global financial system. In highly generalized terms, the Chinese debate on international politics and the construction of a theory "with Chinese characteristics" can thus be subdivided into a group of articles that discuss the current state of international politics and criticize the existing structures, and those that define ways to reformulate China's foreign strategy and to upgrade China's status in world politics. Although both debates are highly heterogeneous, one can assume that at least some elements of these debates will be included in the re-evaluation and, potentially, also in the remodelling of China's strategy under the new fifth generation.

Notes

* This article was originally published in *The China Quarterly* 222, 2015: 430–448. I am grateful to *The China Quarterly* for its kind permission to reprint the article here in this volume.
1 For an overview of the characteristics of the different generations of Chinese IR scholars, see Fang 2005.
2 Online, available at: http://oversea.cnki.net/kns55/brief/result.aspx?dbPrefix=CJFD.
3 On the "clash of civilizations", see Huntington 1996.
4 Zheng Bijian (Central Party School) is said to have been the key architect of the idea of a "peaceful rise", which he first used in a speech at the Bo'ao Forum in 2003 (Zheng 2003). It became officially presented as a new foreign policy doctrine by Wen Jiabao in his speech at Harvard University in December 2003. The "harmonious world" was introduced by Hu Jintao at the sixtieth anniversary of the founding of the UN in September 2005. Chinese scholars, however, have pointed out that the notion had been tested before in various bilateral diplomatic meetings. See Zhao *et al.* 2007: 253.
5 See the related entries in the encyclopaedic dictionaries *Hanyu Da Cidian* and *Zhongguo Da Baike Quanshu*.
6 Zhao, Tingyang 2003. Zhao's critics remark that this argument – i.e. the failure of the "Western" concept of global order and the moral superiority of *tianxia* – lacks empirical foundation and applies a dual standard to the evaluation of "Western" and "Chinese" IR concepts. See Zhou, Fangyin 2008; Xu, Jianxin 2007: 137. His supporters, however, try to integrate Zhao's *tianxia* with global IR theorizing. They argue that Zhao's writings, which upgrade *tianxia* from a regional institutional framework to an abstract global model, overcome the shortcomings of theory approaches that continue to rely on a state-centric construction of the international order. See Liu and Wang 2011.
7 The ideational background of his utopian imagination is to be found in the *Liji* (*Book of Rites*), which contains a whole chapter on the ideal order of society (*liyun*). The passage describes the decline of the old order and the subsequent transition from the era of the *datong* (great unity) to the *xiaokang* (well-off) society. The *Gongyang* commentary on the *Liji*, on which Kang Youwei bases his utopia, argues that the development from *datong* to *xiaokang* is reversible. The return to the paradise lost, the old order, has always been, and continues to be, a guiding principle in Chinese state philosophy. One of the most prominent examples comes from Sun Yatsen, the founding father of the Chinese Republic, who referred to the passage *tianxia wei gong* (meaning that All-under-Heaven form a communality) from the *Liji* to illustrate his vision of China's future state constitution. See Bell 2008: 24.
8 In the late imperial era, China underwent a forced transformation and had to adapt to a "new" global environment. The changes in the international system since 2007–2008, catalysed by the global financial crisis, pose a similar challenge that requires China's elites to rethink the country's foreign strategy and to reformulate its international role conceptions.
9 One of the few IR scholars who integrated the Chinese case with the comparative history of IR in different regional contexts was Martin Wight. See Zhang, Yongjin 2014b.

10 For a collection of post-colonial IR approaches that focus on non-Western regions, see Acharya and Buzan 2010; Jones 2006; Shilliam 2011; and Tickner and Wæver 2009.
11 Observation based on searches for the combination of "theory", "strategy" and "International Relations" on the China Academic Journals database: online, available at: http://oversea.cnki.net/kns55/brief/result.aspx?dbPrefix=CJFD.
12 For a case-based examination of the relationship between "Chinese" IR theory and Chinese foreign politics, see Wang, Hung-Jen 2013b.
13 Given the movement of ideas and nomothetic assumptions between Asia and Europe and processes of learning, emulation and eclectic indigenization, it would be rather misleading to conceive of both philosophical traditions as insulated sets of norms and values. The Sinification of Marxism and its merging with legalist, Daoist and Confucian-Mencian philosophy, as practised by contemporary Chinese IR scholars either intentionally or unintentionally, indicates that one has to think of China's strategic culture as a hybrid amalgam that combines different, often even antagonist, streams of thought.
14 On philosophy and tradition in Chinese foreign policy, see the 2013 special issue of the *Journal of Chinese Political Science* 17(2), online, available at: http://link.springer.com/journal/11366/17/2/page/1.
15 Again, others, most likely (external) observers who operate with different analytical lenses, might argue that the official story that China never practised any kind of expansionism is easily disproved by comparing the territory enlarged by the post-Qin dynasties with the one currently claimed by the PRC (which inherits the border lines of the late Qing dynasty that incorporate Taiwan, Tibet and Xinjiang).
16 This has also been formulated in Hu Jintao's report to the eighteenth Party Congress in November 2012.

Part II
Towards sociological realities

7 The English and Chinese Schools of International Relations
Comparisons and lessons[1]

Wang Jiangli and Barry Buzan

Introduction

In Chinese discussions about International Relations (IR) theory, the 'Chinese School' and the English School are often mentioned in the same breath (Zhang 2003; Pang 2003; Ren 2003, 2009a; Callahan 2004b; Shih 2005b; Wang, C. 2005; Wang, Z. 2012). The obvious reason for this is that their names seem to validate national approaches to IR theory. The less obvious, but no less important reason, is that both are positioned as challengers to mainstream IR theory – particularly realism/neorealism and liberalism/neoliberalism – which is largely American-based, but does not carry the label 'American School'. It hence seems worthwhile to conduct a comparison to see what lessons the English School might or might not offer to those working to construct a Chinese School and to those seeking to develop IR theory in China more generally.

Having been in existence for more than half a century, the English School has a clear and widely accepted identity and a long track record (Dunne 1998; Buzan 2014). The idea of a 'Chinese School' is much newer and still hotly contested. The first problem with this exercise, therefore, is to determine exactly what is being compared. The English School does not represent the totality of IR in Britain, but is just one well-established body of thought that operates within Britain and in the global IR community. It is aimed at system level IR theory, and despite the label has little interest in pursuing foreign policy theory. The picture on the Chinese side is quite different. The term 'Chinese School' has been used to promote the development of theoretical IR thinking within China about systemic IR theory and foreign policy theory for China. The context for the emergence of the Chinese School is one where China needs to find its feet as a major power in a global international system, and in which the whole field of IR in China is relatively new and needs to establish its voice in a well-developed global IR community. Given the lively and diverse IR debates in China, it seems highly unlikely that a single monolithic 'Chinese School' will come to dominate IR thinking there. From present developments, a more likely outcome seems that of 'Chinese Schools' in which there might be two or more lines of theory development that are 'Chinese' in the sense of drawing on distinctive elements of Chinese history, culture and philosophy. In addition to this, there are already

'IR Schools in China', in the sense that Chinese IR scholars identify themselves with existing theoretical approaches to IR, such as realism, liberalism, constructivism, Marxism and indeed the English School. The label 'Chinese School' might well disappear if emergent lines of IR theory acquire more specific names, as the Tsinghua Approach seems keen to do. The lesson from both the English School and the Copenhagen School is that names are given by others, often those opposed to such development. We will nevertheless use the term 'Chinese School' in the discussion that follows, but will differentiate it where appropriate, and readers should keep in mind the diversity that this represents.

In the longer run, Chinese IR might well look somewhat like IR in Britain, with a mixture of theoretical approaches and schools, some global and some reflecting indigenous developments. It might be argued that it is too early to compare the well-developed English School with a diverse Chinese development still in its formative stages. But the comparison is already being made, and therefore needs authoritative discussion. And the history of the English School can still offer insights to those in China trying to become differentiated from mainstream IR. There is indeed concrete content in various 'Chinese Schools' to compare, so although the different stages of development might be a problem, they also constitute an opportunity. In this chapter we focus on academic histories, comparing Chinese IR theory developments and the English School in six dimensions: origins, founders and organization; naming; context; aims/intentions; theoretical sources; and historical projects. The opportunity, therefore, is to apply the experience of the English School to the formative process of Chinese IR theory, at the same time making clear the considerable differences that time, place and circumstance make to the two projects. The chapter concludes by looking at possible lessons for Chinese IR, both from what the English School has done well and from things for which it has been criticized, and at the utility of the comparison.

Comparisons

Why these six dimensions? They are not derived from any theory about theories, but are empirical categories reflecting the purposes of this article. Since the English School and the Chinese School are discussed together, our first aim is to give a comprehensive introduction of each school to their respective members. That is the main point of the first four headings – origins, founders and organization; naming; context; and aims/intentions – which cover the fundamental academic histories, and would apply to a comparison of any schools of thought. Unless these histories are understood, the virtue (or not) of associating the two schools cannot be properly assessed. The first four headings are largely about differences between the two schools. The last two headings – theoretical sources and historical projects – are more about their similarities. Most mainstream IR theories have their roots in political theory, so this is both an interesting point of comparison and a gateway topic to how different theories fit into the wider picture of IR theory. Historical projects are not so common in mainstream IR theory, but are strong features of the Chinese and English Schools, making this a particularly important point of comparison.

Origins, founders and organization

The English School

If one wants to specify a date for the beginning of the English School, then 1959, when the British Committee on the Theory of International Politics (hereafter, the British Committee) first met, is probably the best choice. But the origins of the British Committee can be traced back to the mid-1950s (Vigezzi 2005: 109–116; Epp 2010). The idea of 'international society' is often seen as the flagship concept of the English School, but is not original to it. Thinking along these lines was developing inside several heads well before the first meeting of the British Committee, partly among international lawyers such as Schwarzenberger (1951), and also within IR: Martin Wight and Charles Manning, both teachers at the London School of Economics (LSE). The British Committee was a self-selected group of scholars and practitioners mixing history, philosophy and IR academics with practitioners from the Foreign Office and the Treasury (Dunne 1998: 89–135; Suganami 2003; Vigezzi 2005; Cochran 2009; Epp 2010). It inspired independent, but linked projects, most notably a parallel group on the idea of international society based at the LSE (Donelan 1978; Mayall 1982; Navari 1991; see also Navari 2009: 7–8). The key players in the British Committee were Herbert Butterfield, Hedley Bull, Adam Watson and Martin Wight. The principal exclusions from it were Charles Manning and E.H. Carr, both of whom have their backers as foundational figures of the English School. Manning (1975) was an influential thinker who did much to establish IR as a distinct field of study in Britain and also to embed a sociological, constructivist way of thinking about 'international society' as a 'double abstraction', with imagined states imagining themselves as members of an international society. Carr had no obvious sympathy for the idea of international society, seeing it as an artefact of the dominant powers, which he described as 'masters in the art of concealing their selfish national interests in the guise of the general good' (Carr 1946: 79, 95–97, 167). Yet his dialectical critique of both utopianism (as dangerously divorced from the reality of things) and realism (as politically sterile and fatalistic), and his argument for the necessity of blending power and morality in IR, seemed to leave room precisely for a *via media* of the type offered by the English School's idea of international society (Dunne 1998: 23–46).

The British Committee ceased operation in the early 1980s, after which the English School became more dispersed: a school in the form of an international network rather than a club. Geographically, the English School retains a strong position in British IR, with notable concentrations at Aberystwyth, LSE and Oxford, and a presence in most places where IR is taught. In Europe, there is significant interest in Denmark, Germany and Italy, with outposts in Norway. Further abroad it has a solid presence in Canada and Australia, and some outposts in Turkey, Israel and India. It struggled somewhat to get established in the intensely parochial US IR market, despite having a scattering of followers. But with the establishment of the International Studies Association section, it seems now to have found its feet. More recently, the English School has acquired followers in China, Japan and Korea. Within the United Kingdom, neither universities nor the government played any role in supporting or promoting the English School, other than in their general funding for research of all kinds. Interestingly, given that the English School was in part about finding an alternative to IR theory as it developed in the United States, the American Ford and Rockefeller Foundations played a role in its evolution. Funding for the British Committee's meetings came initially from Rockefeller, and later from Ford.

The Chinese School

The origins of the Chinese School are to be found in the discussions about the development of IR and IR theory that emerged in China around the end of the 1980s. There has since then been ongoing debate about 'whether China has IR theory or not' or 'how to build Chinese IR theory' (Shi 2006; Wang and Dan 2008; Ren 2009b; Ni *et al.* 2009). Some scholars advocated building 'an IR theory with Chinese characteristics' or 'the Chinese School of IR theories', and these ideas gave rise to much debate.

Perhaps the first public move was made in 1986; when Wang Jianwei and others published the paper, 'Make efforts to build Chinese IR theory' (Wang *et al.* 1986). This was shortly followed in 1987 with the first national conference held in Shanghai to discuss constructing Chinese IR theory with Chinese characteristics, in which many scholars expressed views on this theme (Huan 1991; Li 2003). This conference can be regarded as the formal beginning of discussions about IR theory with Chinese characteristics (Shi 2006: 521). Mainly in the 1990s, Liang Shoude and other scholars pushed forward the discussion of IR theory with Chinese characteristics (Liang 1994, 1997a, 1997b, 2005a, 2005b; Liang and Hong 2004; Song 2001). Zhang Minqian suggested building a Chinese School of IR in 1991 (Wang and Dan 2008: 343), perhaps the first use of the term 'Chinese School'. Within a decade, use of this label had become widespread. Through analysis and comparison of IR theories originated in the United States, Mei Ran emphasized the theoretical value and practical implications of constructing a Chinese School, and the need for Chinese scholars to take a creative and independent line (Mei 2000). Ren Xiao, Qin Yaqing, and Wang Yiwei are proactive advocates and promoters of a Chinese School (Ren 2000, 2003, 2009a, 2009b; Wang and Ni 2002; Wang, Y. 2004; Qin 2005, 2006, 2007, 2008, 2009, 2011a, 2012a, 2012b). Qin Yaqing, in particular, has made the most systematic case for both the possibility and necessity of a Chinese School, but many other scholars are also involved in this endeavour. Although the name has changed from building 'IR theory with Chinese characteristics' to constructing a Chinese School, the starting point and aim are the same, i.e. to build China's own IR theory.

This task is still in its early stages. During the 30 years from 1978 to 2007, only 5 per cent of study results were about a Chinese theoretical paradigm, and had not become influential. Yet during the 1990s, Chinese IR academia basically reached a consensus on constructing Chinese IR theory in some way. After 2000, the discussion turned towards exactly how to construct Chinese IR theory (Qin 2008: 17–19). Yan Xuetong emphasizes that IR theories should be universal, hence that the aim of creating a Chinese School is not feasible (Yan 2006: 1). He is not agreeable to using the 'Chinese School' label as a name for his studies and those conducted by the Tsinghua Approach, but the different approaches of Yan and Qin are nevertheless regarded as leaders in giving content to the Chinese School (Kristensen and Nielsen 2013a: 24–30).

There is no equivalent in China to a self-organized group of scholars like the British Committee that pursues an agreed theme. Since the Chinese School has no single core content, its placement in Chinese universities is inseparable from IR theory centres of strength generally. Beijing and Shanghai are predominant in IR study, the former, for example, including Peking University, Tsinghua University, China Foreign Affairs University, Renmin University, Chinese Academy of Social Science, and China Institute of International Studies; and the latter, Fudan University, Shanghai Jiao Tong University, Shanghai International Studies University, and Shanghai Institutes for International Studies. But important IR theory work goes on in other Chinese universities as well, such as Nankai, Nanjing, Jilin and Zhejiang University, etc. Since the end of the 1980s, these universities and organizations have promoted the development of IR in China generally. They have organized academic seminars, set up IR-focused bodies such as the China National Association for International Studies, the Shanghai IR Institute and the International Politics Society of National Colleges and Universities, and published IR journals (such as *World Economics and Politics*, *International Politics Quarterly*, *Journal of European Studies*, *Quarterly Journal of International Politics*, *Journal of China Foreign Affairs University* and *International Studies*).

The National Social Science Foundation (NSSF) and the Humanities and Social Science Foundation of China (HSSF) under the Ministry of Education do not play a direct role in promoting the construction and development of Chinese IR except, as in the United Kingdom, through their general funding and project preferences for academic research generally. Interestingly, there is also a link between the Ford and Rockefeller Foundations and the development of the Chinese School, though it is less direct than in the case of the English School (Shambaugh 2011: 342–344). After China's opening and reform, these same foundations played a role in encouraging the development of IR generally in China. The China office of the Ford Foundations invited three Chinese and American scholars to assess the status of IR in China, and published a book on *International Relations Studies in China* (Ren 2007; Ford Foundation 2003: 92–97).

Naming

The English School

Why 'English' and why 'School'? The name 'English School' was not coined until a critic, Roy Jones, used it in calling for its closure (Jones 1981). In a notable irony, it was after that that it became a label accepted by those both within and outside the School (Suganami 2003: 253–271), and Jones's call for closure was forgotten. Like many such labels, including 'realism' and indeed 'International Relations' itself, 'English School' is a poor fit for what it represents.[2] Some of its founding figures were not English – Hedley Bull was Australian, Charles Manning South African – and its focus has always been on history and theory at the global level of IR. It never had any particular interest in British foreign policy and, to the extent that it was prescriptive, was aimed generally at international society more than at foreign policy making. Aside from a certain degree of pragmatism, neither is there anything particularly English about its ideas, which might be better understood as a European amalgam of history, law, sociology and political theory. The key classical theorists with whom the English School is most closely associated are Grotius, a Dutchman, and the German historian Heeren, whose discussion of states-systems was influential on early English School thinking. But 'English School' has now become an established brand name, pushing alternatives ('British School', 'Classical Approach', 'International Society School') to the margins.

If 'school' has the narrow meaning of a group of people representing a specific line of thought on which all adherents are agreed, then the English School is probably too big and too diverse to fit. Even the British Committee did not represent a single line of thought. By the 1970s, and certainly during the 1980s and 1990s, the English School was becoming more a network of scholars than a specific club, and increasingly a succession of scholars across generations rather than a particular grouping in place and time. The English School is perhaps best seen as a 'great conversation' comprising anyone who wants to talk about the concepts of international and world society, and who relates in some substantive way to the foundational literature on those topics from Bull, Butterfield, Manning, Wight and Watson. Those concepts define a conversation that is distinct from others in IR, and in that general sense the English School might be thought of as a 'school', though not one with strict membership criteria. Some will identify themselves closely with it, others will occasionally engage with it in parts of their work.

The Chinese School

The name Chinese School came out of the debate about IR with Chinese characteristics. After the revival of IR in China, and with the desire to develop further, Chinese scholars generally recognized that China had no IR theory comparable to Western mainstream IR theories. This inspired the thinking and debate in academia at the end of 1980s. IR scholars generally held the positive attitude that it was necessary to construct a Chinese IR theory, but exactly how to construct and how to name this project has been debated for some time (Shi 2006). Many names have been put forward, including 'IR theory with Chinese characteristics', 'Chinese localization (or nativization) of IR theory', 'China's exploration of international political theory', Chinese view of International Relations or international politics' and 'the Chinese School'.

Scholars like Wang Yizhou and Zi Zhongyun took a negative view of any specifically Chinese IR theory, arguing that while there were real gaps between China and Western IR, theory had to be understood as universal. It is still necessary for China to learn and study Western IR theories, which does not prevent Chinese from joining the theoretical discussion at the global level and bringing Chinese history, thinking and concepts to that discussion. The characteristics of theory should not be specified in advance, but should form naturally (Zi 1998: 41–44; Wang 1998b: 28–32). Su Changhe and Peng Zhaochang are even more direct. They hold that the debate over 'International Relations with Chinese characteristics' or 'Chinese School' is not the key point for the current development of IR in China. A school is not self-given but has to be accepted within academia (Su and Peng 1999: 19). Some scholars also object to 'Chinese School', arguing that indeed there is a 'Frankfurt School', a 'Chicago School' and suchlike, but that one seldom hears of such academic schools associated with a country. Even the English School does not represent the IR study of Britain (Shi 2006: 529).

By the beginning of the twenty-first century, the controversy about the name died down, and more scholars accepted the label Chinese School. Yet Qin Yaqing's definition somewhat blurs the distinction: 'the Chinese paradigm refers to the theory study with Chinese ideology and philosophy, ... its characteristic concept should be from unique Chinese international thought or Chinese perspective' (Qin 2008c: 18).

Yan Xuetong criticized the name argument, arguing that

> Every IR theory should be considered like a baby. Before we give birth, we cannot be sure of the name we should give the baby. In my opinion, what Chinese scholars should worry about most is not the name but rather giving birth to the baby.
>
> (2011d: 256)

Other scholars say that the study results created by Chinese scholars necessarily have a Chinese brand, and that although they have no labels of 'characteristics' or 'school', the key is to have China's own IR theory (Yu and Chen 1999; Chen, Y. 2011).

The naming debate has thus been much more prominent in China than in Britain. As the name debate shows, in China the central issue was about how to develop a Chinese voice in IR theory, and whether it was a good idea or not to name this in an aspirational way, before the development of substantive content. That was never an issue in Britain, even though there was some sense of pursuing an alternative to the US mainstream developments of the time. In a sense, the English School followed Yan's advice, and did not worry about a name. Even when the name was given by a critic, it took quite some time to become an accepted label, and this process did not trigger much discussion. The difference is perhaps explained by the fact that the English School started with a definite theoretical idea in mind – international society – and got on with developing that. It was not a late starter, and therefore was not driven by the need to catch up or close gaps. The more intense debate in China also reflects the underlying controversy over what content the label should represent, which was again not an issue in Britain. 'Chinese School' now represents the consensus that IR theory should be developed within China, and that this should be independent from government ideology and related to the wider pursuit of theory in IR globally. But it does not yet represent a single-core idea or approach, and most likely it will become a vehicle for several approaches linked mainly by the fact that they represent Chinese voices, and/or draw on Chinese sources, in the debates in IR theory. Probably also there will remain some tension between those who want to develop a theory that is in some sense for China – a national IR or foreign policy theory – and those who want mainly to develop a significant Chinese voice in the global IR theory debates. The well-known idea from Robert Cox, that all social theory is for someone and for some purpose, plays quite strongly in Chinese thinking about IR.

Context

The English School

The English School emerged early in the development of IR theory after the Second World War. Two prevailing debates defined the context for its emergence: the so-called 'first debate' between realists and liberal idealists about the nature of IR; and the so-called 'second debate' between traditionalists and behaviouralists about what epistemology and what methods were the most appropriate for studying IR.

On the realist–idealist debate, the English School positioned itself as a *via media*, in some senses taking a middle position between the two. But it was also expanding the linear spectrum into a triangle of differentiated positions, the 'three traditions', in which international society was a third way. All general theories of IR identify some basic mechanism or driving force that explains how and why things work the way they do. For realism, this is power politics, *raison d'état*, and relative gains. For liberalism it is rational choice and absolute gains. For Marxism it is the materialist dialectics of class struggle. For post-structuralists it is discursive process and the creation of intersubjective meaning. For the English School it is the social dialectics of the desire to create a modicum of both order and justice beyond the level of the state. This might be understood in terms of Watson's concept, contra realism's, of *raison de système* ('the belief that it pays to make the system work') (Watson 1992: 14). This concept encapsulates the English School's core normative debate between pluralism and solidarism and differentiates English School thinking from other lines of IR theory.

Some IR theories offer a general picture of what the international system looks like and might look like. The English School's picture of IR, like realism's and liberalism's starts with the state, but through its concepts of international and world society and primary institutions, it has a deeper and more social vision of international order than either (Buzan 2014: 25–38). The idea of primary institutions makes it considerably more than just a *via media* between them. Because international societies can come in a great variety of forms, the English School can offer various visions of the future and contains no teleological assumptions about how things will unfold. The balance between the provision of order and justice could get better or it could get worse, and the influence of *raison de système* could get weaker or stronger.

On the methodological debate between traditionalists and behaviouralists, the English School was, and broadly remains, firmly on the side of the traditionalists. It rejected 'scientific' and quantifying approaches that were mainly materialist in basis and assumed that IR could be treated as a branch of physics. Hedley Bull took a robust stance against the behaviouralist approaches and methods that were coming to dominate American IR during the 1950s and 1960s (Bull 1966a: 361–377). Bull defended a 'classical approach' to the subject, based more on history, law and political theory, a tradition carried on by Jackson and Hurrell (Jackson 1992, 1996, 2000, 2009; Hurrell 2001, 2007). Bull's view was fairly representative of the attitude in the British Committee (Dunne 1998; Linklater and Suganami 2006: 97–108; Navari 2009: 5–14), and so from an early point set the English School apart from mainstream American IR theory, and marginalized it within the American-dominated IR discourse.

The Chinese School

By contrast, the Chinese School is coming onto the scene quite late in the development of IR theory. Global IR debates and approaches are now more numerous, with many paradigms and epistemological approaches already in play. Realism and idealism, and the tension between them, are still mainstream, as is behaviouralism. Marxism has been pushed to the margins in much of the global IR debate, and of course the English School itself is now part of the landscape of established IR theory. Within the global IR community, the main lines of epistemological and methodological debate are now between constructivist and post-structuralist 'reflectivists' on the one hand, and materialist neorealist and neoliberal 'rationalists' on the other. Various more specialized approaches, such as feminism and post-colonialism, are also in play. Quite how the 'Chinese School' will relate to this global context remains to be seen, though some lines are becoming clear.

Qin Yaqing (2008c: 18–19) points out that there are three distinctive approaches within the Chinese School: classical, traditional and integrative (*xueheng*). The classical approach explains the international strategy and diplomatic thought of Chinese leaders through the classical theory of Marxism. The traditional approach tries to bring traditional Chinese thought into the era of globalization, and to use traditional Chinese political theory to examine the current world system and order. The integrative approach uses a combination of Chinese and Western theories to explain the world, and China's experience within it. Qin's classification is similar to certain other studies of current Chinese IR theory, suggesting the emergence of a stable pattern (Ni 2001; Li 2011).

Before the 1990s, Marxism occupied a dominant position in China's IR study, but this has diminished since reform and opening-up (Qin 2008c: 15–16; Wang, C. 2011: 95–96). Marxism nevertheless remains active, perhaps still more so than in the West. Marxist IR theory studies include the international thought of classical Marxist authors, new Marxism and the IR theories and practices of Chinese contemporary leaders. A few scholars still promote this approach, but generally it has been pushed to the margins of IR. According to Qin, between 1978 and 2007 Marxist IR theory accounted for just 6 per cent of total Chinese IR theory research (Qin 2008c: 18).

The loosening of the Marxist straightjacket since the late 1970s has allowed a much wider range of theoretical discourse to flourish within China's political system. That, in turn, has created a demand for authenticity and Chinese content. This demand has in part been met by a return to Chinese history and political theory, now once again allowable, even encouraged sources of knowledge within China. The traditional approach has thus been expanding and attracting more attention. Many scholars, including Yan Xuetong and those associated with the Tsinghua Approach, and Ye Zicheng, are applying Chinese history and traditional political theory to the analysis of Chinese IR (Yan and Xu 2008, 2009; Yan 2011a; Ye 2003, 2005). Zhao Tingyang likewise seeks theoretical foundations for IR research by exploring traditional Chinese political theory (Zhao 2005).

Most Chinese IR scholars fit best into the integrative approach but, unlike Qin Yaqing, few raise the flag of the Chinese School. Qin Yaqing is optimistic about forming a Chinese School that is both Chinese and open to global debates. He argues that the key to constructing the Chinese School lies in finding a core theoretical problematic. The core problem of American mainstream IR theory is hegemonic maintenance; that of the English School is the form and development of international society. What, then, should the key problematic to define a Chinese School of IR theory be? One candidate might be '*Guanxi*', which is a core concept of Chinese traditional society and culture (Qin 2005, 2009a). The emergence of such a core as an agreed focus would make the Chinese School appear like the English School. Shi Yinhong holds that China's IR studies should centre on the key issues related to China, but that they should also learn from and embrace other IR theories. Universal theories, of course, also apply to China's issues and China's IR studies, so there will never be a wholly new Chinese IR theory (Shi, Y. 2004). This view is largely shared by Zhu Feng (Zhu 2003).

So developments up to this stage give no clear answer to the question of how the Chinese School will relate to the context in which it finds itself. The Marxist approach has so far largely failed to connect with some of the more interesting Marxist IR scholarship in the West (Rosenberg 1994, 2010, 2013). Chinese realists, liberals, constructivists, followers of the English School, and suchlike, relate to ongoing global debates and can be classed as schools of IR theory in China. There are two developments that might be classed as 'Chinese Schools' in that they build on distinctively Chinese elements: Qin Yaqing's relational approach seeks to generalize an aspect of behaviour that is strong in Chinese culture, but also found elsewhere; the Tsinghua Approach seeks to recover Chinese history and political theory as resources for thinking about both China's foreign policy and world politics more generally. This traditional approach is expanding, and at a minimum should help to bring both China's history and its political theory into the wider IR debates, perhaps along with new concepts such as *tianxia* (All-under-Heaven). Qin's relationalism can be understood as a critique of and corrective to the inherent cultural Euro-centrism of rationalist IR theory. In addition, there is the independent theoretical work of Tang Shiping, which is done in China but fits no categories and, so far, unusually for Chinese IR scholarship, is mainly published in the West. Tang does not draw on Chinese elements specifically, but aims at universal theories that critique and transcend the existing IR mainstream (Tang 2013).

So there are many Chinese voices rather than one, and at this point it looks as though there will be both schools of IR theory in China and perhaps two or more approaches that might be labelled 'Chinese Schools' (Pang 2003: 25). In this sense it remains difficult to see big differences between or progress in either 'the Chinese School' or 'IR theory with Chinese characteristics'. It is still too early to tell whether or how work based on Chinese history, political theory and culture will play into global debates in IR theory, but the foundations for such influence are being laid. The dynamism of IR thinking already evident in China suggests that it may be the site wherein innovative developments in IR theory next take place. As Yan Xuetong points out, Chinese scholars have been making progress on IR theory innovation in the last decade. This is a significant change from earlier times, when the major job of Chinese IR academics was translating and introducing IR theories into China, and therefore basically repeating and following Western IR studies (Yan 2013a). Wang Yizhou and Qin Yaqing have the same view on this point. They argue that the Chinese IR community has drawn heavily on Western IRT, especially that imported from the United States, since 1978, but with reform and opening-up, Chinese society has become increasingly pluralistic, and open debates have been unfolding among scholars on different views and understandings of international politics. So there is now a rapid development of IRT in China, and the conditions for a Chinese IRT school are riper than before (Wang, Y. 2009; Qin 2011b). According to statistical analysis on the articles of 11 IR journals in China from 2008 to 2011, there were 65 articles related to theoretical innovation that made up 14 per cent of 463 theoretical articles (Yang 2012: 91).

Aims/intentions

The English School

The aim of the English School is suggested by the full title of the British Committee: the British Committee on the Theory of International Politics. The intention was to develop a social theory of IR, and the core concept that emerged for this was international society (and later also world society). This was partly about reflecting the roots of English School thinking in history, international law and political theory, and partly about countering the IR theory becoming dominant in the United States about positivist methodology and the concept of an international system. The English School had, as Epp puts it, right from the beginning been seen as 'a somewhat different subject all along' (Epp 2010). Robert Jackson (1992: 271) nicely sums up this conception of the subject of IR as

> a variety of theoretical inquiries which conceive of International Relations as a world not merely of power or prudence or wealth or capability or domination but also one of recognition, association, membership, equality, equity, legitimate interests, rights, reciprocity, customs and conventions, agreements and disagreements, disputes, offenses, injuries, damages, reparations, and the rest: the normative vocabulary of human conduct.

The basic idea of an international society is quite simple: just as human beings as individuals live in societies that they both shape and are shaped by, so also states live in an international society that they shape and are shaped by. International society is therefore about the institutionalization of a shared interest and identity amongst states, and puts the creation and maintenance of shared norms, rules and institutions at the centre of IR theory. But because states are very different entities from individual human beings, this international society is not analogous to domestic or first order societies, in which the members are individual human beings and which are the principle subject of sociology (Bull 1966b: 35–73; Suganami 1989). International societies are second order societies in which the members are durable collectivities of humans, such as states, which are possessed of identities and actor qualities that are more than the sum of their parts. Such societies have to be studied as a distinct form. This social element has to be put alongside realism's raw logic of anarchy if one is to get a meaningful picture of how systems of states operate. When units are sentient, how they perceive one another is a major determinant of how they interact. If the units share a common identity (a religion, a system of governance, a language), or even just a common set of rules or norms (about how to determine relative status, and how to conduct diplomacy), then these intersubjective understandings not only condition their behaviour, but also define the boundaries of a social system.

To study international society requires another pair of concepts: primary and secondary institutions. This distinction relates to the common usage of 'institution', which can be understood either in specific terms as 'an organization or establishment founded for a specific purpose', or in more general ones as 'an established custom, law, or relationship in a society or community' (Buzan 2004: 161–204). Primary institutions are those talked about by the English School and reflect the second usage of 'institution' above. They originate as deep and relatively durable social practices in the sense of being evolved more than designed, and they are constitutive of both states and international society in that they define both the basic character of states and their patterns of legitimate behaviour in relation to each other. For second order societies such institutions define both the units that compose the society and what kinds of behaviour are, and are not, considered legitimate. The classical 'Westphalian' set of primary institutions includes sovereignty, territoriality, the balance of power, war, diplomacy, international law and great power management, to which could be added nationalism, human equality and the market. Primary institutions can be found across history wherever states have formed an international society. Their variety is potentially infinite: in earlier times in Europe, dynasticism, human inequality and imperialism/colonialism were key primary institutions. Both the classical Chinese tribute system and the classical Islamic world had their distinctive primary institutions. Secondary institutions are those talked about in regime theory and by liberal institutionalists, and relate to the organizational usage of the term. They are the products of certain types of international society (most obviously liberal, but possibly other types as well), and are for the most part intergovernmental arrangements consciously designed by states to serve specific functional purposes. They include the United Nations, the World Bank, the World Trade Organization and the Nuclear Non-proliferation regime. Secondary institutions are a relatively recent invention, first appearing as part of industrial modernity in the latter decades of the nineteenth century.

Its gaze firmly fixed on creating a general social theory of IR, the British Committee was famously disinterested in giving policy advice on current affairs (Dunne 1998: 90, 96; Epp 2010). It was most successful as a discussion group, sharpening up and pushing forward the thinking of its individual members. One cannot divorce the outstanding individual works of those who participated in it from the deliberations of the British Committee (Bull 1984a; Gong 1984; Wight 1977, 1979, 1991; Vincent 1986; Watson 1997, 2007). It did, however, produce two landmark-edited volumes in its own right: *Diplomatic Investigations* and *The Expansion of International Society* (Butterfield and Wight 1966; Bull and Watson 1984).

Perhaps the best way to understand the aim and intentions of the English School is as an ongoing, indeed permanent, conversation about how best to balance the demands for order and justice in international society. These demands are in continuous evolution, under pressure from shifts in both the normative and power landscapes of world politics. Think for example, about how the rise of nationalism during the nineteenth century changed the ideological landscape of world politics (Buzan and Lawson 2015). The English School aims to be both part of the normative debate, and also to be engaged in analysis of how the social structure of international society is evolving. The latter task is done by tracking the evolution of primary institutions as they rise (e.g. nationalism, the market, human rights, environmental stewardship), adapt and change (e.g. sovereignty, diplomacy, war), and sometimes fall into obsolescence (e.g. colonialism, human inequality, dynasticism) (Holsti 2004). Classical examples of the English School's order/justice debate as it applies to contemporary world politics can be found in works by Bull, Vincent, Mayall, Jackson, and Hurrell (Bull 1971, 1977, 1984b; Vincent 1986; Mayall 2000; Jackson 2000; Hurrell 2007).

The Chinese School

The aims and intentions of the 'Chinese School(s)' reflect circumstances very different from those that shaped the English School. Where the English School was in at the beginning of the development of IR theory, the Chinese Schools are late entrants with a strong need both to catch up and assert their own identity (Qin 2007). And the English School did not come out of any great break with intellectual tradition, whereas modern Chinese IR emerged as a result of a major political transformation in the country after the late 1970s. The English School might be thought of, at least in part, as a response to the end of empire, and the mass decolonization and decline in Britain's position as a great power that followed the Second World War. But it represented continuity rather than revolution of intellectual tradition, and saw itself as being at the cutting edge rather than as trying to catch up.

This difference of circumstance matters a lot to aims and intentions and can perhaps be captured as three interlinked needs distinctive to Chinese IR: the need to radically redevelop the study of IR in China; the need to recover China's history and political theory as they relate to the study of IR; and the need to think about the rapidly changing position of China in the international system/society.

The need to radically redevelop the study of IR in China followed on from the reform and opening-up beginning at the end of 1970s. Part of this arose from the need to establish academic independence both from the state and from the hegemony of Western, particularly American, IR theory. Before that time, the study of IR in China was very limited, mainly restricted to a Marxist framework, and with the aim of serving the ideological demands of the day. After reform and opening-up, Western IR theories were introduced into China and more scholars went to the West to study IR. While this undoubtedly broadened Chinese scholars' understanding of IR, it put Chinese IR in a position almost of starting from scratch, with much catching up to do. Yuan Ming pointed out that this accumulation of knowledge and experience made the Chinese realize that they needed to perceive the relations between China and the world from a more rational perspective (Yuan 1992). Although this period of learning from Western theories was unavoidable, it also raised the question of how to construct Chinese theory (Qin 2007, 2011a; Ren this volume).

As with the English School, although for different reasons, the 'Chinese School' idea was about contesting the hegemony of US IR theory and building alternatives to it. This was partly motivated by status concerns to construct a Chinese IR theory capable of standing on a par with mainstream Western IR theory. At the same time, Chinese IR needed to establish its independence from the state and ideology, which put priority on acquiring scientific methodology. Only with reliable scientific foundations could it provide the theoretical basis for China's diplomatic policies and practice. Ren Xiao argues that the debate about appropriate methods for the Chinese School was in part spurred by the desire to escape from the close links to policy that prevailed before the mid-1990s (Ren 2007: 301–304).

Possibly other factors were also at play behind the promotion of the Chinese School. Some hold that the construction of IR with Chinese characteristics, or the Chinese School, was a result of anti-colonial attitudes in the academy (Su and Peng 1999: 19; Zheng 2012: 15–21). Kristensen and Nielsen argue that Chinese scholars are trying to innovate the Chinese theory of IR because the debate on developing Chinese IR theory provides a useful opposition line through which to carve out intellectual attention (Kristensen and Nielsen 2013a: 36). Given the almost clean slate of Chinese IR in the 1980s and its need to develop and catch up, even as an empty signifier the idea of a Chinese School had the power to provide motivation and focus for the development of Chinese IR generally. The fact that 'Chinese School' rhetoric is closely bound to the development of IR in China as a whole denotes a significant difference between it and the English School, which never saw itself as representing British IR as a whole or as somehow trying to organize or promote a distinctively British IR.

Closely related to the development of IR study in China was the need to recover China's history and political theory as they related to the study of IR. There can be no doubt that if IR had originated in China it would look significantly different from that which developed in the West. China's long history has more hierarchy and less anarchy than the West, a differently rooted tradition of philosophy and political theory, and arguably a more central role for culture in IR. Although there might be some shared themes (e.g. the order/justice debate plays strongly in the Chinese classics), China's history and culture should produce a different perspective on IR. China's long and distinctive history makes it necessary for China to have its own IR theory or the Chinese School, both for its own self-understanding and as a contribution to global debates in IR theory (Wang 1998a, 1998b; Qin 2006, 2007). This move parallels the development of Western IR theory, including the English School, which also builds on its own history and traditions of political theory.

The collapse of the Chinese empire and the period of strong Marxist domination resulted in the severing of Chinese thinking in many areas from China's history and literature (Qin 2007: 324–326). There was therefore a need to recover Chinese history and political theory and see what could be used. Western IR theory had made some use of the parts of Chinese history that paralleled its own (the pre-Qin 'Warring States' period) while ignoring the rest. Chinese scholars have also given certain prominence to the pre-Qin period, not least because it was a particularly rich time in the development of Chinese political theory. But some take a wider view, looking at the whole of Chinese history for specific perspectives on IR, whether in terms of the worldview (*tianxia*) by Zhao Tingyang, the relationship (*Guanxi*) of Qin Yaqing, or the studies on traditional IR ideas and practices from the pre-Qin period by Yan Xuetong and those associated with the Tsinghua Approach. All hope to find sources of theory from traditional Chinese thought and history, and on that basis make their distinct contribution to IR alongside and in competition with Western IR theories.

They also hope to find better terms and concepts for dealing with Chinese history than were available within Western theories. The practices of the Chinese tribute system, for example, cannot be accurately captured by the Western vocabulary of power politics. Western IR theories are in important ways culturally Western, and therefore not able to explain many questions of concern to other countries, including China. If Western IR theories reflected Western history and culture, then China needed its own theory to reflect its inherent culture and history (Mei 2000; Ren 2000, 2009b). Certain foreign scholars are optimistic about the function of Chinese culture and history. Callahan holds that because China not only represents another states system, but also another civilization, it is the most obvious candidate to build an independent IR theory based on its unique philosophical tradition, although the construction now of independent IR theory is still weak in China (Callahan 2004b: 51).

Third, a Chinese School needs to think about the rapidly changing position of China in the international system/society. It is almost certainly no accident that IR theory has developed most strongly in the two leading Western powers of the last two centuries, Britain and the United States. The dominant position of the United States in IR theory is closely related to the United States' power status (Hoffmann 1977). As China rises, it needs to develop a better relationship between political power and knowledge production. The development of a Chinese School of IR thus becomes part of the power transition process: as Callahan points out, the Chinese School is proactively joining the deconstruction by the English School and critical theory of 'an American social science' (Callahan 2004b: 49). Just as Western concepts do not fit certain aspects of Chinese history and culture, so also do they differ from contemporary Chinese practice, and this easily leads to misreading or misunderstanding of China. Chinese IR needs to develop its own native concepts and paradigms to provide analytical frameworks and theoretical tools for such concepts as the 'peaceful rise of China', 'China model', 'Harmonious World' and so on. China lacks its own knowledge system to explain itself to the outside world, and this is a key problem for China's rise (Zheng 2012). The English School faced none of these pressures.

Theoretical sources

The English School

Even a superficial reading of the English School literature, both classical and contemporary, quickly reveals a deep grounding in the classics of Western political theory and international law. Its third source is world history, on which more in the following section. It is no accident that the school's 'three traditions' (realism, rationalism, revolutionism) are named after Hobbes/Machiavelli, Grotius and Kant. Also to be found are many references to Arendt, Berlin, Burke, Cobden, Elias, Gentili, Hart, Heeren, Hume, Locke, Marx, Mill, Oakeshott, Oppenheim, Popper, Pufendorf, Rawls, Rousseau, Schwarzenberger, Vattel, Weber and many others (Bull 1966b, 1977; Vincent 1986; Wight 1991; Halliday 1992; Brown 1995a, 1995b, 1998; Linklater 1998; Mapel and Nardin 1998; Jackson 2000; Rengger 1992, 2011). Hurrell rightly observes that 'within English School writing the emphasis on the history of thought about International Relations occupied a particularly important place' (Hurrell 2001: 493), and as Wilson observes, many English School writers have themselves contributed directly to the literature on political theory (Wilson 2015). This strong link with political theory is the foundation of the English School's commitment to normative debate around the order–justice question.

In drawing on these sources the English School was playing to well-established and coherent traditions of thought. Yet De Almeida argues that the British Committee was not just constructing a *via media* between realism and liberalism (de Almeida 2003: 277–279). Under Wight's leadership it was recovering a fully-fledged third position of thinking about IR, and its roots in the works of Grotius, Locke, Hume, Burke and de Tocqueville, which had been lost during the two world wars of the twentieth century. In this sense there may be some parallel between the English School and those in China aiming to recover China's history and political theory, though China's circumstances of intellectual disconnection between past and present are much more extreme. These sources in political theory and law have been particularly important in structuring the normative debate that is one of the key features of the English School, and one of the things that differentiates it from constructivism (Reus-Smit 2002: 499–502; 2005: 82–84; 2009: 58–59; Dunne 2008: 279–282; Cochran 2009: 221). This normative approach to English School theory has been strongly influenced by the core questions of political theory: 'What is the relationship between citizen and state?', 'How do we lead the good life?' and 'How is progress possible in international society?'.

Within the idea of international society, and particularly related to discussion of order and justice, human rights and (non)intervention, this debate revolves around two positions, labelled pluralism and solidarism. The terms were coined by Bull (Bull 1966b; Wheeler 1992; Dunne and Wheeler 1996; Bain 2010). Put simply, pluralism represents the communitarian disposition towards a state-centric mode of association in which sovereignty and non-intervention serve to contain and sustain cultural and political diversity. It is in this general sense status quo orientated, and concerned mainly about maintaining inter-state order. As a rule, pluralists, following Bull, will argue that although a deeply unjust system cannot be stable, order is in important ways a prior condition for justice. Solidarism represents the disposition either to transcend the states system with some other mode of association, or to develop the states system beyond logic of coexistence to one of cooperation on shared projects. In principle solidarism could represent a wide range of possibilities (Buzan 2004: 121, 199–200), but in practice within the English School it has been mainly linked to liberal cosmopolitan perspectives and to concerns about justice. Solidarists typically emphasize that order without justice is undesirable and ultimately unsustainable. It is important to see pluralism and solidarism *not* as opposed and mutually exclusive positions. The debate defines the central, permanent tension in the English School's 'great conversation' about how the sometimes conflicting and sometimes interdependent imperatives for order and justice can be met in international society (Bull 1971, 1977, 1984a; Butterfield 1972; James 1973; Vincent 1988; Miller and Vincent 1990; Suganami 1989). More specifically, given that non-intervention is almost a corollary of sovereignty, what is the role of intervention in international society (Vincent 1974; Little 1975; Bull 1984b)?

The Chinese School

The main theoretical sources for the Chinese School are Western IR theories and traditional Chinese political theory, particularly the IR ideas in pre-Qin writings. From 1978 to 2007, research on liberalism, realism, and constructivism accounted for 78 per cent of IR theory work in China (Qin 2008c: 18). This created a somewhat copycat culture, mechanically applying Western concepts without questioning their appropriateness. Recently this has begun to give way to questioning whether or not the concepts and theories of mainstream Western IR are appropriate for analysing China, what Zheng calls: 'the problem of talking about an orange by facing an apple' (Zheng 2012: 1–11). For instance, it is not easy for realism and liberalism to explain fully the peaceful rise of China and its impact on the world. Therefore, for the construction of the Chinese School, how to integrate Western theories into the Chinese native culture is becoming a key question.

Although Western IR theory is still the predominant source, Chinese IR has since the mid-1990s mined traditional political thought to enrich current IR theories and find theoretical sources for Chinese IR. One problem of this approach is China's dual history, which, to oversimplify, has several hundred years of anarchic structure in the pre-Qin period, and a mainly hierarchical tribute system for two millennia thereafter. This raises interesting questions for the project to recover traditional Chinese political theory. Most of China's classical political theory comes from the pre-Qin Spring and Autumn and Warring States periods, which occupy a relatively short span compared to the tribute system period. Does this matter? Luttwak (2012) argues that, at least in relation to strategic thinking, it does, because the classical Chinese logic of strategy was designed to work *within* Chinese culture, and does not work well *between* China and foreign cultures. The emphasis on IR political theory from an anarchic period perhaps makes Chinese political theory more compatible with Western IR political theory, but leaves questions about what political theory emanates from China's imperial epoch, which is more distinct from Western history.

One influential move in this recovery project was by political philosopher Zhao Tingyang, who discusses core IR issues from the point of view of All-under-Heaven (*tianxia*) in *Daodejing*. This involves thinking about the original state of society, the analytical units of world politics, the institutions, conflicts, and cooperation in world, globalization and global governance (Zhao 2005, 2006, 2007a, 2007b, 2009a, 2009b). Zhao's views have developed into what he calls an All-under-Heaven theory (*tianxia Guan*), which has been influential both inside and outside of China. Another move is the process-oriented constructivism proposed by Qin Yaqing, which attempts to combine Western theory with Chinese traditions. He calls his approach an integrative analogical interpretation (Kristensen and Nielsen 2013a: 27). Qin's relational theory derives from the behavioural characteristics of Chinese and much other Asian culture, and which he sets up as a specific counter to what he sees as the distorting dominance of rational choice theory in Western IR. He argues that a blend of rationalism and relationalism would give a more accurate theoretical understanding of how IR are actually conducted, and integrate Chinese concepts and insights into IR theory (Qin 2012a, 2012b). Parallel work on Chinese culture or relationalism has also been done by Shih Chih-yu in Taiwan (Shih 1990, 1999, 2010a; Shih and Huang 2011).

A third project is the excavation and interpretation of pre-Qin traditional thought and practice from the IR standpoint. Ye Zicheng holds that the West and the East constitute two different international systems, and that the emergence and development of an international system came much earlier in China than it did in Europe. He hopes that an analysis of classical history and thinking can provide basic principles and concepts for contemporary Chinese diplomatic policies and practice (Ye 2003).

The work of Yan Xuetong and those associated with the Tsinghua Approach proceeds in the same vein. In 2005, Yan and his team started their studies of Chinese traditional IR thought. They basically interpreted and researched the political thought of pre-Qin dynasties, with the aim of providing traditional resources for Chinese scholars to enrich current IR theories (Yan and Xu 2009: preface). This has become known as the Tsinghua Approach (Zhang 2012: 71–72), which seeks theoretical innovation based on exploring ancient Chinese thought and practice leading to either the creation of a new theory or revision of existing theories (Xu 2011).

This move towards Chinese sources was, and is, necessary if a Chinese School is to establish its distinctive foundations. It is also necessary to fill the gap, if the claim that Western concepts do not fit China is valid. And, as noted earlier, it was an orthodox move paralleling the use made by Western IR theories, including the English School, of Western history and political theory. Just as Western IR theories draw upon classical thinkers such as Thucydides, Machiavelli, Hobbes and Kant, so the Chinese School should draw on the wisdom and insight of classical Chinese thinkers: Lao Zi, Confucius, Mencius, Sun Zi and so forth. Doing so would both supply resources to justify the label 'Chinese School', and make this unfamiliar thinking available to the global IR community. Some of this work has opened space for normative debate about both Chinese foreign policy and order/justice questions more broadly a turn that opens up a parallel between the emerging Chinese School and the English School's strong normative tradition, yet it also exposes problems within Chinese IR of inadequate training and resources to deal properly with the vast archive of classical literature (Wang Jiangli 2013).

Historical projects

The English School

Political theory is of course not the only, or necessarily even the best, way of looking back to find resources for IR theory. History, mainly Western history, has always been an implicit, and sometimes explicit, background for Western IR theory, and this is true for the English School as well, though at least some effort has been made to take a wider view (Bull and Watson 1984; Gong 2002; Watson 1992; Suzuki 2009; Zhang and Buzan 2012). IR concepts such as the balance of power, great power management and indeed international society itself, derive as much, or more, from empirical observation of historical practice as they do from political theory.

As part of its exploration of the international society approach to IR, the English School has developed two historical projects. One, mainly comparative, was initiated by Martin Wight and carried forward by Adam Watson. This project looked back into history to find other cases of international society that could be compared with one another and with the European case (Wight 1977; Watson 1992). The other, mainly in the form of developmental history, looked more specifically at the formation, and expansion to global scale, of the European ('Westphalian') international society. Here the key theme was how, from the late fifteenth century, European international society expanded to dominate the whole planet. As Epp notes, this project sustained a specific English School interest in the consequences of decolonization, and a more general one in the role of culture in world politics (Epp 1998: 49). The expansion project gave rise to a number of more conceptual and normative themes, so linking the English School's theoretical and historical development. Considerable attention was given to the five primary institutions of the classical Westphalian international society: war, diplomacy, the balance of power, international law and great power management (Butterfield and Wight 1966; Bull 1977; Wight 1977). How had these institutions evolved in Europe, and what kind of order did they produce both there and in the global international society that Europe imposed on the rest of the world? These classical five institutions did not satisfy everyone as a complete set, and other candidates for this status also came into play early in the development of the English School: those of sovereignty (James 1986), and nationalism (Mayall 1990).

Two big normative questions came out of the expansion project. The first was that the legitimacy of contemporary international society is based on the principles of the sovereign equality of states and, up to a point, post decolonization, on the equality of people(s) and nations. Yet it is still riddled with the hegemonic/hierarchical practices and inequalities of status left over from its founding process, largely favouring great powers in particular and the West in general. Clark notes the contemporary problem of US dominance in 'the absence of a satisfactory principle of hegemony – rooted in a plausibly wide consensus – in which that actuality would be enshrined' (Clark 2005: 227–243, 254). This disjuncture between hegemony and sovereign equality is a key theme in English School literature (Watson 1992: 299–309, 319–325; 1997, 2007: 7–21; Clark 1989, 2009: 203–228, 2009b, 2011; Hurrell 2007: 13, 35–36, 63–65, 71, 111–114; Buzan 2010). Simpson's work also has a lot to say about this tension over the last two centuries, providing a useful link between English School concerns and International Law (Simpson 2004). Clark (1989) notes the contradiction in English School thinking between a strong commitment to anti-hegemonism as a condition of international society, and its simultaneous acceptance of great power management as an institution, with the inequality of status that implies. The key to both great power management and hegemony as institutions of international society is that the powers concerned attract legitimacy to support their unequal status as leaders. They do this by both displaying good manners and efficiently providing public goods (Clark 2009a).

The second normative question was about culture, and came out of the expansion project. It was about how to deal with the apparent weakening of international society when the expansion to global scale, and the subsequent bringing in of all peoples through decolonization, undermined the cultural cohesion of the original European/Western formation. Decolonization tripled the membership of international society, not only making it multicultural, but also bringing into it many postcolonial states that were both politically weak as states and economically poor and underdeveloped. As Riemer and Stivachtis argue, 'the logic of anarchy, operating in the international system, has brought states into international society; once in, the logic of culture has determined their degree of integration into international society' (Riemer and Stivachtis 2002: 27). According to this logic, if culture were diverse, then international society could be only weakly integrated. The pessimistic view of the post-1945 expansion belongs mainly to the pluralist wing of the English School and is clearly evident in some chapters in Bull and Watson (1984), most notably those by Kedourie and Bozeman. Bull and Watson accepted the negatives of weak states and cultural fragmentation, but tried to balance them with the positive development of the general acceptance by Third World elites of some of the key institutions of international society – sovereign and juridical equality and, up to a point, also of

Western norms. They read the Third World as wanting more to improve its position than to overthrow the system. Linklater and Suganami, and Buzan, argue for a more positive view of expansion (Linklater and Suganami 2006: 147–153; Buzan 2010).

From these historical projects came also another key English School concept: the '*standard of civilization*'. The '*standard of civilization*' is a term taken from diplomatic and international legal practice during the nineteenth century. Its usage in IR was synonymous with the English School, though it is now also used in the postcolonial literature. It originates in the practice of differentiating among states and peoples, in terms of 'civilized', 'barbarian' and 'savage', and using these classifications to gate-keep on entry to European, and later Western, international society. The blatancy of such designations has more or less disappeared from polite international discourse, but the substance very much remains, with regards to conditionality of entry to various clubs, and much of the discourse around human rights (Gong 1984: 90–93, 2002; Donnelly 1998; Jackson 2000: 287–293; Keene 2002: 112–113, 147–148; Clark 2007: 183). For the English School this concept provides useful leverage against an overly easy assumption that sovereign equality is a simple or uniform practice. We put 'standard of civilization' in inverted commas to signify that it is always the construct of one party, usually the dominant one, in a relationship, and not a statement about some essential condition.

The Chinese School

It is fair to say that if IR had been invented in China and based on Chinese history it would not look as it does now. China also has a long and distinctive history to draw on, and to construct a Chinese School of International Relations scholars need to study Chinese history seriously (Hui 2010: 134–135). Hui is also critical of Yan's attempt to mobilize classical Chinese political theory for IR, arguing strongly that history provides a much better empirical resource (Hui 2012a). As for the recovery of China's political theory, one problem with this historical approach is that, as noted above, China has two histories with sharply different structures to draw on. The Warring States period is anarchic, like post-Medieval Europe, while the tribute system is a distinct form of hierarchy perhaps comparable to other imperial systems of the classical era. Yet at this point the study of Chinese history in an IR context is relatively new in China, and an approach pursued by far fewer people than are engaged in Western IR theory.

Three historical projects are helpful in forming a Chinese School and might be regarded as major elements of a Chinese School in the future. The first is the traditional study of the tribute system initiated by John K. Fairbank. This project looked back at hierarchical relations between ancient China and its neighbours, and the East Asian order they generated. Its key theme was that the tribute system, with ancient China at the centre, was different from the international system generated by European history. Fairbank's project has subsequently been taken up by Chinese scholars' studies of the tribute system, bringing to it their personal perspectives. Although here, as with other social sciences in China after 1949, there was discontinuity of study, the topic of the tribute system is relatively persistent compared to other research fields. Huang Chi-lian's study is still widely accepted in Chinese academia as the most systematic theoretical research on ancient China's Tributary System (Quan 2005: 131). Huang argues that the system of the dominant Chinese dynasty through the rule of rites is a concept of IR that contains the relations between ancient China and Korea, Vietnam, Ryukyu, Siam and the Asia-Pacific area, including the Silk Road and the maritime Silk Road (Huang 1992, 1994, 1995). He Fangchuan investigates the 2000-year-long ancient Chinese order and holds that it is an ancient IR system with the Chinese empire at its centre. It is also the most complete system in the development of IR from the Han to the late Qing dynasty of China (He 1998). Li Yunquan discusses the history of the tribute system in ancient China, noting that it originated in the enfeoffment system in the pre-Qin period, and that the structure of the tribute system spread to different levels centred on the capital of many dynasties in ancient China (Li, Y. 2004, 2014). Hao Xiangman argues that the history of relations between China and Japan constitutes a construction and deconstruction process of the tribute system (Hao 2007). After analysing the relations between China and Korea in different dynasties, Fu Baichen holds that this relationship is typical of a tributary system (Fu 2008). There is much literature by historians on the tributary system, especially about that of a specific dynasty of ancient China. Some IR scholars are also interested in this topic (see Yu 2000: 55–65; Jian 2009: 132–143; Zhang 2009; Shang 2009; Chen 2010; Zhou 2011b).

The second historical project focuses on discussing Chinese history and traditional thought and comparing it with Western IR theories and concepts. For instance, Ye Zicheng (1998) analyses the relationship between ancient China and its neighbours from a 'geopolitics' perspective; Wang Zhengyi (2000) uses Wallerstein's 'world system theory' to illustrate the tribute system of ancient China and East Asia; Wang Rihua (2009) studies the relationship among China's ancient countries from the concept of 'international system', and Hu Bo (2008) uses this concept to discuss the origin of the IR system in ancient East Asia; Shang Huipeng (2009) uses the 'world' and 'humans' to interpret the international order of ancient East Asia; Chen Qi and Huang Yu (2008) discuss interference problems among Chinese kingdoms in the Spring and Autumn Period, from the concept and theory of 'interference'; Sun Lizhou (2007) uses the concept of 'pattern' to investigate two major governments of the Western Han and Xiongnu (Mongolians) in ancient China; Meng Weizhan (2012) discusses the applicability of IR theories to the study of inter-state relations of ancient China. Qin Yaqing's *Guanxi* study and research done by Yan Xuetong and those associated with the Tsinghua Approach on traditional Chinese IR thought also can be regarded as belonging to this project, because they are both based on Western theories and concepts.

The third project concerns the more recent turn to ancient Chinese history, but is closer to history, discussing ancient Chinese thought, history, diplomacy, force, strategy and their evolution in the hope of finding guidance for contemporary Chinese foreign policy and diplomacy. Ye Zicheng's study belongs to this project. Many Chinese scholars are working in this field. For example, Zhang Xiaoming (2006) discusses the historical evolution, pattern and process of the relationship between China and its neighbours on the basis of the relations between real strength and the tributary system. Some scholars carry out case studies on the relationship between China and its neighbours during the Ming and Qing Dynasties (Chen, W. 1986; Chen, S. 1993; Gao 1993; Wan 2000). Besides the pre-Qin period, this project is now expanding to dynasties after the pre-Qin, like the Han, Song and Yuan (Meng 2012: 22).

There is indeed at this point a direct link between the English School project on comparative international societies and the Chinese School's recovery of China's history as an IR theory resource. Within the English School there is work attempting to recover and develop in international society terms the story of the tribute system in East Asia (Zhang, Y. 2001; Zhang, F. 2009, 2014; Zhang and Buzan 2012).

Possible lessons

What the English School has done well

The English School has performed well in five ways that proponents of the Chinese School(s) might want to think about when making their own plans.

First, the English School has produced a large and lively literature around its central ideas and stories. It has three foundational theoretical texts (Bull 1977; Butterfield and Wight 1966; Manning 1962) and others that seek to carry its theoretical tradition forward (Buzan 2004; Linklater and Suganami 2006). Its comparative history project has two core works (Wight 1977; Watson 1992), and there is a large literature on its flagship story about the expansion and evolution of international society (Gong 1984; Bull and Watson 1984; Mayall 1990; Keene 2002; Holsti 2004). There is also a body of works analysing contemporary global international society (Jackson 2000; Mayall 2000; Hurrell 2007). These books, and the much larger literature surrounding them,[3] give the English School both a distinctive identity and a solid position in the wider IR literature. It has not only developed a distinctive theory, but has also used that theory to unfold a characteristic way of telling international history.

Second, and as detailed above, the English School has generated several distinctive concepts: international and world society, pluralism/solidarism, primary institutions, the 'standard of civilization', and *raison de système*. These concepts provide the vocabulary that not only links the school together, but also differentiates it from other IR theories and marks out its contribution to how we study and understand IR. In effect, the English School sets out a distinctive taxonomy of what it is that IR should be taking as its principal objects of study: the triad of international system, international society and world society; first and second order societies; and primary and secondary institutions. Taxonomy is not currently fashionable in IR theory, but because it identifies exactly what is to be theorized about, it is absolutely foundational to any theoretical enterprise. To the extent that taxonomy is flawed or wrong, the whole foundation of theory is weakened. The English School deserves more theoretical credit than it gets for its distinctive taxonomy. Since one element of the Chinese School is dissatisfaction with the fit between Western concepts and Chinese practices, various threads within the Chinese School development look well placed to make original conceptual contributions to IR theory.

Third, the English School has inspired a conversation that now spans several generations of scholars, and most countries where the study of IR is taken seriously. As Stephen Krasner acknowledged, the English School is the 'best known sociological perspective in IR' (Krasner 1999: 46). More recently, the English School has attracted interest in Northeast Asia, particularly in and about China. In these countries it resonates with historical approaches to IR, and also serves as an antidote to what some see as the excessive influence of American IR theory in their universities (Zhang 2014). Whether rightly or not, the existence of an 'English School' is taken as justification for developing more national approaches to IR theory, including the 'Chinese School' (Qin 2005). This success reflects both the intrinsic interest of the approach it offers, and the fact that it is a global theory, not a parochial one.

Fourth, the English School has avoided falling into any narrow orthodoxy that would straightjacket its conversation. It has cultivated an open conversation with several different and sometimes contending strands, and has become an active site for normative IR debates about world society, human rights and the environment. By embracing the permanent tension between order and justice as necessary to talking about IR, the English School has become a lively site for ongoing moral debates about how best to balance their conflicting demands.

Fifth, the English School has provided an alternative to mainstream US IR theory. As IR goes global, the English School can claim some credit for having led the way in the process of bringing the cultural distribution of the discipline into better alignment with the global nature of its subject matter. Its attraction lies in an approach to the subject that is more holistic, more historical and less detached from international law than most others. As Wæver (1992: 99–100, 121) puts it, the English School has the ability to

> combine traditions and theories normally not able to relate to each other ... It promises to integrate essential liberal concerns with a respect for a fair amount of realist prudence; it promises to locate structural pressures in specific historical contexts and to open up for a structural study of international history.

Criticisms of the English School

On the other side of the balance sheet, the English School has received three criticisms that the advocates of a Chinese School might want either to try to avoid or be prepared to receive.

First, the English School has been accused of being too imprecise in defining and specifying its concepts and methods (Finnemore 2001). How exactly does one know when an international society or a world society exists? What exactly are the criteria by which one can say that something has become an institution of international society? How does one tell who is and who is not a member of international society? These criticisms are justified, and are being addressed (Holsti 2004; Buzan 2004; Navari 2009), but they do not invalidate the concepts. There is no satisfactory measure of power in IR, but that hardly prevents it from being a useful mainstream concept.

Second, the English School has been accused of failing to meet the standards of positivist theory because it does not generate much in the way of hypotheses, in terms of cause–effect logics. This is an epistemological critique. It is true, but not very interesting unless you think there is only one correct path to knowledge in IR. Positivist methods are more appropriate for studying international systems. The study of societies requires different epistemological approaches: normative, historical and constructivist. In its constructivist and normative theory aspects, English School theory cannot (and does not want to) meet the criteria for positivist theory. Nevertheless, this criticism has played a significant role in the English School's difficulty in penetrating the US IR market, where positivism is almost a kind of 'standard of civilization'. Not until the rise of constructivism to respectability in American IR made intersubjective understanding fashionable, and stood mutual constitution against cause–effect logic, did the English School achieve real recognition there as a distinctive, respectable approach to the subject. That of course led to the further critique that the English School was merely an early, primitive form of constructivism. While there are certain necessary similarities between them, in as much as any study of society must be constructivist, the two have very different origins and are distinct in important ways.

Third, the English School has been weak in dealing with two key concerns in IR: international political economy, and the regional level. Some work has now been done on the regional level of international society (Zhang, Y. 2011; Diez and Whitman 2002; Hurrell 2007; Wang, Q. 2007; Buzan and Gonzalez-Pelaez 2009; Zhang, F. 2009; Suzuki 2009; Stivachtis 2010; Buzan and Zhang 2014). So far not much has been done to build International Political Economy (IPE) into the English School's understanding of international society, a notable exception being Hurrell (2007). These neglected topics are opportunities for new work in the English School tradition, and perhaps also for the Chinese School.

Conclusions

We can conclude that the English School does not make the case for national approaches to IR theory. Indeed, a good part of the explanation for its success is precisely that it eschewed parochial concerns and aimed to construct theory at the global level. Along the way it generated a characteristic taxonomy and set of concepts. Another reason for its success has been that it validates an explicit turn to history as both a source for IR theory and an important part of the study of IR. This historical dimension makes the school's work easily accessible to others and gives it a distinctive way of understanding the structures and dynamics of world politics. Linked to its validation of history is its validation of an explicit turn to classical political theory as a source for normative IR theory. Its embracing of normative debate has been a key source of energy and inspiration for many who associate themselves with the English School tradition, and is a key distinction between it and constructivism (Wæver 1999: 17). The experience of the English School thus offers support for the general history/theory approach adopted by the Tsinghua Approach, and suggests strongly that such an approach will necessarily generate normative debate.

Whatever comes under the label 'Chinese School' will not look like the English School, and that is as it should be. But, that said, there are various ways in which certain strands of IR theory development in China might intertwine with English School themes. The normative orientation arising out of engagement with history and political theory is one. Another is overlapping interests both in relation to Chinese history as a model for types of international society that differ from those in Western history, and to the contemporary rise of China and its impact on regional international society in Asia and on the Western-global international society. Yet another is the problem of how to relate anarchy and hierarchy to international order and harmony. As noted, the English School debates hierarchy as an institution of international society, and this might mesh with Chinese thinking on order and harmony under the Tribute System. There might also be synergies between the English School and emergent Chinese thinking about relationalism. Relationalism might be understood as a primary institution of some types of international society. Both relationalism and primary institutions are forms of power structure, and both are prone to creating insider/outsider structures.

Perhaps these intertwinings and synergies will develop as the Chinese School becomes global. It is already apparent that more and more foreign scholars are joining in the Chinese discussions on Chinese history and political theory. Some are Chinese living in overseas countries, such as Gerald Chan, Zhang Yongjin, Victoria Tinbor Hui, Fen Huiyun, Wang Yuan-Kang, and Zhang Feng (Chan 1999; Zhang 2001; Zhang and Buzan 2012; Hui 2005, 2010; Feng 2007; Wang, Y-K. 2010, 2012; Zhang, F. 2009, 2012, 2014). Others are foreigners from different countries such as Alastair I. Johnston, William A. Callahan, Barry Buzan, Brantly Womack, Jeremy Paltiel, Rana Mitter, Luke Glanville, Robert E. Kelly, David Kang, Linsay Cunningham-Cross, Nele Noesselt, Luke Glanville,

Peter M. Kristensen, and Ras T. Nielsen (Johnston 1995; Callahan 2004a, 2004b, 2008a, 2008b; Callahan and Barabantseva 2011; Zhang and Buzan 2012; Womack 2012; Paltiel 2010, 2011; Mitter 2003; Glanville 2010; Kelly 2012; Kang 2003; Cunningham-Cross and Callahan 2011; Noesselt 2012; Kristensen and Nielsen 2013a, 2013b). As Chinese Schools and IR schools in China develop and evolve they might learn lessons from both the things that the English School has done well and the things it has done not so well. They might thereby avoid certain problems, prepare themselves for those that cannot be avoided, and more safely and effectively chart their way into the global debates in IR.

Notes

1 This is a lightly updated and edited version of an article that was first published in the *Chinese Journal of International Politics*, 7: 1 (2014) 1–46. The earlier version has more extensive referencing than this one, but this one includes a few recent additions. We would like to thank Huang Feifan for helping to reformat the references.
2 Another difficulty is that Chinese translations do not differentiate 'English' from 'British' and tend to use 'British School', thus further emphasizing the national theme.
3 A much fuller listing of English School works can be found in the bibliography online, available at: www.leeds.ac.uk/polis/englishschool/.

8 Navigating the core-periphery structures of "global" IR
Dialogues and audiences for the Chinese School as traveling theory

Peter Marcus Kristensen

Introduction

The Chinese School debate has become more outward-looking than the more defensive and inward-looking debates about "IR with Chinese Characteristics" (Chan 1997; Geeraerts and Men 2001: 269). Interventions in the Chinese School debate seek to enter "global IR" and this chapter reads the Chinese School as an effort to become a "traveling theory"; a theory rooted in the Chinese geocultural context but able to travel and to carve out a space in the "global" IR discipline. The prospect of becoming a traveling theory depends on the Chinese School's navigation of the core-periphery structures of "global" IR, however. There is not really a "global" IR discipline in which ideas and theories, or at least the best ones, travel seamlessly through space. As I will further argue below, IR is a stratified space with asymmetric core-periphery structures of communication. In the most simplistic formulation, there is not one IR discipline but several national disciplines, of which the American core dominates most syllabi, textbooks, journals and conferences. The Chinese School and the Chinese IR discipline has largely imported IR from the United States and taken "American IR" as "global IR". This is a problematic assumption and it is necessary to take other national disciplines, and thus potential audiences, into account when situating the Chinese School in "global IR".

This chapter views the Chinese School from the outside-in focusing on its position(ing) in the core-periphery structure of global IR; the Chinese School in relation to the *core* "American social science"; the Chinese School as a "school among schools", mostly schools in the European *semi-periphery*; and finally, the Chinese School compared to IR in other "rising powers" from the *periphery*, like India and Brazil. First, the Chinese School operates in a discipline notoriously dominated by an American core and is put forward as an alternative to this American core. The Chinese IR discipline was virtually imported from the United States and remains deeply influenced by and focused on the US discipline. Chinese School theorizing seems to have recognition in the United States as the primary goal and its focus on theorizing China's "Peaceful Rise" is largely a response to American "China threat" discourses. Second, as a school among schools, the Chinese School is inspired in *form* by European "schools" in the semi-periphery of this US-dominated discipline, notably the English and Copenhagen schools. Even in *substance*, Chinese IR shares some affinities with the English School – which was imported to China from the United States – in the traditionalist focus on theorizing ancient Chinese thoughts and history, but the engagement with other so-called European "schools" such as the Copenhagen, Aberystwyth and Paris schools in critical security studies has been marginal, although some of these theories seem to speak to the concerns of the Chinese School. Third, the Chinese School is often seen as a natural response to China's rising power. But there has been little engagement with IR in other so-called "rising powers", like Brazil and India, where there have been parallel concerns over the dominance of American and Eurocentric theories and voices calling for a recovery of indigenous resources, albeit to a lesser extent and in different ways than in China. The chapter concludes with a call for audience diversity and the exploration of alternative (e.g. South–South) dialogues for the Chinese School as traveling theory.

The core: the Chinese School and the "American social science"

Stanley Hoffmann's argument that IR is an "American social science" has been repeated so many times that it has become an "evergreen" (Friedrichs 2004: 1) and "truism" (McMillan 2012). Long before Hoffmann, French scholars argued that IR was a "spécialité américaine" displaying an "excès de rationalisme et d'esprit systématique" and "quasi mathématique" inclination in some of its work (Grosser 1956: 637, 640; see also Duroselle 1952: 698). Other Americans had also noted that IR was an "American invention" with "patriotic biases" (Neal and Hamlett 1969: 283; see also Olson 1972: 12; Welch 1972: 305–306). And several scholars since Hoffmann argued that IR remained preoccupied by American foreign policy concerns and/or ahistorical, scientific, behaviouralist and quantitative ways of doing IR that were peculiarly American (Gareau 1981; Alker and Biersteker 1984; Krippendorff 1987; Smith 1987; Wæver 1998). Despite its parochial nature, IR produced in the American "core" dominates textbooks, syllabi and journals all over the world, while IR done all over the world rarely travels to the US "core" (Robles 1993; Strange 1995; Biersteker 2009; Holsti 1985).

China is no exception and the quest for a Chinese School can be read against the backdrop of US hegemony. It is well-documented that Chinese IR was built on an American foundation. American foundations played an instrumental role in providing the foundation for Chinese IR by supporting institutions, translations, visiting scholarships and academic exchange in the 1980s (Lampton *et al.* 1986; Zhang 2003: 342–344; Shambaugh 2011). A young generation of Chinese scholars went to the United States to do their doctorate or post-doctorate, some brought American IR theories back and rose to prominence as translation theorizers (Kristensen and Nielsen 2013b). Even scholars who would later lead the theorization of Chinese thoughts and debate the Chinese School were educated in the United States and initially known as proponents of

American theoretical paradigms (e.g. Yan Xuetong as neorealist and Qin Yaqing as constructivist). Many observers note that IR scholarship in the 1980s and 1990s mainly translated and applied Western theories (Johnston 2002: 35; Qin 2007: 316; 2009: 194; Ren 2008: 296; Wang Yiwei 2009: 106). The conventional historiography of Chinese IR is that it did not become an independent discipline until American theories were imported and translated in the 1980s and 1990s (Song 1997, 2001; Zhang 2002, 2003; Qin 2007, 2009). Compared to IR in other countries, and their receptiveness to US imports, it should be noted that Chinese academia had a unique trajectory: it moved from the closedness, isolation and dismantling of academic life of the Cultural Revolution, which created an almost *tabula rasa*, to a policy promoting learning from the West, especially the United States, which also opened for funding from US foundations. The convergence of these conditions is hardly found elsewhere.

The influence of US theories is evident in the three, almost proxy, debates that shaped the history of Chinese IR according to Qin (2011b). In the 1990s, American realism was introduced as a challenger to previously dominant Marxist theories. The translation of Morgenthau's *Politics Among Nations* "attracted intensive attention" and, followed by Waltz and Gilpin, pushed "realism to the most conspicuous height in China's IR studies" (Qin 2011b: 238). Yan Xuetong's *Zhongguo Guojia Liyi Fenxi* (An Analysis of China's National Interest) and other realist works challenged Marxist orthodoxy by focusing on national interest, not class or ideology, as the primary "independent variable" (Qin 2011b: 238–239). Realists won and Marxist IR was marginalized. But then liberal theories were introduced. Keohane's *After Hegemony*, Keohane and Nye's *Power and Interdependence* and Rosenau's *Governance without Government* were translated and Wang Yizhou's *Dangdai Guoji Zhengzhi Xilun* (An Analysis of Contemporary International Politics) is emphasized as an important work introducing liberalism. This led to a "dramatic increase" in liberal IR stressing globalization, economic and non-traditional security, international institutions and related topics (Qin 2011b: 240–244). Liberalism became dominant. But then, if the logic was not already clear, at the turn of the millennium, constructivism was introduced when Qin Yaqing translated Wendt's *Social Theory of International Politics*. Within a few years, constructivism had surpassed realism and liberalism to become the dominant paradigm. This tripartite theoretical constellation, known from American IR, thus emerged in China too and debates about China's role in the world (revisionist or status quo) took place among adherents of each (Qin 2011b: 245–248).

It is somewhat paradoxical that Chinese scholars debate whether China will be a revisionist or status quo power, whether it will overturn the American-led liberal order or integrate into it – all problems infused by a status quo perspective. It is worth emphasizing that not only American theories were imported, but also American debates and security concerns. Chinese scholars have engaged with the American discourse on China and the various "China threat" theories in their culturalist and neorealist guises. In the mid-1990s, Huntington's "clash of civilizations" thesis, along with the democratic peace thesis, became a "hot topic" and several Chinese scholars responded with critiques (Wang, Jisi 2002: 7, 2009: 106). Johnston's (1995) work on China's "cultural realism" that posited Chinese strategic culture as a *parabellum* culture, not a pacifist Confucian culture, also attracted some dissatisfaction. US debates on the "China threat" theory (Bernstein and Munro 1997; Gries 1999; Mearsheimer 2006) also triggered suspicion and opposition from Chinese scholars:

> "The Democratic Peace Theory", "Clash of Civilizations", and "China Threat" arguments and so on all try to enhance the identity of the western world. This is better shown in the argument of "The End of History". Thus, it is no surprise that the western scholars don't believe in the non-western world and look down upon them.
>
> (Wang Yiwei 2007a: 200–201)

Dissatisfaction with American theories led Chinese scholars to ask why there was no Chinese IR theory (Qin 2011b: 250) and if it was time to move from "copying" towards "constructing" (Wang Yiwei 2009)?

A peculiarity of the typical history of Chinese IR is the narrative on development "stages" where the import and learning of American theories is seen as a catching up, or ripening, process where Chinese academics had to undergo the same development stages as Americans (a teleology reminiscent of modernization theory) only later to negate it and bring about a new stage (or perhaps Marxism). The "end" stage, however, is not a post-Western utopia beyond national parochialisms. Rather, in the end a Chinese School will emerge to address Chinese questions. The logic is clear: if "theory is always for someone and for some purpose" (Cox 1981: 128), namely the United States and its purpose of maintaining hegemony, Chinese IR has now "matured" enough to have its own theory or "big idea" that serves *its* purpose of assuming a greater role in the world through peaceful rise (Qin 2007: 328; 2011b: 474). The core problematic for any theory, the Chinese School included, should be "specific, relevant, conspicuous, and present", must concern "the theorist and the policy maker alike" and "needs solutions" (Qin 2007: 328). Theories are seen as problem-solving devices. Hoffmann's argument that IR is "An American Social Science" is invoked to make the same point: "Mainstream American International Relations theories often claim to be universal, but in fact they are rooted in American culture, practices, and problems" (Qin 2012c: 69). It logically follows that a Chinese School would be rooted in the culture, experience and history of the Chinese people.

In a more classical Marxist formulation, Wang Yiwei (2007: 191, 208) argues that existing theories are "vulgar" because they are really Western theories (represented by Anglo-America) that explain only modern Western history, are "problem-solving" only for the United States and, as class theories, legitimize the Western international system. Vulgar theories, therefore, "can only be negated by the so-called Chinese School", which will automatically be produced when China dominates the world's productive forces:

Once these undeveloped countries rise, their wills should be expressed in the international system, making it possible to deconstruct the western system. This will be the real revolution of International Relations. This is the theoretical and temporal background for censuring western IRT and approaching the possibility of a future Chinese School.

(Wang Yiwei 2007a: 194)

The search for a Chinese School is also driven by a Marxist sociology of knowledge, i.e. that theory should guide political practice and that dominant theories are necessarily theories of the dominant class/state (Tickner and Wæver 2009: 336). Some argue that this practico-political concept of theory is particular to Chinese IR. Contrary to "Western epistemology" where the purpose of theory is "explaining and predicting", it is argued, the Chinese concept of theory is ideological: theory must instruct practice the "right" way and must be normative or "revolutionary", not "empty" (Geeraerts and Men 2001: 252). The lingering influence of Marxism as meta-theory, is one of the explanations why the drive towards developing a national theory has been so strong in China. There is nevertheless a certain irony in using Cox's critical theory arguments not only to expose how certain problem-solving theories serve hegemonic classes and nations, but also to argue that China needs to build a problem-solving theory for the Chinese purpose.

Theories are envisioned as political, not in the sense of constituting the worlds they describe, but as a problem-solving tool for one's nation-state and the challenges it faces. The core purpose of the Chinese School is thus seen by many to be the "peaceful rise" of China (Qin 2011b: 245; Acharya and Buzan 2007: 290; Ren 2008: 300–301). The concern with "peaceful rise" is a response to hegemonic American IR theory, particularly "China threat" theories (Qin 2011b: 245–248). Yet this is also a paradoxical way of countering US hegemony because even a theory about "peaceful rise" operates on a discursive terrain defined by the American concern over the rise of new challengers to US primacy. As Zhang Yongjin argues,

Ironically, the analytical concepts and theoretical assumptions of this counter-discourse are defined in the orthodox neorealist terms characteristic of the "China threat" discourse. The constraining power of the "China threat" discourse is so considerable that even recent discussions of China's "peaceful rise", it is argued, have to be conducted in such a way as to avoid "triggering fear that Beijing harbors revisionist intentions".

(2007: 113)

In other words, not only is the Chinese counter-discourse framed by the concepts and concerns of realist American IR discourse (can power transitions be peaceful, is China a revisionist or status quo rising power, will it overturn the liberal world order?), it also operates in a discursive field where even academic statements are read as indicative of China's peaceful or threatening intentions.

The desire is nonetheless to speak back to Western, mostly American, discourse on China. This raises a number of dilemmas apart from the reflexive security dimension. In order to speak back and be taken seriously in Western-American discourse, Chinese IR scholars try to combine a universal and scientific Western IR language about how to know the world (epistemology) with a local Chinese vision of modern China's being in the world (ontology) to construct their own IR theory – simply put, to be "uniquely universal" (Wang 2013a). Arif Dirlik argues that this combination of universal scientism and unique Chinese characteristics is a product of seeking recognition within mainstream IR:

> So long as they are recognized a voice of their own – and whether out of a disposition to scientism that is a legacy of "scientific" Marxism or because of an enchantment with the "advanced" social sciences of the "West" as represented by its mainstream (and influential) representatives – Chinese scholars seem quite prepared to fall in with the universalistic assumptions of Euro/American IR theory.
>
> (Dirlik 2011: 148–149)

The combination of theoretical universality (in order to enter the dominant discourse) and Chinese uniqueness (in order to carve out a unique identity within it) is also a product of a reading of the "American social science" argument that is more critical of the "American" than the "social science" part (Callahan 2004b: 306). The underlying idea is that there is nothing wrong with the science-based hegemonic project per se – if only it could be less American and more Chinese. The resulting hybridization of epistemological identity and ontological difference seeks to produce a "recognizable Other" that speaks the same sophisticated (civilized? modern? advanced?) scientific language as Western-American IR, but retains its Chinese distinctiveness, its exoticism, "its slippage, its excess, its difference" (Bhabha 2004: 122). The exotic Chinese trait distinguishes it and makes it Americanized and Westernized rather than American and Western. Hybrids are, to use Homi Bhabha's (2004: 122) term for mimicry, *"almost the same, but not quite"*.

There is room, and even a desire, for difference but only insofar as it speaks a universal language. The *Chinese Journal of International Politics* (CJIP) and the "Tsinghua Approach" (Zhang 2011) provides one of the most illustrative examples of this hybridization of unique experiences and universal assumptions. The CJIP, which was established with support from MacArthur Foundation, explicitly focuses on "the theoretical, policy, and the analytical implications of China's rise [and] Chinese ideas, historical and contemporary, about International Relations and foreign policy" (CJIP 2010: 2) while also encouraging "modern methodology" such as quantitative-statistical methods (CJIP 2012). Several CJIP articles embody the hybrid logic, such as game-theoretic analyses of the Tributary System (Zhou 2011b) and the Opium War (Zhou 2010), a game-theoretical reading of the ancient Chinese philosopher Mozi (Li 2009), a categorization of pre-Qin philosophers (pre-221 BC) along the lines of Kenneth Waltz's three levels of analysis (Yan 2011a: chapter 1) and a reorganization of the ancient philosopher Xun Zi's thoughts into independent and dependent variables and power formula according to "modern scientific standards" (Yan 2008: 140). Articles often conclude with policy advice for China. The American social science advising the American Prince is replaced by an Americanized Chinese social science advising the Chinese Prince.

CJIP thus provides an outlet for theoretical studies on ancient Chinese thought, history and experience in IR, but the role of "China" is primarily to provide ontological difference within an epistemological and methodological framework set up by the "modern scientific standards" of the West. Chinese experiences and philosophies function as sources of unique local data on which to test and enrich universal theories. The strategy of the Tsinghua Approach and CJIP is to buy into theoretical and meta-theoretical assumptions of American IR and then make a contribution by recovering ancient Chinese thinkers – a project in which Chinese scholars have a comparative advantage in terms of language and access. But the "recovery" of China's different historical modes of being (Spring and Autumn Period, Warring States, Imperial, Revolutionary) within a universal theoretical framework, aiming to "fill in the gaps" missed by Eurocentric IR, eventually produces an even more totalizing and universalizing discourse (Dirlik 2011: 148). It is, at best, "Worlding" IR in the sense of opening up for different ways of being and experiencing the world, but not different ways of knowing the world. This way of navigating the core-periphery structures of IR is a product of seeking recognition mainly in the American core discipline, which, as a subfield of political science, has found unity more in rationalist and statistical methods (game theory, formal modeling, etc.) compared to a more sociologically and historically inclined European IR (Wæver 1998: 713). The US focus is supported by survey data showing that Chinese scholars prefer to publish in Chinese or American journals and by bibliometric data from CJIP showing that most of its cited sources and published authors are either Chinese or American (Kristensen 2015b).

There is no consensus about one Chinese School, one Chinese characteristic or one Chinese tradition but rather a number of debates about it. The Tsinghua Approach represents only one approach, arguably the most extreme one, but most other attempts at Chinese IR theorizing also have recognition by the US mainstream as the primary goal. Such recognition will not come easily if one is to judge from the critique of Jack Snyder, who does not have "confidence in the generalizability of the results when Chinese International Relations scholars state that the core theoretical problem of the Chinese School should be 'China's peaceful rise'". Snyder believes that it misses "the point of what is normally called theory", namely, "value-neutral terms that carry across time and space for comparative purposes" (Snyder 2008: 4–5). Even if it was recognized as a proper universal IR theory, it may still be difficult to achieve *attention* for a Chinese School. As Acharya and Buzan note, "the problem is not to create such theory but to get it into wider circulation" (Acharya and Buzan 2007: 296). This

150 P.M. Kristensen

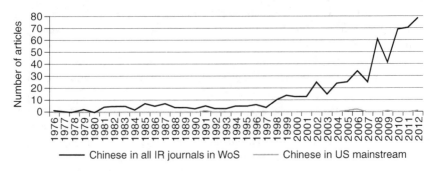

Figure 8.1 China-based scholars in Web of Science IR journals.

requires access to the infrastructure of "global IR", "international" journals primarily controlled by Americans and Europeans. If one looks at IR journals in the Web of Science, however, China-based scholars are rarely published.

As Figure 8.1 indicates, the absolute number of China-based scholars published in IR journals is growing and in 2012 accounted for 78 articles out of 2,990 published articles (2.6 percent). Half of the publications throughout the period 1976–2012 are in journals like *Issues and Studies, World Economy, Chinese Journal of International Law, Chinese Journal of International Politics, Journal of World Trade, Pacific Review, Emerging Markets Finance and Trade, Washington Quarterly* and *Space Policy*. Chinese scholars are less present in the mainstream American IR journals such as *International Organization, International Security, International Studies Quarterly, Security Studies, World Politics* and *Journal of Conflict Resolution*. In fact, only six of 4,505 articles published by these journals from 1976–2012 (0.1 percent) had a geographical affiliation in China. So it is no surprise that CJIP has been established as an alternative outlet for Chinese scholars but modeled on the scientism of American journals.

In sum, the Chinese IR discipline and the Chinese School project has been fixated on American IR, albeit without much success in terms of obtaining recognition. The following sections situate the Chinese School among other non-American schools in the not-so-international discipline.

The semi-periphery: the Chinese School among European schools

The Chinese School is not the only IR theorization following the geography-plus-school formula. Other theories produced outside the United States have also been labeled geographical "schools" and it is interesting also to read the Chinese School in this perspective. Most famous is the English School. The English School gained popularity in China as scholars became aware of the dominance of American approaches to IR (Ren 2008: 297). Ironically, as Zhang (2003: 93) showed, the ideas of Bull and Wight traveled to China via North America (US textbooks and journals) and their increasing popularity is an odd testament to the predominance of US theories. Wang also observes that several younger and Chinese-educated scholars "appreciate but don't fetishize American IR theories and, since they increasingly visit both the United States and Europe, take a broader and comparative look at available theories, drawing heavily on English School and other non-American IR theories" (Wang Yiwei 2009: 109). He further argues that

> China can probably learn more from the English School than from American IR theory since China enjoys more historical and cultural similarities with the UK than the US. In addition, the English School is more open to the idea of variations between different international systems that can accommodate non-Westphalian politics.
>
> (Wang Yiwei 2009: 117)

The English School is seen as a historically nuanced and less deterministic approach to China's rise. Several scholars note that the classical, historical and philosophical approach of the English School is embraced by Chinese scholars as more compatible with Chinese intellectual traditions than American scientific and quantitative approaches (Zhang 2003: 99–100; Wang Yiwei 2009: 109). English School scholarship on China and by Chinese scholars has also traveled back to Europe. The "English School website" (2015) even has two bibliographies; one on the English School in general, and one on the English School for China. The bibliography for China contains 92 articles written about China or by Chinese scholars using the English School by August 2013. Moreover, the *Review of International Studies*, perhaps the closest to a home for the English School, is by far the Western journal that has been most receptive to Chinese scholarship (Kristensen 2015a).

The English School also gained popularity for its form as a geographical "school" that is different from dominant American theories. Proponents and critics of a Chinese School have explicitly mentioned the inspiration from the English School model (Ren 2008: 297; Chen Ching-Chang 2011: 4). In a comprehensive study of the English School's travelogue to China, Zhang argued that the English School was received as an "IR theory with English characteristics" which made it a model for how to theorize in a US-dominated discipline. As a non-American theory that developed independently around the notion of international society and thus distinguished itself from American theories, it was a model for how to develop "IR with Chinese characteristics" (Zhang 2003: 95–96). More recently, when the Chinese School debate gained momentum, Wang argued that advocates of the Chinese School were "Moved by the presence of an English School and a Copenhagen School" (Wang Yiwei 2009: 110). The Copenhagen School has been emphasized as another example of a non-American school that has served as a model for the Chinese School (Wang Yiwei 2009: 110; Paltiel 2011: 376; Qin 2011a: 463).

The mere presence of European schools inspired Chinese IR scholars: if there can be geographical schools in England and Copenhagen why is there no Chinese School? (Ren 2008: 297; Wang Yiwei 2009: 110; Zhang 2011: 3). As a Chinese scholar put it in an interview:

> We Chinese try to argue that we need to have a Chinese School because we have a British school or a Copenhagen school. So why do we not have a Chinese School? So some Chinese try to argue this and also I think it is a good thing for us because Chinese foreign policy is quite different sometimes from the Western countries.
>
> (Cited in Kristensen and Nielsen 2010: 59)

The European geography-plus-school strategy is seen by some proponents of a Chinese School as a blueprint for how to carve out an international niche for different geocultural perspectives. But as a critic argues, the Chinese use of the English School relies on a "(mis)perception that the name implies and supports the construction of a Chinese School of IR" (Alagappa 2011: 211).

While the Chinese School is envisioned as a theory *by*, *about* and *for* China, this was less of a conscious strategy in the case of the English or Copenhagen School. The English or Copenhagen Schools have been developed primarily (but not only) *by* scholars based in England or Copenhagen, but they are not *about* English foreign policy or that of the city of Copenhagen, and it is less clear how they might work *for* the purpose of England or Copenhagen/Denmark (for a critique of the imperialist ideology embedded in the English School, see Callahan 2004b). European schools are also embedded in certain geocultural contexts, indeed, but their concepts like "international society" or "securitization" have also traveled beyond it. In contrast, the Chinese School project of speaking back to the "West" – speaking by, for and about China – seems to reproduce the very hegemonic logic where the "West" remains the place where theory speaks for the entire world, the place of Knowledge and Science, while "China" speaks for itself. Moreover, as critics argue, the Chinese School has been engaged in self-promotion and was coined before much substantive work had been done (Yan 2011d), while the European schools were often coined by others, usually critics, to signify a body of work published by scholars clustered in certain institutions and/or countries: this goes for the English School (Jones 1981), Copenhagen School (Mcsweeney 1996) and also other European schools in critical security studies like the Paris School (Wæver 2004) except perhaps the Welsh/Aberystwyth school (Bilgin 1999; or Smith 1999).

European schools like the Aberystwyth, Paris and Copenhagen Schools in security studies have also been seen as theories that navigate the core-periphery structures of a US-dominated discipline from a certain geocultural standpoint (Wæver 2012). Apart from the common "form" as geographical schools, however, the Chinese School project has little in common with these critical European schools in terms of intellectual substance. Some reasons for this lack of engagement may be that new European schools are more concerned with non-traditional than traditional security threats, tend to be more reflectivist (European) than rationalist (American) by interrogating the very concepts of security, threat and risk, and that they are too critical, constructivist and "academic" and thus not directly policy-relevant and problem-solving (for China's foreign policy), as the common critiques of critical security studies go (Bigo 2008: 118). The emancipatory and critical politics of European schools, in particular, provides a plausible explanation for why they have not been influential in China (Kristensen 2015b). Critical theories are not influential in Chinese IR, primarily due to the import of "problem-solving" American theories (Zhang Yongjin 2007; Wang Yiwei 2009; Dirlik 2011). This marginalization applies not only to critical security "schools" from the geographical semi-periphery (Europe), but also theoretical approaches in the periphery of the American mainstream, such as post-structuralism, feminism and post-colonialism. It is not that there is no criticality in Chinese IR whatsoever, but the room for dialogue with critical theories depends on the object of critique. Critical Chinese scholars direct their critique against international imperialism rather than domestic authoritarianism (Zhang 2007: 118–119). Critical theory is thus invoked mainly to critique American hegemony in IR theory and advocate a Chinese School in its place, not to critically interrogate how a Chinese School might become a servant of the rising Chinese state and its hegemonic project (Qin 2007: 328, 2011b: 474).

Despite these differences, however, there are overlaps in the search for a more international and less US-dominated discipline that takes the local conditions of knowledge production seriously and provides a space for non-US theories. European and Chinese IR would have much to gain from an engaging in further inter-regional dialogue on IR theorizing in a notoriously US-centric discipline. Thus far there has been little such inter-regional engagement, however. This goes not only for Sino-European theory dialogues, but a range of other inter-regional dialogues such as that with IR theorists in other so-called "rising powers" like India and Brazil.

The periphery: the Chinese School and IR theorizing in other rising powers

Stanley Hoffmann (1977) once argued that IR was born and raised as the United States rose to global power post-World War II. The *political circumstances* in a country with expanding global interests combined with *institutional opportunities* for academics to advice policy makers and the *intellectual predisposition* that all problems could be solved with the scientific method led to the birth of IR as a discipline that was to whisper in the ears of the new post-war Prince (Hoffmann 1977). The convergence of these three conditions distinguishes the American trajectory, argued Hoffmann, but his emphasis on the power–knowledge nexus raises the question if today's emerging Princes also need IR research, perhaps even theories, to support their rise to global power? Although the political circumstance of being a "rising power" is a crude macro-political condition for academic production, it is nevertheless worth drawing some comparisons between China and other countries usually perceived as "rising": Brazil and India. As there has been little theoretical engagement between Chinese, Brazilian and Indian IR, the following focuses on potential rather than actual theory travels as in the preceding sections.

IR in Brazil also experienced immense growth in institutions, programs, scholars and research since the 1990s (Herz 2002; Miyamoto 2003; Santos and Fonseca 2009). Like in China, the growth of the discipline has been accompanied by a growing awareness that IR is a ethnocentric enterprise dominated by the *North* "American Social Science" (Herz 2002: 9; Jatoba 2013; Lorenzini and Doval 2013: 10–11). While Brazilian IR scholars also express their dissatisfaction with the unequal global structures of production and consumption of IR theory, the drive towards developing a "national theory" is not as distinct as in China. The line of thinking that comes closest to the Chinese School debate is the so-called "Brasília School" (Escola de Brasília) that focuses on what its proponents call "international insertion" through the "logistical state" (some proponents do call it the Brazilian or Argentine-Brazilian School, however, see Saraiva 2009: 30, 32). "International insertion" has long been a dominant topic in Brazilian IR (Herz 2002) and Latin American IR theories on dependency and autonomy more generally (Tickner 2003: 328), so the Brasília School can hardly claim ownership over it nor to represent Brazilian IR or even the diversity of work done in Brasília. The Brasília School is nonetheless interesting for a comparative study vis-à-vis the Chinese School.

Senior scholar at University of Brasília, Amado Cervo, has been called the "author of the Brasília School" (Actis 2012: 403) but he himself also mentions Luiz Bandeira, José Flávio Saraiva, Argemiro Procopio, Antônio Lessa, Antônio Trinidade, Alcides Vaz, Estêvão Martins, Antônio Ramalho and Carlos da Costa Filho as critical, although not unanimous, thinkers related to the school (Cervo 2003: 20; see also Bernal-Meza 2005: 295; Caballero 2009: 21). Cervo has actively promoted the school denomination although he usually refers to Raúl Bernal-Meza as the inventor of the term Brasília School (Cervo 2003: 20, 2005: 216, 2007: 3). Bernal-Meza, a Chilean-born Argentina-based scholar, defines the school as an "epistemic community of foreign policy thinking" (Bernal-Meza 2006: 71, see also 2009: 155). Like some scholars in the Chinese School debate (notably Qin 2007; Wang Yiwei 2007a), Brasília School scholars critique American theories based on the notion that all theories contain certain values, purposes and national interests (Cervo 2003: 5). Critical minds, Cervo argues, require "introspective formulations derived from cultures or national interests" (Cervo 2003: 5). In Bernal-Meza's description of Cervo, the development of indigenous Brazilian concepts should support Brazil's foreign policy as an "emerging nation" and those "Brazilian concepts would replace the macro-theories of (supposed) universal scope, developed by the academic thinking of the 'centers', mainly the United States" (Bernal-Meza 2010: 201). Saraiva also maintains that concepts and theories in IR have national origins. American theories ranging from Morgenthau's realism to post-modern constructivism "are useful to the national strategic apparatus" of the United States, but "function to those outside the system, especially to peripheral capitalist countries, as hegemonic accommodation theories" (Saraiva 2009: 20). These "old and arrogant" American theories that reflect the "desires and wants" of Americans experienced a crisis in the twenty-first century and now Brazilian, Latin American, Asian, African and European scholars seek to build new visions and concepts for IR (Saraiva 2009: 22–24).

Like in China, there was also resistance to the "Clash of Civilizations" thesis in Brazil, but the response was the vision of a "multicultural and multiracial Brazil" (Bernal-Meza 2010: 195). Generally, however, culture and East–West difference plays a lesser role in Brazilian IR than the North–South cartography and the corollary concern with economic insertion into the global capitalist system. The focus on North–South rather than East–West identities is a product of multiple factors: first, Brazil is seen as Western but multiracial and part of the global South; second, it is a legacy of dependency and core-periphery theories that stress international political economy over both culture and security concerns; third, it is a product of the fact that there are no culture-based "Brazil threat" theories in the American mainstream that scholars feel compelled to counter. As Saraiva argues, the school is characterized by studying international *insertion* rather than international *conflict* (Saraiva 2009: 30).

The central problematique of international insertion (inserção internacional) relies on a different worldview than that of China's peaceful rise. Brazil is articulated as a periphery country that is economically, politically and even academically excluded from the core of the international system, if not entirely outside it, and the main project is to formulate strategies of insertion. More weight is given to political economy and development than to security and war, a characteristic perspective of the global South compared to the North, argues Cervo. Inspired by Latin American structuralism and dependency theory, the Brasília School starts with a critique of how global capitalism, through Ricardian notions of comparative advantage and free trade, instigated center-periphery structures that perpetuated underdevelopment (Cervo 2003: 9; see also Saraiva 2009: 29–32; Giacalone 2012: 338–339). In a hybrid of structuralist theory and an approximation of realist IR theory, the strong "logistical state" paradigm is envisioned as the tool for Brazil's international insertion (Cervo 2003: 22). The logistical state "does not go passively to market forces and the hegemonic power" but envisions the state as an active instrument to "insert" Brazil in the twenty-first-century world, including "the design and management of world order" (Bernal-Meza 2010: 208). While the discourse of "inserting Brazil" conveys an image of being outside of the system and seeking to penetrate its barriers of exclusion, the discourse on the "peaceful rise of China", by contrast, does not imply that China was outside but rather that it stumbled for a century – due to Western and Japanese imperialism – and is now erected to its rightful place. Both "rise" and "insertion" have a peculiar Freudian ring, but a psychoanalytical exploration of rising power discourses must be a topic for further research.

Metatheoretically and methodologically, the Brasília School is quite different from the Chinese School. While Chinese IR was built on American scientific foundations, the Brasília School is historical and inspired by French scholars Duroselle and Renouvin (Saraiva 2009: 33–35). It is characterized by a narrative-conceptual and historiographical, rather than "theoricist", approach (Saraiva 2009: 30). Several scholars associated with the Brasília School see their discipline as "History of IR", which is closer to diplomatic history, not "IR" (Santos 2005). Saraiva traces how what was to become a "Brazilian School of History of International Relations" was imported by Cervo from France (Saraiva 2003: 21–23). It is also striking, especially compared to the Chinese case, that all of the above-mentioned scholars have their doctorates from either Europe or Brazil. Apart from the inspiration from this "French School" (Bernal-Meza 2005: 295), the English School also provides inspiration for national and regional conceptualizations, even though it remains another "Northern" theory that "serves this part of the world only as another national reference" than American IR (Saraiva 2009: 28–29, 36). The link to French and British *historical* traditions partly explains why "Brasília School" proponents do not advocate a Brazilian theory, but a move away from universal theory towards locally "rooted" concepts (Cervo 2008).

The Brasília School and its development of Brazilian concepts is, like the Chinese School, intended as a guide to Brazilian foreign policy (Cervo 2003: 7). The emphasis on policy relevance has been called the "Brazilian Way" of doing IR, where the focus is on finding the "best foreign policy", not the "best theory" (Fonseca 1987: 273–274). The problem-solving impetus of the Brasília School is thus open to many of the same critiques as the Chinese School, namely of being uncritical, ideological and nationalist by serving the state project. Also similar to the Chinese School, this has primarily been an internal debate, which has attracted little attention from mainstream scholars and journals – even from outside Brasília and not all scholars at the University of Brasília identify with the school. However, other IR "schools" were also more introvert in their early years, which may be a necessary condition for developing a distinct school of thought. Another condition is that of debate, competition and opposition. Schools of thought are defined in opposition to each other. While there has actually been debate about the Chinese School (Kristensen and Nielsen 2013; we even argue that opposition is its main driver), this is less obvious in the case of the Brasília School, which appears more like a group of like-minded scholars, some of whom are keen on promoting their unity and profile through the school label. Nevertheless, there are overlaps and potentials for dialogue between the Brasília and Chinese Schools and there is certainly a potential audience for the Chinese School in Brazil. As Saraiva concludes: if IR is to become a world, rather than American, discipline "one must still study (and this is an excellent working agenda for the next years) the Chinese thought in depth, its concepts and five thousand year-old perception" (Saraiva 2009: 38).

The discontent with the Eurocentrism of IR has a longer history in India. Scholars have long criticized the reliance on theories imported from the West.

Navigating "global" IR 157

One of the founding figures of Indian IR, M.S. Rajan, argued already in the 1970s that the state of Indian IR was "inadequate when we consider India's size and the place India occupies in the comity of nations and the role India plays in in international affairs" (Rajan 1979: 77; see also 1997a: 2; 1997b: 157). It was puzzling why India as a leading non-aligned nation could be satisfied by relying on knowledge imported from abroad (Rajan 1979: 84; 1994: 213–214) and why India played a leading role in decolonization but did not set in motion a parallel process of "intellectual decolonization" (Harshe 1997: 74). The sense of paradox has been growing in recent years. While India is emerging as a power in world politics, stock-takers are puzzled that the discipline of International Studies has not kept pace (Alagappa 2009a: 3; Mattoo 2009a: 37; Shahi 2013: 50). Like in China, there is an expectation that India's geopolitical rise will eventually lead to stronger conceptualization and theorization in the Indian IR discipline, that "India's aspiration to attain major power status in the contemporary world order offers a promise for its [IR discipline's] take-off" (Shahi 2013: 50). The power–knowledge linkage leads to the expectation that "rising powers seem to get the IR they need" (Bajpai cited in Mattoo 2009b). This logic is evident when Indian scholars compare themselves to their Chinese colleagues.

Indian comparisons to China provide an interesting outside-in view on the Chinese School. In a stocktaking exercise on Indian IR, Muthiah Alagappa deplores that "In comparative terms, India, which had the more developed international studies programs and institutions in Asia in the 1950s and 1960s, has since fallen behind East Asian countries, particularly China" (Alagappa 2009a: 4). Prominent Indian scholar, Kanti Bajpai, also laments that Indian IR, which was leading in the developing world until the 1980s, has recently been overtaken by China, Korea and Japan (Bajpai 2009: 109). India's lagging behind China is seen as disappointing given India's linguistic advantages, its comparatively longer history of IR and political advantages such as academic freedom (Alagappa 2009a: 4). In terms of theory, Alagappa's benchmarking against China notes that "the number of Chinese scholars doing conceptual and theoretical work has increased dramatically", that Chinese scholars have *both* imported and translated "Western IR classics" and made "a concerted effort to reclaim Chinese traditions and classical thought to develop a Chinese School of IR" (Alagappa 2009b: 12). These scholars further argue that India should learn from the Chinese who are recovering and theorizing their own tradition in IR. While cautious about the pitfalls of the Chinese School project, Alagappa admires its seriousness and the project of recovering indigenous traditions, which might be a fruitful common ground for Sino-Indian theory dialogue. To argue that "China has been at the forefront in elevating the importance of IS as a field of study" (Alagappa 2009b: 9) ignores the frustrations of Chinese IR scholars about Western dominance in IR and that there has so far mostly been *debates* about how to develop a Chinese School. Nevertheless, the Chinese School project serves as a role model.

Like in China and Brazil, Indian calls for indigenous theorizing also start with a critique of dominant American and Western theories. Familiar critiques invoke

Hoffmann's argument that IR is an "American Social Science" (Mattoo 2012) and argue that "global IR, a US-dominated discipline, reflects American policy interests" such as non-proliferation and not India's policy interests such as security or development (Basrur 2009: 105; see also Paul 2009: 133–134). Specifically on nuclear issues, Rajesh Basrur argues that a major weakness in the literature is "the tendency to lean heavily on Western, especially American, Cold War discourse on the basic concepts of deterrence despite the enormous difference in the practice of deterrence" (Basrur 2009: 101). He suggests that "IR in India needs to examine its own experience thoroughly and jettison the lens of American deterrence theory if it is to be truly productive" (Basrur 2009: 102). T.V. Paul suggests that Indian IR should challenge American IR theories in areas where India has its own experiences, e.g. "democratic peace, nuclear deterrence, peaceful rise and civilizational IR" (Paul 2009: 134). Moves to develop "indigenous research programs" are motivated by an awareness that IR theories taught and researched in India should not only be "received discourse" (Alagappa 2009b: 18; Mallavarapu 2009: 173). Instead, indigenous Indian theorizing should focus on "India-situated puzzles" that can enrich existing IR concepts and theories and develop new ones (Alagappa 2009b: 18).

It is still widely acknowledged that "There is no Indian school of IR" (Shahi 2013: 51). There is generally less interest in developing a national school or theory (Acharya 2011: 626), but there are some elements of an Indian School *debate* even though it is far from as dominant as in China. Some scholars see the lack of an Indian school as disappointing considering India's civilizational history and heritage. Amitabh Mattoo, for example, who explicitly compares to Chinese IR debates over how to develop a Chinese theory based on traditional philosophy argues that "Tragically, there is no recognizable Indian school of IR despite the rich civilizational repository of ideas on statecraft and inter-state relations" (Mattoo 2009b). More recently, however, Mattoo argued that Indian IR scholars have been "unusually productive" and are now at the "tipping point" of emerging as an intellectual power (Mattoo 2012). The time has come to speak back to the West, to produce rather than consume: "Having absorbed the grammar of Western International Relations, and transited to a phase of greater self-confidence, it is now opportune for us to also use the vocabulary of our past as a guide to the future" (Mattoo 2012). Mattoo encourages Indian scholars to develop an "Indian grammar" based on rich civilizational resources and ancient Hindu scriptures like the Mahabharata. He criticizes Hoffmann's argument that IR is an American Social Science for ignoring that "thinking on International Relations went back, in the case of the Indian, Chinese and other great civilizations, to well before the West even began to think of the world outside their living space" (Mattoo 2012).

Other scholars oppose the construction of an Indian School, but nevertheless agree that IR is Americocentric and that the Indian tradition provides a rich and under-theorized resource. For example, Basrur argues that "While I do not advocate the notion of an Indian 'way' in IR, I do believe that IR in India as a discipline would benefit immensely if it were to be less an Indian variant of a

US-dominated discipline" (Basrur 2009: 105–106). Navnita Behera also encourages the recovery of indigenous Indian thoughts, but opposes the creation of an Indian School per se. Behera attributes the poor conceptualization of Indian IR to the Gramscian hegemony Western IR theories have acquired over the "disciplinary core of Indian IRT" and argues that this has produced a situation where Indian IR scholars do not recognize their own history and philosophical traditions (such as Kautilya) as a potential source of IR theory (Behera 2007: 341). By implication, an "Indian School" attempting, like the Chinese School, to hybridize Western and Indian traditions would remain caught within a Western discourse that suppresses radically alternative, local visions. There should be no Indian school, Behera argues, because re-imagining IR from India is not about creating an Indian School. It is about redefining IR itself. The road to a truly post-Western IR is not "native" theory but a more thorough rethinking of the discipline, the cultural embeddedness of its theories and a more fundamental problematization of the West/non-West dichotomy between a dominant West and a dominated non-West (Behera 2007). The goal is "post-Western" IR, not for Indians to get a niche within the traditional discipline, like the Chinese School, which essentially seeks to supplement (or substitute) American parochialism with Chinese parochialism. In line with this argument, the keynote address at the 2013 Indian Association of International Studies conference "Re-imagining Global Orders: Perspectives from the South" by Amitav Acharya urged Indian scholars to promote "syncretic universalism, rather than create a distinct Indian School of IR. It is in this sense that India offers a potentially rich source of the development and advancement of the Global IR" (Acharya 2013: 10).

Although there is a general resistance to the label "Indian School", most scholars seem to favor the recovery of Indian civilizational, cultural, philosophical and religious traditions if it steers free of nativism. One of the first to emphasize this was Bajpai, who argued that even though it is not recognized as IR theory, "there is a long recorded, and respectable body of Indian thought which can profitably be interrogated" (Bajpai 1997: 43). Bajpai proposed a "program of recovery" of these Indian ancient traditions if Indian IR is to move beyond the notion that "theory is something that Westerners do" but simultaneously warned against "lapsing into uncritical nativism or seeking some essentialist 'Indian' vision" (Bajpai 1997: 43–44). Similarly, Siddharth Mallavarapu suggests studying Indian "traditions of implicit theoretical thinking" rather than "theory" per se to open up for alternative modes of communicating knowledge from other times and spaces, for example Ancient India, that may not conform to theory as we know it today (Mallavarapu 2009: 167). "Civilizational IR" is seen as an area where Indian scholars can contribute to global IR by theorizing Indic civilization, India's religious traditions and Gandhian and Nehruvian traditions that all "offer powerful counterpoints to Western approaches" (Paul 2009: 139).

Like in China, the recovery of an Indian tradition serves the dual purpose of differentiation vis-à-vis Western IR and of conferring a sense of identity, history and pride to Indian IR. It provides difference, something "Westerners" cannot easily understand or access (cf. Kristensen and Nielsen 2013b). The logic of comparative academic advantage infuses Bajpai's argument that "a recovery of a 'tradition' will help construct a research program in which Indians should have physical, linguistic, and philosophical access, particularly to the older materials which outsiders, in general, will find it hard to match" (Bajpai 1997: 44). The recovery of ancient Indian history and philosophy also serves the purpose of giving Indian IR a history: "it will invigorate the view that Indians have a history of thought" (Bajpai 1997: 44). Here one can point to the revival of "Indian ways of knowing" composed by a non-violent ethos (Behera 2007). In a puzzle reminiscent of China's peaceful rise, Gandhian non-violent resistance is seen as a promising approach to "peaceful change" and power transition: "The need of the hour is for comparative theorizing of the logical bases of Gandhian and other non-violent approaches, and about the conditions under which peaceful transitions take place" (Paul 2009: 139). The recovery of Indian traditions also reflects Indian policy making where "reference to Ashoka, Buddha, and Gandhi continues to be a diplomatic catchphrase" (Upadhyaya 2009: 79).

As should be evident in this case, too, there are parallel conversations in Chinese and Indian IR: There is a common resistance to American-Western dominance, a feeling that a "rising power" should have its own perspective on IR and that ancient cultural resources offer promising resources for this. Thus far these conversations have run on parallel but disconnected tracks, however, and there has been little Sino-Indian (not to mention Sino-Brazilian) dialogue, primarily because the Chinese School has taken the American mainstream to be "global IR" and thus its primary audience. This is not surprising given the core-periphery or "hub-and-spokes" patterns of IR communication in which most peripheries are connected to the core, most often as receivers of discourse, while few of them are connected to IR in other periphery settings (Kristensen 2015b). Theories do not travel completely random routes. But these core-periphery structures are not inevitable, they can be navigated, and the Chinese School would benefit from broadening its audiences in its search to become a traveling theory.

Conclusions: audience diversity and the Chinese School as traveling theory

While IR with "Chinese Characteristics" was more defensive, a protective shield against the inflows of Western IR theory in the late 1980s and 1990s, today's Chinese School project is more offensive and outward-looking. The Chinese School debate aims not to ignore global IR debates completely, but "to participate in theoretical debate in the global IR community while addressing theoretical issues in terms of China's national experience" (Zhang 2002: 104), not to replace, but to enrich existing IR theories with China's unique experiences (Qin 2011b: 250). However, the Chinese theory debate is still mainly an internal Chinese debate and when seeking to enter "global IR" it has mostly focused on one particular audience: the United States. This is no surprise given the clout of American IR and its historical influence in China. The Chinese School, and

Chinese IR more generally, has had little success entering the American mainstream IR theory discourse, however. The Chinese School may therefore benefit from a broadening of audiences. Other theoretical schools in the European "semi-periphery" or similar theory debates in other rising powers in the "periphery" of global IR are just some of the potential audiences that are currently very marginal.

The relevance of engaging in inter-regional dialogues depends on whether the Chinese School is envisioned as "something they do in China" that serves only China or whether it aims to develop ideas that scholars elsewhere would be able to use as thinking tools. The former vision of a Chinese School – by, for and about China – will probably find non-Chinese audiences only among China-watchers, while the latter could inspire wider theoretical debates and even be useful to Indians, Germans or Brazilians. It is not that in order to travel a theory must necessarily be universal and devoid from context. Quite the contrary, it is not obvious that universal knowledge claims detached from all traces of tempo-spatial origins travel more easily than particular and geoculturally rooted ones. As Edward Said argued, traveling theories always bear a trace of their geocultural origins and, at the same time, are transformed and modified as they travel to other conditions (Said 1983b). Whether a theory will travel successfully depends also on the "conditions of acceptance", the tolerance or resistance it confronts in different locales (Said 1983b: 157–158). In that respect, it is remarkable that a theory project as instrumental and self-promoting as the Chinese School has not given much consideration to the conditions of acceptance or resistance it will encounter in different contexts. This is not to argue that the Chinese School should strategically engineer its travels and audiences, but that knowledge is never made exclusively in one place and consumed in its original version in another place, it is made as it travels.

9 The Tsinghua Approach and the future direction of Chinese International Relations research

Xu Jin and Sun Xuefeng

In 2005, under the direction of Professor Yan Xuetong and a group of scholars based at Tsinghua University began research on pre-Qin interstate relations. Over the last ten years, the Tsinghua Team has made significant achievements in its research. In 2011, the publication of Yan Xuetong's edited volume, *Ancient Chinese Thought, Modern Chinese Power* by Princeton University Press represented a major breakthrough for the Tsinghua Team, generating significant interest in the research from scholars around the globe (Yan 2011a). At the beginning of 2012, Dr Zhang Feng of Murdoch University in Australia referred to Yan Xuetong and his team's research as the Tsinghua Approach in a review essay (Zhang 2012: 75). He defined the Tsinghua Approach as having three key characteristics: (1) enriching modern International Relations (IR) theory and drawing policy lessons for China's rise today; (2) drawing on China's political thought from the pre-Qin period, which he notes might be considered the most unique aspect of the Tsinghua Approach; and (3) Applying the scientific method to the analysis of pre-Qin thought on interstate relations.

Both authors of this chapter are members of the Tsinghua Team, and we continue to apply the Tsinghua Approach in our work. We endorse Zhang Feng's reference to the Tsinghua Approach, as well as his critique of the Tsinghua Team's scholarship. As members of the Tsinghua Team, though, we are in a better position to discuss the likely future direction of its research, to review its achievements, and point out some of its current limitations, and we are very willing to share our perspectives on these points with those who are interested in the development of Chinese international studies in the global academic community. We argue that the Tsinghua Team is no longer following a single thread in its research, but that scholars are now moving in two directions: one focuses on theory, the other, on history. To adapt Zhang Feng's reference, we would say that it has "One Approach and Two Directions". In terms of key challenges faced by the Tsinghua Approach, it is presently struggling to find an optimal means of applying ancient Chinese thinking to empirical research on contemporary international issues, to refine and streamline its work into one or several core concepts that can be used to bridge historical and theoretical discourses. Finally it struggles to organically weave the concepts, thinking and history of the pre-Qin period into a systematic theory of IR.

Research on pre-Qin theories of interstate relations

From 2005 to 2010, under the leadership of Professor Yan Xuetong, the Tsinghua Team focused research on theories of interstate relations in China's pre-Qin period. During the Spring and Autumn Period, a number of states existed side-by-side in a confined geographical space known as ancient China and maintained complex interactions with one another (including exchanges of people, trade and war). Parallels can be drawn between interstate relations during this period and the modern international system that has emerged after 1648. This period also represents the golden age of Chinese political theory and philosophy. While some pre-Qin philosophers actually participated in political relations between states, and others were observers, each thinker had his own view of interstate politics, which can be discovered through studying the pre-Qin classics.

The first phase of our research focused on identifying the thinking of various pre-Qin writers on interstate relations. Anyone with basic understanding of the pre-Qin classics knows that scholars of that age were encyclopedic, and that the strict disciplinary specializations that are dominant today simply did not exist. A single piece of writing might speak of domestic politics, interstate politics and governance. Careful reading of the pre-Qin classics reveals that there was no systematic theory of IR, but only a large collection of disparate theories and hypothesis. As such, our first task was to compile an edited volume that extracted from the pre-Qin classics readings that might be relevant to scholars of interstate politics. These were compiled into an edited volume by Yan Xuetong and Xu Jin titled *Pre-Qin Chinese Thoughts on Foreign Relations* and published by Fudan University Press in 2008 (Yan and Xu 2008).

Throughout the process of preparing this volume, a general principle was applied: we did not attempt to force the thinking of pre-Qin philosophers into the categories offered by the schools of thought found in modern IR theory. There are simply no parallels between the debates among pre-Qin thinkers and those between different schools of contemporary IR theory. While there may be some similarities between theories of Confucians, Legalists and Daoists of the pre-Qin era and contemporary theories of idealism, realism, and constructivism, the intellectual divide is vast. For example, while the Confucian concept of *Li* ("Rites") is similar to the idealist concept of an international norm, the Confucian concept of *Ren* (Benevolence) cannot be found in idealism.

Extracting pre-Qin thought as found strictly within its original context nonetheless proved problematic, and to a certain extent we needed to apply or draw parallels to contemporary frames in order to explain pre-Qin thought. For example, in explaining Xunzi's selection, Humane Governance (*Wangzhi*), Yan and Xu (2008: 42–43) point out that

> Xunzi argues that the hierarchy of norms (*Li*) is fundamental to maintaining stability and harmony in the international system ... both domestic and international norms are essentially hierarchical. There is a general consensus

in contemporary International Relations theory that a strict hierarchy of power functions to prevent military conflict. This point of view is equivalent to Xunzi's notion that the establishment of a hierarchical system is a prerequisite of maintaining international order.

Continuing the example of the explication of Xunzi's Humane Governance, Yan and Xu (2008: 59) further point out that

> Xunzi argues that the power of the monarch is the highest form of power, and is based on morality and justice (*Daoyi*). Monarchy is obtained through the sovereign's practice of morality and justice. Hegemony is a form of international power that is lesser than monarchy. A ruler is a hegemon rather than a monarch when his practice of morality and justice is lacking. While there is no parallel to Xunzi's view of the influence of the morality of leaders on the international system in contemporary International Relations theory, area studies research does consider similar types of questions.

Regardless of whether there are parallels between Xunzi's theories and contemporary theories of IR, we still need to use contemporary theories as a frame of reference for research on the classics. Doing so can help us better understand and organize the thinking of the ancient philosophers. One difficulty is that comparisons between historical and contemporary thinking are often criticized as subjective, and as violating the integrity of classical thought. This view holds that de-contextualizing particular elements of classical theories undermines our ability to systematically comprehend them, and that comparisons with contemporary thought are completely unnecessary.

Our response to such criticisms is twofold. First, obtaining a comprehensive understanding of the classics should be the work of historians, philologists and scholars of the history of political theory. Their role is to develop comprehensive commentaries on the ancient Chinese classics so that later generations might be able to study and understand them. As students of IR, we borrow from their research and commentaries in order to create or develop our theories. Second, these concerns are misplaced. Thinking on interstate relations in the pre-Qin period is scattered throughout the pre-Qin classics, and no systematic body of theory exists. If we want to understand this thinking, we must first "parse out" many references to interstate relations scattered throughout from the classics, which will inevitably result in isolating them from the broader body of pre-Qin thought. Even so, if our critics were to carefully review the commentary that we have provided along with each sentence or paragraph that we have extracted from the classics, they might find that we have been very cautious in our explications, and have gone out of our way to avoid inappropriate analogies or extreme interpretations.

The second phase of our research was to carefully analyze the writings we found throughout the pre-Qin classics on interstate relations. As scholars of that period were philosophers rather than theorists, their writings are not systematic or complete, and in some cases can be contradictory. Our role here was to turn these bits of writings into a systematic body of theory. In doing so, we had no choice but to carefully apply modern scientific research methodology. Over the past several years, this work was published in a number of scholarly journals, including the *Quarterly Journal of International Politics*, and *World Economics and Politics*, and in a collection of essays titled *Under the Heavens: Chinese Theories of Global Order and Their Implications* (Yan and Xu 2009). A comprehensive overview of this phase of our work is provided by Professor Yan Xuetong in chapter 13 of *A Comparative Study of Pre-Qin Political Philosophy*. Publication of these articles attracted the attention of international scholars to our work, and we decided to compile these works into an English language volume titled *Ancient Chinese Thought, Modern Chinese Power*, which was published by Princeton University Press 2011.

Following the publication of this book, a number of scholars wrote articles that were critical of our work, some of which were particularly pointed (Cunningham-Cross and Callahan 2011; Paltiel 2011; Zhang Feng 2012; He 2012; Hui 2012a; Zou 2011). These critiques can be placed into four different categories, the first being conceptual. Linsay Cunningham-Cross and William Callahan (2011: 361) remark that many are wary of the large states making moralistic arguments, such as the highly ethical and culturally rich concepts of Humane Authority and Hegemony. In their words,

> Chinese ideas thus are interesting to critical IR theorists as one of many pluralistic "alternatives" – but not if Euro-centrism is simply to be replaced by the singular notion of Chinese piety, or if the dominance of the US is replaced by the new hegemony of China.

The reason, Cunningham-Cross and Callahan (2011: 362) note, is that it is simple to characteristically code China as fundamentally moral and all other ways as immoral. Instead, participants in an ethical conversation first need to respect the plurality of values and the multiplicity of alternative understandings of politics. Cunningham-Cross and Callahan (2011: 365) also criticize Yan Xuetong for failing to provide a clear definition of "politics", for he includes nearly all China's ancient values in his definition, and making it difficult, if not impossible, to distinguish clearly political power from other forms of power or influence.

Our response to this criticism is that while a pluralism of values and political systems can be found across the globe, undoubtedly one (or several) system(s) of values and political ideology plays a leading role. In the contemporary global order, it is obvious that liberalism, democracy and peace are the dominant political discourse, and accordingly that the number of republics far exceeds that of monarchies. While a certain level of cultural and political pluralism or even relativism is necessary, it cannot be too extreme. At the same time, it is important to recognize that values change over time. It may not be possible for us to predict what will replace Euro-centrism, but it is clear that no "ism" will be dominant forever.

Regarding claims that our definition of "politics" is not clear, this may actually be a misunderstanding on the part of the two scholars. We do not actually offer our own definition of "politics", but only attempt to generalize about how pre-Qin thinkers define politics. The focus of this phase of our research is on understanding and describing pre-Qin theories of interstate relations, and is not on constructing new theories or engaging in applied practical research. As such, if some concepts are unclear, it is because pre-Qin thinkers were not so strict in defining these concepts.

The second type of criticism comes from scholars like He Kai (2012), who questions whether or not some of the concepts advanced by Yan Xuetong really applied to the contemporary context. In particular, He Kai looks at the concept of morality, which Yan Xuetong commends as the foundation of the classical order. He Kai questions whether Yan overlooks the morality of the state when he equates the individual morals of the dominant ruler with universal morals. He points out (2012: 188) that assessing the level of morality of a ruler is problematic in the absence of some operational standard for doing so. He Kai (2012: 193) also questions another concept discussed by Yan Xuetong – that of hierarchy – which he feels is only a utopia in the modern international society.

We acknowledge that He Kai is correct in stating that there is currently no standard for assessing the level of morality of a ruler, and agree that assessments of morality should be based on prolonged historical research. With regard to hierarchy on the other hand, we point out that Yan Xuetong does not argue for it as a replacement for the equality of states, but instead that the two concepts should be integrated. It would be incorrect to say that the concept of hierarchy has already departed from the stage of IR (see Lake 2007, 2009; Khong 2013).

A third line of criticism relates to the potential policy implications of the book. Cunningham-Cross and Callahan (2011: 362) point out that both the Western world as well as China's Asian neighbors will find it difficult to accept the hierarchical order appealed by Yan Xuetong, particularly when equality is the fundamental principle of the contemporary international society. Yan Xuetong's proposal "voluntary submission for small states in a China-led hierarchy" is not welcome in East Asia. A clear illustration of this is that after China's "provocative" acts in the East and the South China Sea, many East Asian states are balancing China's growing power by strengthening their military ties with the United States.

We argue that while the equality of states is a basic doctrine of modern international law, it does not prevent powerful states from establishing hierarchy where core interests are concerned. The United Nations Security Council, the International Monetary Fund, the World Bank, NATO and the WTO are all examples of hierarchical institutions. As to whether small states are willing to follow the leadership of powerful states, this depends entirely on the latter's relative power advantage and whether it adopts appropriate policies. If China comes to enjoy an enormous power advantage in Southeast Asia, but small states continue to prefer American rather than Chinese leadership, we will need to reflect on the problems with China's foreign policy in the region, and not simply assert that a hierarchical order is not feasible.

Related to these points, Zou Lei (2011: 140) poses a number of interesting questions: how is an international system led by a Humane Authority governed and maintained? Does the very existence of a Humane Authority automatically result in peace within the international system? If a Humane Authority co-exists with a hegemonic power, how does the former respond to challenges from the latter? How do we assess the morality of a Humane Authority? Does a Humane Authority have the right to promote its values as global values?

We acknowledge that answering the above questions in the absence of the emergence of a Humane Authority is impossible, just as it is impossible to determine the nature of the relationship between nuclear powers before the emergence of nuclear weapons. Nonetheless, all of these questions are worth considering, especially as reflecting on them will help us be prepared in the event that such an international order emerges.

Fourth are criticisms of the application of scientific research methods to studies of pre-Qin thought on interstate relations. Zhang Feng (2012: 83, 88) warns of the dangers of approaching the classical texts with preconceived paradigms, and one's own familiar criteria of classification and discrimination. In Zhang's view, a correct way is to understand classical writers in their own terms and their own context. He argues that Yan and his collaborators almost completely overlook the historical and political background against which Xunzi wrote, as well as the significance and consequences of this background. Zhang Feng (2012: 84) critiques Yan Xuetong's application of the level of analysis to pre-Qin thought on interstate relations, noting that while placing pre-Qin thinkers into an ultramodern framework for analyzing IR may produce innovative results, it is equally possible that it will conceal some unique aspects of pre-Qin thought. As such, he suggests that we need to reflect on the potential limitations of modern methodological assumptions in the light of pre-Qin thought.

Zhang Feng's critique is actually similar to the debate over de-contextualization discussed above. Pre-Qin thought is exceptionally rich conceptually, and when we draw upon it, we can only select some content that has parallels to contemporary IR theory or practice. This is of course determined by the objective of our research. However, we cannot come to the conclusion that such selective drawings from the pre-Qin classics harm our observation of contemporary IR. For example, we need to consider more closely whether or not Yan Xuetong's borrowing of the typology of "Humane Authority, Hegemon, and Strong State" from Xunzi actually helps deepen our understanding of phenomena in IR. In other words, we are more concerned about whether our application of scientific research methods to pre-Qin thought on interstate relations helps us better understand the contemporary context. However, we must concede that there is a certain logic to Zhang Feng's critique. Fortunately, the first two phases of our research provide a foundation for interested researchers to advance research in response to Zhang Feng's concerns.

We would like to end our discussion of efforts to describe and classify pre-Qin thought on interstate relations here. The third phase of our research is to apply the products of the first two phases to conduct theoretical or empirical IR research. Our goal is to borrow from the classics in order to enrich understandings of contemporary phenomenon, or in other words, to innovate by applying classical thinking to develop, supplement or even replace current theories. At the beginning of 2011, Professor Yan Xuetong published an article titled "International Leadership and Norm Evolution", marking the beginning of this third phase of the research project (Yan 2011b, 2011c). In this article, Professor Yan Xuetong applies Xunzi's typology of states as "Humane Authority, Hegemon or Strong States" to illustrate how the nature of the dominant state in the international system determines the direction of the evolution of international norms, and that the state's actions are the primary means through which such influence is exerted.

Since he began his research on pre-Qin thought on interstate relations, Yan Xuetong has become disillusioned with realist theories of IR, which only consider state power, and do not reflect on morality. He is particularly frustrated with developments in realism after Kenneth Waltz introduced the theory of structural realism, which gave no consideration to morality or justice. Prior to Waltz, Hans J. Morgenthau (1978: 14–15) actually considered the relationship between ethics and state behavior in the fourth of his six principles of political realism. According to Morgenthau, there is an inevitable conflict between ethical demands and successful political actions. As such, principles of morality and justice cannot be applied universally to state behavior, but must be applied on a case by case basis, carefully considering the specific context. Yan Xuetong's understanding of this principle is that interests (referring to material interests) and justice are both components of state interests. When the two agree with one another, the state can pursue both interests and justice; when the two disagree, the state generally seeks to ensure interests. Based on this understanding, he argues that the dominant state and a rising state will compete for the moral high ground, and work to institutionalize their own principles of justice as international norms.

In his article "International Leadership and Norm Evolution", Yan Xuetong (2011b: 10–11) argues that dominant states influence the evolution of international norms through three means, namely, "a process of demonstration – imitation; a process of support – strengthening; a process of punishment – maintenance". Of these, he argues, the first (demonstration – imitation) is the traditional Chinese approach, as at its essence is the traditional Chinese saying "lead by example". In Yan's words, "demonstration – imitation is fundamentally different from what G. John Ikenberry and Charles Kupchan (1990) identified as the process of persuasion", through which a hegemon uses discursive dominance to persuade a state to accept a particular type of behavior as a norm. Demonstration – imitation, on the other hand, refers to the dominant power setting an example through its own behavior, which other states may find appropriate to follow or not and eventually accept as a behavior norm. In contrast, persuasion involves providing incentives and/or issuing threats. What is more, with the persuasion approach, the dominant state may seek to persuade other states to follow norms that the dominant state does not even follow. For example, the United States violated the nuclear nonproliferation treaty in its nuclear cooperation with India, but at the same time can still persuade the Republic of Korea not to develop nuclear weapons in response to North Korea's nuclear tests. Demonstration – imitation is only effective if the dominant power actually follows a particular international norm.

Yan's arguments here have clear policy implications. They help us reflect on what type of moral principles China might advocate following its rise, and how it may act to change international norms. With respect to this point, Yan Xuetong has yet to develop a number of his ideas into formal theories. Yan (2012: 21) notes that

> Within the contemporary international system, liberalism enjoys a position of absolute dominance. However, this does not imply that China has no space to promote the emergence of new international norms. At the core of liberalism are freedom, equality and democracy, which represent the theoretical basis for contemporary international norms. Yet there is still room to transcend these concepts. On the basis of classical Chinese theories of *Li* (rites), *Ren* (benevolence), and *Yi* (justice), China can promote new international norms based on the principles of equity, civility and justice.

Yan Xuetong (2013: 12) further explicates in detail means through which a system of universal values appropriate to the contemporary context may be developed on the basis of traditional Chinese culture, and argues that the core principles of this system should be "equity, justice and civility". He is confident that this value system is superior to the values of "freedom, equality and democracy", which are characteristic of liberalism.

Research on relations between China and East Asia states in ancient times

Victoria Tin-bor Hui (2012b: 426) asserts that Yan Xuetong's ahistorical effort to borrow from pre-Qin thought on interstate relations to develop contemporary IR theory is the equivalent to "building a skyscraper on the beach: its foundation will be unstable". Zhang Feng (2012: 88) also cautions that "We do have to be concerned with the events, not those events as recounted by the philosophers, but those which have been carefully established by rigorous historical research conducted by both traditional and modern historians." While both of these critiques are reasonable, the objective of the first two phases of our work was to identify and classify pre-Qin thought on interstate relations, and not to observe history. As we enter the third phase of the project, it will be essential to pay equal attention to both theory and history. Yan Xuetong (2011b) evokes many examples from Chinese history to demonstrate his points of view, even though it is more preoccupied with theory than history.

The publication of Zhou Fangyin's (2011a, 2011b) "Equilibrium Analysis of the Tributary System" marks the beginning of the Tsinghua Team's research on historical relations between China and East Asian states. It applies a game theoretic model to analyze the equilibrium state of the classical Chinese tributary system and to assess its stability. The article is significant both in terms of its scholarly contribution, and its policy implications. Its scholarly significance is that it moves beyond established frameworks for understanding the tributary system, illustrating the internal logic of the tributary system through consideration of strategic interaction between China and its neighboring states. Previously the tributary system had been mostly the purview of historians, with scholars of IR rarely giving it any consideration. Historians concentrated their research on the concept, institutions and rites of the tributary system, as well as on the number of foreign tributary states China maintained under each dynasty, their activities, gifts, travels and trade. However, very rarely did scholars consider strategic interactions between China and its neighboring states against the backdrop of the tributary system – precisely the type of analysis in which political scientists excel. Zhou Fangyin (2011a, 2011b) found that the optimal strategy for small states vis-à-vis great powers is to create a disturbance, but only to a limited extent so as to avoid prompting the great power from adopting a strategy of military punishment. As for great powers, their optimal strategy is to reassure small states, but only to a limited extent so as to avoid prompting small states from developing unrealistic expectations. By balancing these interests, great powers and small states find an equilibrium point in their bilateral relations.

In terms of policy implications, Zhou's findings can be applied to the post-1949 period to explain China's relations with states with which it has territorial or maritime dispute. Often such states have attempted to encroach upon China's territory and interests, but have also been cautious to avoid provoking a strong response from China. Meanwhile, on the basis of political and economic considerations, China has proven unwilling to adopt a strong response, and in some cases has even temporarily acquiesced to the actions of these states. However, as such states become more egregious in their actions, China begins to reach the limits of its tolerance, and will react strongly (generally through military operations) as a means of deterring states, causing such states to relinquish all or some of the Chinese interests they encroached on. At this point the two sides return to equilibrium, and a new round of the game begins.

Zhou Fangyin (2012) offers an analysis of the "Zunwang" (Respect the King of Zhou Dynasty) strategy of the Warring States Period. "Zunwang" is a type of hegemonic behavior unique to the Spring and Autumn Period. According to Zhou, "Zunwang" was an effective strategy states used to obtain hegemonic status under a loose hierarchical system, which involved reducing the concerns and opposition of small and medium sized states, while isolating and deterring competitors. Such an approach of rising as a hegemon was seen as legitimate. While Zhou focuses on the history of the Spring and Autumn Period, his findings still have important practical implications. At the end of the article, Zhou (2012: 34) points out that his research "helps ensure that we do not understand the rise of a great power and hegemonic competition only through the European experience ... and it also provides insights into understanding the evolution of the future regional order in East Asia".

In a recent email to the authors of this chapter, Zhou explained further as follows:

> This article discusses a rather unique circumstance of hegemonic competition, which may illustrate differences in the historical experiences of Europe and East Asia. During the Spring and Autumn Period, hegemonic competition between great powers was relatively mild, with the focus being on identifying a legitimate path to obtaining authority. The historical experience of hegemonic competition between European powers is not necessarily the future of Asia. Power transition in East Asia may take place peacefully, and the evolution of the East Asian order (as well as competition over regional leadership) may parallel the power transition of the Spring and Autumn Period, especially when it comes to the means and conditions according to which great powers compete for authority. Future research in this direction might offer more insights.

The reality is that China is currently adopting a strategy of "Zunwang" as it makes its own respective rise. For example, China has tremendous respect for the United Nations and the role of all kinds of international organizations, and emphasizes its observance of international law and international principles.

Xu Jin (2012) also analyzed the effectiveness of the "Zunwang Rangyi" strategy ("Respect the King of Zhou Dynasty and Expel the Barbarians") based on the historical record of the Spring and Autumn Period. In his research, Xu Jin finds that the effectiveness of the "Zunwang Rangyi" strategy depends on the value of its strategic objectives. When the value of the strategic objective is great, the strategy tends to be effective; when the value is small, the strategy tends to be less effective; when there is no value or the strategic objective disappears, this strategy must be abandoned. This finding is similar to the findings of Zhou Fangyin (2012: 34) on the "Zunwang" strategy, when he points out that the looser the international hierarchy in the Spring and Autumn Period, the lower the effectiveness of the "Zunwang" strategy.

Findings of Xu Jin (2012) also have important policy implications. He argues that if we put aside *Hua* (China), *Yi* (non-Chinese) and other distinctively Asian political constructs, and merely consider the way in which *Hua* and *Yi* political systems (ideologies) competed during the Spring and Autumn Period, this may help us understand and predict a number of contemporary phenomena in international politics. For example, China's practice of treating Sino-US relations as the most important element of its foreign policy is similar to the "Zunwang" strategy of the Spring and Autumn Period. Extrapolating from the Spring and Autumn example, as China continues its rise, it will result in a decline in

America's relative power, and the effectiveness of a policy which treats Sino-US relations as the most important element of foreign policy will be less effective. According to this view, as China rises, it will increasingly pay less attention to Sino-US relations. To offer another example of potential policy implications, the story of the non-Chinese state of Chu transforming itself to a civilized state tells us that contemporary China should continue to increase the pace of its reform and opening, and reduce its gap with the United States in terms of politics, theory, education and culture such that it will be increasingly difficult for the United States to invoke ideology as a reason for developing alliances to hedge against China (Xu 2012: 60–61).

Research on China's relations with East Asian states is by no means new – some scholars have already made great contributions in this field (Johnston 1995; Hui 2005; Wang Yuan-Kang 2010). The Tsinghua Team can only be considered rookies when it comes to work in this area, and its research has yet to attract significant attention from international scholars. China's long history and its rich experiences in foreign policy represent a treasure-trove of data that can be mined in advancing IR research. We have reasons to believe that members of the Tsinghua Team and other like-minded Chinese scholars will leverage this treasure-trove to produce more valuable scholarly contributions.

Outstanding problems and potential directions

While the Tsinghua Team led by Professor Yan Xuetong has made numerous achievements through the "Tsinghua Approach", it still faces a number of challenges that it needs to respond to through the development of new research agendas. These are reviewed in this section.

1 Slowed pace of innovation

During the first two phases of this research, the Tsinghua Team had a large number of members involved, morale was very high, and the team made a large number of contributions to the field. A significant number of articles were published, as were three edited volumes. After entering into the phase of theoretical innovation in 2011, the number of articles published by team members began to decrease, and quite a few team members moved on to work on other research projects. There are two explanations for this. First is that theoretical innovation is more difficult than academic work focused on description or generation of typologies. While creating such typologies requires significant patience, careful attention to detail and a great investment of time in reviewing the relevant literature and developing a better means for presentation of the relevant findings, not a great deal of innovation is required. Such work is the precursor of innovation, and is a highly laborious task. It depends on having a large number of people. Unlike more innovative research, however, it does not require the same level of unique skills or abilities to identify and resolve problems.

Another challenge is that the team members need to further develop their research capacity. Borrowing from thinking and history found in classical Chinese texts related to interstate relations to develop contemporary theories of IR requires that researchers are proficient in both IR theory as well as knowledgeable of ancient Chinese political thinking and history. This further means that scholars need to have the ability to engage in interdisciplinary research. Almost all members of the Tsinghua Team were trained in the study of IR, and lack the requisite knowledge of Chinese history and history of political theory. While they can borrow from commentaries on historical classics written by contemporary scholars, gaining a deep understanding of the classics, and applying such an understanding to contemporary IR theory will be extremely difficult.

We already grasp the challenges discussed above, and are now working to attract the interest of researchers from across the country to contribute to this project; however response has been limited. As such, it is likely that in the future the team will rely on the enduring efforts of a small number of highly committed researchers. The number of articles published will not necessarily be as numerous as it was previously, and longer periods of time may pass in between publications. However, what is lost in quantity will be made up for in quality – these articles will hopefully attract the attention and criticism of scholars from around the globe.

2 Need to integrate research agendas

As discussed above, as the members of the Tsinghua Team continue to apply the Tsinghua Approach, two research agendas – one focused on theory and the other on history have emerged. While researchers can certainly make contributions in each of these areas, we argue that it is possible to integrate these two agendas, and that doing so will likely open new prospects for research.

There are two possible ways for integrating these agendas: focusing on theoretical development while considering history; and focusing on history while also considering theoretical development. Yan Xuetong has already conducted some preliminary experiments with the first of these two possibilities. In Yan (2011b), he borrows Xunzi's concepts of "Humane Authority, Hegemon and Strong State" to construct a theory of international leadership, and further borrows from historical materials from China's Western Zhou and the Spring and Autumn Period to illustrate the theory. In addition, he also proposes to construct a new international norm of the principles of equity, civility and justice on the basis of the classical Chinese concepts of *Li* (rites), *Ren* (benevolence) and *Yi* (justice). In his efforts to develop a systematic theory to support this, drawing on cases from ancient Chinese history will be essential.

Members of the Tsinghua Team have yet to make any achievements with respect to the second means of integrating the two agendas. International scholars have attempted a parallel comparative research project, though, which involves the comparison of contemporary IR phenomena with historical cases of China's interstate relations. For example, it is possible to compare America's relations with its contemporary allies and the relations between the Qing empire and its neighboring tributary states during the early to mid-Qing period in the seventeenth and eighteenth centuries. Should a member of the Tsinghua Team advance such research, he needs to place his primary emphasis on history, while giving secondary consideration to theory. For example, a history of the role that ideology or values played during a particular Chinese dynasty between China and its tributary states may be compared with the role of ideology or values in the contemporary relations among nation-states.

3 Lack of a core concept

Zhang Feng (2012: 75) refers to the work of the Tsinghua Team as the Tsinghua Approach rather than the Tsinghua School because, as he argues, the three characteristics he identifies as comprising the Tsinghua Approach are not sufficient to be considered a school of thought.

A school of thought must have a unique and systematic research methodology in a particular field, and must have already established a flagship methodology and line of argumentation. At the same time, it must also offer space for future scholarly advancement. For example, the English School of IR is well-known for its pluralistic research methods and its flagship concept of international society (see Wang and Buzan this volume). The Copenhagen School borrows from linguistic behavioral theory to develop a theory of "securitization", and uses discursive analysis to illustrate how security problems are socially constructed. The Cambridge School of history of political theory integrates political history and history of thought through its unique blend of discursive and linguistic analysis. At present, the Tsinghua Approach lacks a distinct methodology and a deep theory with respect to its work on classical Chinese thought, contemporary IR theory and contemporary Chinese foreign policy. To establish the Tsinghua School, considerable work is still needed with respect to theory, methodology and empirical research.

We completely agree with Zhang Feng's argument above. The Tsinghua Approach lacks a core concept such as "international society" or "securitization" in order to develop the Tsinghua Approach into a Tsinghua School. Zhang Feng (2012: 95, 98) calls Yan Xuetong as a proponent of moral realism, and suggests not only that such a notion is theoretically tenable, but that it has considerable policy implications. The challenge for Yan Xuetong is to develop a new concept as a bridge between morality and realism to organically integrate the two. We believe that Yan Xuetong's emphasis on global leadership and emerging international norms (equity, justice, civility), might well develop into a core conceptual focus in the future.

Conclusion

This chapter has reviewed the development of the Tsinghua Approach to IR research, and provided an overview of its achievements and deficiencies, while pointing out likely directions for future research and challenges. We argue that if they want to develop the Tsinghua Approach into a Tsinghua School, Professor Yan Xuetong and his Team will need to devote more energy to integrating theory and history, as well as morality and realism. The goal of the next phase of this research should be to develop a systematic theory of the emergence of new international norms, to conduct more direct comparative research and, most importantly, to propose a core theory, possibly of a theory of moral realism.

The dissemination of the Tsinghua Approach within the Chinese IR academia is quite slow. It is basically a niche group without many followers, and will be so in the future. It is also slow for the scholars to conduct researches by the positivist methodology because of its high threshold. The latest achievement is a journal article written by Zhou Fangyin and Li Yuanjing (2014). Yan Xuetong (2015) will publish his monograph on moral realism in 2015, which will indicate the final formation of this theory. Of course scholars outside of Tsinghua Team can also use the Tsinghua Approach to conduct their researches. For example, using the Tsinghua Approach, Chen Zheng (2015) from Shanghai Jiao Tong University brought forth a new explanation on the degeneration of international norms in the Spring and Autumn Period in China. More broadly, the Tsinghua Approach has exerted important influence among the IR academia in China. It has stimulated other Chinese IR scholars to devote themselves to theoretical innovation, to explore new theoretical approaches, and to construct a new school of IR theory in China. For example, some scholars have proposed that the achievements of a group of scholars from Shanghai are sufficient to be the basis of a "Shanghai School" of IR theory (Zhang *et al.* 2014; Ren this volume).

The advance of the Tsinghua Approach is a valuable endeavor made by Chinese IR scholars represented by Yan Xuetong, who attempt to apply the indigenous resources in China to enrich and develop IR theories. This endeavor is paralleled by notable attempts by other Chinese scholars for innovative theorization of IR. Two are particularly worth mentioning here. Professor Qin Yaqing from the China Foreign Affairs University has devoted himself in recent years to integrating social constructivism and Chinese traditional philosophy to construct a new theory with Chinese characteristics: Processual constructivism (Qin 2009a). Professor Tang Shiping from Fudan University has developed a social evolutionary approach to provide an endogenous explanation for the systemic transformation of international politics (Tang 2013).

A recent review essay on the development of Chinese IR research points out that although there has not yet been a great theoretical breakthrough in Chinese IR after the new millennium, Chinese IR scholars have produced some innovative and high quality scholarship, and made notable attempts at the creation of original theory at the systemic level (Yang 2012: 62). At the same time, it is also critical that many publications, which offer no new ideas and are full of slogans, have found their way in the top IR journals in China, and articles and monographs without any innovation still constitute the mainstream of such Chinese media (Yang 2012: 106).

The goal of the scientific research is the production of knowledge, and to help human beings to understand the world better by the innovation of theories. Thus theoretical breakthrough is very critical to the development and progress of any discipline. The precondition of the establishment of an original theory and even a school of theory is to find an important core theoretical question and try to solve it. It is regrettable that Chinese IR scholars have not found such a research question after 30 years' efforts, therefore a school of IR theory in China is yet to be achieved. We hope that we will see glimmers of hope on the horizon before the coming of the third decade of new millennium.

10 Balance of relationship and the Chinese School of IR

Being simultaneously Confucian, post-Western and post-hegemonic

Chih-yu Shih and Chiung-chiu Huang

In 2005, the United States gave the Democratic People's Republic of Korea, designated by the United States as a terrorist state, the promise not to attack it with either nuclear or traditional weapons (Cha 2009). Such a rigid pledge contradicts both the realist calculus of the balance of power and the idealist undertaking not to negotiate with terrorists. Just a few years before this, the United States had invaded Afghanistan (2001) and then Iraq (2003) on the grounds that they trained terrorists and possessed weapons of massive destruction (according to the fabricated evidence) while neither country was capable of or had intent for a war with the United States. Again, these were incompatible with either realism or idealism. It is apparent that realism has not been exclusively the principle of International Relations (IR) for the United States. Since 2011, the United States has adopted the strategy of rebalancing toward Asia. This has included both partnership building with Myanmar, Malaysia, China and so on, on the one hand, and realist balancing against China via cooperation with Japan, the Philippines and Vietnam on their maritime disputes with China, on the other hand. Accordingly, balance of power (BoP) and balance of relationships (BoR) together characterize the United States' endeavors to remain influential in spite of a relative power decline. However, in the current study of IR there is no systematic discourse on BoR.

This chapter provides such a discourse. It will draw on Confucianism to map the route to the discovery of a general theory of BoR. Specifically, BoR is the process via which nation states stabilize reciprocal relationships with each other. Their purpose is to reduce uncertainty in the long run. We use Confucianism for three reasons: First, Confucianism contains clear doctrines that illustrate both the rationales of BoR and how the rational system of BoR can be culturally sensible. However, we argue that cultural and ideological routes to reach BoR are various and multiple. BoR can be universally accessible, if not universally practiced at any given time. Second, we want to reject the stereotype of Confucian pacifism and its alleged negligence of rationality for the sake of morality. We argue that BoR is a rational system of international politics, but definitely not about pacifism. Third, assessing Confucianism could be useful in surmising the impact of China rising on international politics. We believe that the much discussed Chinese School of IR in recent years would be misleading if China's claimed quest for relational security is mistaken as an exclusively Chinese phenomenon. We will demonstrate that BoR is not just Chinese. In this last regard, we will also draw implications of BoR for post-Western IR.

The chapter proposes an IR theory as a parallel to the more familiar narratives of BoP, balance of interests, and balance of threat. These other narratives conceive of IR as structures independent of the maneuvering of individual nations. BoP, for example, typically conceives of structures as ultimate constraints that render the human choice at best a spurious process. Alternatively, BoR considers nation states as managers of mainly bilateral relationships that transcend structural constraints. We believe that the BoR theory not only incorporates non-structuralist ways of thinking more effectively, but also transcends all civilizational divides and the epistemological gap between rationality and culture, with the exception that routes toward BoR could be localized or even individualized. We believe that BoR is more accessible and feasible than the above-mentioned structuralist narratives. Nation states always try to decide how to stabilize bilateral relationships regardless of whether or not the existing relationships are reciprocal. Current IR theories are biased toward estranging relationships, overlooking both the necessity of relational security as well as nations' possessing the agency to achieve it (Yan 2011a; Hui 2005).

Conceptualizing BoR

BoR is a concept that explains the limited relevance of differences in ideas, institutions, identities and material forces as variables that matter in IR since they can readily be disregarded for the sake of long-term stability. However, BoR acknowledges that all these elements still have mundane implications in daily policy making. BoR is a general theory of long-term IR. It is in direct contrast with the pursuit of a synchronized world or regional order. Synchronization is the modernist version of rationalism and universalism. It informs most general theories in IR. It refers to the diffusion of a simultaneous executed or promoted pattern of rational thinking embedded in an idea, an institution, a collective identity or a perceived arrangement of material force. Synchronization is presumably a process whereby unrelated national actors conjunctionally fulfill their self-assigned functions in order to interact orderly. However, the balance of relationships is a system exempt from such synchronized rationality. It prescribes ontological tolerance and epistemological sensibility in IR.

Accordingly, BoR predicts that national actors will not consistently stick to any specific synchronic ways of rational thinking in the long run. This is especially relevant in the post-hegemonic order, referred to as a condition under which nation states subscribe to a basically US-led liberal institution and yet do so without either the capacity or will to consistently sanction its enforcement. Rather, they will from time to time try to achieve stabilized reciprocal relationships no matter how deterministic or opportunistic they might appear in the short run in their pursuit of security, prosperity, global governance, peace, etc. It is a system of bilateral relations that relies on reciprocal tolerance instead of shared values, implying inconsistency in enforcing one's own values when facing different countries at different times. BoR is a system parallel to BoP, just as for all nations the social system is parallel to the political system. In the following discussion, we will begin with a discussion of the significance of Confucianism in post-hegemonic IR and the relevance of Confucian relational sensibilities to the post-Western quest for re-Worlding sites of geocultural distinction. The chapter then proceeds with analyzing how Confucianism leads to the discovery of a generalized thesis on BoR.

Classic Confucianism and Chinese IR

Confucianism hoped to instill moral consciousness into the elite stratum and ensure that duties are performed as prescribed by institutional roles. This moral consciousness, according to Confucius, could arise from enhanced benevolence in the heart of the kings and their officials. To promote benevolence, Confucius turned to blood kinship, hence blood kinship was a solution in his institutional design. For Confucius, anyone within the kinship circle who wished to establish himself would instinctively want to establish his family and clan. Such a kinship circle thus could breed the virtue of self-restraint. When all people in the ruling position practiced self-restraint, the levy would not exceed the minimum that is necessary to maintain the kingdoms and the expansion would not take place between them.

Confucianism, among most other Chinese classics, was already quasi-IR theory in its time, to the extent that it began as a philosophy to rescue the All-under-Heaven order from decaying into a warring system among kingdoms. Kingdoms were initially feudal domains bestowed to the kin of Zhou. The emperor of Zhou received no respect from his kin – each assigned to their land and yet each announcing their own kingship. It was a period of transition from a hierarchical world order dominated by a few major kings to a warring period of many competing powers. This can be related analogously to the collapse of the so-called "European Concert" or the end of the Cold War. In contrast to other contending schools of the time that achieved fame among the elite strata, Confucianism stressed morality but nonetheless shared with them one important platform – restoring the order via rectifying names. Names presumably provided the population a code of propriety, which enabled them to interact in an orderly way. Confucius and his disciples believed that the best way to promote propriety was to embed it in moral consciousness. Confucians of later generations disagree on how to enhance moral consciousness. Confucius himself had conviction in kinship, which he argued arose from spontaneous love. He insisted that spontaneous self-restraint in everyone's caring and loving families be essential to the restoration of order. He hoped that a metaphor of kinship abiding by the classic Book of Rites could breed benevolence via spontaneous self-restraint. Subsequent followers of Confucius appealed to rituals and teaching, instead of kinship, to breed moral consciousness (Fu 1994; Tu 1996: 8; Nuyen 2007; Rubin 1976: 17–18; Ho 1968). Further away from Confucianism was the School of

Legalism, which turned to strict law in order to enforce the named duties. Self-restraint became compulsory, not spontaneous, under the legalist circumstances.

Classic Confucianism and contemporary post-Western IR face almost exactly the same situation and mission – the breakdown of a hegemonic order and the quest for post-hegemonic order, not to be unilaterally enforced by a hegemonic center. Post-Western IR attends to the geocultural distinction of all sites in its re-appropriation of hegemonic order for its own purposes, and the hegemonic order is exposed to be no more than a provincial site, called the West (Tickner and Blaney 2012, 2013). To achieve post-Zhou identities, Confucianism appealed to specific nostalgia for a bygone utopia as its reference so as to appropriate the Zhou values and institutions. However, post-Western IR relied on retrieving so many varieties of nostalgia, each embedded in a sited genealogy, that no hegemonic theorization could possibly incorporate, synchronize or convert all of them. Incidentally, the advocacy of the Chinese School of IR in China shared the same Confucian nostalgia for either a relational order (Qin 2009a) or a benevolent hierarchy (Yan 2011c) regardless of the Marxist indoctrination of those scholars in their earlier career. In the light of post-Western determination to resist any plausible hegemonic order, the Chinese School's propensity for hierarchy understandably sends an alert.

Nevertheless, Confucianism coped with the arriving of anarchy and endeavored to control it. The conviction that anarchy should and could be controlled lay in the imagined state of nature in accordance with the ancient classics over a thousand years before Confucius. For Confucianism and contemporary neo-Confucianism, anarchy was not the state of nature but the reality to be controlled. A revisit to Confucianism in the twenty-first century can thus inform both post-hegemonic and post-Western theorization in the sense that post-hegemonic theorization is preoccupied likewise with anarchy, though as the state of nature rather than a deviation from it, and post-Western theorization, by the pursuit of multiple sites of genealogy each rooted in its own geocultural distinction. The Confucian notion of benevolence rings the post-Western bell of geocultural genealogy on one hand (Shih 2010b), and alerts the post-Western IR on the other to the danger of the emergence of another hegemony that would name duties and enforce their requests for self-restraints around the world (Callahan 2008a). In the sense that Confucianism houses a mainstream IR's anarchical sensibility and a post-Western identity of sited genealogy, it can contribute at least to the explanation of the post-hegemonic IR in the self-reflection of a Chinese School on China's own strategy of survival, either hegemonic or sited.

To a significant extent, Confucius and his contemporaries coped with both international and domestic politics. Self-restraint was their advice for kings in order to maintain order internally and attain reputation internationally. Internally, benevolence could be reified through the reduction of levies. Externally, the population elsewhere would long for the arrival of a benevolent king. As a result, no one would treat the naturally self-restraining king and his clans as tyrants internally or threat externally. The relationship between warring states would eventually calm down, with such states returning to their named duties in a spontaneous order symbolized by the presumably selfless emperor of Zhou. This attested to what Confucius called the Way, which should be so broad due to the voluntary self-restraint of all that all can relax on walking along with one another (Ivanhoe 2004: 197).[1] Needless to say, the Western counterpart similarly has its utopia, for example the idea of critical peace (Behr 2014) or the world government (Wendt 2003), both of which obscure the international from the internal. Transcending the territorial boundary seems to characterize all post-hegemonic versions of utopia, be it Confucianism or post-Western IR.

Confucianism is concerned with the preparation of foreign policy for relationality, mutuality, embeddedness and contextuality, unfailingly making Sinification, historical as well as contemporary, an all-directional movement void of teleology (Katzenstein 2012). Consequently, China is hardly a distinctive analytical entity, but a cosmology (Callahan 2004a). These cultural processes either introduce or rejuvenate Chinese worldviews as defined by the values of harmony, group orientation and *guanxi* culture (Qin 2009a). *Guanxi*, a metaphor of kinship, is particularly pertinent to BoR. It refers to the cultural belief, in the IR context, that nations cannot survive without coupling their existence to each other in certain mutually agreed and practiced relationships. The quest for *guanxi* makes reciprocity an intrinsic component in any rational, bilateral exchange. In the subsequent discussion, however, we will not aim to assert China's distinctiveness, but to arrive at a general thesis that one can discover via a Confucian route.

BoR vis-à-vis BoP

The belief that, ultimately, states should strive to establish harmonious relations is the distinctive feature of BoR. This belief could either reflect the Confucian calculus of long-term interest or provide a cognitive resource to manage IR where BoP fails. The idea of a BoR originally derived from Confucian lessons is the ability to extend the horizon of BoP. BoP prescribes for states facing the rise of another power to either engage in balancing or a deviant strategy of bandwagoning. Balancing is aimed at defending against the potential aggression exerted by the rising power to maintain one's own security. Bandwagoning is aimed at joining the side of the rising power to avoid becoming its target. The goals of BoR, like BoP and bandwagoning, also include the preservation of the independence and security of state. More importantly, however, BoR aims to create peaceful and constructive relationships between states. Although both strategies focus on apparent and immediate national interests, such as survival, security and economic benefits, among other things, BoR does not take such interests as priorities or ultimate ends.

The strategy of BoP or bandwagoning is often triggered by fear; the fear that external powers can deprive a nation-state of its survival is similar to what Thucydides described in such a rationale thousands of years ago. The classical realist assumption in IR theory has unremittingly followed the idea that, "the strong do what they can and the weak suffer what they must" (Thucydides quoted in

Donnelly 2000: 23). However, the motivation that applies to BoR is completely different. When a state applies the strategy of BoR, it may temporarily shelve apparent and immediate national interests for the preservation of relationships. When a state adopts the strategy of BoP and bandwagoning, the strategy always targets a specific other. The state either attempts to weaken a specific other's capability or influence or to aspire to the release of the pressure resulting from being threatened by a stronger external power.

By contrast, the rationale for applying BoR is to achieve reciprocation and harmony. Such a rationale could only appear when the state's need for survival can be met by an enhanced sense of relational security. When the state is denied a reciprocal relationship, it senses the threat of survival because of the reemerging anarchy. Balancing and bandwagoning are strategies adopted when the international system remains in the Hobbesian state of nature. In reality, rarely do states continue to hold survival as the primary national interest at stake because they usually possess relational security of various kinds and to certain degrees. On the other hand, when the survival is really an issue, few states would not seek support via social, religious and ideological relationships. Confucianism considers a degree of relational security as the state of nature. In this latter regard, the soft power does not refer to cultural resources under one's control, but those that lie in one's capacity to provide relational certainty in response to the common desire for stability defined by existing relationships. If anarchy is a system of nature in which the state in solitude is compelled to adopt a self-help strategy, harmony should likewise be a system of nature in which the state in reciprocal relationships is inclined to avoid the disruption of relationships (Qin 2009a, 2009b).

Under anarchy, the foundation of strategic calculation is about the capability and relative weakness in physical power resources as indicators of danger. If realists believe that nations must live in anarchy and thus nations cannot help but resort to BoP for survival, they could alternatively seek to control anarchy by establishing reciprocal relationships so that self-help actually means mutual help. The same fear toward the potentially unrestrained violence of anarchy therefore leads to the system of self-restraint upon which they could rely to manage their survival. BoP is a systemic aptitude for realists to live with anarchy as nature; BoR is a systemic resource for realist states to control or reverse anarchy as an undesirable, but not inevitable condition. They are parallel to each other. The abortion or failure of either leads to strategic thinking leaning towards the opposite. Under the aforementioned Confucian circumstance, anarchy does not define the state of nature. Compared with power undergirded by self-help, relationships undergirded by self-restraint in the Confucian state of nature are the systemic parameters of BoR. Therefore, if a country subscribes to a specific idea, e.g. liberalism, or institution, e.g. capitalism, and acts with determination to synchronize the ways of rational thinking of all other nations in order to operate IR accordingly, BoR will predict that its determined pursuit will not continue in the long run.

Under the system of BoR, nations that seek to diffuse a distinctive value or institution always need to coordinate with other nations and therefore inevitably

Balance of relationship 183

act inconsistently when coping differently with complying and revisionist actors that coexist. All the inconsistencies are indicators of BoR, which explains why one should compromise on the deviant behavior of a perceived ally. Compromises and confrontations that deviate from synchronizing forces attest to the system of BoR. Compromise is a widespread practice anywhere and anytime. This is because compromise with a complying nation could secure its continued support; compromise with a revisionist nation could warm up feelings conducive to future synchronization. The latter is usually called peaceful evolution or engagement. Whether or not and how much to compromise necessarily involves human judgment, which compels one to think in the longer term and in relational terms.

BoR is a peculiar system that pushes all the other systems to realize and observe their limits. There can be higher moments in which nations stick with a particular way of rational thinking at the expense of bilateral reciprocity. However, they are always capable of retrieving reciprocity through BoR in the aftermath of – or during an interval in between – high moments. BoR enables the nations to recover from the fatigue or uncertainty caused by overcommitment. Those other systems of rationality based on power, institutions or identity have to retrieve specific bilateral relationships when systemic constraints fail to provide guidance. The deepest danger during the systemic failure is the loss of relationship or of the possibility to stay related. Even though harmony is hardly attainable or fixable in the IR dynamic, it remains a policy goal in practice. The quest for relationships is too strong to allow synchronization to continue consistently, indiscriminately or teleologically. Being an indicator of the failure of states to comply with the theory of BoP, inconsistency in enforcing a value or a rule is actually intrinsic to BoR because judgment and its indefinite consequences are systemic parameters of BoR. That's why Confucianism's harmony is a systemic goal regardless of states' consciousness, and anarchy cannot be the state of nature since states can always find relational exits.

In the system of BoR, even the national leaders who subscribe to BoP tactics will find it rational to seek reciprocal relationships. To renounce a claim, to concede a right, or to compromise on a dispute, is an investment or a cost-efficient way of the stronger party to preserve a long-term, reciprocal relationship. For example, Israel's decision to refrain from military strike to counter Iran's acquisition of nuclear weapons in 2012 was likewise a pursuit of relational security with both Tehran and Washington at the expense of territorial security (Gladston 2012).[2] The United States, for another example, at times adopts a cautious BoR policy to avoid containing China even though it has superior military power (Nye 2013).[3] Thus, in addition to being a system, BoR could be a strategy adopted by any states. Once the stability of relational security develops, the loss of trust of other members of the group is a danger. Between the two imagined extremes of anarchy and harmony, the states typically strive to dismiss uncertainty through negotiated or assimilated convention and institutions on the one hand, and to guard against two potential threats on the other. These threats are the breach in an extant reciprocal relationship and the emergence of those not yet assimilated. The latter threat, which is caused by an undefined relationship, is also a source of opportunity.

In those societies arising from Confucian historiography, BoR becomes the main theme of foreign policy more easily. This is because their domestic culture (politically as well as socially) provides strong support for the application of such a relationship-oriented strategy. BoR emphasizes the importance of reciprocal interaction and harmony in one's kin circle. The goal of harmony does not signify the ethical and virtuous aspects of states' acts. On the contrary, achieving harmony is a comprehensively realistic consideration with the hope for better future gains or fewer future losses by preserving positive relations with all concerned parties. Therefore, BoR is a strategy with a genuinely pragmatic logic that takes seriously national interests into account. Such logic treats the sequence of interests differently.

Stabilized relationships are not the same as rigid relationships. Rather, adjustment is essential to stabilization because the emerging needs of the other side should and must be taken into account to demonstrate benevolence. Accordingly BoR should be adjusted and readjusted according to the conditions that vary across time and space. Moreover, when an actor applies such a strategy, the response from the other side has a crucial impact on the subsequent adjustment of "balancing". If, for instance, when both sides possess negative mutual perceptions, the operation of BoR tend to focus on cooling down the dissatisfaction, making the relations between them seem lukewarm or even alienated. In such a circumstance, if one party decides to initiate the readjustment of its relation with the other party, some apparent and immediate interests might be relinquished in exchange for a better and reconnected relationship with the other side. The occurrence of temporary turbulence from time to time is healthy if it clarifies one's intention to the other side or insinuates the direction of restoration. In comparison, BoP always witnesses the same kind of testing, indicating the relational component of the BoP alliance making.

The relational approach to international rules

The rules of IR threaten relationships. Willingness to make room for the other side best testifies the existence of relationship. BoR encourages arrangements that pragmatically relax the rule enforcement. The national interest calculus is not just about realist BoP or liberal balance of interests. It transcends specific values or systems of power in order to stabilize relationships. Familiar theorists of international systems tend to defend strategies that improve one's power relative to that of others. Classic realists prioritize apparent national interests in relation to other countries' interests in order to determine the costs and benefits of BoP within each state as well as between states. To achieve a BoR, however, a nation will always be ready to concede on issues of power or interests in order to protect relational security and reduce uncertainty in the long run. In the age of global governance, the purpose of BoR pragmatism, for example, is to find a plausible solution to the dilemma between (1) the quest for stable borders, which intervention would undermine, and (2) the quest for recognition by great powers, which resistance to intervention would undermine.

BoR directs one's attention to conflicts of relationships or roles. For example, China's adaptation of pragmatism reflects a realist influence that even an ascendant China cannot escape, as no state can avoid the synchronizing demand of global governance led by great powers, whether it is perceived to be hypocritical or not. China has to learn how to care exclusively for its own relational security in the face of interventionist global forces by supporting them only partially. Simultaneously, China is trying to change the style of global intervention in order to reduce the potential impact of intervention on China's relationships with either great powers or the target state. Pragmatism is thus translated into adapting to both international conditions and the conditions of others in order to ease their worries about one's own intentions. This means that one should avoid creating one rational global society by enforcing specific principles of justice or orders for global governance that seek to synchronize values or procedures between nations.

Chinese pragmatism is at the same time cultural and, to the extent of being cultural, post-Western. Pragmatism of this kind ill fits with multilateral relations, whereby a universal type of norm is called for to synchronize the internal conditions of all parties in that multilateral relationship. China continues to have faith in its ability to protect its national interests by cultivating long-term stability. A stable relationship that ensures certainty and reciprocity is believed to benefit both China and its partners. Chinese pragmatism defines China's style of soft power, which builds on its reputation for never deliberately standing in the way of other states' goals. This means that China is reluctant to attempt any synchronic arrangement in accordance with China's own vision of order. In this way, its leaders hope that China is never a threat to others even though they may dislike Chinese values or institutions. Chinese soft power stands in dramatic contrast to American soft power, which prevails in the IR literature. American soft power emphasizes the capacity of the United States to synchronize other nations' ways of rational thinking into following American values and institutions voluntarily, even though they may dislike the United States itself.

In addition, BoR privileges bilateral relationships over multilateral ones, although it does not preclude multilateral BoR, which is a system composed of multi-bilateral relationships. To lead or even participate in multilateral relations requires one to take an intervening attitude regarding how to synchronize the domestic practices of all the countries (Carlson 2005), unless all relevant parties are applying BoR at the same time, as illustrated by the ASEAN.[4] Any notion of the allegedly right values or procedures positions countries against one another by dividing them into followers and revisionists. Whenever there is a perceived revisionist, there is perceived confrontation. To enhance one's relational security, one minimal strategy is to avoid treating anyone else as a revisionist. The quest for justice undermines relational security, so overly zealous involvement in regulating multilateral relations is always dangerous. In the same vein, hierarchy in IR is usually bilateral (Lake 2009). The sensibility toward bilateral relationship marks BoR's distinctive contribution to the understanding of post-hegemonic IR.

Establishing a bilateral relationship is instrumental to balancing potential threats via alliance formation under the BoP system, but it is a goal in itself under the BoR system. A bilateral relationship benefits both sides if it does not fluctuate in accordance with the perceived power shift or emerging alliance reformation in a multilateral setting. To engage in bilateral relations is at the same time to neutralize multilateral synchronization so that the scenario of global interference with domestic or bilateral relationships can generate little threat. China, for example, does not have to resist the hegemonic order imposed by a superpower, i.e. the United States, if all countries bordering China do not have to take sides between China and the United States. Even though a neighboring country seemingly complies with the hegemonic request for cooperation, it will not seek a change in its reciprocal relationship with China. All-round stabilized bilateral relations along the borders not only reduce the threat of containment by the United States, but would also help render China's own bilateral relationship with the United States less confrontational. This is in sharp contrast with the strategy of BoP, which recommends seeking allies in the face of a rising power or alerts at new strategic alliances between others.

However, the United States is not a stranger to BoR. For example, the US–Mexican and US–Canadian relationships have different foci. For countries under BoR, there is no need to choose sides when coping with two different countries in two different patterns, i.e. a multi-bilateral system. This is particularly relevant to both the United States and China today. As a rising power experiencing expansive interactions, China cannot enforce any value consistently. The United States' rebalancing in Asia likewise has to avoid promoting single values in order to negotiate support from a whole range of partners. Wherever there is a will to retrieve the loose reciprocal relationship, there is regression toward BoR. BoR, instead of BoP, is an ultimate resort for a nation under threat to avoid the dreaded anarchy. One incident that shows the salience of bilateral relationships is when Beijing comments on arms sales by Russia to India. According to the Chinese diplomatic spokesman, "both India and Russia are China's friendly neighbors … China welcomes the growing friendly relationship between India and Russia and believes that the growing of their bilateral relationship is conducive to the world's peace and stability" (EWS 2012). This means that a nation can rationally consider a stable bilateral relationship between its potential enemies conducive to its interests.

International order is maintained under BoR through stable bilateral relationships so that the national security of one country is not threatened by good relationships between others. Investment in BoP would be redundant in the long run. Nevertheless, investment in hard power is always wise because bilateral relationships can still break down and hegemonic power can still coerce neighbors on the borders. This combination of pragmatic preparation for confrontation and pragmatic renouncement of benefits for the sake of any particular relationship appears inconsistent. Their coexistence is the reason that once led the late Lucian

Pye (1988) to misperceive a China that perplexingly tolerates cognitive dissonance and the literature on strategic culture to debate whether or not China has a peaceful strategic culture (Johnston 1995; Mearsheimer 2006; Hui 2008; Wang Yuan-Kang 2010; Buzan 2010). A stable bilateral relationship necessarily follows patterns and rituals, and their emergence as well as their reproduction involves coincidence, volition and consensus. Each stable bilateral relationship has its own history and distinct features that the post-Western IR lauds. That is why the salience of bilateral relationships inevitably causes inconsistency between different countries' bilateral relationships (Wendt 1999).[5]

Theoretical propositions of BoR

In terms of policy, BoR is twofold: to show self-restraint in order to give credit to the relationship and to renounce self-restraint in order to destroy the credit of the other side that betrays the relationship. The BoR quest for security does not necessarily involve an expansion of its influence or an increase in its capacity for control. Instead, the entire or part of the BoR foreign policy orientation involves reciprocal mutuality as opposed to sovereign estrangement between nations. Immediate and concrete gains are considered less useful than stable relationships, which are sometimes achieved even at the expense of such immediate and concrete gains. Based upon the need for a stable relationship, we propose the following three principles of BoR as guidelines for any nation coping with disruptive conditions:

1   In order to enable a return to the long-term calculus that makes little sense of mutual encroachment, when a condition is perceived as potentially threatening, one should resort to compromise to repair it. This principle explains how it is appropriate for a rising power to exercise self-restraint when facing a weaker partner's threat to break the relationship.
2   In order to give credibility to one's commitment to the original relationship as well as relationships elsewhere, when a condition is perceived as being directly threatening, one should resort to restoring via destruction. This principle is an appropriate strategy in the situation of a declining power facing the challenge to its familiar order.
3   In order to avoid the embarrassment in the case where neither one-sided concession nor unilateral sanctions is effective, when a condition is perceived as indirectly threatening, one should resort to a mix of sanctions and repair to rectify it. This principle is an appropriate strategy in the situation of a deadlock between two nations, equal in power, facing a relational problem.

For a nation practicing BoR, determining how threatening a condition may be requires judgment on the possibility of recovery from lost reciprocity. This judgment should be based on both the strength of the extant reciprocal relationships and the resources available for carrying out sanctions as well as compromise. Different leaderships may arrive at different judgments under similar conditions.

Therefore, BoR, aside from being a system, is also a skill, an attitude and a decision.

Judgment on the nature of the threat to the existing reciprocal relationship is critical in the play of BoR. By contrast, the BoP theory is presumably an analytical tool used by scholars to explain the occurrence of a specific policy. Unlike in the BoP theory, in which policy options are considered structurally constrained, the policy under BoR involves judgment. Policy makers need to rationalize whether a particular situation is a total threat that requires the total termination of a relationship, or a minor threat that requires only pampering to repair. What prepares a policy choice is not the power change, but the judgment on the specific relationship. At times, one can observe that smaller powers refuse to concede or that stronger powers renounce the use of sanctions. China is one such country that uses relational consideration deliberately and in accordance with a doctrine.

All nations practice BoR in accordance with the perceived reciprocal role expectations of one another. After 9-11, the United States began to consider terrorist attacks as extremely threatening and responded by invading Afghanistan, which was neither a major power, nor a rising power, nor an owner of energy, but was an actor to be punished for allegedly hosting the enemy of the United States, i.e. Al Qaeda. The United States inflicted on Afghanistan a thorough severing of their relationship. The destruction of a wrong relationship is not a BoP, but a balance of relationships. The Falklands war of 1982 between the United Kingdom and Argentina is another example testifying to the protection of the bilateral relationship with the United Kingdom by the United States. The victorious United Kingdom did not incur the perception of being a threat to the United States despite the display of UK power in America defying the Monroe Doctrine. Rather, the United States facilitated such a display in accordance with the existing reciprocal relationship with the United Kingdom, even at the expense of the long-held principle of refusing any European force to interfere with American affairs.

Confucianism is not required at all to exercise BoR outside the greater Confucian cultural area, though. In contrast, the English School of IR advises on how a nation understands the world order instead of any relational sensibility of a much practical and thus smaller scope. However, the United Kingdom always faithfully stuck with the United States in the latter's interventionist policy, for example. It is not clear if the United Kingdom adopted a world order approach by supporting the US world order or a relational approach to support the United States. Nevertheless, the United Kingdom once relied on enhancing a bilateral relationship to dissolve a multilateral crisis: the United Kingdom's hasty recognition of the People's Republic of China in 1950 at its birth, despite that Communism was the major threat to the US-embraced world order of the time. The early bird effect successfully dissolved the potential crisis of the PRC taking over the British colony of Hong Kong. Preventing the loss of Hong Kong at the time exempted the United Kingdom from the image of decline and also the domino effect on its multilateral empire of African colonies and elsewhere.

By contrast, even if the capacity of a major power to intervene is insufficient, intervention will nonetheless proceed if the violation of its order is judged as direct. After all, an apparently bad relationship has to be made anew by destroying it completely. US intervention in Iraq in 2003, out of at best dubious interest calculus based upon a false intelligence that Iraq possessed weapons of massive destruction, exemplifies the BoR thinking of restoring via destruction. The United States withdrew in 2014 despite the fact that the liberal project was far from being successful. The intervention indicated the higher priority registered in relational rather than value concerns; withdrawal indicated the arrival of the post-hegemonic age.

A major power may refrain from intervention when it judges that a challenge to its cherished order can be better handled if a relationship can be established. This is how China was able to contrive the framework of the Six-Party Talk to bring the United States together with North Korea to the same table. The United States went along not because it did not have the capacity to intervene or sanction but because a relationship with North Korea, once emerging, could bring a longer-term solution. North Korea, in comparison, never hesitates to threaten the much more powerful United States in order to demonstrate its disapproval at a perceived act of betrayal on the United States' side.

For a nation deciding which side to take, the policy of BoR is to avoid enforcing synchronization. BoR leads a nation to cherish bilateral relationships with both the intervening major power and its target states. An extant relationship with the target state encourages caution. An extant relationship with the interventionist country encourages some contribution to intervention. All foreign policy debates over intervention demonstrate the negotiable nature of interventionist policies. Each round of negotiation provides hints about how stable a relationship is or can be. Interventionist practices in accordance with BoR have to be highly individualized and contextualized.

BoR as a system vs BoR as a Chinese School of IR

A plausible Chinese School of IR embedded in Confucianism acquires post-Western characteristics of being post-hegemonic as well as geoculturally distinctive, and yet it also has universal implications. The post-hegemonic order that Confucius endeavored to contrive was to remind kings of their named duties in order for each to ensure security in face of the collapse of All-under-Heaven reigned over by the Son of Heaven. The Son of Heaven continued to symbolize the harmonious state of nature. However, the enforcement no longer relied on his performance, but on the major kings to act together with self-restraint in relational reciprocity. The post-hegemonic order that the post-Western IR has proposed is to re-World sited geocultural distinction in order to trace the re-appropriation of rules of global liberalism and explain the uneven and inconsistent continuation of the hegemonic order. BoR further explains inconsistency as both systemic and bilateral.

While kinship-bred spontaneous benevolence is uniquely Confucian, relational security that eases anxiety toward anarchy under BoP is familiar to all nations, Confucian, Western and post-Western. The readiness to resort to punishment in a seriously disrupted relationship is neither necessarily peaceful nor necessarily violent. BoR is widespread all over the world and throughout history. However, both because BoR predicts inconsistent rather than synchronic ways of rational thinking and because BoR guarantees no immediate consequence of gain, rationality is not as apparent as BoP in the immediate run. The bilateral approach to restoring order no longer places trust on multilateral arrangements where consistency is important. However, the view on what exactly constitutes the proper relationship evolves over time. That is probably the reason why even though nations resort to BoR all the time, students of international politics have not been ready yet to consider it as a system. The obvious tendency of bilateralism is to refrain from taking side in the multilateral setting so that all the other countries can feel secured. Actions are called for only in order to cope with a threatened bilateral relationship. Inconsistency is in actuality a systemic feature.

BoR is not new, nor is it restricted to a few Confucian cultural areas, but IR theorists have failed to acknowledge its ubiquity and longevity. In sum, the relationship in BoR can be defined now – it is a practically governable pattern of mutually agreed reciprocal tolerance. But, to discuss how universally applicable BoR can be in IR misses the point of studying BoR. This is because BoR is mainly bilateral and contextual. Whether or not a stable bilateral relationship can emerge is the result of both coincidence and volition. This is why BoR as a theory is not necessarily universally present or recognized, but as a practice it is plausible, pragmatic, sporadic and therefore universally ready. In this sense, BoR is retrievable anywhere there is inconsistency or incomprehensible compromise/sanction. The Confucian culture, which cherishes long-term reciprocal relationship, prepares Confucian leaders to think and desire BoR in substitution for a BoP or a balance of interest. Each other culture has its own route to such realization. This is why BoR is different from repeated Prisoners' Dilemmas or transaction-cost institutionalism, both of which advocate a synchronic measure of rationality likewise of a longer term.

The Christian tradition that stresses ontological integrity rather than a relational self can still incorporate BoR as long as the historical moment enables a pair of countries to appreciate their relationship more than the immediate national interests of each. That BoR and BoP are parallel systems in international politics resembles the political system and the social system in domestic politics or individual self-actualization and group-belonging within individual identity. Such a situation is not rare because the quest for stability and certainty answers directly to the desire of controlling the potentially unrestrained violence of anarchy. The decision to enter a particular system depends on judgment but the decision in itself is inescapable. BoP and BoR together complete the theory of international systems. The question for IR scholars to study is how a nation opts for a particular system. In actuality, this means that the post-hegemonic order relies more on a nation state to decide first ontologically about which kind of state it wants to be – a participant of hegemonic order, or a relational agent engrossed in geocultural distinction.

The Chinese IR defined by relational sensibility participates in the quest for post-hegemonic order via its double-edged engagements. It engages the post-Western quest via a geoculturally distinctive belief in the spontaneity of mutual benevolence between nation states complying with the metaphor of kinship. It engages the hegemonic liberal order via a revisit to a pre-modern hierarchy that stresses harmony and self-restraint. Under BoR, BoP only takes place when a reciprocal bilateral relationship is not enforceable. On the other hand, the reciprocal bilateral relationship is the solution to cases whereby nations subscribing to BoP fail to control anarchy. The two systems necessarily switch in cycles. The Chinese IR thus predicts the use of compromise to reproduce bilateral relationships regardless of one party's even stronger power status. It also predicts the use of sanction to restore a reciprocal bilateral relationship regardless of one party's even weaker power status. BoR is a skill that all can possess, a decision that reflects one's choice of system, and a spontaneous order of self-restraint that relies on a stable bilateral relationship to control anarchy.

Notes

1 Such arguments could been found in Confucius' saying, which was recorded in *The Analects of Confucius*, 13.5, 14.1, and 14.42.
2 Israel has viewed Iran as its most dangerous enemy. Iran's pursuit of nuclear weapons has caused serious tensions not only between Jerusalem and Teheran, but also between Jerusalem and Washington. Yet in October 2012, Israel's defense minister has announced that Israel "interpreted Iran's conversion of some enriched uranium to fuel rods for civilian use as evidence that Iran had delayed ambitions to build a nuclear weapon" and decided to soften its position of imposing military strikes on Iran (Gladston 2012).
3 Joseph Nye, for example, praises the policy signals that "ensure that China doesn't feel encircled or endangered.... sometimes America's power is greater when we act with others rather than merely over others" (Nye 2013).
4 The Association of Southeast Asian Nations (ASEAN) was established in 1967, the founding states (Indonesia, Malaysia, Philippines, Singapore and Thailand) had made it clear that "noninterference in the internal affairs of one another" is one of the six fundamental principles for ASEAN members. For more details about ASEAN and the founding principles, visit its official website, online, available at: www.asean.org/asean/about-asean.
5 To a certain extent, this lack of consistency is not unlike Wendtian constructivism whereby Lockean and Hobbesian orders may coexist (Wendt 1999). However, there is a specific order in each of the Wendtian sub-systems, while there is no such order under BoR.

11 Constructing a Chinese School of IR as sociological reality

Intellectual engagement and knowledge production

Yongjin Zhang

> We must never forget that genuine schools [of thought] are sociological realities. They have their structures – relations between leaders and followers – their flags, their battle cries, their moods, and their all-too human interests. Their antagonisms come within the general sociology of group antagonisms and of party warfare. Victory and conquest, defeat and loss of ground, are in themselves values for such schools and part their very existence.
>
> (Joseph Schumpeter 1994: 783)

This chapter provides an alternative, and perhaps also complementary, narrative that looks at the growth of the discipline and the construction of a Chinese IR epistemic community as constitutive of the long march towards theoretical innovation in Chinese international studies today. It takes Chinese intellectual engagement with trans-Atlantic IR and the diffusion of ideas as a central analytical focus. Through this interpretative lens, I argue, in particular, that there have been three epistemic turns in Chinese intellectual engagement with trans-Atlantic IR in the last 35 years. More specifically, I argue that the diffusion of trans-Atlantic IR constitutes part of, and has been driven by, a critical move from epistemic optimism to epistemic discontent, and from epistemic skepticism to epistemic reflexivity in international studies in China. The latest epistemic turn to purposive reflexivity has led to promising indigenous production of knowledge in China. These epistemic turns, I further argue, are integral to the long social processes of constructing Chinese approaches to theorizing IR, as international studies in China have moved decisively from simply knowledge acquisition to knowledge production/creation. In so doing, I also examine the extent to which the Chinese School of IR has become a constructed sociological reality.

Like many other intellectual enterprises, the disciplinary growth of IR in China has had its fair share of pitfalls, contentions, conflicts, anxieties, agonies as well as triumph, joys and accomplishments. While I maintain that the arrival of a Chinese School of IR remains a promise to be fulfilled, it is hardly disputable that the intellectual world of Chinese IR has changed dramatically in this social process. International studies as new lines of intellectual action, the emergence of a self-conscious intellectual community, and the growing global networks of IR scholars working in China are but part of the dramatic intellectual changes of Chinese IR. In advancing this set of arguments, the chapter also aims to show that the painstaking search for new theoretical knowledge in Chinese IR promotes greater inclusiveness and diversity in the discipline, a shared aspiration of a global IR epistemic community. It is this shared aspiration that drives intellectual changes in Chinese IR, which have in turn contributed to making IR 'a vibrant, innovative, and inclusive enterprise that reflects the voices, experiences, interests, and identities of all humankind' (Acharya 2014: 657) and to reimagining IR as a more inclusive global discipline.

Only in China

International studies is widely regarded in China today as a hot subject of inquiry and an influential discipline in Chinese foreign policy making. In the last 35 years, the disciplinary development of IR in China and the growth of the Chinese IR epistemic community have both had accomplishments and frustrations, which are constitutive of their very existence; and both can claim battles won and lost as their achievements and disappointments. How a new and burgeoning intellectual enterprise in the early 1980s has grown into a thriving discipline in China today has a story of its own (Wang and Yuan 2006). It is a story that cannot be told separately either from China's opening and reform in the first instance, or from the rise of China in the twenty-first century. To the extent that some aspects of this story have already been told in this volume or elsewhere, four existing accounts with different interpretation are worth considering briefly in our discussions.

Qin Yaqing (2011b) looks at the development of IR theory in China since 1979 as framed by three debates. The first was between orthodox (i.e. conservative) and reformist scholars on the assessment of what characterized the international order of the day, 'war and revolution' or 'peace and development'. The second was between 'Chinese realists and liberals' on how best to realize China's national interest. And third is a tripartite contention, between Chinese realists, liberals and constructivists, on China's peaceful rise. Wang Yiwei's (2009) narrative divides the evolution of Chinese IR studies into four stages, which he calls respectively, the starting–Marxism period (the 1960s to the 1980s), the learning–copying period (the 1980s), the stimulus–response period (the 1990s), and the reflecting–constructing period (the 2000s). Wang Yizhou (2006a) emphasizes the historical continuity of international studies in China more than its fragmentation. He sees five periods in the development of international studies in China in the twentieth century, i.e. the pre-1949 period (individual exploration and gradual awareness of the subject), the 1949 to 1963 period (early government efforts at disciplinary building), the 1963 to 1978 period (the leftist intervention), the 1978 to the early 1990s period (learning from and introducing trans-Atlantic IR), and the post-Cold War period (the millennium change and new era in IR). Finally, Shi Bin (2006) constructed his story centered on the enduring, and sometime divisive, contention about the necessity and imperatives of 'Sinicizing' IR theory in pursuit of either IR theories 'with Chinese characteristics', or a Chinese School of IR. .

While these accounts tell the same story of the disciplinary growth and theoretical development of IR in China in different manners, all of them note the diffusion of trans-Atlantic IR to China through Chinese learning and the introduction of Western IR scholarship after China's opening and reform in 1978 as crucial in knowledge acquisition and dissemination in China. They offer, however, only passing observation, if at all, of the unique historical and political circumstances that made the diffusion of trans-Atlantic IR to China possible and under which such diffusion began to have an impact on the disciplinary growth of IR in China. A proper understanding of the 'Western impact', to borrow from John King Fairbank (Teng and Fairbank 1954), on the birth and growth of IR as a discipline in China needs to start from an appreciation of the inhospitable terrains in the late 1970s that opposed and resisted the diffusion of Western ideas in China.

Politically, post-Mao China remained a revolutionary power and repressive state hostile to Western ideas. It continued to champion a Marxism-induced revolutionary outlook of the world order. Intellectually, China between 1949 and 1979 was regarded as what Wu Daying (2000) called 'the desert of social sciences'. Little genuine social science research existed during this period. Disciplinary destruction rather than disciplinary construction was the order of the day. Internationally, China had been alienated from international society after 1949. Full diplomatic relations between China and the United States was not established until the end of 1978. Although China returned to the United Nations in 1971, it did not have membership in key international economic institutions such as the International Monetary Fund and the World Bank until 1980 (Zhang 1998). Such alienation had an unfortunate intellectual consequence, that is, there had been virtually no 'professional communication' between Chinese scholars and scholars in the West, not just in IR but also more broadly in social sciences, until the late 1970s, not to speak of shared production or consumption of ideas, concepts or theories.

How were the seeds then first sewn in China's 'desert of social sciences' in 1979 for different social science disciplines to grow? And how to explain the rapid diffusion of trans-Atlantic IR in such inhospitable political and intellectual terrains? Answers to these two questions can be usefully sought through exploring the Hoffmannian explanatory variables, namely, 'the convergence of three factors: intellectual dispositions, institutional opportunities and political circumstances' (Hoffmann 1977: 45). In China's case, though, it is the changing political circumstances that are decisive in either creating or securing institutional opportunities, which are in turn conducive to bringing into full play intellectual predispositions in promoting the diffusion of trans-Atlantic IR to China.

The opening and reform launched in December 1978 is conventionally regarded as the single most important political change in the post-Mao China, the start of China's second revolution (Harding 1987). This is undoubtedly the single most important socio-political change that opened the possibility of the diffusion of trans-Atlantic IR to China. Equally important, however, are the battles to reconfigure Chinese politics that had prepared politically and intellectually for China's historical opening and reform. Among them are the re-evaluation of the Cultural Revolution, the debates on Marxist humanism, the repudiation of the 'two whatevers' ('We will resolutely uphold whatever policy decisions Chairman Mao made, and unswervingly follow whatever instructions Chairman Mao gave') and the triumph of 'practice is the sole criterion of truth' (Baum 1994; Su 1996). It is none other than Deng Xiaoping himself who personally and purposively instigated these changing political circumstances that prove to have had direct bearing on the birth and growth of IR as a discipline.

Deng also put a personal mark on the restoration and development of social science disciplines in China. In a speech made on 30 March 1979 at the Chinese Communist Party's theoretical works meeting, Deng (1994: 180–181) remarked,

> We have neglected for many years research of political science, law, sociology as well as world politics. We need to catch up now in a timely manner. We have admitted that we lag behind the West in natural sciences. We should also admit that we also lag behind the West in social sciences.

These words articulated by Deng, China's would-be paramount leader, politically sanctioned the rebuilding of social sciences as an integral part of China's opening and reform. They legitimized the disciplinary (re)construction, encouraged learning from the West and shopping for ideas as indispensable in catching up with the West. Though the ideological straightjacket remained very tight, political circumstances in general became more tolerant and encouraging for the revitalization of social science research in China. Deng's highlighting of both political science and world politics as in need of advancement is particularly significant in our analytical context.

These political changes opened up a number of institutional opportunities, which were seized upon quickly to institutionalize international studies in China, although there was widely shared awareness of acute challenges for rebuilding or constructing social sciences in China. The Chinese Academy of Social Sciences (CASS), established only in May 1977, took the lead in the revival and reorganization of social science research in China. The Institute of Sociology and the Institute of World Economics and Politics were among the first research arms to be established within the CASS in January and December 1980 respectively. Also in 1980, the Chinese Association for the Studies of History of IR was inaugurated. By the time the Institute of Political Science was established rather belatedly in 1985, CASS could claim a cluster of research institutes that engaged in IR research in addition to the Institute of World Economics and Politics. These range from the Institute of American Studies, to the Institute of European Studies, and to the Institute of Asia-Pacific Studies, as well as institutes of Japanese Studies, of African Studies, of Latin American Studies, and of Soviet and Eastern European Studies. These institutes promoted mostly area-focused studies of IR. They proved less conducive to more systemic level enquiries and theoretical exploration of IR. Interestingly, CASS still claims no institute of international studies/politics. This is a severe limit of institutional invention within CASS in promoting theoretical studies of IR.

Chinese universities, which began to take in undergraduates and graduate students through the restored nationwide exams system in 1978, started to explore these institutional opportunities too. Departments of IR/politics were established one after another in universities other than Peking, Renmin and Fudan, the three universities that had set up international studies departments at the government direction in 1963. Most recent accounts claim that around 60 Chinese universities now have IR related degree awarding programs (Wang Yiwei 2009; Shambaugh 2011). The success of institutionalizing international studies in Chinese universities can perhaps best be seen in the recognition of both IR and international politics as two independent 'sub-disciplines' (tier-two disciplines) within the primary (tier-one) discipline of political science on the disciplinary list authorized for circulation by the Ministry of Education. It should be noted that in China, teaching and research in international politics/relations is institutionally separate from political science in most universities. This proves rather problematic for disciplinary building of IR.

The idea of a research-led university, imported mainly from the United States, would later inspire the establishment of various research centers in Chinese universities; the establishment of the Institute of International Studies at Tsinghua University in 1997 is a prime example. In the 1980s, beyond universities, national foreign and security policy research bureaucracy, both civilian and military, was revamped. Research institutes under the Ministry of Foreign Affairs and the CCP International Liaison Department were either revived or reorganized. Out of such reorganization emerged, for example, the China Institute of Contemporary International Relations (CICIR) in the late 1970s, which would be put under the newly established Ministry of State Security in 1982. In the 1980s, a cluster of research institutes affiliated with various government ministries and the PLA constituted an integral part of the evolving institutional landscape of Chinese international studies. Though networking its various constituent parts would take time and conscious efforts, this rapidly changing institutional landscape heralded the emergence of an IR epistemic community in China. Institutional and intellectual networks have become ever since an integral part of the IR disciplinary evolution in China. For all intents and purposes, the first national conference on international studies in China held in Shanghai in 1987 was a precursor to such an eventuality.

One other crucial institutional opportunity that was created was for Chinese social science scholars to exchange ideas with their counterparts in the West, which has proven to have lasting effects in exerting the 'Western impact' on China's international studies. Such 'exchange' historically meant mostly importing ideas from the West. The sense of crisis in the wake of the devastation of the Cultural Revolution and the imperative for enlightened decision-making in China as China pursued its opening and reform generated the demand for ideas, and indeed the need for shopping for ideas. This is an opportunity and an imperative applicable to sociology, political science and international studies alike (Zhao 2008; Deng 2010). As I have argued elsewhere (Zhang 2003: 101–103; see also Shambaugh 2011: 343–346), this institutional opportunity was also exploited effectively by a condominium of American foundations and academics to promote American studies of IR in China. The diffusion of trans-Atlantic IR has, in other words, sociological explanations.

It is therefore not pure coincidence that key works of trans-Atlantic IR, particularly its theoretical canons produced in the United States, were quickly introduced into China through 'a translation boom' (Qin 2007: 317). They 'were imported *en mass*', to use Deng Zhenglai's (2010) description of the diffusion of Western political theories in China at its early stages. In Qin Yaqing's (2012c: 68) description, 'new ideas in humanities and social sciences in the West, and especially in the United States, were pouring into China's intellectual communities, helping to establish or re-establish most of the academic disciplines, IR included'.

It should be noted, however, that to an important extent, the condominium of American foundations and academics only catered to the needs of Chinese scholars with particular intellectual predispositions at the time when social sciences in China were going decisively beyond, if not totally rejecting, orthodox Marxist/Mao ideologies. After over 30 years of insulation from IR epistemic communities in the West, the intellectual hunger was palpable in the nascent Chinese scholarly community. The possibility of learning from the developed West in terms of theories, ideas and methods of international studies held a tempting appeal to Chinese scholars, an appeal that was further intensified by the imperative to build IR as a new discipline from scratch in China. This may explain why, even though the ideological straightjacket was still rather tight in the 1980s, there was little real resistance to the diffusion of Western ideas in international studies in China. Trans-Atlantic IR was more or less embraced, not just because of its appealing theories and newish ideas, but also because it provided a disciplinary model to follow.

Pervasive among certain groups of Chinese IR scholars at the time was a kind of epistemic optimism, believing that scholarship, and therefore knowledge, was already provided for them in trans-Atlantic IR, and they could simply obtain it through learning. Constructing Chinese IR was therefore first and foremost a matter of knowledge acquisition and dissemination. There were, in other words, great intellectual expectations that China could borrow from the West not just ideas, but also theories and structures to lay the foundation for the disciplinary growth of IR in China. This was a period when a tenacious effort was made to introduce trans-Atlantic IR theories from abroad. Qin (2007) listed 85 key theoretical works in English that were translated into Chinese and published by five major presses in China by March 2007. In the characterization of Wang Yiwei (2009: 105), 'a romantic view of the West dominated, and scholars copied Western scholarship without much regard for Chinese perspectives and ideas'. As I will argue later in this chapter, this epistemic optimism would be replaced before long by epistemic skepticism, as intellectual discontent mounted gradually with the universalist claims of trans-Atlantic IR, and the hegemonic nature of rationalist theoretical discourse.

Be that as it may, the tentative start of the diffusion of trans-Atlantic IR in China in the early 1980s must be understood against the convergence of a set of unique historical, political and intellectual circumstances that gave birth to the discipline of IR in China. Only in China could such a tentative diffusion of trans-Atlantic IR have played so central a role in providing Chinese IR as an emerging field of studies with some of the general intellectual foundations it needed to claim its disciplinary status. More importantly, perhaps, it started an intellectual engagement between IR epistemic communities in and outside China for the mutual understanding and cross-fertilization of ideas. In so doing, trans-Atlantic IR was firmly embedded in the Chinese knowledge repertoire of IR and became indispensable in the IR disciplinary construction in China. As is discussed below, further diffusion of trans-Atlantic IR would lead to more epistemic turns in Chinese scholars' long march in advancing Chinese knowledge of IR and in their tortuous search for theoretical innovation.

Even in China

Writing in 1998, Ole Wæver (1998: 723) lamented that national IR scholarly communities around the world 'still follow the American debates, and teach American theories'. China is no exception. Qin Yaqing (2011b) captures rather eloquently, if also unwittingly, the internalization and the entrenchment of American theoretical discourse in China. In his account of the 'progress' made in the construction of Chinese IR theory, Qin (2011b) notes two particular debates since the 1990s. One is between Chinese realists and Chinese liberals, focusing on whether China should assume the identity of a Hobbesian power or a Lockean state in pursuit of its vital national interest. The other is contention among three groups of Chinese theorists, which in Qin's formulation are Chinese realists, Chinese liberals and Chinese constructivists, over the question of whether a rising China is and/or should be a revisionist challenger or a status quo power in international society.

It is telling that Qin divides Chinese theorists into either the two- or the three-group formation largely according to the theoretical orientations, as he understands, of those Chinese theorists informed principally by neo-realism (Kenneth Waltz), neo-liberal institutionalism (Robert Keohane and Joseph Nye), and constructivism (Alex Wendt). In Qin's narrative of debates among Chinese IR theorists, critical, reflectivist and non-positivist approaches are largely invisible or non-existent. Qin's account is equally telling of the dominance of American theories in another way. That is, even when the empirical question is unequivocally about China, there is simply no escape for Chinese IR discourse to be overwhelmingly informed by the mainstream IR theoretical perspectives and insights diffused and disseminated to China mostly from the United States.

The prevailing influence of trans-Atlantic IR in Chinese IR theoretical discourse has one other expression, i.e. many meta-theoretical debates and quests of trans-Atlantic IR have been reproduced in China in different fashions and on different scales. The quest for science, which equally troubled political science in China (Deng 2010), raised important questions of methodology and epistemology as vital in constructing IR as a scientific discipline in China (Zhou 2006).

It led to a fierce, but ultimately inconclusive debate about whether IR is science or art in China (Zhou 2006; Wang 2007a; Ren 2008; Ren this volume). Understanding and explaining as two contending forms of analysis in IR were also discussed as part of this debate (Yuan 2003). The claim of value-free social enquiry was similarly contested and debated. One other meta-theoretical question that was raised, but not much debated, is the importance of ontology in the theoretical construction. Noting the central role played by ontological questions in sustaining the theoretical hegemony of trans-Atlantic IR, Li Yihu, for example, argued that a breakthrough in inventing an alternative ontology is 'a precondition for constructing a Chinese School of IR' and in overcoming Western hegemony in IR discourse (Li 2005; see also Shi 2006).

These accounts of dominance and reproduction are, however, only a partial picture of the evolving Chinese IR discourse. The theoretical landscape of Chinese IR is much more pluralistic and contentious than Qin's tripartite formation suggests, even if one concedes that they are three dominant theoretical orientations among Chinese IR scholars. As one rather comprehensive survey shows, the diffusion of ideas of trans-Atlantic IR in China is multifarious. *IR Studies in China, 1995–2005* edited by Wang and Yuan (2006) includes detailed accounts in individual chapters on the diffusion and dissemination of feminism and the English School, for example, in Chinese IR theoretical discourse (Li 2006; Miao 2006). It provides abundant evidence to show that Chinese IR scholars took an increasingly eclectic theoretical approach in their analysis of important questions in global politics.

The accounts in this survey and other recent writings also reveal that as the diffusion of trans-Atlantic IR moved from importation to internalization and indigenization in China, there was growing awareness among Chinese IR scholars of the contentious nature of theoretical discourse of trans-Atlantic IR and disputations among contending mainstream theoretical claims. There emerged mounting intellectual discontent among Chinese IR scholars about trans-Atlantic IR. Most acutely, such intellectual discontent was about the intellectual hegemony of the American IR discourse, about some knowledge claims of both universality and neutrality, and about the inability of existing theories to help explain the most important puzzles central to Chinese IR. Such intellectual discontent heralded a shift from epistemic skepticism about knowledge claims to epistemic reflexivity in Chinese IR. It is an important driver that prompted a decisive turn from simple knowledge acquisition to attempts at knowledge production/creation in the Chinese IR epistemic community.

First, dynamic contentions within the Chinese IR epistemic community were inspired, partially at least, by disputations among contending schools of thought in trans-Atlantic IR. It led to the questioning of the legitimacy of the intellectual hegemony of rationalist theories, in terms of both the production and the dissemination of ideas, which happened to be produced mostly in the United States. It encouraged an interest in a search for alternative theories and worldviews. Arguably, it is such discontent that helped develop an appreciation among Chinese IR scholars of the English School of IR, and subsequently, its diffusion in China

(Zhang 2003). The English School is, as is widely acknowledged among Chinese IR scholars, a Euro-centric approach and an integral part of trans-Atlantic IR. Its diffusion in China owes much, however, to its insistence on philosophical enquiry, its legitimation of historical research in theorizing IR, its emphasis on ethic and normative questions, and its methodological pluralism. Ultimately, the English School shows that a different kind of theoretical knowledge can be and has been produced of IR. Rightly or wrongly, the English School, as a non-mainstream IR theoretical approach, is also seen as an anti-hegemonic discourse (Wang and Buzan this volume). The diffusion of the English School serves a specific purpose, i.e. as a counter-balance to otherwise overwhelmingly American enterprise (Miao 2006; Ren 2009a; Zhang Qianming 2009).

Second, there was growing skepticism about the claims of neutrality and the universal applicability of theoretical knowledge produced in trans-Atlantic IR. As discussed earlier, the value-free enquiry in social science had already been contested in the methodological debates among Chinese IR scholars. For Chinese scholars, the English School proves the contingent nature of knowledge claims by demonstrating that alternative theoretical knowledge is possible. Chinese scholars also increasingly questioned the relationship between power and the production of knowledge in IR. '[The] theory of international politics is always the theory of, for and by great power', Wang Yizhou (1998a: 4) asserted. Tracing the development of IR theories in the United States, Mei Ran (2000) came to the conclusion that 'IR theories' conventionally referred to in the Chinese discourse are no other than American IR theories; and that IR as an American social science is in essence a great power social science. These understandings come tentatively close to Ken Booth's (1996: 331) claim that 'the institutionalization of the subject [of IR] and its development underlines simply and clearly the crucial relationship between the global distribution of power and global production of knowledge'. For Wang Yiwei (2009: 116), Western IR theories reflect but a partial truth. One of the imperatives for the theoretical knowledge creation in China is therefore to help 'restore Western IR to the status of local theories'.

Third, Chinese scholars were increasingly unhappy that the theoretical knowledge they acquired from trans-Atlantic IR offered little help in making sense of ongoing debates such as the clash of civilizations or the China threat in the 1990s. Nor could it provide insights into the prospect of the peaceful rise of China or the policy challenges China is likely to confront as a rising power. This is so not only because trans-Atlantic IR theories are 'deeply rooted in the particularities and peculiarities of European history, the rise of the West to world power' (Acharya and Buzan 2007: 293), but also because seeing, knowing and doing international politics in the national site of the United States is clearly different from seeing and doing that from a distinctively Chinese perspective. Historical circumstances (China's search for wealth and power after the Opium War), political demands (exercise of sovereign rights) and policy concerns (national and regime survival and economic development) dictate that China has distinctive 'master research narratives' in IR (Alagappa 2011: 204), which generate and entail disciplinary knowledge of IR that is appreciably different from that of the United States.

International studies, in other words, serve different social purposes and should have something to say about foreign policy agenda in China. IR studies in Asia, Alagappa (2011: 196) observes,

> Has had a predominantly practical orientation with emphasis on understanding and interpreting the external world to develop suitable policy responses. Knowledge production through development of a hierarchy of law-like propositions has not been priority. Strong practical orientation contributed to emphasis on historical, area and policy studies.

This strongly resonates Wæver (1998: 694) that IR 'is specifically influenced by the foreign policy orientation of a country'.

The diffusion of trans-Atlantic IR in this manifestation has therefore paradoxically dual effects on the Chinese IR discourse. While it reinforces the dominance of American IR theories in China, it also provokes intellectual discontent and stimulates debates that go to the heart of the relationship between power and the production of knowledge, and of the contingent nature of social knowledge. Chinese scholars began to reflect on Karl Popper's arguments about the central role of refutation and disputation in the growth of scientific knowledge in IR (Wang Yizhou 2006c). There was a decisive epistemic turn from optimism to skepticism. 'A state of dissatisfaction', claims Stanley Hoffmann (1977: 59), 'is a goad to research'. In the case of Chinese IR, it is also, one could add, a goad to theoretical 'innovation by opposition' (Collins 2000). This is an argument that has been extensively developed by Peter Kristensen and Ras Nielsen (2013a) in understanding Chinese scholars' search for theoretical innovation.

For better or worse, trans-Atlantic IR was further entrenched in this fashion in IR disciplinary growth in China and in advancing Chinese knowledge of IR. In the Chinese IR epistemic community, as in many others on the margins of the global IR epistemic community, there have long been articulations of complaints about and resistance to the much criticized intellectual hegemony of American IR. Yet, it is only recently that trans-Atlantic IR theories have been increasingly seen as inadequate in explaining the systemic transformation of the unipolar world, in understanding foreign policy challenges a rising China has to confront, and more broadly, in meeting the needs distinctive to Chinese IR. Yet, in so far as IR is part of the 'colonial expenses' of social sciences (Grovogui 2013: 248), challenges are formidable for Chinese IR scholars as latecomers to the IR theorization enterprise, as they cannot escape from the existing vocabulary, concepts, categories and theoretical tools, and they can hardly dispense with the existing 'universals' in their attempts at theorization. They have to wrestle with an acute intellectual dilemma, i.e. trans-Atlantic IR is both indispensable and inadequate in their intellectual attempts at knowledge production and theoretical innovation.

Because of China

There has been longstanding discomfort within the Chinese IR epistemic community that Chinese experience in modern IR after the Opium War in 1840 has been neglected in the theorization of IR. Chinese debates on whether the distinctive national social experience should be taken into consideration in pursuit of constructing China's own international theory can be traced back to the 1980s. It was at the first national conference on IR theory in Shanghai in 1987 that the question of constructing an IR theory 'with Chinese characteristics' was first raised. One could argue with some persuasion that in the 1980s the call was intuitive, and it is mainly the politics of legitimation of the subject that is behind this call. More than 20 years later, the similar call, whether it is for constructing an IR theory 'with Chinese characteristics', or for 'indigenizing' IR in China, or for constructing a Chinese School of IR, is no longer just a reflection of political concerns. It is backed up by intellectual justifications. It is consciously reflective and is driven by a notable turn from epistemic skepticism to epistemic reflexivity. Theoretical innovation was explicitly called for at a national conference on IR theories held in Shanghai in 2004, which would 'embody the Chinese characteristics, incorporate both Marxist international thought and the scientific core of Western IR theories, and cultivate the Chinese cultural heritage' (Shi 2006).

Cultural and civilizational heritage, as will be discussed later, have indeed become important resources for theoretical innovation of Chinese IR for knowledge production. There is, however, also a political logic facilitating the turn to epistemic reflexivity. 'The growth of the discipline' in the United States, Stanley Hoffmann (1977: 47) once remarked, 'cannot be separated from the American role in world affairs after 1945'. Hoffmann (1977: 49) also cautioned that scholars should be aware of 'their intellectual dependence on the status of their country, and the ambitions of their political elite' in their attempts to produce knowledge. By the same token, the changing great power status of China in global politics would have significant implications for the growth of Chinese IR, as global disparities in material power and wealth between China and the US – and more broadly the democratic West – are narrowing significantly and changing rapidly. In sociological terms, large-scale political and economic transformations are important because they 'indirectly set off periods of intellectual change', although ideas 'do not reduce to surrounding social conditions' (Collins 2000: 82) nor can they be attributed to purely contingent local construction of meaning. For Randall Collins (2000: 51),

> the outmost level of macro-causality does not so much directly determine the kinds of ideas created as give an impetus for stability or change in the organizations which support intellectual careers, and this moulds in turn the networks within them.

The rapid rise of China and China's changing role in global politics, in this reading, provides stimulus for the latest epistemic turn in Chinese IR in three ways. It accentuates Chinese scholars' awareness of the deficiency of the explanatory power of existing trans-Atlantic IR theories. It makes it imperative to have a theoretical construct and research agenda that cater to understanding a rising China's strategic challenges and meeting the policy needs of a rising power. It has provided central empirical problems and analytical puzzles to theorize IR from a distinctive Chinese perspective, among which are China's changing identity in global politics, its integration into international society, and the prospect of its peaceful rise (Qin 2011b). One could add also the question of the legitimacy of rising Chinese power and therefore also the legitimacy of the post-American liberal global order (Zhang 2015b). To the extent that IR theory constructs the world that it purports to describe and is constitutive of the reality that it addresses, to paraphrase Acharya and Buzan (2007: 290), Chinese scholars have a major interest in being part of the game.

Insistence on IR theory with 'Chinese characteristics', however, has its own perils. One particular dilemma has troubled the Chinese IR epistemic community in the last 35 years in both their knowledge acquisition and knowledge production. That is, which is the key question that knowledge acquisition and knowledge production should try to address: 'What should we know?' or 'What should we do?' This was a dilemma that used to confront American IR. American scholars, Hoffmann asserted, 'have tried to know as much as we needed in order to know how to act – rarely more' (Hoffmann 1977: 58–59). Given the historical and political circumstances of the disciplinary rebirth and growth in China, and the challenges that have confronted Chinese elite and policy establishments as China rises rapidly, knowledge acquisition and production in Chinese IR has clearly skewed towards addressing what should we do, that is towards what Qin Yaqing (2007: 314) calls 'action-oriented' theory. The 'practical orientation' of theoretical and disciplinary knowledge rooted in China's traditional philosophy and statecraft further amplifies this problem.

There is, therefore, a real risk of IR in China 'sloping from research-with-practical-effects to practical-advocacy-derived-from-research' (Hoffmann 1977: 56) in constructing IR theory as 'guidelines for action' (Qin 2007: 314). Even if the Chinese IR epistemic community collectively avoids the peril of being co-opted by power and absorbed into the policy world (see Noesselt in this volume for more discussion), addressing only China-centered issues and policy concerns in order to answer the 'what should we do' question would relegate Chinese IR to a level of analysis that is not conducive to theoretical innovation. As Acharya and Buzan (2007: 298) caution, 'As a rule, it is perhaps fair to say that the more closely linked the study of IR is to government and foreign policy establishment, the less theoretical it is likely to be'.

Be that as it may, the continued call for an IR theory with Chinese characteristics, together with such poignant question as why there is no Chinese IR theory (Qin 2007; Yan 2011d), have become battle cries in the construction of a Chinese School of IR. To the extent that these battle cries have been answered, three distinctive research projects are worth considering briefly below, which are representative of the collective efforts of Chinese scholars at facilitating theoretical innovation. They have produced considerable theoretical ferment around the questions of local IR knowledge production in China.

Yan Xuetong: the Tsinghua Approach and rediscovering Chinese international thought

The so-called Tsinghua Approach has been led and advocated by Yan Xuetong, a leading Chinese IR scholar and a self-identified realist (see Xu and Sun this volume for more detailed discussion). It is labelled the Tsinghua Approach by one of its critics (Zhang 2012) because a distinctive research program aimed at rediscovering ancient Chinese international thought has been conducted by a small group of researchers with institutional links with the Institute of International Studies headed by Yan at Tsinghua University. The Institute runs two key journals, one in Chinese, *Guoji Zhengzhi Kexue* (Quarterly Journal of International Political Science), and the other in English, the *Chinese Journal of International Politics*, now published by Oxford University Press. It is through these two journals that new scholarship and knowledge produced by this research program has been disseminated both in China and internationally. The publication by the prestigious Princeton University Press in 2011 of *Ancient Chinese Thought, Modern Chinese Power*, edited by Daniel Bell, makes available to a global audience selected works by Yan as well as works by his associates and critics. It helps stimulate further debates about the promise and the peril of the Tsinghua Approach to theorizing IR in the global discipline (Chou 2011; Cunningham-Cross and Callahan 2011; Hui 2012).

For Yan and his associates, the common philosophical and political discourse among all contending schools of thought in pre-Qin China (771–221 BC) represents a valuable and unexplored intellectual source for theoretical innovation. The 'battle of ideas' among ancient Chinese philosophers in this period prompted in particular the growth of what is referred to as an inter-state political philosophy in ancient China. More specifically, it is the ideas and conceptualizations of power, authority, hegemony, war and justice by ancient Chinese philosophers that they are interested in exploring for producing new theoretical knowledge. For this purpose, they have interrogated how morality informs interest and is related to order, why hierarchy is conducive to stability, and why and how moral leadership fosters humane authority as supreme power.

One crucial finding of this archaeology of knowledge is that the conceptualization of power by ancient Chinese philosophers differs conspicuously from that of classical and contemporary Western thinkers. While not denying the importance of material power, ancient Chinese philosophical discourse sees power as derived mostly, if not exclusively, from non-material sources with a firm moral claim. Morality therefore is the core of any claim to political power, as it gives legitimacy to the claim of power. There is, in other words, an ethical dimension in any claim to power, if the legitimacy of power is not based on coercion. There is at the same time an emphasis on 'the context sensitivity of Confucian ethics' (Roetz 2012: 258).

It follows that there are three distinctive ways of exercising power in constructing a hierarchical international order: humane authority (*wangquan*), hegemony (*baquan*), and tyranny (*qiangquan*). Humane authority, based on the power of persuasion rather than coercion, is the highest form of rulership with strong moral claims, for example from the Mandate of Heaven, for its legitimacy and leadership. Most interestingly, the exercise and acceptance of humane authority does not rest on claims to material power. International order based on the exercise of humane authority is the most stable and long lasting. 'A humane authority under heaven relies upon its ultra-powerful moral force to maintain its comprehensive state power in first place in the system' (see Bell's chapter in Yan 2011a: 13). Tyranny (*qiangquan*) on the other hand is 'the lowest form of rule, relying exclusively on military force and stratagems'. For such understanding and interpretation of the centrality of power in ancient inter-state relations, Yan has been labelled a 'moral realist' (Zhang 2012).

The Tsinghua Approach clearly seeks to make a distinctive contribution to IR theorization through exploring valuable indigenous sources related specifically to ancient Chinese history and philosophy. In Yan's own words, the Tsinghua Approach aims to 'provide new resources for Chinese scholars to enrich existing International Relations theory' through rediscovering pre-Qin inter-state political thought (quoted in Paltiel 2011: 11). Yan does envision a more ambitious goal for the study of ancient Chinese political thought in the long run. That is 'to create a new International Relations theory on the basis of both pre-Qin thought and contemporary International Relations theory', for 'it is only by creating a new theory that we can fully prove the value of studying pre-Qin thought' (Yan 2011a: 221). Yan is unenthusiastic about the idea of constructing a Chinese School of IR. In his words, 'if we envision IR as a scientific inquiry, then IR theory should be universally applied. If we do not need a Chinese School of physics or chemistry, why do we need a Chinese School of IR theory?' (Yan 2011d: 259).

Qin Yaqing: reinventing Confucian relationalism

As a leading Chinese IR theorist and self-identified constructivist, Qin Yaqing shares with Yan Xuetong the aspiration of theoretical innovation through 'an inter-cultural dialogue with more critical reflections' and by 'taking its inspiration from Western theories and engaging them with Chinese culture, practices and worldviews' (Qin 2012c: 78, 86). His research project aims at developing a theoretical model of processual constructivism 'informed by social constructivism and Chinese philosophical traditions' and 'by incorporating and conceptualizing two key Chinese ideas – processes and relations' (Qin 2009a: 5) in constructing 'a theory on relationality to understand the dynamic International Relations'. Relationality, Qin argues, is 'the pivotal concept in Chinese society, developed over millennia, and practiced by generations' (Qin 2012c: 85) and it is deeply 'rooted in traditional Chinese practices and thought', which can be traced back to *Yi Jing* (Book of Change), where the fundamental concept for governance was deliberated and understood by ancient Chinese philosophers.

In contrast to trans-Atlantic IR theorization that takes rationality as its hard core, Qin takes the Chinese idea of 'relationality' as the hard core of his theoretical construct by giving 'relations' some ontological status, and theorizes it 'following social science principles' (Qin 2012c: 79–81).

Qin identifies three components of his theory of relationality: process in terms of relations, meta-relationship, and relational governance. On the Chinese dialectics of meta-relations, that is the 'relation of relations', Qin (2012c: 81) contends that

> Like Hegelian dialectics, it sees things in opposite and interactive poles; but unlike Hegelian dialectics, it assumes that the relations between the two poles (yin and yang) are non-conflictual and can co-evolve into a harmonious synthesis, a new form of life containing elements of both poles and which cannot be reduced to either.

Chinese dialectics thus 'allows room for a "process approach"', making harmony possible 'by combining opposites and thwarting conflict'. In IR, 'Chinese dialectics does not assume the non-existence of conflict. Rather it takes conflict as representing progressive steps toward harmony, which is the highest form of life' (Qin 2012c: 80–82).

Relational governance, Qin argues, is 'a more culturally oriented behaviour' rather than merely based on cost–benefit calculation. It is

> a process of negotiating socio-political arrangements that manage complex relationships in a community to produce order so that members behave in a reciprocal and cooperative fashion with mutual trust that evolves through a shared understanding of social norms and human morality.

Relations should be taken as the basic unit of analysis. Taking global governance as a social environment, governance is more of a process of balancing, maintaining and managing relations rather than just that of controlling and regulating the behavior of rational actors through networks of institutions to realize rule-based governance. Qin emphasizes, however, that relational governance is complementary to rule-based governance in IR (Qin 2012c: 82–83, Qin 2011c).

Like Yan, Qin is emphatic that his theorization combines rediscovering China's traditional thought and practice and inspirations from trans-Atlantic IR theories. His theory provides a complementary account of the dynamics in IR and enriches the existing theories rather than displaces any of them. Unlike Yan, Qin is unequivocal that theory of social sciences has its own geographic and cultural birthmarks based on the living experience and practice of people (Qin 2009d: 18). Only when a specific theoretical innovation eventually transcends local traditions and experiences can it become universally valid. Qin is also a strong advocate for constructing a Chinese School of IR.

Zhao Tingyang: reinterpreting tianxia

Unlike Yan and Qin, Zhao is not an IR scholar. A philosopher by training, Zhao has pursued his career as a researcher at the Institute of Philosophy at the Chinese Academy of Social Sciences. His intervention in the construction of Chinese international theory from a cognate discipline in 2005, in the first instance with the publication of *Tianxia Tixi* (The System of All-under-Heaven), is largely unanticipated but most productive in generating debates about how ancient Chinese history and philosophy as a critical resource could and should be drawn upon for innovative theorization of IR. Zhao's works since 2005 has sought to advance a philosophical critique of the worldview prevailing in Western philosophy and IR theory. It is his sustained attack on the ontology and epistemology of Western political thought that inserts him in the meta-theoretical debate in trans-Atlantic IR.

The key claim that Zhao has made is that today's world is a non-world, i.e. philosophically and institutionally it is not a world in its true sense. The only world that prevails today is geographical one, institutionally failed and politically abandoned. The ontological world understood and interpreted by Western philosophy is a problematic one because it is a world constituted by rational state actors, who pursue their narrow national interests. The world-ness of the world is sadly missing because Western political theory and international theory justify national interest in governing world politics, thus denying the world its world-ness. The existing institutions created by powerful states and for powerful states do not promote universal wellbeing (Zhao 2005). 'The failure of world politics is essentially the failure of [Western] philosophy' (Zhao 2009c: 7). The Kantian vision of perpetual peace and its modern incarnation (i.e. democratic peace), for example, fail to transcend, least of all overcome, the cultural and spiritual divides among civilizations. The idea of a 'federation of free states', constructs insiders and outsiders in the world and does more to divide than unite the world. So does Western philosophy.

Zhao calls for 'a philosophical renewal of All-under-Heaven' (Zhao 2009c: 9) and argues for an imaginative and creative use of ancient Chinese political thought, particularly the idea of *tianxia* (All-under-Heaven) to foster an all-inclusive worldview and to imagine a world that is of all and for all, where nothing is 'foreign' or 'pagan'. 'Viewing the world as a whole is an epistemological principle first used by Laozi'. As Chinese philosophy always considers the world more as a political body than a scientific object, it is a political epistemology not a scientific one that informs ancient Chinese philosophy. 'Chinese philosophy deals more with the problems of relations [how close is this view to Qin!] and the heart, whereas Western philosophy concentrates more on the truth and the mind' (Zhao 2009c: 10). A global political philosophy constructed around the idea of *tianxia* is to cultivate a worldview equivalent to, in his words,

> a mind at peace, free from the trap of thinking in terms of war, enemy, winner and loser. It is different as political mentality from those of Machiavelli, Hobbes, Marx, Freud, Schmitt, Morgenthau, and Huntington, and

different in a practical sense from the hegemonic order of *Pax Romana*, Christian cosmopolitanism and democratic peace under US leadership'.

(Zhao 2005: 7; translation from Qin 2012: 74)

For Zhao, 'a philosophical renewal of All-under-Heaven' is indispensable in search of such a global political philosophy. It entails 'rethinking China'; and 'the historical significance of "rethinking China" lies in recovering China's own ability to think (Zhao 2005: 7).

If it is intellectual intuition that directs Yan, Qin and Zhao to ancient Chinese history and philosophy in pursuit of new knowledge production, trans-Atlantic IR proves to be both positive and negative sources of inspiration for them to draw upon for theoretical innovation. Intellectually, all three projects assert, and attempt to establish, the epistemological legitimacy of resurrecting ancient Chinese philosophy and history as critical resources to draw upon to construct new knowledge and to contest exclusive epistemological claims of trans-Atlantic IR. For both Qin and Yan (but not so much for Zhao), the purpose of their attempts at (re)discovering international thought in ancient China is to enrich, not to substitute, the existing IR theories developed in trans-Atlantic IR (Yan 2011d; Qin 2012c). As one critic puts it, for them, 'Chinese experiences and philosophies function as sources of unique local data on which to test and enrich universal theories'. Worlding IR in this fashion, therefore, may open up 'different ways of being and experiencing the world, but not different ways of knowing the world' (Kristensen this volume).

Nonetheless, in so doing, they offer an implicit critique of the historicism – 'Europe first, then elsewhere' in Chakrabarty's formulation – in the development of IR theory (Chakrabarty 2001: 28–30). In no small measure, all three try to reverse the subject–object relationship in the studies of IR. To assert the identity as the knower is to overcome one particular intellectual challenge and dilemma for Chinese scholars – what Tu Weiming (1991) called the Enlightenment mentality – that came to dominate Chinese intellectual thinking about the world and the world history and by the same token the interpretation of Chinese history. This is what Zhao Tingyang calls 'China's ability to think'. For all three, it is through consciously and purposively engaging in inter-cultural dialogue that they seek new knowledge production and theoretical innovation. It is in such a dialogue, however, that one senses a historical motion and political, intellectual, and even personal, struggle with the presence of the indispensable yet inadequate trans-Atlantic IR. Little wonder it is to see how much the West is embedded in these distinctively non-Western and Chinese approaches to theorizing IR!

Conclusion

The foregoing constructed narratives are no more than a set of personal reflections on the long march that Chinese IR has embarked upon towards theoretical innovation and knowledge production rather than a systematic examination or even a capsule history of the evolution of IR as a discipline in China. One key argument I seek to advance here is the contingent role of the diffusion of trans-Atlantic IR in the disciplinary building and IR epistemic community construction in China, which can hardly be overestimated. As an effective and stimulating mode of intellectual engagement, this diffusion has effected and facilitated three epistemic turns in Chinese IR, namely, epistemic optimism, epistemic skepticism and epistemic reflexivity. As Chinese IR moves from knowledge acquisition and theoretical consumption to knowledge production and theoretical innovation, the diffusion of ideas is no longer a one-way street; but a two-way processes. China is now arguably one of the most promising sites for alternative theorizing of IR beyond the trans-Atlantic epistemic space. These epistemic turns are important in opening up 'the epistemic space for the rise of Chinese IR theory' (Wang Yiwei 2009: 115), and they are constitutive of essential steps towards constructing a Chinese School of IR.

The call for constructing theoretical knowledge that is more sensitive to Chinese historical experience, philosophical tradition and political context is clearly a bold intellectual move. It can, of course, be either commended for or faulted as 'exceptionalist theorizing' (Acharya and Buzan 2007: 291). Yet, in grounding IR theorization in history, ideas, institutions, practices and traditions beyond the West, and in taking seriously voices, experiences, values and intellectual perspectives of peoples hitherto ignored in IR theories, Chinese IR, as an intellectual enterprise, has already addressed what Amitav Acharya (2014) calls 'a new agenda for international studies' in making IR a more inclusive global discipline. In so doing, it has the potential of opening up additional and new perspectives in the search for a better understanding the changing social world that we live in.

Has a Chinese School of IR arrived as sociological reality? It is difficult to question the growth of a self-consciously reflexive Chinese IR epistemic community and the contribution it makes to the globality of IR as a discipline. It is beyond dispute that there have been battle cries, the structure is emerging, and flags have been waved. There is no doubt that promising attempts have been made at theoretical innovation and new knowledge production. To the extent that constructing a Chinese School of IR is consequential as an intellectual enterprise, it has not only raised, but also offered a tentative 'yes' answer to, the fundamental question of whether it is possible 'to build understandings of IR based on their [non-Western] histories and social theories, and even to project these in the form of universalist claims' (Acharya and Buzan 2007: 300). Nevertheless, the arrival of a Chinese School of IR as sociological reality remains more of an aspiration than a promised fulfilled. Constructing this sociological reality is a long social and historical process. All those who aspire to contribute to constructing the Chinese School as sociological reality will do well to remember that 'The social scientist is a part of the history from which his knowledge is constructed, and at any moment that knowledge may have to be revised or abandoned altogether' (Runciman 1969: 73).

Conclusion
The Chinese School of IR as an intellectual project – a critical assessment

Hun Joon Kim and Yongjin Zhang

The investigations conducted in this volume offer a glimpse into the raging debates about IR theorization within China and the distinctive visioning of a global order by Chinese thinkers and their dream about the future of the world. They also demonstrate that the Chinese School of IR is a deeply contested project. It is a product-in-process that is susceptible to political dynamics and intellectual change – domestic, international and global. It is characterized by ongoing debates about whether it is the research methods, key research puzzles, core analytical concepts, or theoretical constructs that make the Chinese School of IR distinctive from and different to Western IR. Theorization under the umbrella of the Chinese School is marked notably by multiple contentious approaches. There is no single monolithic 'Chinese School' that comes to dominate IR theorization in China. There are, rather, competing accounts and different understandings of what theory is and what theory can and should do. 'Naming' remains a contentious issue. There is even no agreement about what 'Chinese-ness' means in the putative Chinese School of IR project. It is nevertheless also clear that the Chinese School represents a consensus that the Chinese voices, experiences, values and sources should be brought to bear on IR theorization from a distinctive geocultural site. Further, IR theory could and should be developed within China as an integral part of the global pursuit of IR theories drawing upon the Chinese ways of seeing and experiencing global politics, thus challenging the boundary-drawing practices of IR that privilege the historical experience and scholarly folklores of the 'West'. In engaging in such a pursuit, and in articulating this theoretical aspiration, the Chinese School of IR, as a viable project, contributes to revealing the parochialism of Western IR and to the disciplinary reflexivity on its provincialism. Chinese IR has built up in this fashion a significant stake in making IR a truly global discipline. Foundations have thus also been laid for rendering the flows of IR knowledge produced no longer just 'one-way streets' from the West to the rest.

As a number of contributing chapters in this volume make clear, among the specific goals that the Chinese School project has strived to achieve from the disciplinary margins are 'greater inclusiveness and diversity in our discipline' and 'greater respect for diversity in our knowledge sources and claims, historical experiences, and beliefs and approaches about world order'. It is a shared aspiration of Chinese scholars, including those who are sceptical about the construction of a Chinese School of IR, to make IR 'a vibrant, innovative, and inclusive enterprise that reflects the voices, experiences, interests, and identities of all humankind' (Acharya 2014: 649, 656–657). One assertion that Chinese voices have made is indeed that local knowledge and historical experience are not simply there for researchers to 'delve into', as Johnston (2012: 56) states, for theory-building and theory-testing and for expanding 'the conceptual tools for theorizing about IR more generally'. They should be also investigated as alternative intellectual and historical sources for the 'discovery of new ideas and approaches' (Acharya 2014: 648). In grounding their knowledge claims firmly on Chinese and Asian history, three distinctive projects of theoretical innovation carried out by Chinese scholars, Yan Xuetong, Qin Yaqing and Zhao Tingyang, among others, discussed in a number of contributing chapters of this volume, have taken IR theorization purposefully beyond Greco-Roman, European, or US history in investigating 'distinct and diverse cultural and historical experiences that inform their [non-Western] conceptions of and approach to world order'. One of the principal purposes of these projects is precisely 'to challenge us to rethink the concept and practice of power, legitimacy, and international orders, all of which are central concepts in IR' (Acharya 2014: 653).

The rise of China is likely to continue to provide both enabling and impeding socio-political conditions and context for further evolution of the Chinese School of IR. The unprecedented global power shift, the future of the emerging global order, and China's role in the making of such an order will continue to provide central intellectual puzzles and stimulate demand for reflexive knowledge of IR for the Chinese School project. The exigencies of policy imperatives for China as a rising power, on the other hand, will continue to generate demand for instrumental knowledge of IR. At the same time, Chinese IR in general has to negotiate with the state constantly for its relative autonomy as a discipline. The Chinese School project has to work within a tightly regulated and restricted space easily subject to political influence and manipulation of the state and the state-sponsored scholarship. It has to guard against being hijacked by power, as its legitimacy as an intellectual pursuit will be seriously jeopardized if the project becomes overtly political.

To the extent that the evolution of the Chinese School of IR illustrates the complexity of knowledge formation within a specific political and intellectual setting and geocultural site, it is closely connected to and clearly reflective of a particular political imagination of world politics and utopia. There is, however, a significant convergence of disciplinary practice and knowledge in the instance of constructing and structuring IR as a discipline in China, as Chinese IR has now become theory-literate and theory-concerned, if not yet theory-led. In the rest of this concluding chapter, we offer a critical assessment of the Chinese School of IR as an intellectual project in a summary fashion as a continuation of the conversation and debate. We address three questions: Why is the Chinese School at this particular historical juncture? How is the Chinese School 'differently different'? What are intellectual risks of the Chinese School of IR project? By way of articulating our intellectual discontents with the Chinese School project, we identify a number of specific obstacles to overcome in order for the Chinese School of IR as an intellectual project to move forward.

The Chinese School of IR: why now?

Wang and Buzan (Chapter 7 this volume) argue that a set of historically contingent circumstances created

> three interlinked needs distinctive to Chinese IR: the need to radically redevelop the study of IR in China; the need to recover China's history and political theory as they relate to the study of IR; and the need to think about the rapidly changing position of China in the international system/society.

In terms of the specific geopolitical circumstance, it is generally argued and commonly accepted in the contributing chapters that the rise of China and China's growing global ambition, i.e. China's rapidly changing position in international society, provide an indispensable socio-political context within which the Chinese School of IR emerges and evolves. There is certain degree of truth in this contention. As John Agnew (2007: 142) argues, massive socio-political changes in the world are 'shaping changes in how we (whomever and wherever we are) engage in how knowledge is ordered and circulated' and surprises unleashed in world politics often expose 'anomalies in established theories' and 'the subsequent limits to the conventional theoretical terms in which social science theories have been organized'. That the real world change in global politics leads to the developments of new theories can best be seen in the rise of a host of post-positivist and reflectivist approaches to theorizing IR after the end of the Cold War.

There is no doubt that global power shift triggered by and in favour of the rise of China is historically unparalleled. It is changing the uneven global power distribution that has historically favoured the West in an unprecedented manner. Global disparities in material power between China and the United States – and more broadly the democratic West – are undoubtedly narrowing significantly and changing rapidly. Will the rise of China bring 'a renewed conflict of geopolitical visions of the world'? What will China's new 'script' for world politics be, as it rises in a world not of its own making? How will China challenge and change 'the groundwork for a global geopolitics of knowledge' laid down in the first instance by colonialism (Agnew 2007: 143–145)? What does the rise of China mean for the future of liberal global order (Ikenberry 2014)? By all accounts, the rise of China is certainly a kind of international experience never experienced before that has brought up new puzzles, demanding new attempts at theorizing.

It is, however, too facile to suggest that the rise of Chinese international theory in such a context is only natural, not in the least because it cannot explain how and why the construction of the Chinese School of IR has taken the direction it has. Nor can it tell us why there should have been particular drives for theorizing in Chinese academia. It has also ignored other political conditions under which knowledge of IR in China is produced and disseminated, namely, domestic political change. Both Chang (Chapter 5 this volume) and Noesselt (Chapter 6 this volume) have shown how IR knowledge production in China has been made to serve power and Communist Party interests in the historical context of China rising, and why the boundaries between knowledge production and politics are always blurred in contemporary China's socio-political milieu. It is nevertheless incorrect to assume a priori that scholarship produced in China is irredeemably ideological and political. It is advisable to remember that 'Much IR production globally is linked to it [the state] via factors such as obedience to state directives for knowledge production and attempts to mirror its foreign policy needs' (Tickner and Blaney 2013: 4). Further, domestic political change sometimes opens more space and opportunities for knowledge production in China, as was the case in the 1980s. Still, IR knowledge production is arguably political 'with Chinese characteristics' in the sense that scholars in China working in an environment inhospitable to academic freedom of speech must carefully navigate through and negotiate with the tricky constraints and limitations imposed and the limited incentives and opportunities provided by the changing Chinese domestic politics. These complex political dynamics of knowledge production and dissemination in China should be further explored and appropriately appreciated.

In this regard, China's peaceful rise can be said to be both a political and an intellectual project. It is a political project not in the sense that it is politically commissioned and controlled, but because it has been pursued as a counter-discourse to the China threat discourse, which originated principally from the United States, and as it fulfils a particular policy need in developing China's grand strategy. It is an intellectual project, as it provides a genuine central analytical and historical problematique with which to mobilize the construction of a Chinese School of IR.

Simply stating that the rise of China and the rise of Chinese international theory are intrinsically linked, then, does not tell us much about what intellectually drives theoretical innovation within the Chinese School of IR project. What are the intellectual drivers for theoretical exploration/proliferation in China? One obvious answer is the need to develop and institutionalize Chinese IR as an academic discipline from scratch in the contingent historical circumstances of China's opening and economic reform after 1979. IR disciplinary construction in China is therefore a significant driver, as it opens up a number of institutional opportunities for learning and knowledge production. If theoretical exploration, contention and proliferation are commonly accepted indicators of disciplinary maturity, then the growth of IR as a discipline in China should be marked by vigorous pursuit of growing theoretical knowledge, like the development of the discipline at the heartland of disciplinary IR, the United States. Intellectual curiosity has also played a big part. The initial driver for Zhao Tingyang's reinterpretation of *tianxia* is to provide a philosophical critique of the worldview prevailing in Western philosophy, particularly the Kantian vision of perpetual peace and its contemporary incarnation. It is perhaps through largely unanticipated engagement with IR scholarship that a theoretical ambition emerges in Zhao's intervention to provide an indigenous Chinese perspective on IR and to prepare China intellectually for a greater, more constructive and distinctive role in world affairs.

Zhao's aspiration to recover China's ability to think through reconsidering the Chinese philosophical thought articulates a strong resistance to interpretive projections from the knowledge experiences of specific places/times onto all places/times. More specifically in the case of IR, such resistance is increasingly shared among Chinese IR scholars to the hegemony of IR scholarship produced in the United States with bitter complaints about its claim of universality and deficiency of its explanatory power in understanding and solving the challenges confronted by a rising China. One intellectual driver for the Chinese School of IR is therefore to challenge the dominance, power and privilege of Western IR. The Chinese School of IR emerges, to paraphrase Mignolo (2000: 95), as none other than 'a diverse set of theoretical practices emerging from and responding to hegemonic imposition of Western IR at a particular intersection of contemporary Chinese and Euro/American history'. This resistance to and protest against such hegemonic impositions is also a struggle for the recognition of alternative knowledge claims and sources from different geocultural sites. It amounts to a call to add Chinese voices to the global discipline of IR as indispensable to demarginalize histories, knowledge claims and ideas of the non-Western world.

These political and intellectual accounts still cannot explain why and how a particular kind of theoretical knowledge has been promoted and produced in China. 'The need to recover China's history and political theory as they relate to the study of IR' may be intuitive. However, why should there be three different approaches to theoretical innovation pioneered respectively by Yan Xuetong, Qin Yaqing and Zhao Tingyang that draw upon traditional Chinese philosophy and ancient Chinese history in distinctive manners? This question remains unexplained. It is too simplistic to say that this is because 'As academics we make choices about which theories are legitimate partners to be engaged, that is, which are allowed entry into the marketplace and which are to be excluded' (Dunne et al. 2013: 414).

In other words, there should be a sociology-of-science account of theoretical exploration, innovation and proliferation that is constitutive of the Chinese School. This is arguably the least explored in the contributing chapters of this volume. How are individual scholars driven for theoretical innovation by, for example, their desire for personal fame and national and international recognition? In which way have professional ambition, career opportunities and available funds shaped their research? To what extent can a social theorist's theory be understood as 'constituted at the intersection of biography and history' (Burawoy 2013: 780)? As Peter Kristensen and Ras Nielsen (2013a: 19) argue with persuasion, a sociology-of-knowledge account of theoretical innovation of the Chinese School of IR needs to look into 'the internal academic context [that] comprises intellectuals pursuing prominence, with each intellectual trying to carve out a maximally distinct position in order to receive attention from their peers'. Their research, which takes Randall Collins' (2000) micro-sociological theory of intellectual innovation to a field trip in China, is revealing of how positioning oneself in Chinese theory debate as the central line of opposition and rivalry in structuring the attention space drives individual research agendas. It provides enlightening accounts of why and how Yan Xuetong, a self-professed neorealist and strong believer of theoretical universalism, should have embarked on an exploratory journey in rediscovering the international in ancient Chinese thought. Yan allegedly told one of his colleagues that 'if you want to do a real [theoretical] achievement, you need to do something that the Westerners cannot understand' (Kristensen and Nielsen 2013a: 27.) There is an equally enlightening account of how 'relationality' came to be the theoretical core of Qin Yaqing's search for theoretical innovation, drawing upon ancient Chinese philosophical wisdom and political thought (Kristensen and Nielsen 2013a: 28–29).

How is the Chinese School 'differently different'?

To the extent that the Chinese School represents some manifestly different ways of theorizing IR, there has been a constant struggle for it to be different from the dominant theoretical traditions and approaches. At a deeper level, the 'naming' contentions between 'IR theory with Chinese characteristics' and 'a Chinese School of IR' are contentions between scientific socialism and social scientism (Kristensen and Nielsen 2013a: 24). The adoption of the Chinese School label, inspired and legitimated by such role models as the English School and the Copenhagen School, asserts a particular local identity claim, but also ironically domesticates any radical promises it may have at the same time, as Chinese IR moves from the resigned marginality to seeking from the margins participation in and recognition of the existing global discipline.

If there is any attempt at unthinking of traditional conceptions of world politics in the Chinese School, there is little offering of any radically different alternative script of global politics by Chinese scholars. The political imagination of the world in Chinese IR remains conservatively state-centric, mired in the Westphalian myth. For most Chinese scholars, who speak from a very different geocultural location and tradition, the idea of the 'international' central to the disciplinary discourse looks surprisingly similar to the hegemonic imposition. The ideas at the root of modern Western worldview such as state, sovereignty, power, order, security, globalization, etc. remain pivotal to Chinese IR. Largely because of the unique pathway of the disciplinary growth in China, 'academic Chinese knowledge of the "international" largely remains refracted through intellectual lenses made in the United States' (Agnew 2007: 146; see also Zhang 2003). The colonial character of IR remains largely intact, even when it seems to be being chipped away somewhere. The Chinese School simply cannot escape from the bondage of global geopolitics of knowledge production: who decides what is authorized and accepted as genuine knowledge of IR. This is an inescapable political and intellectual conditioning of what can be accepted as legitimately differently different that Chinese theoretical innovation can bring to the global discipline. It dictates the terms of engagement and lays down the frame of reference of debate. It is impossible to imagine that, under such political and intellectual conditioning, Chinese scholars could come up with a 'totally alternative scripting to world politics' (Agnew 2010: 570).

Any subversive potential of the Chinese School is further limited by its desire to be heard and to be able to speak back to the putative global discipline, particularly American IR (Kristensen 2015a). As Tickner and Blaney (2012: 3) note, Gayatri Chakravorty Spivak (1988) already argued, in her influential essay 'Can the Subaltern Speak?', that 'the main prerequisite of being heard is the ability to speak in the West's (or the powerful's) own language'. Homi Bhabha's (2004: 122) celebrated dictum 'almost the same but not quite' becomes both an unspoken precondition for any meaningful dialogue to happen between the core and the periphery and a strategy adopted by Chinese theorists to be heard and recognized in the discipline. Qin Yaqing and Yan Xuetong's efforts to cultivate ancient Chinese resources through either constructivist or neorealist analytical frameworks for theoretical innovation best exemplifies the personal and institutional struggle for recognition of distinctively Chinese approaches to theorization as respectfully and legitimately different. These efforts may in fact help perpetuate, rather than subvert, the core-periphery depiction in the discipline, as they reinforce, wittingly or not, the dominance and hegemony of Western IR they set out to challenge.

The real battle for the Chinese School to be differently different is therefore, to borrow from Michael Burawoy (2015), 'not *against* reigning hegemonies but *on the terrain* of those hegemonies, appropriating, reordering and reconstructing them in new contexts'. The problem is, in other words, not so much with the existing IR theories but with what Chinese scholars do with them once they arrive in China. The story then is not just that of the hegemonic imposition of power and privilege of existing theories, but also their active and transformative appropriation in China. The Chinese School project, in this reading, embodies both resistance and contestation to and acquiescence of the existing world hierarchies of IR knowledge production. It should be unsurprising then that it is 'enriching' the existing theories of IR that most protagonists of the Chinese School principally aim at. As Xu and Sun (Chapter 9 this volume) claim, what the Tsinghua Approach strives for is 'to borrow from the classics in order to enrich understandings of contemporary phenomenon, or in other words, to innovate by applying classical thinking to develop, supplement, or even replace current theories'.

What are intellectual hazards of the Chinese School project?

It may seem ironic to claim that one of the intellectual hazards of the Chinese School project is that it is too 'Chinese', given the discussions above. Arguments in the contributing chapters do contain, however, strong claims of Chinese exceptionalism/particularity and betray dichotomous thinking of China vis-à-vis the West, more of which later. There is legitimate unease that the Chinese School project is driven by too parochial concerns. Jack Snyder's scepticism, noted by Kristensen (Chapter 8 this volume), i.e. whether a Chinese international theory could be constructed around the core theoretical problem such as 'China's peaceful rise', which would have general applicability, cannot easily dismissed. This is doubly so, as the theoretical debate over the last two decades has broadened the agenda of IR beyond traditional concerns of state security and a narrowly defined foreign policy agenda and as explaining and understanding global social forces demands more theoretical knowledge. As Wang and Buzan (Chapter 7 this volume) argue, the English School is successful because 'it eschewed parochial concerns and aimed to construct theory at the global level'. Yet, as China rises, it is likely that Chinese scholars will bring with them a new set of presumptions and parochial concerns about the world that they have experienced as 'Chinese' in their theorization. The intellectual hazard of Chinese scholars projecting these experiences and concerns as 'universals' onto the world at large has to be taken seriously.

There is another kind of intellectual hazard for the Chinese School project that is closely associated with the promise of IR as a discipline that 'makes a difference' to the world, namely, the domination of instrumental knowledge over reflexive knowledge of IR. The failings of US policy intellectuals during the Cold War in the face of the seductions of political and policy influence are well noted. Stanley Hoffmann (1977: 56, 59) warned that American IR risked 'sloping from research-with-practical-effects to practical-advocacy-derived-from-research' as it was 'too close to the fire'. There is a real risk of this nature for Chinese School of IR project, as Zhang (Chapter 11 this volume) notes that 'knowledge acquisition and knowledge production in IR in China have clearly skewed towards addressing what should we do question [rather than what should we know]'. This observation can be further supported by claims made by leading thinkers in China that Chinese IR theory should be constructed as 'guidelines for action' (Qin 2007: 314) and that the purpose of studying the pre-Qin political philosophy is to 'draw lessons for policy today' and to inform China's grand strategy for its peaceful rise (Yan 2011a: 200–221). Such risk is significantly heightened when one considers the convergence of two traditions in China's socio-political context of knowledge production, i.e. a particular Chinese intellectual tradition – 'the intersection of moral philosophy and the statecraft' (Paltiel 2011: 400) and the Marxist conception of theory with a political purpose.

In rushing to make knowledge claims drawing upon ancient Chinese history and philosophy as local resources, which is the main thrust for theoretical innovation under umbrella of the Chinese School of IR, there is also the intellectual risk that 'critical reflection is largely abandoned for excavating this or that experiential difference' and 'a singular history of knowledge associated with a specific world region' is privileged without making a good case why this foundational thought 'has the continuing importance we give to it across a historically evolving world political system' (Agnew 2007: 138–141). Reifying the

Chinese culture also risks making Chinese School theoretical exploration 'a disengaged form of pluralism with each theoretical perspective legitimating its claims solely on its own terms and with little reason to engage in conversations with alternative approaches' (Dunne et al. 2013: 416). Drawing explicitly on Chinese culture could also be seen as a nationalization rather than internationalization of IR that does not and cannot travel (Kristensen Chapter 8 this volume).

The Chinese School of IR and its intellectual discontents

What are the future prospects of the Chinese School of IR as an intellectual project then? By way of articulating our intellectual discontent with the project, we identify four obstacles that we believe it is imperative for the Chinese School to overcome in order to move the project forward. These are exceptionalism, dualism, the romanticization of Chinese tradition, culture, history and thoughts, and great power conceit.

Exceptionalism

In his plea for global IR, Amitav Acharya (2014: 651) argues that one important aspect of IR's aspiration to become a truly global discipline is to eschew 'cultural exceptionalism and parochialism'. Exceptionalism is 'the tendency to present the characteristics of one's own group (society, state, or civilization) as homogenous, unique, and superior to those of others' (Acharya 2014: 651). In order to demonstrate exceptionalism, Acharya uses the examples of concepts such as 'Asian Values', 'Asian human rights', and 'Asian democracy'. One particular example he notes is a tendency to use the 'Chinese tributary system as the basis of a new Chinese School of IR' (Acharya 2014: 651). Feng Zhang (2013) identifies four contemporary characteristics of Chinese exceptionalism in Chinese academic and official thinking about IR – the claims of great power, reformism, benevolent pacifism, and harmonious inclusions. This Chinese exceptionalism, it is claimed at the same time, lacks the offensive characteristics that mark American exceptionalism.

Cultural exceptionalism clearly prevails in some current approaches to building a distinctive Chinese IR, as shown in this volume. Chinese exceptionalism appears strongly in Wang and Han's chapter (Chapter 3 this volume) when they try to explain why there is no Chinese international theory, yet. The first answer they provide is that there is something called Chinese secular culture that is against any universal theory. According to them, this traditional culture is too strong and therefore obstructs theory construction in China. Furthermore, 'the diversity of Chinese culture and the nature of Chinese language', in their words, 'make it impossible for any single theory or school of theory to cover all Chinese experience'.

Chinese exceptionalism is further expressed in the assumption that China will be different from any other great power in its behaviour or disposition. Hu (Chapter 4 this volume) asserts, for example, that the rise of China is exceptional and 'the exceptionality lies in peaceful rising' and that many Chinese scholars believe that 'China is a unique country and its exceptionality would generate a new set of the core problematiques for IR theory-building'. This assumption can also be found in Shih and Huang (Chapter 10 this volume) who see the Chinese School of IR 'embedded in Confucianism' as acquiring 'post-Western characteristics of being post-hegemonic'.

The Tsinghua Approach has a similar assumption when Xu and Sun (Chapter 9 this volume) argue, following Yan (2011b), that the dominant state influences the evolution of international norms through three means: 'a process of demonstration – imitation; a process of supporting – strengthening, and a process of punishment – maintenance'. The emphasis here is on the first two options, where demonstration and supporting are prioritized over punishment. The underlying assumption reveals wishful thinking that, unlike the United States, which heavily relies on punishment, when China rises, a process of demonstration will persuade other countries to follow China's norms and values. However, as Noesselt (Chapter 6 this volume) points out 'whether China possesses a unique (and strategic) culture *sui generis* or whether it emulates elements of strategic traditions similar to the ones practiced (and reflected) by the "Western" world' is an open research question, not something that can be presumed and simply asserted. One way to avoid such conceptual and methodological pitfalls of exceptionalism is to heed Chang's (Chapter 5 this volume) call to 'bring East Asia back in'.

Dualism

The second obstacle is dualism, i.e. a dichotomous understanding of China vis-à-vis the West. Dualism is most apparent in the case of Zhao's explanation of the *tianxia* system. Zhao (2006) proposes the potential revival of the *tianxia* system as an alternative to the existing modern state system. Here, the *tianxia* order is contrasted to the Westphalian order, which is anarchic, zero-sum, military-dominated and amoral. In contrast to external 'anarchy and chaos', *tianxia* is understood to posit, according to Ling (Chapter 1 this volume), 'a worldly world order filled with an intimate network of individuals–families–states–universe, constantly interacting back and forth, both vertically and horizontally'. A dichotomous perspective of the West vis-à-vis China is further represented in Ling's (Chapter 1 this volume) comparison between *Leviathan* and *Sanguo Yanyi*, where it is argued that *Sanguo Yanyi*'s cultural appeal 'surpasses mere power politics'. As Noesselt (Chapter 6 this volume) argues, the claim that 'China's international engagement does not follow the path of military struggle for hegemony and zero-sum power competition also underlies the current reinvention of *tianxia*'. Here, what is good and desirable – order, legitimacy, voluntary submission – are all clustered in the Chinese traditional system and what is bad and undesirable – anarchy, disorder, war – are found in the Westphalian system. Based on this dualism, the *tianxia* order is understood as 'a hierarchical but stable alternative' since the system is run by moral, cultural, and political power (i.e. China) and the participation is voluntary.

As with exceptionalism, dualism and setting up a straw man should be eschewed and overcome, since dichotomous understanding is but gross simplification and dualism is often purposively and socially constructed. A simple contrast is not helpful since most social phenomena we examine are complex. After all, it is difficult to separate out what is purely Chinese and what is purely Western. As Ren (Chapter 2 this volume) argues, building Chinese IR theories does not mean to 'seek the opposite to the Western theories or a difference for difference's sake'.

Romanticization

In relation to the previous two obstacles, a related pitfall is romanticizing things that are uniquely Chinese, such as Chinese tradition, culture, history, and thought. This obstacle, of course, is not unique to Chinese scholars. We all tend to get our own history and tradition wrong and romanticize our history and culture. Here we can refer to Zhao's reinterpretation of the *tianxia* system. It can be also seen in Ling's claims (Chapter 1 this volume) that under the *tianxia* system, 'the state is not a self-enclosed, self-interested institution' but is one component within a worldly world order. However, such romanticization leaves unproblematized the concept of *tianxia* and the state as its constitutive component in a contingent historical context. Throughout Chinese history, various types and forms of the *tianxia* system were conceptualized and practised, often depending on China's military and economic power. In addition, hierarchy was neither stable nor steady since the emperor did not always have the intention or power to rule or reign. As Zhao's critics pointed out, the *tianxia* system as Zhao conceptualized is more like something constructed in late nineteenth century in the course of China's encountering with the expanding European international system.

In addition to the *tianxia* system, one other example of romanticizing Chinese tradition and history is the concept of 'harmony', which is said to be central to the principles embodied in the traditional 'doctrine of mean'. Wang and Han (Chapter 3 this volume) argue that there is something called 'harmonious mentality' in China and the aim of Chinese mind is 'of not mere compromise, but harmony'. They also assert that 'Chinese cosmopolitanism is inclusive, and favours culture to force, free-choice to coercion'. Yan's conceptualization of *wangdao* or moral leadership in traditional Chinese political thought follows similar logic. However, whether the moral and benevolent leadership is truly moral and benevolent is an open research question; as is how these historical concepts can be used to explain IR in the twenty-first century. Xu and Sun (Chapter 9 this volume) note, for example, that Yan's critics question whether his concept of 'moral leadership' can 'really apply to the contemporary context'. Hu (Chapter 4 this volume) also finds the concept such as *tianxia* or harmonious society 'neither realistic nor operational in today's International Relations reality'.

Great power conceit

The fourth point is what we call great power conceit. This is also related to exceptionalism since exceptionalism justifies 'the dominance of the powerful states over the weak' (Acharya 2014: 651). It is well observed that China has become more and more self-conscious of its global power status, as China has become 'self-assured in defending its national interests', and 'Beijing is more confident and straightforward in championing for international institutional reforms and power sharing in world politics' (Hu Chapter 4 this volume). Ren (Chapter 2 this volume) talks about a kind of self-consciousness that is 'on the rise in almost all the fields in Chinese humanities and social sciences' for knowledge creation inspired by the growing awareness of China's global power status. The search for a Chinese School has therefore become 'a part of China's quest for national identity and global power status' (Noesselt Chapter 6 this volume). Healthy and moderate self-consciousness is surely conducive to the production of new theoretical knowledge. There is, however, a conceptual difference between the self-consciousness of a great power status and the self-conceit of a great power.

Does power necessarily produce theoretical knowledge? Is there any truth in the claim that 'IR theories are produced by scholars from big powers and big power practice enables scholars to produce IR theories' (Hu Chapter 4 this volume)? Is it really true that 'In a big power, usually there is a greater degree of intellectual and theoretical autonomy', and by extension, Chinese scholars are working in a more favourable academic and institutional environment for theoretical knowledge production (Ren Chapter 2 this volume)?

These statements, first of all, are not true and can be easily falsified. First, the relationship between power and knowledge is much more intricate than assumed. Material power alone rarely produces any theoretical knowledge. Further, many interesting theoretical concepts and frameworks, such as dependency theory, were originated and advanced from the geocultural sites of geopolitically weak states, and many important international practices – international human rights, multilateralism, developmental norms – were either invented or promoted by weak states and non-state actors. Stripped off their veneer, these statements can be regarded as explicit expressions of great power conceit, which are detrimental to furthering the advancement of a Chinese School of IR. As Kristensen (Chapter 8 this volume) argues, the success of a Chinese School depends on how many audiences a Chinese academic circle could attract from both the semi-periphery and the periphery. Not only the core (American social science) but also the periphery (rising powers like Brazil and India) or semi-periphery (Europe) is important. For those countries, explicit connection between great power and IR knowledge production would be strongly resisted. There are already some signs of rejection. Xu and Sun (Chapter 9 this volume) acknowledge that Yan's proposal for 'voluntary submission for small states in a China-led hierarchy' is not welcomed in East Asia. Cunningham and Callahan (2011: 362) find 'both Western world as well as China's Asian neighbours will find it difficult to accept the hierarchical order appealed for by Yan Xuetong, particularly when equality is the fundamental principle of the contemporary international society'.

Conclusion

The growth of disciplinary IR in China has undoubtedly contributed to the globalization of IR as a discipline and to the global production of theoretical knowledge about IR. It is now impossible to imagine IR as a genuinely global discipline without reference to Chinese participation and contribution. Neither is it possible to think of the future of Chinese IR without local endeavour at theoretical innovation. Whether there is or there is not a Chinese School of IR is now very much a moot point. The issue at stake is rather *what kind of* Chinese School is likely to evolve, *toward which directions* ongoing Chinese theoretical innovation will be directed, and *whether and how* critical potential of any Chinese international theory, which has ambition to gain a global reach, can be brought into full play.

The scrutiny of the putative Chinese School of IR as an intellectual project conducted in this volume highlights the extent to which all social theories are no more than 'a response to a specific social and historical situation of which an intellectual occasion is a part' (Said 1983b: 237). It acknowledges the singularity of Chinese international theory as invariably rooted in the Chinese geocultural context and intellectual tradition, hence itself a product of specific historical time and place. It also shows clearly that the Chinese School of IR and vibrant attempts at theoretical innovation associated with it are still very much an internal dialogue of theory contestation and construction even when it has become increasingly outward looking. What is conspicuously missing is a meaningful external dialogue of critique through inter-cultural communication, whereby theoretical propositions made by Chinese scholars are subject to the critical gaze of external critics from the global IR epistemic community. In other words, the Chinese School has rarely travelled, as yet, to other cultures, because of a conspicuous absence of the complex dynamics of reception, rejection, reinterpretation and reinvention that characterizes the transfer of ideas and theoretical concepts from one historical and geocultural site to another. Yet, any Chinese international theory that potentially claims to provide a general analytical framework for understanding global problems cannot be constructed exclusively in China and then consumed elsewhere.

This suggests that if the Chinese School wishes to 'carve out a space in the global IR' (Kristensen Chapter 8 this volume) in the discipline's multiple accounts of theory, it is imperative that Chinese international theory travels to other geocultural sites to be challenged, informed and enriched, as well as rejected by knowledge produced there. After all, the potential for theoretical knowledge that draws upon local resources to have any universal claim depends on whether and how such knowledge journeys not just through space but also through time. To the extent that knowledge is made as it travels and circulates, this traveling leads to a transformative process, as ideas and theoretical concepts of Chinese international theory are dis-embedded from their original historical, social and cultural circumstances and are wrested from their original use and are shaped and reshaped by the local conditions of reception, resistance, rejection, reproduction and transmission under different social, cultural, historical and linguistic conditioning and practice, not in the least that of lost in translation. This is particularly so when 'ideas mutate and feed into each other in even more challenging ways' (Tickner and Blaney 2013: 12) in a contemporary global order characterized by more complex and accelerated patterns of exchange. Surely, not all aspects of a traveling Chinese international theory will survive the journey; some are likely to be further advanced, enriched and expanded, while others will be rejected, abandoned and forgotten altogether along the way. To deny such transformative potential of a traveling Chinese international theory is, however, to defeat the very idea of the Chinese School of IR.

Bibliography

Abramowitz, Morton and Stephen Bosworth (2003). 'Adjusting to the New Asia'. *Foreign Affairs*, 82(4): 119–131.

Acharya, Amitav (2003). 'Will Asia's Past be its Future?' *International Security*, 28(3): 149–164.

Acharya, Amitav (2011). 'Dialogue and Discovery: In Search of International Relations Theories beyond the West'. *Millennium – Journal of International Studies*, 39: 619–637.

Acharya, Amitav (2013). 'Imagining Global IR out of India'. Keynote Address in *Re-imaging Global Orders: Perspectives from the South (The Annual International Studies Convention 2013)*, New Delhi, Jawaharlal Nehru University, 10–12 December 2013.

Acharya, Amitav (2014). 'Global International Relations (IR) and Regional Worlds – A New Agenda for International Studies'. *International Studies Quarterly*, 58(4): 647–659.

Acharya, Amitav and Barry Buzan (2007). 'Why is there no Non-Western International Relational Theory? An Introduction'. *International Relations of the Asia-Pacific*, 7(3): 287–312.

Acharya, Amitav and Barry Buzan (2010a). 'Why is there no Non-Western International Relations Theory: An Introduction'. In: Amitav Acharya and Barry Buzan (eds). *Non-Western International Relations Theory: Perspectives on and beyond Asia*. London, UK: Routledge, pp. 1–25.

Acharya, Amitav and Barry Buzan (2010b). *Non-Western International Relations Theory*. New York: Routledge.

Actis, Esteban (2012). 'Los Condicionantes Domésticos En Los Diseños de Política Exterior: La Internacionalización de Capitales Brasileños Como Nuevo Objetivo de La Política Exterior de Brasil'. *Brazilian Journal of International Relations*, 1: 399–423.

Agnew, John (2007). 'Know-Where: Geographies of Knowledge of World Politics'. *International Political Sociology*, 1(1): 138–148.

Agnew, John (2010). 'Emerging China and Critical Geopolitics: Between World Politics and Chinese Particularity'. *Eurasian Geography and Economics*, 51(5): 569–582.

Alagappa, Muthiah (2009a). 'Guest Editor's Note'. *International Studies*, 46: 3–6.

Alagappa, Muthiah (2009b). 'Strengthening International Studies in India: Vision and Recommendations'. *International Studies*, 46: 7–35.

Alagappa, Muthiah (2011). 'International Relations Studies in Asia: Distinctive Trajectories'. *International Relations of the Asia-Pacific*, 11(2): 193–230.

Alker, Hayward and Thomas Biersteker (1984). 'The Dialectics of World Order: Notes for a Future Archeologist of International Savoir Faire'. *International Studies Quarterly*, 28: 121–142.

Ames, Roger T. (ed.) (1998). *Wandering at Ease in the Zhuangzi*. Albany, NY: State University of New York Press.
Ames, Roger T. and Henry Rosemont Jr. (Trans. with an introduction) (1998). *The Analects of Confucius: A Philosophical Translation*. New York: Random House.
Arthur, W. Brian (1989). 'Competing Technologies, Increasing Returns, and Lock-In by Historical Events'. *Economic Journal*, 99(3): 116–131.
Baik, Young-seo, Chen Kuan-shin and Sun Ge (2004). 'Guanyu dongya lunshu de kenengxing' [On the Prospect of East Asian Discourses]. *Book Town*, 12: 35–36.
Bain, William (2010). 'The Pluralist–Solidarist Debate in the English School'. In: Robert A. Denemark (ed.). *International Studies Encyclopedia*. London: Blackwell Publishing.
Bain, William (2014). 'The Pluralist–Solidarist Debate in the English School'. In: Cornelia Navari and Daniel Green (eds). *Guide to the English School in International Studies*. Chichester: John Wiley and Sons, pp. 159–170.
Bajpai, Kanti P. (1997). 'International Studies in India: Bringing Theory (Back) Home'. In: M.S. Rajan (ed.). *International and Area Studies in India*. New Delhi: Lancers Books, pp. 31–49.
Bajpai, Kanti P. (2009). 'Obstacles to Good Work in Indian International Relations'. *International Studies*, 46: 109–128.
Baldwin, David (ed.) (1993). *Neorealism and Neoliberalism – The Contemporary Debate*. New York: Columbia University Press.
Basrur, R.M. (2009). 'Scholarship on India's International Relations: Some Disciplinary Shortcomings'. *International Studies*, 46: 89–108.
Baum, Richard (1994). *Burying Mao: Chinese Politics in the Age of Deng Xiaoping*. Princeton, NJ: Princeton University Press.
Beckley, Michael (2011). 'China's Century? Why America's Edge Will Endure'. *International Security*, 36(3): 41–78.
Beckwith, C.I. (2009). *Empires of the Silk Road: A History of Central Eurasia from the Bronze Age to the Present*. Princeton, NJ: Princeton University Press.
Behera, Navnita Chadha (2007). 'Re-Imagining IR in India'. *International Relations of the Asia-Pacific*, 7: 341–368.
Behnke, Andreas (2008). '"Eternal Peace" as the Graveyard of the Political: A Critique of Kant's *Zum Ewigen Frieden*'. *Millennium – Journal of International Studies*, 36(3): 513–531.
Behr, Hartmut (2014). *Politics of Difference: Epistemologies of Peace*. Abingdon, Oxon: Routledge.
Bell, Daniel (2008). *China's New Confucianism: Politics and Everyday Life in a Changing Society*. Princeton, NJ: Princeton University Press.
Bernal-Meza, Raúl (2005). *América Latina en el Mundo: El Pensamiento Latinoamericano y la Teoría de Relaciones Internacionales*. Buenos Aires: Nuevo Hacer, Grupo Editor Latinoamericano.
Bernal-Meza, Raúl (2006a). 'Aportes Teórico-Metodológicos Latinoamericanos Recientes al Estudio de las Relaciones Internacionales'. *Revista de Historia Actual*, 4: 227–238.
Bernal-Meza, Raúl (2006b). 'Cambiosy Continuidades en la Política Exterior Brasileña'. *Lateinamerika Analysen*, 13: 69–94.
Bernal-Meza, Raúl (2009). 'Latin American Concepts and Theories and their Impacts to Foreign Policies'. In: José Flávio Sombra Saraiva (ed.). *Concepts, Histories and Theories of International Relations for the 21st Century: Regional and National Approaches*. Brasilia: Instituto Brasileiro de Relações Internacionais, pp. 131–177.

Bernal-Meza, Raúl (2010). 'International Thought in the Lula Era'. *Revista Brasileira de Política Internacional*, 53 (special edition): 193–213.

Bernstein, Richard and Ross H. Munro (1997). 'The Coming Conflict with America'. *Foreign Affairs*, 76(2): 18–32.

Bhabha, Homi K. (2004). *The Location of Culture*. London and New York: Routledge.

Biersteker, Thomas J. (2009). 'The Parochialism of Hegemony: Challenges for "American" International Relations'. In: Arlene Tickner and Ole Wæver (eds). *International Relations Scholarship around the World*, London and New York: Routledge, pp. 308–327.

Bigo, Didier (2008). 'International Political Sociology'. In: Paul Williams (ed.). *Security Studies: An Introduction*. London and New York: Routledge, pp. 120–134.

Bilgin, Pinar (1999). 'Security Studies: Theory/Practice'. *Cambridge Review of International Affairs*, 12: 31–42.

Booth, Ken (1996). '75 Years on: Rewriting the Subject's Past – Reinventing its Future'. In Steve Smith, Ken Booth and Marysia Zalewski (eds). *International Theory: Positivism and Beyond*. Cambridge: Cambridge University Press.

Brown, Chris (1995a). 'International Theory and International Society: The Viability of the Middle Way'. *Review of International Studies*, 21(2): 183–196.

Brown, Chris (1995b). 'International Political Theory and the Idea of World Community'. In: Ken Booth and Steve Smith (eds). *International Relations Theory Today*. Cambridge: Cambridge University Press, pp. 90–109.

Brown, Chris (1998). 'Contractarian Thought and the Constitution of International Society Perspective'. In David R. Mapel and Terry Nardin (eds). *International Society: Diverse Ethical Perspectives*. Princeton, NJ: Princeton University Press, pp. 132–143.

Buckley, Chris (2013). 'China Takes Aim at Western Ideas'. *New York Times*, p. A1, 20 August.

Bull, Hedley (1966a). 'International Theory: The Case for the Classical Approach'. *World Politics*, 18(3): 361–377.

Bull, Hedley (1966b). 'The Grotian Conception of International Society'. In: Herbert Butterfield and Martin Wight (eds). *Diplomatic Investigations*. London: Allen and Unwin, pp. 35–73.

Bull, Hedley (1971). 'Order vs. Justice in International Society'. *Political Studies*, 19(3): 269–283.

Bull, Hedley (1977). *The Anarchical Society*. London: Macmillan.

Bull, Hedley (1984a). 'The Revolt against the West'. In: H. Bull and A. Watson (eds). *The Expansion of International Society*. Oxford: Oxford University Press, pp. 217–228.

Bull, Hedley (1984b). *Justice in International Relations: the 1983–4 Hagey Lectures*. Ontario: University of Waterloo.

Bull, Hedley and Adam Watson (eds) (1984). *The Expansion of International Society*. Oxford: Oxford University Press.

Burawoy, Michael (2013). 'Living Theory'. *Contemporary Sociology*, 46(2): 779–783.

Burawoy, Michael (2015). 'Travelling Theory', *Open Democracy*/ISA RC-47: Open Movements 21 March. Online, available at: https://opendemocracy.net/michael-burawoy/travelling-theory.

Butterfield, Herbert (1972). 'Morality and an International Order'. In: B. Porter (ed.). *The Aberystwyth Papers: International Politics, 1919–1969*. London: Oxford University Press, pp. 336–357.

Butterfield, Herbert and Martin Wight (eds) (1966). *Diplomatic Investigations*. London: Allen and Unwin.

Buzan, Barry (1993). 'From International System to International Society: Structural

Realism and Regime Theory Meet the English School'. *International Organization*, 47(3): 327–352.
Buzan, Barry (2004). *From International to World Society? English School Theory and the Social Structure of Globalisation*. Cambridge: Cambridge University Press.
Buzan, Barry (2010a). 'China in International Society: Is 'Peaceful Rise' Possible?' *Chinese Journal of International Politics*, 3(1): 5–36.
Buzan, Barry (2010b). 'Culture and International Society'. *International Affairs*, 86(1): 1–25.
Buzan, Barry (2014). *The English School of International Relations: An Introduction to the Societal Approach*. Cambridge: Polity.
Buzan, Barry and Ana Gonzalez-Pelaez (eds) (2009). *International Society and the Middle East: English School Theory at the Regional Level*. Basingstoke: Palgrave.
Buzan, Barry and George Lawson (2015). *The Global Transformation: History, Modernity and the Making of International Relations*. Cambridge: Cambridge University Press.
Buzan, Barry and Richard Little (2000). *International Systems in World History: Remaking the Study of International Relations*. Oxford: Oxford University Press.
Buzan, Barry and Zhang Yongjin (eds) (2014). *International Society and the Contest over East Asia*. Cambridge: Cambridge University Press.
Buzan, Barry, Ole Wæver and Jaapde Wilde (1998). *Security: A New Framework for Analysis*. Boulder, CO: Lynne Rienner Publishers.
Caballero, Sergio (2009). 'Comunidades Epistémicas En El Proceso de Integración Regional Sudamericana'. *Cuadernos Sobre Relaciones Internacionales, Regionalismo y Desarrollo*, 4(8): 11–26.
Callahan, William A. (2001). 'China and the Globalization of IR Theory: Discussion of "Building International Relations Theory with Chinese Characteristics"'. *Journal of Contemporary China*, 10(26): 75–88.
Callahan, William A. (2004a). *Contingent States: Greater China and Transnational Relations*. Minneapolis, MN: University of Minnesota Press.
Callahan, William A. (2004b). 'Dui guoji lilun de minzuhua – Yingguo xuepai yu Zhongguo tese guoji guanxi lilun de fuxian' [Nationalizing International Theory: The Emergence of the 'English School' and 'IR Theory with Chinese Characteristics']. *World Economics and Politics*, 6: 49–54.
Callahan, William A. (2004c). 'Nationalising International Theory: Race, Class and the English School'. *Global Society*, 18: 305–323.
Callahan, William A. (2008a). 'Chinese Visions of World Order: Post-hegemonic or a New Hegemony?' *International Studies Review*, 10(4): 749–761.
Callahan, William A. (2008b). 'Zhongguo shiye xia de shijie zhixu: tianxia, diguo he shijie' [The World Order with Chinese Perspective: Tianxia, Empire and the World]. *World Economics and Politics*, 10: 49–56.
Callahan, William A. and E. Barabantseva (eds) (2011). *China Orders the World: Normative Soft Power and Foreign Policy*. Washington, DC: Woodrow Wilson Centre Press.
Carlson, Allen (2005). *Unifying China: Integrating with the World*. Stanford, CA: Stanford University Press.
Carr, E.H. (1946). *The Twenty Years Crisis*. London: Macmillan.
Central Committee (2004). 'Guanyu jin yi bu fanrong fazhan zhexue shehui kexue de yijian' [Suggestions for the Further Development of Social Sciences]. Online, available at: www.chinasdn.org.cn/n1249550/n1249739/11013345.html (accessed 13 July 2013).

Cervo, Amadoluiz (2003). 'Política Exterior E Relações Internacionais Do Brasil: Enfoque Paradigmático'. *Revista Brasileira de Política Internacional*, 46: 5–25.
Cervo, Amadoluiz (2005). 'Os Excluídos Da Arca de Noé'. *Revista Brasileira de Política Internacional*, 48: 214–217.
Cervo, Amadoluiz (2007). 'Globalização, Integração E Estado Nacional No Mundo Contemporâneo'. *Meridiano*, 84: 2–6.
Cervo, Amadoluiz (2008). 'Conceitos Em Relações Internacionais'. *Revista Brasileira de Política Internacional*, 51(2): 8–25.
Cha, Victor D. (2009). 'What Do They Really Want?: Obama's North Korea Conundrum'. *Washington Quarterly*, 32(4): 119–138.
Chakrabarty, Dipesh (2001). *Provincializing Europe: Post-colonial Thought and Historical Difference*. Princeton: Princeton University Press.
Chan, Gerald (1997). 'International Studies in China: Origins and Development'. *Issues and Studies*, 33(2): 40–64.
Chan, Gerald (1998). 'Toward an International Relations Theory with Chinese Characteristics?' *Issues and Studies*, 34(6): 1–28.
Chan, Gerald (1999a). 'The Origin of the Interstate System: The Warring States in Ancient China'. *Issues and Studies*, 35(1): 147–166.
Chan, Gerald (1999b). *Chinese Perspectives on International Relations: A Framework for Analysis*. London: Macmillan Press Ltd.
Chan, Stephen (2009). *The End of Certainty: Towards a New Internationalism*. London: Zed Books.
Chang, Chi-shen (2011). 'Tianxia System on a Snail's Horns'. *Inter-Asia Cultural Studies*, 12(1): 28–42.
Chang, Chih-song (2007). 'Dongxi Guoji Zhixu Yuanli de Chongtu: Qingmo Minchu Zhongxian Jianjiao de Mingfen Jiaoshe' [The Contrast of the Eastern and Western Rationales of International Order: Sino-Siamese Negotiation on Diplomatic Status]. *Historical Research*, 2007(1): 88–114.
Chang, Chih-song (2010). 'Zhonghua Shijie Zhixu Yuanli de Qiyuan: Jindai Zhongguo Waijiao Fenzheng Zhong de Gudian Wenhua Jiazhi' [The Origin of Chinese World Order: The Classical Cultural Values in Foreign Conflicts of Modern China]. In: Wu Zhipan (ed.). *Dong Ya de Jia Zhi [The Value of East Asia]*. Beijing: Peking University Press, pp. 106–146.
Chang, Chih-song (2011). 'Jindai chuqi dongfang waijiao wenshu zhong suo chengxian de rihan mingfen zhixu lunzheng: cong xianwen shuqi dao jianghua tiaoyue de guoji wenshu fenxi' [The Korean-Japanese Status Disputes in Modern Diplomatic Documents: A Case Study]. Paper published at *International Conference on the Relations between China and Surrounding States*, Taipei, Academia Sinica, 25 November 2011.
Chang, Simon Teng-chi (2002). 'Zhongguo gainian de neihan yu liubian xiaokao' [A Review of the Conceptual Evolution of 'China']. *Mainland China Studies Newsletter*, 11: 17–20.
Chang, Simon Teng-chi (2004). 'Zhongguo daguo waijiao de leixingxue fenxi' [A Typology of China's Great Power Diplomacy]. *World Economy and Politics*, 288: 76–80.
Chang, Simon Teng-chi (2010). 'Qingdai menggu mengqi zhidu jianli de yihan: yizhong 'tianxia tixi' guannian xia de guoji zhengzhi zhidu chuangxin' [The Implications of Qin's Mongolian Banner System: An Institutional Innovation of the 'Under Heaven System']. *Mongolian and Tibetan Quarterly*, 19(4): 34–49.
Chang, Teng-chi (2013a). '"Zaipingheng" dui zhongmei guanxi zhi yingxiang: yige lilun yu zhengce de fenxi' ['Rebalance' and Its Impacts on Sino-American Relations: An Analysis of Offensive Realism]. *Prospect Quarterly*, 14(2): 53–99.

Bibliography 229

Chang, Teng-chi (2013b). 'A Responsible Great Power Not Hiding Light Anymore? China's Foreign Policy after the Xi-Li Administration's Inauguration'. *Prospect Journal*, 9: 77–106.

Chang, Teng-chi and Chen Yin-si (2012). 'Chaogong tixi zaixian yu "tianxia tixi" xingqi? Zhongguo waijiao de anli yanjiu yu lilun fansi' [Tribute System Revitalized and the Rise of the 'Under-Heaven System'? Cases Studies and Reflections on China's Diplomacy]. *Mainland China Studies*, 55(4): 89–123.

Chen, Bo-yu (2014). 'Sovereignty or Identity? The Significance of the Diaoyutai/Senkaku Islands Dispute for Taiwan'. *Perceptions: Journal of International Affairs*, 19: 107–120.

Chen, Ching-Chang (2011). 'The Absence of Non-Western IR Theory in Asia Reconsidered'. *International Relations of the Asia-Pacific*, 11: 1–23.

Chen, Li-fu (1986). *The Confucian Way: A New and Systematic Study of 'The Four Books'*. London: Routledge and Kegan Paul Inc.

Chen, Po-yu (2011). 'Guoji guanxi yazhou xuepai shifou keneng: guoji guanxi yanjiu de wenming zhuanxiang' [The Possibility of the Asian Schools of the IRT: A Civilizational Turn]. Kaohsiung: National Sun Yat-Sen University Institute of Political Science PhD Dissertation.

Chen, Qi and Huang Yuxing (2008). 'Chunqiu shiqi de guojiajian ganshe – jiyu Zuozhuan de yanjiu' [Intervention in the Spring and Autumn period – Researches on Tso Chuan]. *Quarterly Journal of International Politics*, 1: 33–73.

Chen, Shangsheng (1993). *Bisuo yu kaifang: Zhongguo fengjian wanqi duiwai guanxi yanjiu [Isolated and Open: Study on Foreign Relations in Late Feudal China]*. Ji'nan: Shandong People's Publishing House.

Chen, Tingxian and Zhou Ding (2008). *Tianxia, shijie, guojia: jindai zhongguo duiwai guannian yanbian shilun* [*Under Heaven, World and the States: A History of Modern Chinese Foreign Ideas*]. Shanghai: Joint Publishing.

Chen, Weifang (1986). 'Jiawu zhanqian chaoxian de guoji maodun yu qingzhengfu de shice' [Korea's International Contradiction and the Missteps of Qing Government before the Sino-Japanese War of 1894]. In: Historical Association of Shandong Province (ed.). *Jiawu 'jiushi zhounian jinian lunwenji [Commemorative Symposium on the 90th Anniversary of the Sino-Japanese War of 1894]*. Ji Nan: Qilu shushe, pp. 24–50.

Chen, Xu (2012). 'Jinnian guonei Makesizhuyi guoji guanxi lilun yanjiu pingshi' [Notes on Marxist IR research in China]. *Shehuizhuyi Yanjiu*, 3: 136–139.

Chen, Yugang (2011). Speech in Liu Yue, '"Zhongguo guoji lilun yanjiu: xianzhuang, wenti he qianjing" xueshu yantaohui zongshu' [A Transaction of the Symposium Themed with 'Studies of IR Theories in China: Status Quo, Issues and Prospects']. Online, available at: www.cssn.cn/news/420953.htlm (accessed on 5 May 2012).

Chen, Zheng (2015). 'Chunqiu huaxia zhixu wajie yu guoji shehui tuihua jizhi' [Collapse of International Order during the Spring and Autumn Era and the Study of International Society's Disintegration]. *World Economics and Politics*, 2: 41–64.

Chen, Zhigang (2010). 'Guanyu Fenggong tixi yanjiu de jige lilun wenti' [Theoretical Issues in a Study of the Tributary System]. *Journal of Tsinghua University (Philosophy and Social Sciences Edition)*, 6: 59–69.

Cheng, Zhe and Guo Shuyong (2012). 'Dangdai Zhongguo Makesizhuyi guoji guanxi lilun yanjiu: zou xiang duihua yu lunzhan' [Research on Modern Chinese Marxist IR: Dialogue and Controversy]. *Qianyan*, 7: 24–27.

Chiu, Kun-shuan and Simon Teng-chi Chang (2013). 'Taiwan zhonggong waijiao yanjiu de huigu: xin fazhan, yu xin tiaozhan' [Review of Studies on China's Foreign Relations in Taiwan: Challenges and Prospects]. In: Yushan Wu, Lin Jiwen and Leng Zegang (eds). *Political Science: The State of the Discipline*. Taipei: Wunan Publisher, pp. 439–462.

Chou, Mark (2011). 'Theorising China's International Relations'. *Australian Review of Public Affairs*. Online, available at: www.australianreview.net/digest/2011/09/chou.html.

Chowdhry, Geeta and L.H.M. Ling (2010). 'Race(ing) Feminist IR: A Critical Overview of Postcolonial Feminism'. In: Robert A. Denemark (ed.). *The International Studies Encyclopedia*. London: Blackwell Publishing, pp. 6038–6057.

Chowdhry, Geeta and Sheila Nair (eds) (2002). *Power, Postcolonialism, International Relations: Reading Race, Gender, Class*. London: Routledge.

Christensen, Thomas J. (1996). 'Chinese Realpolitik: Reading Beijing's World-View'. *Foreign Affairs*, 75(5): 37–52.

CJIP (2010). 'Editor-in-Chief Statement on the Transition to Quarterly Publication'. *Chinese Journal of International Politics*, 3: 1–2.

CJIP (2012). 'About the Journal'. *Chinese Journal of International Politics*. Online, available at: www.oxfordjournals.org/cjip/about.html.

Clark, Ian (1989). *The Hierarchy of States: Reform and Resistance in the International Order*. Cambridge: Cambridge University Press.

Clark, Ian (2005). *Legitimacy in International Society*. Oxford: Oxford University Press.

Clark, Ian (2007). *International Legitimacy and World Society*. Oxford: Oxford University Press.

Clark, Ian (2009a). 'Towards an English School Theory of Hegemony'. *European Journal of International Relations*, 15(2): 203–228.

Clark, Ian (2009b). 'Bringing Hegemony Back In: The United States and International Order'. *International Affairs*, 85(1): 23–36.

Clark, Ian (2011). *Hegemony in International Society*. Oxford: Oxford University Press.

Clinton, Hillary (2011). 'America's Pacific Century'. *Foreign Policy*. Online, available at: http://foreignpolicy.com/2011/10/11/americas-pacific-century/ (accessed 18 August 2012).

Cochran, Molly (2009). 'Charting the Ethics of the English School: What "Good" is there in a Middle-Ground Ethics?' *International Studies Quarterly*, 53(1): 203–225.

Collins, Randall (2000). *The Sociology of Philosophies: A Global Theory of Intellectual Change*. Cambridge, MA: Belknap Press of Harvard University Press.

Collins, Randall (2002). 'On the Acrimoniousness of Intellectual Disputes'. *Common Knowledge*, 8(1): 47–70.

Cox, Robert W. (1981). 'Social Forces, States and World Orders: Beyond International Relations Theory'. *Millennium – Journal of International Studies*, 10(2): 126–155.

Cox, Robert W. (1986). 'Social Forces, States and World Orders: Beyond International Relations Theory'. In: Robert O. Keohean (ed.). *Neorealism and Its Critics*. New York: Columbia University Press, pp. 204–254.

Cox, Robert W. (1996). 'A Perspective on Globalization'. In: J.H. Mittelman (ed.). *Globalization: Critical Reflections*. Boulder, CO: Lynn Rienner, pp. 21–30.

Crawford, Neta C. (1994). 'A Security Regime among Democracies: Cooperation among Iroquois Nations'. *International Organization*, 48(3): 345–385.

Cui, Zhongping (2003). *The Translation and Interpretation of Lao-tzu's Tao Te Ching*. Haerbing: Heilongjiang People Press.

Cunningham-Cross, Lingsay and William A. Callahan (2011). 'Ancient Chinese Thought, Modern Chinese Power'. *The Chinese Journal of International Politics*, 4(4): 349–374.

De Almeida, João Marques (2003). 'Challenging Realism by Returning to History: The British Committee's Contribution to IR Forty Years On'. *International Relations*, 17(3): 273–302.

Dellios, Rosita (2011). 'International Relations Theory and Chinese Philosophy'. In: Brett McCormick and Jonathan H. Ping (eds). *Chinese Engagements: Regional Issues with Global Implications*. Robina, Queensland: Bond University Press, pp. 45–66.

Deng, Xiaoping (1994). *Selected Works of Deng Xiaoping, Volume II*. Beijing: People's Publishing House.

Deng, Zhenglai (2010). 'The State of the Field: Political Science and Chinese Political Studies'. *Journal of Chinese Political Science*, 14(4): 331–334.

Diez, Thomas and Richard Whitman (2002). 'Analysing European Integration, Reflecting on the English School: Scenarios for an Encounter'. *Journal of Common Market Studies*, 40(1): 43–67.

Dirlik, Arif (2011). 'Culture in Contemporary IR Theory: The Chinese Provocation'. In: Robbie Shilliam (ed.). *International Relations and Non-Western Thought*. London and New York: Routledge, pp. 139–156.

Donelan, Michael (ed.) (1978). *The Reason of States*. London: Allan and Unwin.

Donnelly, Jack (1998). 'Human Rights: A New Standard of Civilization?' *International Affairs*, 74(1): 1–23.

Donnelly, Jack (2000). *Realism and International Relations*. Cambridge: Cambridge University Press.

Douzinas, Costas (2007). *Human Rights and Empire: The Political Philosophy of Cosmopolitanism*. New York: Routledge.

D'Souza, R. (2014). 'What Can Activist Scholars Learn from Rumi?'. *Philosophy East and West*, 64 (1): 1–24.

Dunne, Tim (1998). *Inventing International Society: A History of the English School*. London: Macmillan.

Dunne, Tim (1999). 'A British School of International Relations'. In: Jack Hayward, Brian Barry and Archie Brown (eds). *The British Study of Politics in the Twentieth Century*. Oxford: Oxford University Press, pp. 395–424.

Dunne, Tim and Nicholas Wheeler (1996). 'Hedley Bull's Pluralism of the Intellect and Solidarism of the Will'. *International Affairs*, 72(1): 91–107.

Dunne, Tim, Lene Hansen and Colin Wight (2013). 'The End of International Relations Theory?' *European Journal of International Relations*, 19(3): 405–425.

Duroselle, Jean-Baptiste (1952). 'L'étude Des Relations Internationales: Objet, Méthode, Perspectives'. *Revue Française de Science Politique*, 2: 676–701.

Egan, Ronald C. (1994). *Word, Image, and Deed in the Life of Su Shi*. Cambridge: Harvard University Press.

Engels, Friedrich (1998). 'A New English Expedition to China'. In: *The Complete Works of Marx and Engel*. Beijing: People's Publishing House.

English School Website (2015). English School Resources: Politics and International Studies (POLIS): University of Leeds. Online, available at: www.polis.leeds.ac.uk/research/international-relations-security/english-school/.

Epp, Roger (1998). 'The English School on the Frontiers of International Relations'. *Review of International Studies*, 24(Special Issue): 47–63.

Epp, Roger (2014). 'The British Committee on the Theory of International Politics and Central Figures'. In: Cornelia Navari and Daniel Green (eds). *Guide to the English School in International Studies*. Chichester: John Wiley and Sons, pp. 25–36.

Escobar, Arturo (2011). *Encountering Development: The Making and Unmaking of the Third World*. Princeton, NJ: Princeton University Press.

EWS (2012). 'China Hopes Russia-India Ties Conducive to Asian Stability'. *Xinhua News*, 26 December 2012. Online, available at: http://news.xinhuanet.com/english/china/2012-12/26/c_132065055.htm (accessed 8 January 2013).

Fairbank, John K. (1942). 'Tributary Trade and China's Relations with the West'. *Far Eastern Quarterly*, 1(2): 129–149.

Fairbank, John K. (ed.) (1968). *The Chinese World Order: Traditional China's Foreign Relations*. Cambridge, MA: Harvard University Press.

Fang, Changping (2005). 'Zhongguo guoji guanxi lilun jianshe: wenti yu sikao' [Constructing a Chinese IR Theory: Problems and Reflections]. *Jiaoxue yu yanjiu*, 6: 46–51.

Feng, Hui-yun (2007). *Chinese Strategic Culture and Foreign Policy Decision-Making: Confucianism, Leadership and War*. London: Routledge.

Finnemore, Martha (2001). 'Exporting the English School'. *Review of International Studies*, 27(3): 509–513.

Fonseca, Gelson (1987). 'Studies on International Relations in Brazil: Recent Times (1950–80)'. *Millennium – Journal of International Studies*, 16: 273–280.

Ford Foundation (ed.) (2003). *International Relations Studies in China: A Review of Ford Foundation Past Grantmaking and Future Choices*. Beijing: Ford Foundation Beijing Office.

Friedrichs, Jörg (2004). *European Approaches to International Relations Theory: A House with Many Mansions*. London: Routledge.

Fu, Baichen (2008). *Zhongchao lidai chaogong zhidu yanjiu [Study on the Tributary System and Relations between China and Korea in Different Dynasties]*. Changchun: Jilin Renmin Chubanshe.

Fu, Zhengyuan (1994). *Autocratic Tradition and Chinese Politics*. Cambridge: Cambridge University Press.

Fukuyama, Francis (1992). *The End of History and the Last Man*. New York: Free Press.

Gan, Chunsong (2012). *Back to Wangdao: Confucianism and the World Order*. Shanghai: East China Normal University Press.

Gao, Shangtao (2010). 'Guanxi zhuyi yu zhongguo xuepai' [Guanxiism and the Chinese School]. *World Economics and Politics*, 8: 116–160.

Gao, Weinong (1993). *Zouxiang jinshi de Zhongguo yu chaogong guo guanxi [The Relations between China and Its Tributaries as China Entered the Modern Era]*. Guangzhou: Guangdong Education Press.

Gareau, Frederick (1981). 'The Discipline International Relations: A Multi-National Perspective'. *Journal of Politics*, 43: 779–802.

Ge, Zhaoguang (2001). *Chinese Intellectual History*. Shanghai: Fudan University Press.

Geeraerts, Gustaaf and Jing Men (2001). 'International Relations Theory in China'. *Global Society*, 15(3): 251–276.

Giacalone, Rita (2012). 'Latin American Foreign Policy Analysis: External Influences and Internal Circumstances'. *Foreign Policy Analysis*, 8: 335–354.

Gill, Stephen (ed.) (1993). *Gramsci, Historical Materialism and International Relations*. Cambridge: Cambridge University Press.

Gilpin, Robert (1981). *War and Change in World Politics*. Cambridge: Cambridge University Press.

Gilpin, Robert (1994). *War and Change in World Politics* (Chinese Edition). Beijing: Renmin University of China Press.

Gladston, Rick (2012). 'Israeli Defense Chief Says Iran Postponed Nuclear Ambitions'. *New York Times*, 30 October. Online, available at: www.nytimes.com/2012/10/31/world/middleeast/israel-says-iran-has-postponed-nuclear-ambitions.html?r=1& (accessed 13 March 2013).

Glanville, Luke (2010). 'Retaining the Mandate of Heaven: Sovereign Accountability in Ancient China'. *Millennium*, 39(2): 323–343.

Glasser, Charles (2011). 'Will China's Rise lead to War?' *Foreign Affairs*, 90(2): 80–91.

Gong, Gerrit W. (1984). *The Standard of 'Civilization' in International Society*. Oxford: Clarendon Press.

Gong, Gerrit W. (2002). 'Standards of Civilization Today'. In: Mehdi Mozaffari (ed.). *Globalization and Civilization*. New York: Routledge, pp. 77–96.

Grazia, Sebastian de (1973). *Masters of Chinese Political Thought*. New York: Viking Press.

Gries, Peter Hays (1999). 'A "China Threat?": Power and Passion in Chinese "Face Nationalism"'. *World Affairs*, 162: 63–75.

Griffiths, Martin (1995). *Realism, Idealism and International Politics: A Reinterpretation*. London and New York: Routledge.

Griffiths, Martin (2007). 'Worldviews and IR Theory: Conquest or Coexistence?' In: Martin Griffiths (ed.). *International Relations Theory for the Twenty-First Century*. London: Routledge, pp. 1–10.

Grosser, Alfred (1956). 'L'étude Des Relations Internationales, Spécialité Américaine?' *Revue Française de Science Politique*, 6: 634–651.

Grovogui, Siba (2013). 'Postcolonialism'. In Tim Dunne, Milja Kirki and Steve Smith (eds) *Theories of International Relations*. Oxford: Oxford University Press.

Gu, Yue (translated and annotated) (1997). *Tao Te Ching*. Xi'an: World Publishing Xi'an Corporation.

Gu, Yufen (2005). 'Guo ji ge ju yu xin shi qi zhong guo wai jiao zheng ce de yan bian' [International Structure and the Evolution of Chinese Foreign Policy in the New Era]. *Northeast Normal University (Philosophy and Social Science)*, 2: 23–26.

Guo, Qingxiang (ed.) (2012). *The Doctrine of the Mean*. Beijing: Dongfang Press.

Haass, Richard (2008). 'The Age of Nonpolarity: What will Follow US Dominance?' *Foreign Affairs*, 87(5): 44–56.

Halliday, Fred (1992). 'International Society as Homogeneity: Burke, Marx, Fukuyama'. *Millennium*, 21(3): 435–461.

Han, J. and L.H.M. Ling (1998). 'Authoritarianism in the Hypermasculinized State: Hybridity, Patriarchy, and Capitalism in Korea'. *International Studies Quarterly*, 42(1): 53–78.

Han, M. (ed.) (1990). *Cries for Democracy: Writings and Speeches from the 1989 Chinese Democracy Movement*. Princeton, NJ: Princeton University Press.

Hao, Xiangman (2007). *Chaogong tixi de jiangou yu jiegou – lingyan xiangkan Zhong Ri guanxi [Construction and Deconstruction of the Tributary System: New View on Relations between China and Japan]*. Wuhan: Hubei Renmin Chubanshe.

Harding, Harry (1987). *China's Second Revolution: Reform after Mao*. Washington, DC: Brookings Institution Press.

Hardt, M. and A. Negri (2000). *Empire*. Cambridge: Harvard University Press.

Harshe, Rajan (1997). 'The Status of International Relations Studies: An Agenda for the Future'. In: M.S. Rajan (ed.). *International and Area Studies in India*. New Delhi: Lancers Books, pp. 68–80.

He, Baogang (2011). 'The Dilemmas of China's Political Science in the Context of the Rise of China'. *Journal of Chinese Political Science*, 16(3): 257–277.

Bibliography

He, Fangchuan (1998). '"Huayi zhixu" lun' [On the Sinocentric System]. *Journal of Peking University Humanities and Social Sciences Edition*, 6: 30–45.

He, Kai (2012). 'A Realist's Ideal Pursuit'. *Chinese Journal of International Politics*, 5(2): 183–197.

Hegel, G.W.F. (1983a). *The Speeches of Philosophical History*, Chinese edition. Beijing: Shangwu Publishing House.

Hegel, G.W.F. (1983b). *Lectures on the History of Philosophy*, Chinese edition. Beijing: Commercial Press.

Herz, Mônica (2002). 'O Crescimento Da Área de Relações Internacionais No Brasil'. *Contexto Internacional*, 24: 7–40.

Hevia, James (1995). *Cherishing Men from Afar: Qing Guest Ritual and the MacArtney Embassy of 1793.* Durham: Duke University Press.

Ho, Ping-ti (1968). 'Salient Aspects of China's Heritage'. In: Ping-ti Ho and Tang Tsou (eds). *China in Crisis*, vol. 1. Chicago: University of Chicago Press, pp. 1–92.

Hobbes, Thomas (1642). 'De Cive'. Online, available at: www.constitution.org/th/decive.htm (accessed 27 May 2013).

Hobbes, Thomas (1988 [1651]). *The Leviathan.* Buffalo, NY: Prometheus Books.

Hobson, John M. (2002). 'What's at Stake in "Bringing Historical Sociology Back into International Relations"? Transcending "Chronofetishism" and "Tempocentrism" in International Relations'. In: Stephen Hobden and John M. Hobson (eds). *Historical Sociology of International Relations*. Cambridge: Cambridge University Press, pp. 3–41.

Hobson, John M. (2012). *The Eurocentric Conception of World Politics: Western International Relations Theory, 1760–2010.* Cambridge: Cambridge University Press.

Hobson, John M. and George Lawson (2008). 'What is History in International Relations?' *Millennium – Journal of International Studies*, 37: 415–435.

Hoffmann, Stanley (1977). 'An American Social Science: International Relations'. *Daedalus*, 106(3): 41–60.

Holsti, Kalevi (1985). *The Dividing Discipline: Hegemony and Diversity in International Theory*. Boston: Allen & Unwin.

Holsti, Kalevi (2004). *Taming the Sovereigns: Institutional Change in International Politics*. Cambridge: Cambridge University Press.

Hu, Bo (2008). 'Gudai dongya guoji guanxi tixi de zhaoshi' [The Beginning of the Ancient East Asian International System]. *Foreign Affairs Review*, 1: 50–59.

Hu, Shoujun (2006). *Shehui gongsheng lun [A Theory of Social Symbiosis]*. Shanghai: Fudan University Press.

Hu, Weixing, Gerald Chan and Daojiong Zha (eds) (2000). *China's International Relations in the 21st Century: Dynamics of Paradigm Shifts*. Lanham, MD: University Press of America.

Hu, Zongshan (2003). 'Hou lengzhan shidai de guoji guanxi xin sichao yu waijiao xin zhanlüe' [New Thoughts on International Relations and Foreign Strategy in the Post-Cold War Period]. *Xinyang shi-fan xueyuan xuebao*, 23(6): 7–10.

Huan, Xiang (1991). 'Guanyu jianli guoji guanxixue de jige wenti' [Several Questions about the Establishment of the Studies of IR]. In: Shanghai Society of the Studies of IR (ed.). *Guoji guanxi lilun chutan [The Preliminary Exploration of IR Theories]*. Shanghai: Shanghai Foreign Language Press, pp. 1–7.

Huang, An-hao and Chen Chung-chi (2010). 'Guoji guanxi yanjiuzhong yingguo xuepai dianfan ji qi dui zhongguo xuepai zhi qishi' [The IR Paradigm of the English School and its Implication for Establishing a Chinese School]. *Prospect Quarterly*, 11(1): 41–86.

Huang, Chi-lian (1992). *Tian chao li zhi ti xi yan jiu Vol. 1: Yazhou de huaxia zhi xu–Zhongguo yu yazhou guojia guanxi xingtai lun [Study on the System of the Dominant Chinese Dynasty by the Rule of Rites: Cathay Order in Asia – On the Relations between Ancient China and Asian Countries]*. Beijing: China Renmin University Press.

Huang, Chi-lian (1994). *Tian chao li zhi ti xi yan jiu Vol. 2: Dongya de liyi shijie – Zhongguo fengjian wangchao yu chaoxian bandao guanxi xingtai lun [Study on the System of the Dominant Chinese Dynasty by the Rule of Rites: The World of Rites and Morality – On the Relations between Chinese Feudal Dynasties and the Korean Peninsula]*. Beijing: China Renmin University Press.

Huang, Chi-lian (1995). *Tian chao li zhi ti xi yan jiu Vol. 3: Chaoxian de ruhua qingjing gouzao – chaoxian wangchao yu manqing wangchao de guanxi xingtai lun [Study on the System of the Dominant Chinese Dynasty by the Rule of Rites: The Circumstances of Confucianismized Process – On the Relations between the Korean Dynasty and Qing Dynasty]*. Beijing: China Renmin University Press.

Hui, Victoria Tin-bor (2005). *War and State Formation in Ancient China and Early Modern Europe*. New York: Cambridge University Press.

Hui, Victoria Tin-bor (2008). 'How China Was Ruled?' *American Interest*, 3(4): 44–52.

Hui, Victoria Tin-bor (2010). 'Goujian "Zhongguo xuepai" bixu zhengshi lishi' [Chinese History Must be Taken Seriously in the Construction of a Chinese School of International Relations] (Xu Jin trans.). *World Economics and Politics*, 5: 124–138.

Hui, Victoria Tin-bor (2012a). 'Building Castles in the Sand: A Review of *Ancient Chinese Thought, Modern Chinese Power*'. *Chinese Journal of International Politics*, 5(4): 425–449.

Hui, Victoria Tin-bor (2012b). 'History and Thought in China's Traditions'. *Journal of Chinese Political Science*, 17: 125–141.

Huntington, Samuel (1996). *The Clash of Civilizations and the Remaking of World Order*. New York: Simon and Schuster.

Hurrell, Andrew (2001). 'Keeping History, Law and Political Philosophy Firmly Within the English School'. *Review of International Studies*, 27(3): 489–494.

Hurrell, Andrew (2007). *On Global Order: Power, Values and the Constitution of International Society*. Oxford: Oxford University Press.

Ikenberry, G. John (2008). 'The Rise of China and the Future of the West'. *Foreign Affairs*, 87(1): 23–37.

Ikenberry, G. John (2011). 'The Future of the Liberal World Order: Internationalism after America'. *Foreign Affairs*, May/June. Online, available at: www.foreignaffairs.com/articles/67730/g-john-ikenberry/the-future-of-the-liberal-worldorder.

Ikenberry, G. John (2014). 'The Rise of China and the Future of Liberal World Order'. The C. Douglas Dillon Lecture, Chatham House, London, 7 May 2014. Online, available at: www.chathamhouse.org/sites/files/chathamhouse/field/field_document/20140507RiseofChina.pdf.

Ikenberry, G. John and Charles A. Kupchan (1990). 'Socialization and Hegemonic Power'. *International Organization*, 44(3): 283–315.

Ikenberry, G. John and Anne-Marie Slaughter (2006). 'Forging a World of Liberty under Law: US National Security in the 21st Century'. Final Report of the Princeton Project on National Security. Princeton: Woodrow Wilson School of Public and International Affairs. Online, available at: www.princeton.edu/~ppns/report.html.

Inoguchi, Takashi (2010). 'Why Are There No Non-Western Theories of International Relations? The Case of Japan'. In: Amitav Acharya and Barry Buzan (eds). *Non-Western International Relations Theory*. London: Routledge, pp. 51–68.

Ivanhoe, Philip J. (2004). 'Filial Piety as a Virtue'. In: Alan Kam-leung Chan and Sor-hoon Tan (eds). *Filial Piety in Chinese Thought and History*. London: Routledge Curzon, pp. 189–201.
Jackson, Robert H. (1992). 'Pluralism in International Political Theory'. *Review of International Studies*, 18(3): 271–281.
Jackson, Robert H. (1996). 'Is There a Classical International Theory?' In: S. Smith, K. Booth and M. Zalewski (eds). *International Theory: Positivism and Beyond*. Cambridge: Cambridge University Press, pp. 203–218.
Jackson, Robert H. (2000). *The Global Covenant: Human Conduct in a World of States*. Oxford: Oxford University Press.
Jackson, Robert H. (2009). 'International Relations as a Craft Discipline'. In: Cornelia Navari (ed.). *Theorising International Society: English School Methods*. Basingstoke: Palgrave, pp. 21–38.
Jahn, Beate (2013). *Liberal Internationalism*. London: Palgrave Macmillan.
James, Alan (ed.) (1973). *The Bases of International Order: Essays in the Honour of C.A.W. Manning*. London: Oxford University Press.
James, Alan (1986). *Sovereign Statehood: The Basis of International Society*. London: Allen and Unwin.
Jatoba, Daniel (2013). 'Los Desarrollos Académicos de Las Relaciones Internacionales En Brasil: Elementos Sociológicos, Institucionales Y Epistemológicos'. *Relaciones Internacionales*, 22: 27–46.
Jia, Qingguo (2005). 'Learning to Live with the Hegemon: Evolution of China's Policy toward the US since the End of the Cold War'. *Journal of Contemporary China*, 14(4): 395–407.
Jian, Junbo (2009). 'Zhonghua chaogong tixi: Guannian jiegou yu gongneng' [Chinese Tributary System: Ideational Structure and Function]. *International Politics Quarterly*, 1: 132–143.
Jin, Haimin (2010). *The Translation and Interpretation of the Analects of Confucius*. Nanchang: Baihuazhou Literature and Art Publishing House.
Jin, Yaoji (2013). 'Shehuixue de zhongguohua: yige shehuixue zhishilun de wenti' [The Sinicization of Sociology: An Epistemic Sociological Question]. In: Jin Yao-i (ed.). *Zhongguo xiandaihua de zhongji yuanjing – Jin Yaoji zixuanji [The Ultimate Vision for China's Modernization – Selected Works of Jin Yaoji]*. Shanghai: Shanghai People's Publishing House.
Johnston, Alastair I. (1995). *Cultural Realism: Strategic Culture and Grand Strategy in Chinese History*. Princeton, NJ: Princeton University Press.
Johnston, Alastair I. (2002). 'The State of International Relations Research in China: Considerations for the Ford Foundation'. In: Ford Foundation (ed.). *International Relations in China: A Review of Ford Foundation Past Grant-Making and Future Choices*. Beijing: Ford Foundation.
Johnston, Alastair I. (2003). 'Is China a Status Quo Power?' *International Security*, 27(4), 5–56.
Johnston, Alastair I. (2007). *Social States: China in International Institutions, 1980–2000*. Princeton, NJ: Princeton University Press.
Johnston, Iain (2012). 'What (If Anything) Does East Asia Tell Us about International Relations Theory?'. *Annual Review of Political Science*, 15: 53–78.
Jones, Branwen G. (ed.) (2006). *Decolonizing International Relations*. Lanham, MA: Rowman & Littlefield.
Jones, Roy E. (1981). 'The English School of International Relations: A Case for Closure'. *Review of International Studies*, 7(1): 1–13.

Kan, Huai-chen (ed.) (2004). *Huangquan, liyi yu jingdian quanshi: zhongguo gudai zhengzhishi yanjiu [Imperial Power, Rites, and the Interpretations of Classics: A Study of Ancient China's Political History]*. Taipei: National Taiwan University Press.

Kan, Huai-chen (ed.) (2007). *Dongya lishi shang de tianxia yu zhongguo gainian [The Concepts of 'All-under-Heaven' and 'China' in East Asian History]*. Taipei: National Taiwan University Press.

Kang, David (2003). 'Hierarchy and Stability in International Relations'. In: G. John Ikenberry and Michael Mastanduno (eds). *International Relations Theory and the Asia-Pacific*. New York: Columbia University Press, pp. 163–190.

Kang, David (2007). *China Rising: Peace, Power and Order*. New York: Columbia University Press.

Kang, David (2010). *East Asia before the West: Five Centuries of Trade and Tribute*. New York: Columbia University.

Kang, David (2013). 'International Relations Theory and East Asian History: An Overview'. *Journal of East Asian Studies*, 13: 181–205.

Kant, Immanuel (2011). *Pepertual Peace: A Philosophical Essay*. Seattle, WA: Amazon.

Kaplan, Robert D. (2005). 'How We Would Fight China?' *Atlantic Monthly*, 29(5): 49–64.

Katzenstein, Peter J. (2006). 'Meiguo zhudao tixi xia de yazhou' [Asia under US Primacy]. *Journal of International Studies*, 2006(2): 10–20.

Katzenstein, Peter J. (2012). *Sinicization and the Rise of China: Civilizational Processes Beyond East and West*. London and New York: Routledge.

Keene, Edward (2002). *Beyond the Anarchical Society: Grotius, Colonialism and Order in World Politics*. Cambridge: Cambridge University Press.

Kelly, Robert E. (2012). 'A "Confucian Long Peace" in pre-Western East Asia?' *European Journal of International Relations*, 18(3): 407–430.

Keohane, Robert O. (1988). 'International Institutions: Two Approaches'. *International Studies Quarterly*, 32(4): 379–396.

Keohane, Robert O. (2005 [1984]). *After Hegemony: Cooperation and Discord in World Political Economy*. Princeton, NJ: Princeton University Press.

Keohane, Robert O. and Joseph S. Nye (1992). *Power and Interdependence: World Politics in Transition*. Boston, MA: Little, Brown & Co.

Khong, Yuen Foong (2013). 'The American Tribute System'. *Chinese Journal of International Politics*, 6(1): 1–47.

Kindleberger, Charles (1981). 'Dominance and Leadership in the International Economy'. *International Studies Quarterly*, 25(2): 242–254.

Kissinger, Henry A. (2012). 'The Future of US–Chinese Relations: Conflict Is a Choice, Not a Necessity'. *Foreign Affairs*, 91(2): 44–55.

Krasner, Stephen (1999). *Sovereignty: Organized Hypocrisy*. Princeton, NJ: Princeton University Press.

Krippendorff, Ekkehart (1987). 'The Dominance of American Approaches in International Relations'. *Millennium – Journal of International Studies*, 16: 207–214.

Krishna, Sankaran (1999). *Postcolonial Insecurities: India, Sri Lanka, and the Question of Nationhood*. Minneapolis, MN: University of Minnesota Press.

Krishna, Sankaran (2008). *Globalization and Postcolonialism: Hegemony and Resistance in the Twenty-First Century*. Plymouth: Rowman & Littlefield Publishers.

Kristensen, Peter M. (2015a). 'How Can Emerging Powers Speak? On Theorists, Native Informants and Quasi-Officials in International Relations Discourse'. *Third World Quarterly*, 36(4): 637–653.

Kristensen, Peter M. (2015b). 'International Relations in China and Europe: The Case for Interregional Dialogue in a Hegemonic Discipline'. *Pacific Review*, 28: 161–187.
Kristensen, Peter M. and Ras T. Nielsen (2010). 'Writing on the Wall: Prominence, Promotion, Power Politics and the Innovation of a Chinese International Relations Theory'. Copenhagen: Master's Thesis in Political Science, the University of Copenhagen.
Kristensen, Peter M. and Ras T. Nielsen (2013a). 'Constructing a Chinese International Relations Theory: A Sociological Approach to Intellectual Innovation'. *International Political Sociology*, 7: 19–40.
Kristensen, Peter M. and Ras T. Nielsen (2013b). '"You Need to Do Something That the Westerners Cannot Understand" – The Innovation of a Chinese School of IR'. In: Nicola Horsburgh, Astrid Nordin and Shaun Breslin (eds). *Chinese Politics and International Relations: Innovation and Invention*. London: Routledge, pp. 97–118.
Kurlantzick, Joshua (2007). *Charm Offensive: How China's Soft Power is Transforming the World*. Binghamton, NY: Yale University Press.
Lai, Sing Lam (2011). *The Romance of the Three Kingdoms and Mao's Global Order of Tripolarity*. Oxford: Peter Lang AG.
Lake, David A. (2007). 'Escape from the State of Nature: Authority and Hierarchy in World Politics'. *International Security*, 32(1): 47–79.
Lake, David A. (2009). *Hierarchy in International Relations*. New York: Cornell University Press.
Lampton, David M., Joyce A. Madancy, Kristen M. Williams and Committee on Scholarly Communication with the People's Republic of China (1986). *A Relationship Restored: Trends in US–China Educational Exchanges, 1978–1984*. Washington, DC: National Academies Press.
Levy, Jack S. (1997). 'Too Important to Leave to the Other: History and Political Science in the Study of International Relations'. *International Security*, 22(1): 22–33.
Leonard, Mark (2008). *What Does China Think?* London: The Fourth Estate.
Li, Bin (2005). 'Shenme shi Makesizhuyi de guoji guanxi lilun' [What is Marxist IR theory?]. *World Economics and Politics*, 5: 37–44.
Li, Bin (2009). 'Insights into the Mozi and Their Implications for the Study of Contemporary International Relations'. *Chinese Journal of International Politics*, 2: 421–454.
Li, Jie (2007). 'Ruanshili jianshe yu Zhongguo de heping fazhan' [Soft Power Building and China's Peaceful Development]. *China International Studies*, 49(1): 19–24.
Li, Ming (2008). 'Zhuge Liang "qiqin meng huo" chuanshuode wenhua nei han chutan' [An Initial Examination of the Cultural Implications of Zhuge Liang's 'Seven Captures of Meng Huo']. *Journal of Lincang Teachers College*, 17(1): 9–10.
Li, Shaojun (2011). Speech in Liu Yue, '"Zhongguo guoji lilun yanjiu: xianzhuang, wenti he qianjing" xueshu yantaohui zongshu' [A Transaction of the Symposium Themed with "Studies of IR Theories in China: Status Quo, Issues and Prospects"']. Online, available at: www.cssn.cn/news/420953.htlm (accessed 5 May 2012).
Li, Shisheng (2003). 'Guanyu guoji guanxixue jiaoyan de sikao – guoji guanxi xue tansuo wenji qianyan' [Thinking of IR Teaching and Research – Preface to The Anthology of IR Explorations]. *International Politics Quarterly*, 4: 112–117.
Li, Yihu (2004). 'Guoji geju yanjiu de xianshi zhuyi quxiang he zhongguo xuepai' [The Realist Approach of International 'Geju' and the Chinese School]. *Journal of International Studies*, 92: 28–36.
Li, Yihu (2005). 'The Question of Ontology in International Relations Theories'. *International Observer*, 1.
Li, Yingtao (2006). 'Research on Feminism in International Relations in China'. In:

Wang, Yizhou and Yuan Chunqing (eds). *Zhongguo guoji guanxi yanjiu (1995–2005) [IR Studies in China (1995–2005)]*. Beijing: Peking University Press, pp. 225–254.
Li, Yunquan (2004). *Chaogong zhidu shilun – Zhongguo gudai duiwai guanxi tizhi yanjiu [History of Tributary System – Study of the Foreign Relations System in Ancient China]*. Beijing: Xinhua Press.
Li, Yunquan (2014). *Wanbanglaichao: Chaogong Zhidu Shilun [The Tributary System in Ancient China]*. Beijing: Xinhua Press.
Li, Zehou (1987). *Zhongguo Xiandai Sixiang Shi Lun [On Modern Chinese Intellectual History]*. Beijing: Dongfang Press.
Li, Zehou and Liu Xuyuan (2011). *Gai zhongguo zhexue dengchang le? [Time for the Arrival of Chinese Philosophy? Dialogues with Li Zehou in 2010]*. Shanghai: Shanghai Translation Publishing House.
Li, Zehou and Liu Xuyuan (2012). *Zhongguo zhexue ruhe dengchang? [How Should Chinese Philosophy Come onto the Stage? Dialogues with Li Zehou in 2011]*. Shanghai: Shanghai Translation Publishing House.
Liang, Qichao (1901). *Complete Works of Liang Qichao*, Chinese edition, Beijing: Beijing Press.
Liang, Shoude (1994). 'Lun guoji zhengzhixue de zhongguo tese' [On IR with Chinese Characteristics]. *International Politics Quarterly*, 1(1): 15–21.
Liang, Shoude (1997a). 'Guoji zhengzhixue zai zhongguo: zaitan guoji zhengzhixue lilun de "Zhongguo tese"' [Studies of International Politics in China: A further Discussion on IR with Chinese Characteristics]. *International Politics Quarterly*, 1: 1–9.
Liang, Shoude (1997b). 'Lun guoji zhengzhixue lilun de "Zhongguo tese"' [On the International Relations Theory with Chinese Characteristics]. *Journal of China Foreign Affairs University*, 2: 40–46.
Liang, Shoude (2005a). 'Zhongguo guoji zhengzhixue lilun jianshe de tansuo' [Exploring the Construction of International Relations Theory in China]. *World Economics and Politics*, 2: 16–21.
Liang, Shoude (2005b). 'Lun zhongguo guoji zhengzhixue lilun jianshe' [On Constructing Chinese International Theory]. *Journal of Tongji University Social Science Edition*, 16(5): 84–88.
Liang, Shou-de and Hong Yinxian (2000). *Guoji zhengzhixue lilun [Theories of International Politics]*. Beijing: Peking University Press.
Lin, Daizhao (1994). 'Changes of International Relations in East Asia and China's Foreign Policy' [Dong ya di qu guo ji guan xi de bian hua yu zhong guo de wai jiao zheng ce]. *Studies of International Politics*, 2: 84–92.
Lin, Hsiaoting (2011). 'Chaogong zhidu yu lishi xiangxiang: liangbainianlai de zhong guo yu kanju ti' [The Tributary System and Historical Imagination: China and Kanjut, 1761–1963]. *Bulletin of the Institute of Modern History Academia Sinica*, 74: 41–82.
Lin, Justin (2012). *New Structural Economics: A Framework for Rethinking Development and Policy*. Washington, DC: The World Bank.
Lin, Yifu (2013). 'Xin jiegou jingjixue – fazhan jingjixue de fansi yu chonggou' [New Structural Economics: Rethinking and Restructuring Development Economics]. *Guangming Daily*, 10 November 2013.
Ling, L.H.M. (1994). 'Rationalizations for State Violence in Chinese Politics: The Hegemony of Parental Governance'. *Journal of Peace Research*, 31(4): 393–405.
Ling, L.H.M. (2014). *The Dao of World Politics: Towards a Post-Westphalian, Worldist International Relations*. London: Routledge.

240 Bibliography

Ling, L.H.M. (2016). 'Border Pathology: Ayurveda and Zhongyi as Strategic Therapies'. In: *India and China: New Connections for Ancient Geographies*. Ann Arbor, MI: University of Michigan Press.

Linklater, Andrew (1998). *The Transformation of Political Community*. Cambridge: Polity Press.

Linklater, Andrew and Hidemi Suganami (2006). *The English School of International Relations: A Contemporary Reassessment*. Cambridge: Cambridge University Press.

Little, Richard (1975). *Intervention: External Involvement in Civil Wars*. London: Martin Robertson.

Liu, Han, and Wang Cungang (2011). 'Lun Yingguo xuepai de guoji zhixu guan – jian yu tianxia tixi lilun de zhixu guan bijiao' [A Study of the View of the English School on the International Order and Comparison with the View of the Tianxia System Theory]. *Guoji luntan*, 13(6): 41–46.

Liu, Lydia H. (2004). *The Clash of Empires: The Invention of China in Modern World Making*. Cambridge: Harvard University Press.

Locke, John (1991 [1689]). *Two Treatises of Government*. North Clarendon, VT: Tuttle.

Lorenzini, María Elena and María Gisela Pereyra Doval (2013). 'Revisitando Los Aportes de Las Teorías Del Sur: Nexos Entre Teoría Y Praxis En Argentina Y Brasil'. *Relaciones Internacionales*, 22: 9–26.

Lu, Peng (2014). 'Pre-1949 Chinese IR: An Occluded History'. *Australian Journal of International Affairs*, 68(2): 133–155.

Luttwak, Edward N. (2012). *The Rise of China Vs. The Logic of Strategy*. Cambridge MA: The Belknap Press of Harvard University Press.

MaGann, James G. (2014). *2013 Global Go To Think Tank Index Report*. Online, available at: http://gotothinktank.com/dev1/wp-content/uploads/2014/01/GoToReport2013.pdf.

Major, J.S., S.A. Queen, A.S. Meyer, and H.D. Roth (trans and eds) (2010). *The Huainanzi: A Guide to the Theory and Practice of Government in Early Han China*. New York: Columbia University Press.

Mallavarapu, Siddharth (2009). 'Development of International Relations Theory in India: Traditions, Contemporary Perspectives and Trajectories'. *International Studies*, 46: 165–183.

Mancall, Mark (1984). *China at the Center – 300 Years of Foreign Policy*. New York: Free Press.

Manning, C.A.W. (1962). *The Nature of International Society*. London: London School of Economics.

Mao, Zedong (1937a). 'On Practice: On the Relation between Knowledge and Practice, between Knowing and Doing'. In: *Selected Works of Mao Zedong*, vol. 1. Beijing: Foreign Language Press, pp. 295–309.

Mao, Zedong (1937b). 'On Contradiction'. In: *Selected Works of Mao Zedong*, vol. 1. Beijing: Foreign Language Press, pp. 310–347.

Mapel, David R. and Terry Nardin (eds) (1998). *International Society: Diverse Ethical Perspectives*, Princeton, NJ: Princeton University Press.

Marchand, Marianne and Anne Sisson Runyan (eds) (2011). *Gender and Global Restructuring: Sightings, Sites, and Resistances*. London: Routledge.

Mattoo, Amitabh (2009a). 'The State of International Studies in India'. *International Studies*, 46: 37–48.

Mattoo, Amitabh (2009b). 'Upgrading the Study of International Relations'. *The Hindu*. Online, available at: www.hindu.com/2009/04/21/stories/2009042156680800.htm (accessed 27 February 2013).

Mattoo, Amitabh (2012). 'An Indian Grammar for International Studies'. *The Hindu*. Online, available at: www.thehindu.com/opinion/op-ed/an-indian-grammar-for-international-studies/article4185358.ece.

Mayall, James (1990). *Nationalism and International Society*. Cambridge: Cambridge University Press.

Mayall, James (2000). *World Politics: Progress and its Limits*. Cambridge: Polity.

Mayall, James (ed.) (1982). *The Community of States: A Study in International Political Theory*. London: George Allen and Unwin.

Mcmillan, Kevin (2012). 'Beyond Geography and Social Structure: Disciplinary Sociologies of Power in International Relations'. *Journal of International Relations and Development*, 15: 131–144.

Mcsweeney, Bill (1996). 'Identity and Security: Buzan and the Copenhagen School'. *Review of International Studies*, 22: 81–93.

Mearsheimer, John J. (2001). *The Tragedy of Great Power Politics*. New York: Norton Press.

Mearsheimer, John J. (2006). 'China's Unpeaceful Rise'. *Current History*, 105: 160–162.

Mearsheimer, John and Stephen Walt (2013). 'Leaving Theory Behind: Why Simplistic Hypothesis Testing is Bad for International Relations'. *European Journal of International Relations*, 19(3): 427–457.

Mei, Ran (2000). 'Gai bu gai you guoji zhengzhi lilun de zhongguo xuepai – jian ping meiguo de guoji zhengzhi lilun' [Should There be a Chinese School of IR Theory? Remarks on American Theories of International Politics]. *International Politics Quarterly*, 1: 63–67.

Meng, Honghua (2005). 'Hui gui guo ji guan xi yan jiu de zhong guo zhong xin: jia qi li lun yu shi' jian de qiao liang [Let's Refocus on China in IR Research Work: Bridging Theory and Practice]. *Teaching and Research*, 11: 28–31.

Meng, Weizhan (2012). 'Guoji guanxi lilun zhiyu zhongguo gudai guojiajian guanxi yanjiu de shiyongxing wenti' [International Relations Theories and Applicability in the Study of Inter-State Relations of Ancient China]. *Journal of Central South University Social Science Edition*, 6: 22–31.

Miao, Hongni (2006). 'Research on the English School in China'. In: Wang, Yizhou and Yuan, Zhengqing (eds). *IR Studies in China, 1995–2005*. Beijing: Peking University Press, pp. 196–224.

Mignolo, Walter D. (2000). *Local Histories/Global Designs: Coloniality, Subaltern Knowledges, and Border Thinking*. Princeton, NJ: Princeton University Press.

Miller, J.D.B. and John Vincent (eds) (1990). *Order and Violence: Hedley Bull and International Relations*. Oxford: Clarendon Press.

Mitter, Rana (2003). 'An Uneasy Engagement: Chinese Ideas of Global Order and Justice in Historical Perspective'. In: Rosemary Foot, John Gaddis and Andrew Hurrell (eds). *Order and Justice in International Relations*. Oxford: Oxford University Press, pp. 207–235.

Miyamoto, Shiguenoli (2003). 'O Ensino Das Relações Internacionais No Brasil: Problemas E Perspectivas'. *Revista de Sociologia e Política*, 20: 103–114.

Morgenthau, Hans J. (1978). *Politics Among Nations: The Struggle for Power and Peace*. 5th Edition. New York: Alfred A. Knopf.

Navari, Cornelia (ed.) (1991). *The Condition of States*. Buckingham: Open University Press.

Navari, Cornelia (2009). *Theorising International Society: English School Methods*. Basingstoke: Palgrave.

Bibliography

Neal, Fred Warner and Bruce Hamlett (1969). 'The Never-Never Land of International Relations'. *International Studies Quarterly*, 13: 281–305.

Ni, Shixiong (2001). *Dangdai xifang guoji guanxi lilun [Contemporary Western IR Theories]*. Shanghai: Fudan University Press.

Ni, Shixiong and Xu Jia (1997). 'Zhongguo guoji guanxi lilun yanjiu: lishi huigu yu fazhan' [IR Research in China: Historical Retrospective and Development]. *Ouzhou*, 6: 11–15.

Ni, Shixiong, Su Changhe and Jin Yingzhong (2009). 'Zhongguo guoji wenti yanjiu 60 nian' [China's International Studies in Sixty Years]. In: Yang Jie-mian (ed.). *Duiwai guanxi yu guoji wenti yanjiu [Foreign Relations and International Studies]*. Shanghai: Shanghai People's Publishing House.

Niou, Emerson M.S. and Peter C. Ordershook (1987). 'Preventive War and the Balance of Power: A Game-Theoretic Approach'. *Journal of Conflict Resolution*, 31(3): 387–419.

Nixon, Richard (1967). 'Asia after Vietnam', *Foreign Affairs*, 46(1): 113–125.

Noesselt, Nele (2012). 'Is There a "Chinese School" of IR?' GIGA Working Paper No. 188. Online, available at: http://dx.doi.org/10.2139/ssrn.2134863 (accessed 24 August 2012).

Noesselt, Nele (2015). 'Mapping the World from a Chinese Perspective? The Debate on Constructing a Theory of International Relations with Chinese Characteristics'. *China Quarterly*, 222: 430–448.

Nuyen, A.T. (2007). 'Confucian Ethics as Role-Based Ethics'. *International Philosophical Quarterly*, 47(3): 315–328.

Nye, Joseph Jr. (2013). 'Work with China, Don't Contain It'. *New York Times*, 26 January p. A19. Online, available at: www.nytimes.com/2013/01/26/opinion/work-with-china-dont-contain-it.html?_r=0.

Olson, William (1972). 'The Growth of a Discipline'. In: Brian Porter (ed.). *The Aberystwyth Papers: International Politics 1919–1969*. London: Oxford University Press, pp. 3–29.

Onuf, Nicholas G. (2013). *Making Sense, Making Worlds: Constructivism in Social Theory and International Relations*. London: Routledge.

Paltiel, Jeremy (2010). 'Mencius and World Order Theories'. *Chinese Journal of International Politics*, 3(1): 37–54.

Paltiel, Jeremy (2011). 'Constructing Global Order with Chinese Characteristics: Yan Xuetong and the Pre-Qin Response to International Anarchy'. *Chinese Journal of International Politics*, 4(4): 375–403.

Pan, Chengxin (2013). 'The Asian/Chinese Century from the Chinese Perspective'. *Griffith Asia Quarterly*, 1(1): 30–52.

Pan, Chengxin (2014). 'Rethinking Chinese Power: A Conceptual Corrective to the 'Power Shift' Narrative'. *Asian Perspective*, (38): 387–410.

Pan, Zhongqi (ed.) (2012). *Conceptual Gaps in China–EU Relations*. Basingstoke: Palgrave Macmillan.

Pang, Zhongying (2003). 'Kaifangshi de zizhu fazhan: dui yingguo guoji guanxi lilun de yixiang guancha' [An Open Road of Independent Exploration: An Observation of the English School]. *World Economics and Politics*, 6: 20–25.

Park, Geun-Hye (2013). 'The Exercise of My Despair: Park Geun-Hye Autobiography'. Online, available at: www.goodreads.com/book/show/18138421-the-exercise-of-my-despair (accessed 10 December 2013).

Pateman, Carole (1988). *The Sexual Contract*. Stanford: Stanford University Press.

Paul, Thazha Varkey (2009). 'Integrating International Relations Studies in India to Global Scholarship'. *International Studies*, 46: 129–145.

Peng, Zhaochang and Su Changhe (1999). 'Zhongguo guoji guanxi lilun de pinkun: dui jin ershinian guoji guanxixue zai zhongguo fazhan de fansi' [The Poverty of China's International Relations Theory: A Review of Two Decades' IRT in China]. *World Economics and Politics*, 2: 15–19.

Peterson, V. (1992). *Gendered States: Feminist (Re)Visions of International Relations Theory*. Boulder, CO: Lynne Rienner.

Pouliot, Vincent (2008). 'The Logic of Practicality: A Theory of Practice of Security Communities'. *International Organization*, 62(2): 257–288.

Pouliot, Vincent (2010). *International Security in Practice: The Politics of NATO-Russia Diplomacy*. Cambridge: Cambridge University Press.

Prozorov, Sergei (2014). *Ontology and World Politics*. London: Routledge.

Pye, Lucian (1968). *The Spirit of Chinese Politics: A Psychocultural Study of the Authority Crisis in Political Development*. Cambridge: MIT Press.

Pye, Lucian W. (1988). *The Mandarin and the Cadre: China's Political Cultures (Michigan Monographs in Chinese Studies)*. Ann Arbor, MI: The Chinese Centre for Chinese Studies, University of Michigan.

Qin, Yaqing (1999). *Baquan tixi yu guoji chongtu* [Hegemonic System and International Conflict]. Shanghai: Shanghai Renmin Chubanshe.

Qin, Yaqing (2004). 'Di san zhong wenhua: guoji guanxi yanjiu zhong kexue yu renwen de qihe' [The Third Culture: The Integration of Scientific and Humanistic Methods in IR Research]. *World Economics and Politics*, 1: 19–20.

Qin, Yaqing (2005). 'Guoji guanxi lilun de hexin wenti yu zhongguo xuepai de shengcheng' [The Core Question of IR Theory and the Formation of the Chinese School]. *Social Sciences in China*, 3: 165–176.

Qin, Yaqing (2006). 'Guoji guanxi lilun "zhongguo xuepai" shengcheng de keneng he biran' [A Chinese School of International Relations Theory: Possibility and inevitability]. *World Economics and Politics*, 3: 7–13.

Qin, Yaqing (2007). 'Why is there No Chinese International Relations Theory?' *International Relations of the Asia-Pacific*, 7(3): 313–340.

Qin, Yaqing (2008a). 'Guanyu goujian zhongguo tese waijiao lilun de ruogan sikao' [Reflections on the Development of a Chinese Theory of Diplomacy]. *Foreign Affairs Review*, 101: 9–17.

Qin, Yaqing (2008b). 'Yanjiu sheji yu xueshu chuangxin' [Research Design for Academic Innovation]. *World Economics and Politics*, 2008(8): 75–80.

Qin, Yaqing (2008c). 'Zhongguo guoji guanxi lilun yanjiu de jinbu yu wenti' [Study of International Relations Theory in China: Progress and Problems]. *World Economics and Politics*, 11: 13–23.

Qin, Yaqing (2009a). 'Guanxi benwei yu guocheng jiangou: jiang zhongguo linian zhiru guoji guanxi lilun' [Relationality and Processual Construction: Bringing Chinese Ideas into International Relations Theory]. *Social Sciences in China*, 3: 69–86.

Qin, Yaqing (2009b). 'Development of International Relations Theory in China'. *International Studies*, 46(1–2): 185–201.

Qin, Yaqing (2009c). 'Zhongguo guoji guanxi lilun' [On China's International Relations Theory]. In: Wang Yizhou (ed.). *Zhongguo duiwai guanxi zhuanxing 30 nian [Chinese Foreign Relations: Thirty Years in Transition]*. Beijing: Social Science Academic Press, pp. 306–343.

Qin, Yaqing (2010). 'Why is there No Chinese International Relations Theory?' In

244 Bibliography

Amitav Acharya and Barry Buzan (eds). *Non-Western International Relations Theory.* London: Routledge, pp. 26–50.

Qin, Yaqing (2011a). 'Development of International Relations Theory in China: Progress and Problems'. In: Yizhou Wang (ed.). *Transformation of Foreign Affairs and International Relations in China, 1978–2008.* Brill ebooks.

Qin, Yaqing (2011b). 'Development of International Relations Theory in China: Progress through Debates'. *International Relations of the Asia-Pacific*, 11: 231–257.

Qin, Yaqing (2011c). 'Rule, Rules, and Relations: Towards a Synthetic Approach to Governance'. *Chinese Journal of International Politics*, 4(2): 117–145.

Qin, Yaqing (2012a). *Guoji guanxi lilun: fansi yu chonggou [International Relations Theory: Reflection and Reconstruction].* Beijing: Peking University Press.

Qin, Yaqing (2012b). *Guanxi yu guocheng: Zhongguo guoji guanxi lilun de wenhua jiangou [Relations and Process: Cultural Construction of Chinese International Relations Theory].* Shanghai: Shanghai People's Publishing House.

Qin, Yaqing (2012c). 'Culture and Global Thought: Chinese International Theory in the Making'. *Revista CIDOB d'Afers Internacionals*, 100: 67–90.

Qin, Yaqing (2014). 'Continuity through Change: Background Knowledge and China's International Strategy'. *Chinese Journal of International Politics*, 7(3): 285–316.

Quan, Hexiu (2005). 'Zhongguo gudai chaogong guanxi yanjiu shuping' [A Review on the Tributary Relationships in Ancient China]. *China's Borderland History and Geography Studies*, 15(3): 124–133.

Rajan, M.S. (1979). 'Teaching and Research on International Relations and Area Studies'. *International Studies*, 18: 75–88.

Rajan, M.S. (1994). 'International and Area Studies in India'. *International Studies*, 31: 207–214.

Rajan, M.S. (1997a). *International and Area Studies in India.* New Delhi: Lancers Books.

Rajan, M.S. (1997b). 'Reflections on Development of Area Studies in India'. In: M.S. Rajan (ed.). *International and Area Studies in India.* New Delhi: Lancers Books.

Reiss, Hans (ed) (1970). *Kant's Political Writings.* Translated by H.B. Nisbet. Cambridge, UK: Cambridge University Press.

Ren, Xiao (1998). 'Guoji wenti yanjiu duanxiang' [Fragments on International Studies]. *International Review*, 4: 51–53.

Ren, Xiao (2000). 'Lilun yu guoji guanxi lilun' [Theory and IR Theory: Some Thoughts]. *Journal of European Studies*, 4: 19–25.

Ren, Xiao (2003). 'Xiang yingguo xuepai xuexi' [To Learn from the English School]. *World Economics and Politics*, 7: 70–71.

Ren, Xiao (2004). 'Jiangjiu fangfa, bu wei fangfa' [Stressing Method While Not Sticking to Method]. *World Economics and Politics*, 1: 19.

Ren, Xiao (2005). 'Guoji guanxi xue buneng meiyou renwen diyun' [IR Could Not Be Without A Humanistic Foundation]. *Studies in International Politics*, 4: 145–146.

Ren, Xiao (2008). 'Toward a Chinese School of International Relations'. In Wang Gung-wu and Zheng Yong-nian (eds). *China and the New International Order.* London: Routledge, pp. 293–309.

Ren, Xiao (2009a). 'Guanjian zaiyu zhongguo texing: yetan yingguo xuepai ji qita' [The Chinese Characteristics are Critical: On the English School and Beyond]. *World Economics and Politics*, 1: 69–72.

Ren, Xiao (2009b). 'Zou zizhu fazhan zhilu: zhenglun zhong de "zhongguo xuepai"' [The Road of Our Own Choice: The Chinese School in Debate]. *Journal of International Studies*, 2: 15–28.

Ren, Xiao (2014). 'Lun zhongguo de shijie zhuyi' [On Chinese Cosmopolitanism]. *World Economics and Politics*, (8): 30–45.

Ren Xiao (ed.) (2015). *Gongsheng – shanghai xuepai de xingqi [Gongsheng – the Rise of a Shanghai School of IR]*. Shanghai: Shanghai Yiwen Press.

Rengger, Nicholas (1992). 'A City Which Sustains All Things? Communitarianism and International Society'. *Millennium*, 21(3): 353–369.

Rengger, Nicholas (2011). 'The World Turned Upside Down. Human Rights in International Relations after 25 years'. *International Affairs*, 87(5): 1159–1178.

Reus-Smit, Christian (2002). 'Imagining Society: Constructivism and the English School'. *British Journal of Politics and International Relations*, 4(3): 487–509.

Reus-Smit, Christian (2005). 'The Constructivist Challenge after September 11'. In: Alex J. Bellamy (ed.). *International Society and its Critics*. Oxford: Oxford University Press, pp. 81–94.

Reus-Smit, Christian (2009). 'Constructivism and the English School'. In: Cornelia Navari (ed.). *Theorising International Society: English School Methods*. Basingstoke: Palgrave, pp. 39–57.

Riemer, Andrea K. and Yannis A. Stivachtis (eds) (2002). *Understanding EU's Mediterranean Enlargement: The English School and the Expansion of Regional International Societies*. Frankfurt: Peter Lang.

Ringmar, Erik (2012). 'Performing International Systems: Two East-Asian Alternatives to the Westphalian Order'. *International Organization*, 66(1), 1–25.

Risse, Thomas (2000). '"Let's Argue!": Communicative Action in World Politics'. *International Organization*, 54(1): 5–6.

Robinson, I. William (2005). 'What Is a Critical Globalization Studies? Intellectual Labor and Global Society'. In: Richard P. Appelbaum and William I. Robinson (eds). *Critical Globalization Studies*, New York, Routledge, pp. 11–18.

Robles, Alfredo, Jr. (1993). 'How "International" Are International Relations Syllabi?' *Political Science and Politics*, 26: 526–528.

Roetz, Heiner (2012). 'The Axial Age Theory: A Challenge to Historism or an Explanatory Device for Civilizational Analysis? With a Look at the Normative Discourse'. In Robert N. Bellah and Hans Joas (eds.) *The Axial Age and Its Consequences*. Cambridge, MA: Harvard University Press.

Rosenberg, Justin (1994). *The Empire of Civil Society*. London: Verso.

Rosenberg, Justin (2010). 'Problems in the Theory of Uneven and Combined Development Part II: Unevenness and Multiplicity'. *Cambridge Review of International Affairs*, 23(1): 165–189.

Rosenberg, Justin (2013). 'Kenneth Waltz and Leon Trotsky: Anarchy in the Mirror of Uneven and Combined Development'. *International Politics*, 50(2): 183–230.

Rubin, Vitaly A. (1976). *Individual and State in Ancient China* (Steven I. Levine trans.), New York: Columbia University Press.

Ruggie, John G. (1986). 'Continuity and Transformation in the World Polity: Toward a Neorealist Synthesis'. In Robert O. Keohane (ed.). *Neorealism and Its Critics*. New York: Columbia University Press, pp. 131–157.

Runciman, W.G. (1969). *Social Science and Political Theory*. Cambridge: Cambridge University Press.

Said, Edward W. (1983). *The World, the Text, and the Critic*. Cambridge: Harvard University Press.

Santos, Norma Breda dos (2005). 'História Das Relações Internacionais No Brasil: Esboço de Uma Avaliação Sobre a Área'. *História*, 24: 11–39.

Santos, Norma Breda dos and Fúlvio Eduardo Fonseca (2009). 'A Pós-Graduação Em Relações Internacionais No Brasil'. *Contexto Internacional*, 31: 353–380.

Saraiva, José Flávio Sombra (2003). 'Um percurso acadêmico modelar: Amado Luiz Cervo e a afirmação da historiografia das relações internacionais no Brasil'. In: Estevão Chaves de Rezende Martins (ed.). *Relações Internacionais: Visões Do Brasil e Da América Latina (Estudos Em Homenagem a Amado Luiz Cervo)*. Brazil: IBRI, pp. 17–36.

Saraiva, José Flávio Sombra (2009). 'Are There Regional and National Conceptual Approaches to International Relations?' In: José Flávio Sombra Saraiva (ed.). *Concepts, Histories and Theories of International Relations for the 21st Century: Regional and National Approaches*. Brasilia: Instituto Brasileiro de Relações Internacionais.

Sawyer, Ralph D. (trans.) (1993). *The Seven Military Classics of Ancient China*. Boulder, CO: Westview Press.

Schmitt, Carl (2007). *The Concept of the Political*. Chicago, IL: The University of Chicago Press.

Schram, Stuart (1989). *The Thought of Mao Tse-Tung*. Cambridge: Cambridge University Press.

Schumpeter, Joseph (1994). *History of Economic Analysis*. London: Routledge.

Schwarzenberger, Georg (1951). *Power Politics: A Study of International Society*. London: Stevens and Sons.

Seth, Sanjay (ed.) (2013). *Postcolonial Theory and International Relations: A Critical Introduction*. New York: Routledge.

Shahi, Deepshikha (2013). 'Indian Scholarship on International Relations and Multilateralism'. *Economic and Political Weekly*, 48: 50–58.

Shambaugh, David (ed.) (2005). *Power Transition: China and Asia's New Dynamics*. Berkley, CA: University of California Press.

Shambaugh, David (2011). 'International Relations Studies in China Today: History, Trends and Prospects'. *International Relations of the Asia-Pacific*, 11(3): 339–372.

Shambaugh, David (2013). *China Goes Global: The Partial Power*. Oxford: Oxford University Press.

Shambaugh, David and Wang Jisi (1984). 'Research and Training in International Studies in the People's Republic of China'. *PS: Political Science and Politics*, 17(4): 6–14.

Shang, Huipeng (2009). '"Lunren" yu "Tianxia" – Jiedu yi chaogong tixi wei hexin de gudai dongya guoji zhixu' ['Human Relationships' and 'All-Under-Heaven': An Interpretation of the Ancient East Asian International Order under the Tributary System]. *International Politics Quarterly*, 2: 29–43.

Shi, Bin (2004). 'Guoji guanxi lilun zhongguoshi tansuo de jige jiben wenti' [Basic Questions of Chinese Explorations on International Relations Theory]. *World Economics and Politics*, 5: 8–13.

Shi, Bin (2006). 'Guoji guanxi yanjiu "Zhongguohua" de lunzheng' [Debates in the Nationalization of IR in China]. In: Wang Yizhou and Yuan Zhengqing (eds). *Zhongguo guoji guanxi yanjiu (1995–2005) [IR Studies in China (1995–2005)]*. Beijing: Peking University Press: pp. 518–545.

Shi, Yinhong (2004). 'Guoji guanxi lilun yanjiu yu pingpan de ruogan wenti' [Several Issues in the Studies and Comments on IR Theories]. *Social Sciences in China*, 1: 89–91.

Shi, Yinhong (2009). 'Meiguo quanshi, zhongguo jueqi yu shijie zhixu' [America's Supremacy, China's Rise and the World Order]. In: Gao Quan-xi (ed.). *Daguoce: quanqiu shiye zhong de zhongguo dazhanlue [Statecrafts: China's Grand Strategy from a Global Perspective]*. Beijing: People's Publishing House, pp. 32–39.

Shih, Chih-yu (1990). *The Spirit of Chinese Foreign Policy: A Psychocultural View*. Basingstoke: Macmillan.
Shih, Chih-yu (1999). 'Shijie zhishi de Zhongguo huiying: zhishi, lichang ji qita – Yi zhengzhixue weili' [Chinese Response to World Knowledge: Knowledge, Position and Others – Taking Political Science as an Example]. *Strategy and Management*, 4: 54–61.
Shih, Chih-yu (2005a). 'Post-Chineseness and Mainlandization'. Paper presented at *The Workshop on Culture and Security*. Tsukuba: Tsukuba University, 28 September 2005.
Shih, Chih-yu (2005b). 'Yingguo xuepai yu liang'an guoji guanxi yanjiu' [The English School and IR Studies in both mainland and Taiwan]. *Quarterly Journal of International Politics*, 1: 132–148.
Shih, Chih-yu (2008). *Riben jindaixing yu zhongguo: zai shijie xianshen de zhuti celue [The Modernity of Japan and China: The Strategy of Subjectivity for a Representation in the World]*. Taipei: National Translation and Compilation Center.
Shih, Chih-yu (2010a). 'Guoji guanxi yanjiu de yazhou difangxing xuepai' [The Regional School in Asia of IR Studies]. *Quarterly Journal of International Politics*, 3: 51–73.
Shih, Chih-yu (2010b). 'The West That Is Not in the West: Identifying Self in Oriental Modernity'. *Cambridge Review of International Affairs*, 23: 537–560.
Shih, Chih-yu (2011a). 'Mizoguchi Yuzo's Chinese Kitai Revisited: Worlding the Sinic Order through Multisited Recollections'. Paper presented in *Symposium on Rethinking Asia in the Age of Globalization*. Hong Kong, Baptist University, 1–2 December 2011.
Shih, Chih-yu (2011b). 'Wenming yu guoji guanxi lilun: yazhou xuepai de bu/kexingxing' [Civilization and International Relations Theory: The Im/possibility of Asian Schools]. In: Bao Tzong-ho (ed.). *Guoji guanxi lilun [Theories on International Relations]*. Taipei: Wunan Books, pp. 331–347.
Shih, Chih-yu (2015). 'Chineseness, and Post-Chineseness'. Lecture at the Asia-Pacific Centre for Chinese Studies, Chinese University of Hong Kong, Hong Kong, 12 October 2015.
Shih, Chih-yu and Huang Chiung-chiu (2011). 'Bridging Civilizations through Nothingness: Manchuria as Nishida Kitaro's "Place"'. *Comparative Civilizations Review*, 65: 4–17.
Shih, Chih-yu and Huang Chiung-chiu (2012). 'Balance of Relationships: Accessing International Relations System from China'. Paper presented at the International Workshop *The Chinese School of IR and its Critics*, Beijing, 8–9 July 2013.
Shih, Chih-yu and Huang Chiung-chiu (2014). 'China's Quest for Grand Strategy: Power, National Interest, or Relational Security'. *Chinese Journal of International Politics*, 8(1): 1–26.
Shih, Chih-yu and Simon Tengchi Chang (2010). 'Ganjue zhongguo jueqi: benti xushi ji qi qinggan jichu' [Perceiving China's Rise: Ontological Narratives and Their Affectional Foundations]. In: Ding Shu-fan and Chang Yachung (eds). *Baquan zhihou yu zhongguo jueqi [After Hegemony and China's Rise]*. Taipei: National Cheng-Chi University Institute of International Relations, pp. 1–46.
Shih, Chih-yu and Teng-chi Chang (2011). 'The China Studies that Defend Chineseness: The Im/Possibility of China Centrism in the Divided Sino-phone World'. In: Herbert S. Yee (ed.). *China's Rise – Threat or Opportunity*. New York: Routledge Press, pp. 280–297.
Shih, Chih-yu, Yin Wei and Kuo Ming-Jie (2008). 'Yuanzilun shi guojizhengzhixue de benti? Shehuia jiangou yu minzhuheping de gongmo' [Is Atomism the Ontology of International Politics? The Conspiracy of Social Constructivism and the Democratic Peace]. *World Economics and Politics*, 2008(6): 29–38.
Shilliam, Robbie (ed.) (2011). *International Relations and Non-Western Thought: Imperialism, Colonialism and Investigations of Global Modernity*. London: Routledge.

Simpson, Gerry (2004). *Great Powers and Outlaw States: Unequal Sovereigns in the International Legal Order*. Cambridge: Cambridge University Press.

Smith, Steve (1987). 'Paradigm Dominance in International Relations: The Development of International Relations as a Social Science'. *Millennium – Journal of International Studies*, 16: 189–206.

Smith, Steve (1999). 'The Increasing Insecurity of Security Studies: Conceptualizing Security in the Last Twenty Years'. *Contemporary Security Policy*, 20: 72–101.

Snow, C.P. (1998). *The Two Cultures*. Cambridge: Cambridge University Press.

Snyder, Jack (2008). 'Some Good and Bad Reasons for a Distinctively Chinese Approach to International Relations Theory'. Paper presented at *the Annual Meeting of the APSA 2008 Annual Meeting*, Boston, Massachusetts, Hynes Convention Center, 28 August 2008.

Song, Wei (2013). 'Hexin gainian de chuangzao yu Zhongguo guoji guanxi lilun de fazhan (yantaohui zongshu)' [Conference Summary: The Innovation of Key Concepts and The Development of IR Theory in China]. *Guoji zhengzhi yanjiu*, 4: 175–177.

Song, Xinning (1997). 'International Relations Theory-Building in China'. *Political Science*, 49: 40–61.

Song, Xinning (2001). 'Building International Relations Theory with Chinese Characteristics'. *Journal of Contemporary China*, 10(26): 61–74.

Spivak, Gayatri Chakravorty (1988). 'Can the Subaltern Speak?' In: Nelson, Cary and Lawrence Grossberg (eds). *Marxism and the Interpretation of Culture*, Champaign, IL: University of Illinois Press, pp. 271–313.

Stivachtis, Yannis A. (2014). 'The Regional Dimension of International Society'. In: Cornelia Navari and Daniel Green (eds). *Guide to the English School in International Studies*. Chichester: John Wiley and Sons, pp. 109–126.

Strange, Susan (1995). '1995 Presidential Address ISA as a Microcosm'. *International Studies Quarterly*, 39: 289–295.

Strassler, Robert B. (ed.) (1996). *The Landmark Thucydides: A Comprehensive Guide to the Peloponnesian War*. New York: Free Press.

Su, Changhe (2003). 'Wenti yu sixiang: zaitan guoji guanxi yanjiu zai zhongguo' [Puzzles and Reflections: Rethink the Studies of International Relations in China]. *World Economics and Politics*, 2003(3): 28–30.

Su, Changhe (2005). 'Why Is There No Chinese IR Theory?' *International Review*, (4): 26–30.

Su, Changhe (2012). 'Zai xin de lishi qidian shang sikao Zhongguo yu shijie guanxi' [Exploration of the Relationship between China and the World from a New Historical Starting Point]. *World Economics and Politics*, 26(8), 4–19.

Su, Changhe and Peng Zhaochang (1999). 'Zhongguo guoji guanxi lilun de pinkun – dui jin ershi nian guojiguanxi xue zai zhongguo fazhan de fansi' [The Poverty of China's IR Theory – Reflections on the Recent Twenty Years' Development of IR in China]. *World Economics and Politics*, 2: 15–19.

Su, Shaozhi (1996). *Shinian Fengyun: Wenge Hou de Dalu Lilunjie [Ten Eventful Years: Theoretical Circles in the Mainland China after the Cultural Revolution]*. Taipei: Shibao Wenhua.

Suganami, Hidemi (1989). *The Domestic Aanalogy and World Order Proposals*. Cambridge: Cambridge University Press.

Suganami, Hidemi (2003). 'British Institutionalists, or the English School, 20 Years On'. *International Relations*, 17(3): 253–271.

Suganami, Hidemi (2008). *Globalization and Postcolonialism: Hegemony and Resistance in the Twenty-First Century*. Plymouth: Rowman & Littlefield Publishers.

Suganami, Hidemi (2010). 'The English School in a Nutshell'. *Ritsumeikan Annual Review of International Studies*, (9): 15–28.

Sun, Lizhou (2007). 'Xihan shiqi dongya guoji tixi de liangji geju fenxi – Jiyu hanchao yu xiongnu liangda zhengzhi xingweiti de kaocha' [Han-Xiongnu Bipolarity in Ancient East Asia during the Western Han Dynasty]. *World Economics and Politics*, 8: 17–25.

Sun, Xuefeng (2003). 'Academic Criticism Does Not Mean Moral Condemnation: On the Essay of "Between Science and Art – On a Theory of International Relations"'. *World Economics and Politics*, (1): 31–34.

Sun, Xuefeng (2007). 'He xie shi jie li nian yu zhong guo guo ji guan xi li lun yan jiu' [The Idea of Harmonic Society and the Research on Chinese IR Theories]. *Teaching and Research*, (11).

Sun, Yecheng (2010). *The Translation and Interpretation of Lao Tzu*. Nanchang: Baihuazhou Literature and Art Publishing House.

Suzuki, Shogo (2009). *Civilisation and Empire: China and Japan's Encounter with European International Society*. London: Routledge.

Suzuki, Shogo, Yongjin Zhang and Joel Quirk (2014). *International Orders in the Early Modern World: Before the Rise of the West*. London: Routledge Press.

Tang, Hsin-wei (2010). 'Dingjen Lianqiang de Shuangbian Guanxi: 1660–2006' [Bilateral Relations between Two Great Powers: 1660–2006]. *Taiwanese Journal of Political Science*, 44: 75–104.

Tang, Shiping (2010). 'Yu "kouhaoxing" wenzhang juelie' [To Break off from Slogan-like Articles]. *Newsletter of Chinese Social Science*, 23 December 2010, p. 4.

Tang, Shiping (2013). *The Social Evolution of International Politics*. Oxford: Oxford University Press.

Tang, Xiaosong (2005). 'Ying guo xue pai de fa zhan gong xian he qi shi' [The English School: Its Development, Contribution, and Lessons for Us]. *World Economy and Politics*, (7): 21–27.

Tellis, Ashley J. (2014). *Balancing Without Containment: An American Strategy for Managing China*. New York: Carnegie Endowment.

Teng, Ssu-yu and John King Fairbank (eds) (1954). *China's Response to the West: A Documentary Survey, 1839-1923*. Cambridge, MA: Harvard University Press.

Thomas, E.D. (1927). *Chinese Political Thought*. New York: Prentice-Hall.

Tickner, Arlene (2003). 'Hearing Latin American Voices in International Relations Studies'. *International Studies Perspectives*, 4: 325–350.

Tickner, Arlene and David Blaney (eds) (2012). *Thinking International Relations Differently*. London: Routledge.

Tickner, Arlene and David Blaney (eds) (2013). *Claiming the International*. London and New York: Routledge.

Tickner, Arlene and Ole Wæver (eds) (2009). *International Relations Scholarship around the World*. London: Routledge.

Tickner, Arlene, Carolina Cepeda and Jose Luis Bernal (2013). 'Investigatión Y Política International (TRIP) En América Latina'. *Brazilian Journal of International Relations*, 2: 6–47.

Toby, Ronald (1998). *State and Diplomacy in Early Modern Japan: Asia in the Development of the Tokugawa Bakufu*. Stanford: Stanford University Press.

Tu, Wei-ming (1991). 'The Enlightenment Mentality and the Chinese Intellectual Dilemma'. In Kenneth Lieberthal (ed.) *Perspectives on Modern China*. Armonk, New York: M.E. Sharpe, pp. 103–118.

Tu, Weiming (1996). 'Introduction'. In: Weiming Tu (ed.). *Confucian Traditions in East Asian Modernity*. Cambridge: Harvard University Press, pp. 1–10.

US Senate Committee on Foreign Relations (2008). *China's Foreign Policy and "Soft Power" in South America, Asia, and Africa*. Washington, DC: US Senate Committee of Foreign Relations.

Upadhyaya, Priyankar (2009). 'Peace and Conflict: Reflections on Indian Thinking'. *Strategic Analysis*, 33: 71–83.

Vigezzi, Brunello (2005). *The British Committee on the Theory of International Politics 1954–1985: The Rediscovery of History*. Milan: Edizzioni Unicopli.

Vincent, R. John (1974). *Nonintervention and International Order*. Princeton, NJ: Princeton University Press.

Vincent, R. John (1986). *Human Rights and International Relations: Issues and Responses*. Cambridge: Cambridge University Press.

Vincent, R. John (1988). 'Hedley Bull and Order in International Politics'. *Millennium*, 17(2): 195–213.

Wæver, Ole (1992). 'International Society – Theoretical Promises Unfulfilled?' *Cooperation and Conflict*, 27(1): 97–128.

Wæver, Ole (1998). 'The Sociology of a Not So International Discipline: American and European Developments in International Relations'. *International Organization*, 52(4): 687–727.

Wæver, Ole (1999). 'Does the English School's Via Media equal the Contemporary Constructivist Middle Ground?' Paper presented in *24th BISA Conference*, Manchester, 20–22 December 1999.

Wæver, Ole (2004). 'Aberystwyth, Paris, Copenhagen New "Schools" in Security Theory and Their Origins between Core and Periphery'. Paper presented at *ISA convention 2004*, Montreal, Canada, 17–20 March 2004.

Wæver, Ole (2012). 'Aberystwyth, Paris, Copenhagen: The Europeanness of New "Schools" of Security Theory in an American Field'. In: Arlene Tickner and David Blaney (eds). *Thinking the International Differently*. London: Routledge, pp. 48–71.

Walt, Stephen M. (2013). 'Why the Sunnylands Summit won't stop Sino-American Rivalry'. *Foreign Policy*, 5 June 2013. Online, available at: http://walt.foreignpolicy.com/posts/2013/06/05/the_sunnylands_summit_wont_stop_sino_american_rivalry >.

Waltz, Kenneth (1979). *Theory of International Politics*. Reading, MA: Addison-Wesley Press.

Waltz, Kenneth (1986). 'Reflections on Theory of International Politics: A Response to My Critics'. In: Robert O. Keohane (ed.). *Neorealism and its Critics*. New York: Columbia University Press, p. 339.

Waltz, Kenneth (1991). *Man, The State and War* (Chinese edition). Shanghai: Shanghai Yiwen Chubanshe.

Wan, Ming (2000). *Zhongguo rongru shijie de bulv – Ming yu Qing qianqi haiwai zhengce bijiao yanjiu [The Pace of China's Merging into the World – A Comparative Study on Foreign Policy in the Ming and Early Qing Dynasties]*. Beijing: Social Science Press.

Wang, Cungang (2005). 'Ke jiejian de he ying pipan de: guanyu yanjiu he xuexi Yingguo xuepai de sikao' [What We Can Learn From and Should Criticise?: Thinking of Study on the English School]. *Journal of European Studies*, 23(4): 48–52.

Wang, Cungang (2009). 'Weishenme yao fazhan Makesizhuyi guoji guanxi lilun' [Why Marxist IR will have to be Developed Further]. *Forum of World Economics and Politics*, 5: 6–12.

Wang, Cungang (2011). "Guonei xuejie guanyu makesi zhuyi guoji guanxi lilun ji qi zhongguohua yanjiu" [On the Studies of Marxist International Relations Theories and its Sinicization in China]. *Journal of International Studies*, (3): 81–98.

Wang, Haoliang (2010). *The Translation and Interpretation of Mencius*. Nanchang: Baihuazhou Literature and Art Publishing House.

Wang, Hung-jen (2013a). 'Being Uniquely Universal: Building Chinese International Relations Theory'. *Journal of Contemporary China*, 22(81): 518–534.

Wang, Hung-jen (2013b). *The Rise of China and Chinese International Relations Scholarship*. Lanham, MA: Lexington.

Wang, Jiangli (2013). 'Zhongguo guoji guanxi yanjiu de lishi zhuanxiang' [The Historical Turn of Contemporary IR Study in China]. *Journal of Zhejiang University*, 43(4): 77–92.

Wang, Jiangli and Barry Buzan (2014). 'The English and Chinese Schools of International Relations: Comparisons and Lessons'. *Chinese Journal of International Politics*, 7(1): 1–46.

Wang, Jianwei, Lin Zhimin and Zhao Yuliang (1986). 'Nuli chuangjian woguo ziji de guoji guanxi lilun tixi' [Make Efforts to Build up Chinese IR Theory]. *World Economics and Politics for Internal Reference*, 9: 1–7.

Wang, Jisi (1994). 'International Relations Theory and the Study of Chinese Foreign Policy'. In: Thomas W. Robinson and David Shambaugh (eds). *Chinese Foreign Policy: Theory and Practice*. Oxford: Clarendon Press, pp. 481–505.

Wang, Jisi (2002). 'International Relations Studies in China Today'. In: Ford Foundation (ed.). *International Relations in China: A Review of Ford Foundation Past Grantmaking and Future Choices*. Beijing: Ford Foundation, pp. 1–25.

Wang, Jisi (2006). *Guoji zhengzhi de lixing sikao [A Rationalist Reflection on International Politics]*. Beijing: Peking University Press.

Wang, Jisi (2009). 'Guanyu gouzhu zhongguo guoji zhanlue de jidian kanfa' [A Few Points on the Construction of China's International Strategy]. In: Kao Quan-xi (ed.). *Daguoce: quanqiu shiye zhong de zhongguo dazhanlue [Statecrafts: China's Grand Strategy from a Global Perspective]*. Beijing: People's Publishing House, pp. 14–16.

Wang, Jun (2004). 'Zhong guo de guo ji guan xi li lun yi zhong zhu ti xing shi jiao' [Chinese IR Theories: An Ontological Perspective]. *World Economy and Politics*, (2): 26–30.

Wang, Jun and Dan Xingwu (2008). *Zhongguo guoji guanxi yanjiu sishinian [IR Studies of China in the Past Forty Years]*. Beijing: Central Compilation and Translation Press.

Wang, Qiubin (2007). 'Yi yingguo xuepai shijiao shenshi dongbeiya guoji shehui' [International Society in the Northeast Asia: From the Perspective of the English School]. *Jilin University Journal Social Sciences Edition*, 2: 59–65.

Wang, Rihua (2009). 'Guoji tixi yu zhongguo gudai guojiajian guanxi yanjiu' [International System and International Relations in Ancient China]. *World Economics and Politics*, 12: 58–68.

Wang, Rihua (2011). 'Kongzizhuyi yu guoji guanxi lilun yu Zhongguo waijiao' [Confucianism, International Relations and Chinese Diplomacy]. *Contemporary International Relations*, 31(5): 47–54.

Wang, Rongpei and Ren, Xiuhua (translated and annotated) (1999). *Shi-Jin [The Book of Poetry]*. Liaoning: Liaoning Education Publishing House.

Wang, Xiangsui (2011). 'Biyuan zhengzhi: shijie geju de bianhua yu weilai' [Currency Politics: Change and Future of the International System]. *World Economics and Politics*, 4: 10–24.

Bibliography

Wang, Yiwei (2002). 'Between Science and Art: On a Theory of International Relations'. *World Economics and Politics*, (9): 4–10.
Wang, Yiwei (2004). 'Weishenme meiyou Zhongguo de guoji guanxi lilun?' ['Why Is There No Chinese IR Theory?'], *Shijie jingji yu zhengzhi (World Economics and Politics)*, 1: 21–22.
Wang, Yiwei (2007a). 'Between Science and Art: Questionable International Relations Theories'. *Japanese Journal of Political Science*, 8(2): 191–208.
Wang, Yiwei (2007b). 'Theorization of International Relations Theory'. *World Economics and Politics*, (4): 19–25.
Wang, Yiwei (2009). 'China: Between Copying and Constructing'. In: Arlene B. Tickner and Ole Waever (eds). *International Relations Scholarship Around the World*. New York: Routledge: pp. 103–119.
Wang, Yiwei and Ni Shixiong (2002). 'Lun bijiao guoji guanxi xue ji guoji guanxi lilun de Zhongguo xuepai' [On Comparative IR and Chinese School of IR theories]. *Open Times*, 5: 17–23.
Wang, Yizhou (1995). *Dangdai guoji zhengzhi xilun [An Analysis of Contemporary International Politics]*. Shanghai: Shanghai People's Publishing House.
Wang, Yizhou (1998a). 'Zhongguo guoji zhengzhi lilun yanjiu de jige wenti' [Several Issues in the Research on IR Theories in China]. *Journal of European Studies*, 2: 4–11.
Wang, Yizhou (1998b). 'Zhongguo guoji zhengzhi lilun yanjiu de jige wenti–xu' [Several Issues in the Research on IR Theories in China – Part 2]. *Journal of European Studies*, 3: 28–32.
Wang, Yizhou (1998c). *International Studies in the West: History and Theories*. Shanghai: Shanghai People's Publishing House.
Wang, Yizhou (2006a). 'Xulun' [Introduction]. In: Wang Yizhou and Yuan, Zhengqing (eds). *Zhongguo guoji guanxi yanjiu (1995–2005) [China's International Relations Studies: 1995–2005]*, Beijing: Peking University Press, pp. 1–60.
Wang, Yizhou (2006b). 'Guodu zhong de zhongguo guoji guanxixue' [China's International Relations Studies in Transition], *World Economics and Politics*, 2006(4): 7–12.
Wang, Yizhou and Yuan Zhengqing (eds) (2006). *Zhongguo guoji guanxi yanjiu (1995–2005) [IR Studies in China, 1995–2005]*. Beijing: Peking University Press.
Wang, Yuan-Kang (2010). *Harmony and War: Confucian Culture and Chinese Power Politics*. New York: Columbia University Press.
Wang, Yuan-Kang (2012). 'Managing Regional Hegemony in Historical Asia: The Case of Early Ming China'. *Chinese Journal of International Politics*, 5(2): 129–153.
Wang, Yuesheng and Ma Xiangdong (2015). 'Cong zhuisui dao chuangxin' [From Following to Innovation]. *People's Daily*, 26 January 2015.
Wang, Yukai (2008). 'Zhongguo zhengzhi moshi tiaxian le zishen youshi' [The Chinese Model Shows its Advantages]. *Renmin Luntan*, 28: 36–17.
Wang, Zhengyi (2000). *Shijie tixi lun yu Zhongguo [World System Theory and China]*. Beijing: The Commercial Press.
Wang, Zhengyi (2006). 'Chengwei zhishi de shengchanzhe' [To Be a Producer of Knowledge]. *World Economics and Politics*, 2006(3): 6–11.
Wang, Zhuoyu (2012). 'Goujian "Zhongguo xuepai" de guannian kunjing – jiyu bijiao shiye de fenxi' [The Conceptual Difficulties with Building a "Chinese School": A Comparative Perspective]. *Journal of Contemporary Asia-Pacific Studies*, 2: 60–83.
Watson, Adam (1992). *The Evolution of International Society*. London: Routledge.
Watson, Adam (1997). *The Limits of Independence: Relations Between States in the Modern World*. London: Routledge.

Watson, Adam (2007). *Hegemony and History*. Abingdon: Routledge.
Weinberger, J. (1975). 'Hobbes' Doctrine of Method'. *American Political Science Review*, 69(4): 1336–1353.
Welch, William (1972). 'The Possibility of an International Discipline of International Affairs'. *International Studies Quarterly*, 16: 295–320.
Wells, Audrey (2001). *The Political Thought of Sun Yat-Sen: Development and Impact.* Basingstoke: Palgrave/Macmillan.
Wendt, Alexander (1992). 'Anarchy is what States make of it: The Social Construction of Power Politics'. *International Organization*, 46(2): 391–425.
Wendt, Alexander (1999). *Social Theory of International Politics*. Cambridge: Cambridge University Press.
Wendt, Alexander (2003). 'Why a World State is Inevitable?' *European Journal of International Relations*, 9(4): 491–542.
Wheeler, Nicholas J. (1992). 'Pluralist and Solidarist Conceptions of International Society: Bull and Vincent on Humanitarian Intervention'. *Millennium*, 21(3): 463–489.
Wight, Colin (2006). *Agent, Structure and International Relations: Politics as Ontology*. Cambridge: Cambridge University Press.
Wight, Martin (1960). 'Why Is There No International Relations Theory?' *International Relations*, 2: 35–48.
Wight, Martin (1966). 'Why Is There No International Theory?' In: H. Butterfied and Martin Wight (eds). *Diplomatic Investigations*. London: George Allen & Unwin, pp. 19–34.
Wight, Martin (1977). *Systems of States*. Leicester: Leicester University Press.
Wight, Martin (1979). *Power Politics*. London: Penguin.
Wight, Martin (1991). *International Theory: The Three Traditions*. Leicester: Leicester University Press for the Royal Institute of International Affairs.
Wilson, Peter (2015) 'English School Neo-Neo Style: Symposium on The English School in Retrospect and Prospect'. *Cooperation and Conflict.* Published online before print, 18 November 2015; doi: 10.1177/0010836715610595. Online, available at: http://cac.sagepub.com/content/early/2015/11/14/0010836715610595.
Womack, Brantly (2010). *Chain among Unequals: Asymmetric Foreign Relations in Asia*. Singapore: World Scientific Press.
Womack, Brantly (2012). 'Asymmetry and China's Tributary System'. *Chinese Journal of International Politics*, 5(1): 37–54.
Wong, Edward (2015). 'China Approves Sweeping Security Law, Bolstering Communist Rule'. *New York Times*, p. A12, 2 July 2015.
Wu, Daying (ed.) (2000). *Social Science in the New China: A Fifty Year Perspective*. Beijing: China Social Sciences Press.
Wu, Xiaoming (2014). 'Zhongguo xueshu ruhe zouchu "xuetu zhuangtai"' [How should Chinese Academic Research Go Out Of 'Apprenticeship']. *Wenhui Xueren*, 12 December 2014. Online, available at: www.whb.cn/xueren/20585.htm.
Xi, Jinping (2014). 'Speech by H.E. Mr. Xi Jinping President of the People's Republic of China at the Meeting Commemorating the 50th Anniversary of the Establishment of China-France Diplomatic Relations'. 27 March 2014. Online, available at www.fmprc.gov.cn/mfa_eng/wjdt_665385/zyjh_665391/t1147894.shtml.
Xu, Jianxin (2007). 'Tianxia tixi yu shijie zhidu' [Tianxia and world order]. *Quarterly Journal of International Politics*, 3(2): 113–143.
Xu, Jielin (2004). *Chunqiu bangjiao yanjiu [A Study of Interstate Relations in the Spring and Autumn Period]*. Beijing: China Social Science Press.

Xu, Jin (2011). 'Liyong zhongguo gudai guojiajian zhengzhi sixiang he xingwei fazhan guoji guanxi lilun de shexiang' [A Proposal on Improving IR Theories through Studies on Inter-State Political Thought in Ancient China]. *Sina Blog*, 29 November 2011. Online, available at: http://blog.sina.com.cn/s/blog_60be0aa10100z3by.html (accessed on 12 May 2012).

Xu, Jin (2012). 'Chunqiu Shiqi "Zunwang Rangyi" Zhanlue de Xiaoyong Fenxi' [An Analysis of the Effectiveness of the 'Zunwang Rangyi' Strategy during the Spring and Autumn Period]. *Quarterly Journal of International Politics*, 2: 38–61.

Xu, Lin (2014). 'Top 10 Most Influential Think Tanks in China'. Online, available at: www.china.org.cn/top10/2014-02/03/content_31341799.htm.

Yan, Xuetong (2004). 'Guoji guanxi yanjiu zhong shiyong kexue fangfa de yiyi' [The Meaningfulness of Applying Scientific Method in IR Research]. *World Economics and Politics*, 1: 17–18.

Yan, Xuetong et al. (2004). 'A Forum on the "Rise of Great Powers and China's Choices"'. *Social Sciences in China*, 2: 51–63.

Yan, Xuetong (2006). 'Guoji guanxi lilun shi pushixing de' [IR Theory is Universal]. *World Economics and Politics*, 2: 3.

Yan, Xuetong (2008). 'Xun Zi's Thought on International Politics and its Implications'. *Chinese Journal of International Politics*, 2(1): 135–165.

Yan, Xuetong (2011a). *Ancient Chinese Thought, Modern Chinese Power*. Princeton, NJ: Princeton University Press.

Yan, Xuetong (2011b). 'Guoji Lingdao yu Guoji Guifan de Yanhua' [International Leadership and Norm Evolution]. *Quarterly Journal of International Politics*, 1: 1–28.

Yan, Xuetong (2011c). 'International Leadership and Norm Evolution'. *Chinese Journal of International Politics*, 4: 233–264.

Yan, Xuetong (2011d). 'Why Is There No Chinese School of International Relations Theory?' In: Yan Xuetong (ed.). *Ancient Chinese Thought, Modern Chinese Power*, Princeton, NJ: Princeton University Press, pp. 252–259.

Yan, Xuetong (2012). 'Quanli Zhongxin Zhuanyi yu Guoji Tixi Zhuanbian' [Power Transition and Transformation of the International Order]. *Journal of Contemporary Asia-Pacific Studies*, 6: 4–21.

Yan, Xuetong (2013a). 'Chongyin xuyan' [Reprint Preface]. In: James Dougherty and Robert L. Pfaltzgraff (eds). *Zhenglun zhong de guojiganxi lilun (diwuban) [Contending Theories of International Relations – A Comprehensive Survey, The Fifth Edition]* (Yan Xuetong and Chen Hanxi trans.). Beijing: Shijie zhishi chubanshe.

Yan, Xuetong (2013b). 'Gongping Zhengyi de Jiazhiguan yu Hezuo Gongying de Waijiao Yuanze' [Just and Equitable Values and the Foreign Policy Principle of Win-Win Cooperation]. *International Studies*, 1: 6–14.

Yan, Xuetong (2014). 'Daoyi Xianshi Zhuyi de Guoji Guanxi Lilun' [International Relations Theory of Moral Realism]. *The Journal of International Studies*, 2014(5): 102–127.

Yan, Xuetong (2015). *Daoyi Xianshi Zhuyi Lilun [The Moral Realism of International Relations]*. Beijing: Peking University Press.

Yan, Xuetong and Lu Xin (2005). 'Yan Xuetong: zhizhuo yu kexue yuce de xianshi zhuyi xuezhe' [Yan Xuetong: A Realist Scholar Pursuing Scientific Forecasting: An Interview]. *World Economics and Politics*, 7: 59–64.

Yan, Xuetong and Xu Jin (2008). *Zhongguo xianqin guojiajian zhengzhi sixiang xuandu [Pre-Qin Chinese Thoughts on Foreign Relations Selected Readings]*. Shanghai: Fudan University Press.

Yan, Xuetong and Xu Jin (2009). *Wangba tianxia sixiang ji qi qidi [Thoughts of World Leadership and Implications]*. Beijing: World Affairs Press.

Yang, Chuang (2004). 'Guanyu Zhongguo dui wai zhanlüe yu guoji zhixu lilun' [On China's Foreign Strategy and Theories of International Order]. *Foreign Affairs Review*, 78: 22–29.

Yang, Hu-an (2011). 'Mei Dui Mian "Qiao Waijiao" Xiaoguo Cuiyi Neng Ge Miandian Shihui Shizai Taishao' [The US Doubts on Myanmar's Tricky Diplomacy]. *World News Journal*, 6 December. Online, available at: http://intl.ce.cn/sjjj/qy/201112/06/t20111206_22894919.shtml (accessed 8 December 2011).

Yang, Jiemian (2013). 'Zhong guo wai jiao li lun chuang xin de san chong li shi shi ming' [The Trio Historic Missions in the Innovation of China's Diplomatic Theory]. *Global Review*, (1): pp. 1–11.

Yang, Yuan (2012). 'Zhongguo guojiguanxi lilun yanjiu (2008–2011)' [IR Theories Studies in China (2008–2011)]. *Quarterly Journal of International Politics*, 2: 66–110.

Yao, Xiaoou (2009). *The Translation and Interpretation of Book of Changes (II)*. Beijing: The Contemporary World Press.

Yasunori, Arano (1987). *Nihongata chitsujo hana ebisu no keisei [The Formation of Japanese 'Hua-Yi' Order]*. Tokyo: Iwanami Shoten.

Yasunori, Arano (1988). *Kinsei no nihon to higashi ajia [Japan and East Asia in the Modern Time]*. Tokyo: University of Tokyo Press.

Ye, Zicheng (1998). *Diyuan zhengzhi yu Zhongguo waijiao [Geopolitics and Chinese Diplomacy]*. Bejing: Beijing Publishing House.

Ye, Zicheng (2003). *Chunqiu zhanguo shiqi de zhongguo waijiao sixiang [China's Diplomatic Thought during the Spring Autumn, and Warring States Periods]*. Hong Kong: Hong Kong Social Science Press.

Ye, Zicheng (2005). 'Guoji guanxi yanjiu zhong de zhongguo shiye' [On China's Perspective in International Studies]. *Foreign Affairs Review*, 3: 64–71.

Yu, Changsen (2000). 'Shilun chaogong zhidu de yanbian' [On the Evolution of the Tributary System]. *Southeast Asian Affairs*, 1: 55–65.

Yu, Chi-wei and Simon Tengchi Chang (2011). 'Zhongguo de feizhou zhengce: ruan quanli yu chaogong tixi de fenxi' [China's African Policy: Aspects from Soft Power and the Tribute System]. *Prospect Quarterly*, 12(4): 111–156.

Yu, Jianrong (2006). 'Hu Jintao de shehuizhuyi hexie shehui jianshe sixiang' [Hu Jintao's Ideas on Constructing a Harmonious Society]. *Journal of Yunnan Provincial Committee of the CPC*, 2: 26–28.

Yu, Keping (2008). 'Zhongguo tese shehuizhuyi de shijie lishi yiyi' [The Meaning of Socialism with Chinese Characteristics for World History]. *Renmin Luntan*, 28: 16–19.

Yu, Xintian (2008). 'Ruanshili jianshe yu Zhongguo dui wai zhanlüe' [Soft Power Building and China's Foreign Strategy]. *International Studies*, 2: 15–20.

Yu, Zhengliang (2005). 'Xuyan' [Introduction]. In: Guo Shuyong (ed.). *Guoji guanxi: huhuan zhongguo lilun [International Relations: Inviting a Chinese Theory]*. Tianjin: Tianjin People's Publishing House, pp. 121–132.

Yu, Zhengliang and Chen Yugang (1999). 'Zhongguo guoji guanxi de zhanlue zhuanxing yu lilun yanjiu ershi nian' [Strategic Transformation and Twenty Years' Theories Studies of IR in China]. *Journal of Fudan University*, 1: 12–17.

Yuan, Ming (1992) (ed.). *Kua shiji de tiaozhan: Zhongguo guoji guanxi xueke de fazhan [The Challenge of Transcentury: the Development of IR in China]*. Chongqing: Chongqing Chubanshe.

256 Bibliography

Yuan, Zhengqing (2003). 'Explaining and Understanding Are Both Important in Chinese Studies of International Relations'. *World Economic and Politics*. 3.

Yuzo, Mizoguchi (1999). *Zuowei fangfa de zhongguo [China as Method]* (Lin Chong-yo trans.). Taipei: National Translation and Compilation Center.

Zakaria, Fareed (2009). *Ho Meiguo Shijie [The Post-American World]* (Zhao Guangcheng and Lin Minwang trans.). Beijing: Citic Press.

Zhai, Xuewei (2013). *Renqing, mianzi and quanli de zai shengchan [Human Sympathy, Face and the Reproduction of Power]*. Beijing: Peking University Press.

Zhang, Chun, Yu Hongyuan, Zhang Jian and Zhou Shixin (2014). 'Haina Baichuan, Baorong Gongsheng De "Shanghai Xuepai"' [Inclusive and Symbiotic "Shanghai School" of IR Theory]. *Global Review*, 6: 1–17.

Zhang, Feng (2009). 'Rethinking the "Tribute System": Broadening the Conceptual Horizon of Historical East Asian Politics'. *Chinese Journal of International Politics*, 2(4): 545–574.

Zhang, Feng (2012). 'The Tsinghua Approach and the Inception of Chinese Theories of International Relations'. *Chinese Journal of International Politics*, 5(1): 73–102.

Zhang, Feng (2013). 'The Rise of Chinese Exceptionalism in International Relations'. *European Journal of International Relations*, 19(2): 305–328.

Zhang, Feng (2014). 'International Societies in Premodern East Asia: A Preliminary Framework'. In: Barry Buzan and Yonjin Zhang (eds). *International Society and the Contest Over East Asia*. Cambridge: Cambridge University Press, pp. 29–50.

Zhang, Feng (2015). *Chinese Hegemony: Grand Strategy and International Institutions in East Asian History*. Stanford: Stanford University Press.

Zhang, Jianxin (2009). 'Xifang guoji guanxi lilun fanshi de zhongjie yu "Zhongguo xuepai" chengzhang de kunhuo' [The End of the Western IR Theory Paradigm and the Growing Puzzle of the Chinese School]. *International Review*, 5: 9–16.

Zhang, Qianming (2009). *Yingguo xuepai de guoji shehui lilun [International Society Theory of the English School]*. Beijing: China Social Science Press.

Zhang, Shuguang (2007). 'Lengzhan guoji shi yu guoji guanxi lilun de lianjie – goujian zhongguo guoji guanxi yanjiu tixi de lujing tantao' [Reconciling International Relations Theory with Cold War International History: A Possible Direction for Chinese IR Research]. *World Economics and Politics*, 2: 9–16.

Zhang, Weiwei (2012). *The China Wave: The Rise of a Civilizational State*. Hackensack, NJ: World Century Publishing Cooperation.

Zhang, Wenxiu (ed.) (1995). *The Record of Rites*. Beijing: Yanshan Publishing House.

Zhang, Xiaoming (2006). 'Zhongguo yu zhoubian guojia guanxi de lishi yanbian, moshi yu guocheng' [History, Model and Process of the Relations between China and its Neighbours]. *International Politics Quarterly*, 1: 57–71.

Zhang, Xiaoming (2008). 'Yingguo xuepai haishi yinggelan xuepai' [A Discussion on the Chinese Translation of 'English School']. *World Economics and Politics*, 5: 80–82.

Zhang, Xiao-ming (2011). 'China in the Conception of International Society: the English School's Engagements with China'. *Review of International Studies*, 37(2): 763–786.

Zhang, Yancheng and Dong Shouzhi (eds) (2010). *The Record of Rites*, Chinese edition. Beijing: Jindun Publishing House.

Zhang, Yongjin (1998). *China in International Society since 1949: Alienation and Beyond*. Basingstoke: Palgrave Macmillan.

Zhang, Yongjin (2002). 'Review: International Relations Theory in China Today: The State of the Field'. *China Journal*, 47: 101–108.

Zhang, Yongjin (2003). 'The "English School" in China: A Travelogue of Ideas and their Diffusion'. *European Journal of International Relations*, 9: 87–114.

Zhang, Yongjin (2007). 'Politics, Culture, and Scholarly Responsibility in China: Toward a Culturally Sensitive Analytical Approach'. *Asian Perspective*, 31: 103–124.

Zhang, Yongjin (2011). 'System, Empire and State in Chinese International Relations'. In: Michael Cox, Tim Dunne and Ken Booth (eds.). *Empires, Systems and States: Great Transformations in International Politics*. Cambridge: Cambridge University Press, pp. 43–63.

Zhang, Yongjin (2014a). 'The Global Diffusion of the English School'. In: Cornelia Navari and Daniel Green (eds). *Guide to the English School in International Studies*. Chichester: John Wiley and Sons, pp. 223–240.

Zhang, Yongjin (2014b). 'The Idea of Order in Ancient Chinese Political Thought: A Wightian Exploration'. *International Affairs*, 90(1), 167–183.

Zhang, Yongjin (2015a). 'The "International Turn" in the Chinese and Trans-Atlantic IR – Toward Global Renaissance in the History of International Thought'. Paper presented at the International Workshop on *Is Korean International Relations Theory Possible and Desirable?* Korea, Seoul: Korea University, 3 July 2015.

Zhang, Yongjin (2015b). 'China and the Struggle for Legitimacy of a Rising Power', Chinese Journal of International Politics, 8(3): 301–322.

Zhang, Yongjin and Barry Buzan (2012). 'The Tributary System as International Society in Theory and Practice'. *Chinese Journal of International Politics*, 5(1): 3–36.

Zhang, Yongle (2010). 'The Future of the Past: On Wang Hui's Rise of Modern Chinese Thought'. *New Left Review*, 62: 57.

Zhao, Kejin and Ni Shixiong (2007). *Zhongguo guoji guanxi lilun yanjiu [IR Theory Research in China]*. Shanghai: Fudan University Press.

Zhao, Tingyang (2003). 'Tianxia tixi: diguo yu shijie zhidu' [Tianxia: Empire and World Institutions]. *World Philosophy*, 5: 2–33.

Zhao, Tingyang (2005). *Tianxia Tixi: Shijie Zhidu Zhexue Taolun [The Tianxia System: A Philosophy of World Institutions]*. Nanjing: Jiangsu Education Publishing House.

Zhao, Tingyang (2006). 'Rethinking Empire from a Chinese Concept "All-Under-Heaven" (Tian-xia)'. *Social Identities*, 12(1): 29–41.

Zhao, Tingyang (2007a). 'Xunzi de chushi zhuangtai lilun' [Xunzi's Theory of Original State]. *Social Science Front*, 5: 9–11.

Zhao, Tingyang (2007b). 'Chongtu, hezuo yu hexie de boyi zhexue' [The Philosophy Game of Conflict, Cooperation, and Harmony]. *World Economics and Politics*, 6: 6–16.

Zhao, Tingyang (2009a). 'Cong guojia, guoji dao shijie: Sanzhong zhengzhide wenti bianhua' [From States, the International to World: Changes of Three Kinds of Political Problems]. *Philosophical Researches*, 1: 89–95.

Zhao, Tingyang (2009b). 'Gongzai cunzailun: Renji yu xinji' [Ontology of Coexistence: Relations and Hearts]. *Philosophical Researches*, 8: 22–30.

Zhao, Tingyang (2009c). 'A Political World Philosophy in Terms of All-under-Heaven (Tian-Xia)'. *Diogenes*, 56(1): 5–18.

Zhao, Tingyang (2009d). *Huai shi jie yan jiu zuo wei di yi zhe xue de zheng zhi zhe xue [Investigations of the Bad World: Political Philosophy as the First Philosophy]*. Beijing: Renmin Daxue Chubanshe.

Zhao, Tingyang (2010). 'Tianxia tixi de xiandai qishi' [Modern Enlightenment of the Tianxia System. *Wenhua Zongheng* [Cultural Review], (3): 34–41.

Zhao, Tingyang (2011). *The Tianxia System – An Introduction to the Philosophy of World Institution.* Beijing: Renmin University Press.

Bibliography

Zheng, Bijian (2003). 'A New Path for China's Peaceful Rise and the Future of Asia'. In: *China's Peaceful Rise: Speeches of Zheng Bijian 1997–2005*. Washington, DC: Brookings, pp. 14–20.

Zheng, Yongnian (2011). 'Bian jiang di yuan zheng zhi he zhong guo de guo ji guan xi yan jiu' [Frontiers, Geopolitics and China's IR Research]. *Foreign Affairs Review*, 6: 12–20.

Zheng, Yongnian (2012). *Tongwang daguo zhilu: Zhongguo de zhishi chongjian he wenming fuxing [The Road to the Great Power: the Reconstruction of Knowledge and Revival of Civilization in China]*. Beijing: Renmin Dongfang Chuban Chuanmei Youxian Gongsi.

Zhou, Fangyin (2006). 'Methodological Contentions in Chinese IR'. In: Wang and Yuan (eds). *Zhongguo guoji guanxi yanjiu (1995–2005) [IR Studies in China (1995–2005)]*. Beijing: Peking University Press, pp. 426–458.

Zhou, Fangyin (2008). 'Tianxia tixi shi zui hao de shijie zhidu ma?' [Is the Tianxia the Best World Order?]. *Quarterly Journal of International Politics*, 4(2): 98–104.

Zhou, Fangyin (2010). 'Wars of Attrition and the Timing of Peace Settlements'. *Chinese Journal of International Politics*, 3: 79–123.

Zhou, Fangyin (2011a). 'Chaogong tizhi de junheng fenxi' [An Analysis of Equilibrium on the Tribute System]. *Quarterly Journal of International Politics*, 2011(25): 29–58.

Zhou, Fangyin (2011b). 'Equilibrium Analysis of the Tributary System'. *Chinese Journal of International Politics*, 4(2): 147–178.

Zhou, Fangyin (2012). 'Songsan Dengji Tixixia Hefaxing Jueqi: Chunqiu Shiqi "Zunwang" Zhengba Celue Fenxi' [Legitimate Rise under a Loose Hierarchical System: An Analysis of the Vassals 'Zunwang' Strategy during the Spring and Autumn Period]. *World Economics and Politics*, 6: 4–34.

Zhou, Fangyin and Li Yuangjing (2014). 'Shili, Guannian Yu Buduichen Guanxi De Wendingxing: Yi Mingqing Shiqi De Zhongchao Guanxi Weili' [Power, Values and the Stability of Asymmetric Relationships: China-Korea Relations in the Ming-Qing Period]. *Journal of Contemporary Asia-Pacific Studies*, 4: 29–54.

Zhou, Xiaochuan (2009). 'Reforming the International Monetary System'. *BIS Quarterly Review*, December 2009. Online, available at: www.bis.org/review/r090402c.pdf (accessed 10 October 2012).

Zhu, Feng (2003). 'Guoji guanxi lilun zai Zhongguo de fazhan: wenti yu sikao' [The Development of the Theory of International Relations in China: Problems and Reflections]. *World Economics and Politics*, 3: 23–25.

Zhu, Feng (2009). 'Zhongguo tese de guoji guanxi yu waijiao lilun yanjiu' [International Relations and Diplomacy Studies with Chinese Characteristics]. *Journal of International Studies*, 2009(2): 1–14.

Zhu, Liqun and Nie Wenjuan (2010). 'Guo ji guan xi li lun yan jiu de shi jian zhuan xiang' [A Practice Turn in IR Theoretical Research]. *World Economy and Politics*, 8: 98–115.

Zi, Zhongyun (1998). 'Guoji zhengzhi lilun tansuo zai zhongguo'. [The Exploration of International Political Theories in China]. *International Economic Review*, 6: 41–44.

Zou, Lei (2011). 'Zhongguo Jueqi Yujingxia de Xianqin Guojiajian Zhengzhi Sixiang Yanjiu' [Research on Pre-Qin Theories of Interstate Relations and the Narrative of a Rising China]. *Quarterly Journal of International Politics*, 4: 130–142.

Index

Acharya, Amitav 2, 7, 52, 70, 91, 103, 149, 159, 203, 209, 218
Acharya–Buzan dichotomy 70–1, 86, 91, 103
Agnew, John 212
Al Qaeda 188
Alagappa, Muthiah 104, 157, 201
All-under-Heaven 25–6, 55, 61–2, 77, 90, 92–3, 125, 133, 179, 189, 207–8; *see also Tianxia*
American behaviorism 42
American IR 37, 38, 40, 77, 115, 123, 140, 143, 145, 150, 156, 160, 199, 203, 216, 217; appropriation of 6, 8; Chinese translation of 58, 99, 199; dominance of 10, 128, 139, 201; international of 6; theories 66, 77, 83, 86, 123, 144, 147, 151, 158, 200; and the Tsinghua Approach 149
American Political Science Association (APSA) 44
Asian capitalism 31
Asian democracy 218
Asian Infrastructure Investment Bank 76
Asian Values 218
Association of Southeast Asian Nations (ASEAN) 185, 191n4
atheism 55

Balance of Power (BoP) 12, 20, 88, 108, 134, 177–8; *versus* Balance of Relationship (BoR) 181–4; bilateral relationship 186–7; strategy of 181
Balance of Relationship (BoR) 12, 87–8, 108, 177–8; *versus* Balance of Power (BoP) 181–4; bilateral relationships 186–7; conceptualizing 178–9; goals of 181; idea of 181; international order maintained under 186; principles of 187; strategy of 182; as a system *versus* BoR as a Chinese School of IR 189–91; theoretical propositions of 187–9
balance of threat 12, 88, 178
Beijing Consensus 94
blood kinship 179
Brasília School 154–6
BRICS countries 76, 110
British Committee on the Theory of International Politics 38, 117–20, 123, 126–7
Buddha, Lord 55, 66, 160
Buddhism 56–7, 65
Bull, Hedley 117, 120, 123, 128, 131, 132, 135, 151; and international society theory 69
Burawoy, Michael 216
Buzan, Barry 52, 70

Cao, Cao 22, 27
Chang, Chi-hsiung 90; *Chinese World Order* 90, 92–3
China Academic Journals database 100, 112n11
China Institute of Contemporary International Relations (CICIR) 8, 196
China Institute of International Studies (CIIS) 8, 119
China Model 94, 100, 103, 130
China National Association for International Studies 119
China, rise of 68, 160; "charm offensive" 84; great power diplomacy 91; and influence in regional economic governance 76; military and economic power 220; neo-colonialism 84; policy challenges and 200; positioning in international politics 102; resolution for a peaceful rise 77; status as the world's second largest economy 110

Index

China, rise of: anxieties about 1–2; as a core problematique for Chinese IR 11, 70, 77–8, 80, 82–5, 96, 213, 219; and theoretical innovation of Chinese IR 2–3, 11–13, 213

China's identity: as "Asia's Sickman" 75; the century of humiliation 75; cultural Chineseness 82; development of 57–8; ethnic Chineseness 82; as a leading Third World nation 91; three interchangeable great-power (GP) identities 92

China's 'second revolution' (1978) 5

Chinese Academy of Social Sciences (CASS) 3, 36, 195, 207

Chinese Association for the Studies of History of IR 195

Chinese cultural heritage 4, 202

Chinese culture: and abstractive IR theory 56–7; development of 56–7; pragmatic moderation of 59–60; traditional 55–6; and Western IR theories 60–5; *versus* Western thinking 59–60

Chinese empire 102; collapse of 129

Chinese exceptionalism 10, 13, 216, 218–19

Chinese foreign policy 98–9, 105, 201; cost-benefit calculations 109–10, 206; Five Principles of Peaceful Coexistence 108; theoretical-philosophical narrative of 107

Chinese history 90, 105, 130, 141, 170, 173, 220; ancient 137, 173, 205, 207, 208, 214, 217; and Chinese IR 81, 88, 95, 115, 121, 124, 125, 129, 136, 137, interpretation of 208

Chinese International Relations (IR) 1; Americanization of 58–9; before 1979 7–9; colonization of 6; construction of 4; disciplinary growth of 5, 6, 7, 11, 13, 35, 192, 194, 197, 201, 215; evolution of 193; legitimation, politics of 4; Marxist influence of 4, 59, 73, 76, 91, 92, 97n9, 99–101, 104, 111, 112n13, 116, 123, 124, 125, 128–9, 145–7, 148, 180, 193, 197, 202, 217; methodological debate in 35, 39–43, 85–8, 91, 148–9, 174–5, 198, 200; path dependence development of 58–9; reforms in 1979 3; stages of 193; teaching curricula and syllabi for studies on 7–8; theoretical innovation in 2, 4–6, 12, 13, 36, 43, 46, 47, 50, 72, 125, 133, 172, 175, 192, 198, 201–6, 208–9, 211, 213, 215–17, 222; traditional Chinese thinking on 59–60; *see also* Western IR theories

Chinese IR theory: action oriented theory 11, 69–70, 203; archaeological excavations 101–3; Chinese writings on 104; classic Confucianism and 179–81; core problematique for 77–8, 87; cultural explanations of 55–60; development and growth of 43; dream of 65–6; functional dimensions of 103–6; 'ideology-driven' concept of 53; innovation for the twenty-first century 99–100; knowledge oriented theory 11, 69–70, 71, 77–80, 203; the making of master research narratives 200; original IR theory 73; path dependence development and 58–9; and political action 106–9; practice and the search for 73–7; Qin's theorization of relationality in 88; reformulation of 100, 105; revival of 120; the rise of, 2–7, 11; science and research traditions, philosophy of 99–103; self-consciousness of 44; stages of 91; theoretical innovation of 202; Tsinghua Approach of 137

Chinese Journal of International Politics (CJIP) 86, 142n1, 148–9, 150, 204

'Chinese Mind, Western Techs,' idea of 57

Chinese philosophers 48, 148, 204–5, 206; 'battle of ideas' 204; Pre-Qin 42, 47, 149, 163, 166

Chinese political philosophy 103; Pre-Qin 99, 205, 217; Spring and Autumn period (770–476 BC) 50, 86, 101, 132, 137, 149, 163, 170, 173, 175; Warring States period (475–221 BC) 50, 79, 101, 129, 132, 136, 149, 170

Chinese School of IR 2–3, 17, 70, 115, 136, 192; aims and intentions of 128–30; and "American social science" 144–50; among European schools 150–3; as an intellectual project, 9–10, 13, 53, 150, 152, 157, 160, 210–12, 216–17; challenges faced by 51; Chinese identity and 57–8; Chinese theorists on 17, 31, 92, 118–19, 198, 216; comparisons with English school *see* Chinese *versus* English school of IR; construction of 5, 7, 9–11, 35, 37, 76, 92; context of 123–5; debates at home and abroad on 43–5; development of 89; difference from dominant theoretical traditions and approaches 215–16; dualism in 219–20; emergence of 44, 45, 68, 82; ethical appeals of international studies 93; evolution of 82, 211; exceptionalism 218–19; great power conceit 221–2; importance of 212–15; intellectual discontents of 218–22; intellectual hazards of 216–18; intellectual resources and constraints 91–4; and IR theorizing in other rising powers 153–60; labelling and naming 35–9, 120–2; methodological debate 39–43; methodology/ontology, question of 86–91; ongoing debates 9–14; origins, founders and organization of 118–19; prospects of 45–50, 94–6; scientific research method, procedures of 41; search for central problematiques 83–5; suggestions 94–6; theoretical sources of 132–4; as traveling theory 160–1 (*see also* IR with Chinese characteristics); Tsinghua Approach Chinese universities 5, 7, 119, 196

Chinese *versus* English school of IR 116–38; aims and intentions of 126–30; context 122–5; historical projects 134–8; naming 120–2; origins, founders and organization 117–19; theoretical sources 131–4

Chinese World Order 90, 92–3

Chinese–East Asian relations, in ancient times 169–72

Christian monotheism 55

civilizational state, notion of 102

clash of civilizations 35, 58, 105, 145, 146, 155, 200

Cold War 158; end of 179; failings of US policy intellectuals during 217; ontology 88

Collins, Randall 202, 215

Communist Party of China (CPC) 81, 100, 195

Confucian ethics, sensitivity of 204

Confucian governance 25, 30

Confucian idealism 63

Confucian relationalism, reinventing 179, 205–6

Confucian state: modernization (Westernization) of 18; self-restraint in 182

Confucianism 12, 17, 33n25, 56, 57, 64, 99, 177, 183; China's return to 108; and Chinese IR 179–81; *Li* (rites), concept of 62, 163; and post-Western IR 189; pragmatic attitude of 59; and relational security 182; *Ren* (benevolence), concept of 62, 163; significance of, in post-hegemonic IR 179

Copenhagen School 116, 144, 151–2, 174, 215

cosmopolitanism: ancient 60; Chinese 60–2, 220; modern 60; as strategy of world domination 60; Western 61–2

cost–benefit calculation 109–10, 206

Cox, Robert 11, 53, 76, 81, 82, 122, 146, 147

cultural exceptionalism 218–19

Cultural Revolution 3, 5, 94, 145, 195–6

cultural superiority, concept of 55

daguo 101, 109

Dao De Jing 59, 63, 133

Daoism 17, 25, 28, 33n25, 56, 57, 62, 63, 65, 163; dialectics of 31; ethics of 63

Database of Journal Articles of Chinese IRT (1996–2014) 82

Datongshu 102–3

Daxue (The Great Learning) 25

Deng, Xiaoping 31, 59, 74, 100, 195

Deng, Zhenglai 197

Dougherty, James 73

dualism, in Chinese culture 219–20

East Asia 89, 95; relation with China 169–72

English School of IR 10, 19, 39, 43, 68, 77, 83, 87, 90, 115–16, 129, 135, 144, 150–2, 156, 174, 188, 200, 217; aims and intentions of 126–8; as an alternative to mainstream IR theories 139; beginning of 117; comparison with Chinese school *see* Chinese *versus* English school of IR; context of 122–3; criticisms of 140; diffusion of 199, 200; as a Euro-centric approach 200; historical projects 134–6; international society, idea of 117, 131, 138, 140; lessons for Chinese IR 38, 138–40; naming of 120; origins, founders and organization of 117–18; and national approaches to IR theory 12, 139; as role model 215; 'standard of civilization' 136, 138, 140; theoretical sources of 131–2

Enlightenment 28

ethical idealism 62–4

Euro-centrism, of rationalist IR theory 50, 125, 165–6

European Concert 179

European Journal of International Relations 2

262 Index

Fairbank, John K. 84, 136, 194
Falklands war (1982) 188
Ford Foundation 58, 118, 119

Gang of Four 81
Giddens, Anthony 87
global financial crisis (2007–2008) 110, 111n8
global financial governance 110
global financial system 110
Global Go To Think Tanks Index Report (2013) 3, 8
global IR 3, 6–9, 14, 31, 37–9, 46–7, 86, 91, 115, 122–3, 134, 143, 150, 158–60, 193, 218
global liberalism, rules of 189
"*gong sheng*" (symbiosis) theory 49–50
Guanxi (relationship), Chinese concept of 87, 124, 130, 137, 181

Han dynasty 18, 22, 137
harmony: Chinese concept of 47, 64–5; Western concept of 64–5
Hegelian dialectics 206
hegemonic power 20–1, 37, 49, 68, 77, 155, 167, 186
hegemony (*baquan*), principle of 135, 205
History of the Peloponnesian War (431 BCE) 19, 46
Hobbes, Thomas 18–19, 21
Hoffmann, Stanley 144, 146, 153, 158, 201, 202, 217
Huan, Xiang 83
Huang, Chi-lian 89, 137
human morality, understanding of 206
human rights 76, 78, 131; Asian 218
humane authority (*wangquan*) 205; exercise of 205; "Humane Authority, Hegemon and Strong State," concept of 173
Humane Governance (*Wangzhi*) 163–4
Humanities and Social Science Foundation of China (HSSF) 119
Hundred Years' War 18

Ikenberry, G. John 93, 168
Indian School of IR 158–9
Institute of World Economics and Politics, China 195
intellectual decolonization 157
inter-personal relations 79
International Monetary Fund (IMF) 166, 194
international order, hierarchy of 205
International Relations (IR): Acharya–Buzan dichotomy on 70–1; and another kind of world-making 24–5; Chinese story 70–3; concept of 17; democratization of 100; features of 18; global 31; Hobbesian–Westphalian legacy 31; *Leviathan* in 18–19; Neorealist 20–1, 30; post-colonial assessments of 101; principle of 177; and relational approach to international rules 184–7; *Sanguo Yanyi* and *tianxia* 21–4; school of thought on 43; social actions and practices 72; subject–object relationship 208; theorization of 202, 205; theory and practice of 70–3; Western-paradigm 56
international society, idea of 95, 117, 126, 140; English School's 117, 131, 140
International Studies Association (ISA) 44, 118
interstate system, concept of 137
interstate relations, pre-Qin thought on 163–9
IR with Chinese characteristics 36, 39, 53–4, 83, 86, 91, 94, 98, 118, 110, 120, 121, 125, 129, 143, 151, 160, 175, 193, 202, 203, 215
Iroquois League (1450–1777) 28

Jackson, Robert 123, 126
Jones, Roy 120

Kang, Youwei 7, 102, 111n7
Kant, Immanuel 60–1, 107, 131, 134; perpetual peace, factors for 60–1, 207
Katzenstein, Peter 93
Ken, Booth 200
Keohane, Robert O. 73, 145, 198
Keynes, John Maynard 49
knowledge production: geopolitics of 1, 5, 7, 13–14, 47, 54, 69, 130, 153, 192, 199–200, 202–3, 208–10, 213, 215–17, 221–2
Krasner, Stephen 139
Kupchan, Charles 168

Lao, Tzu 60
Laozi 25, 207; *see also* Daoism, Lao Tzu
"leaning toward one side" strategy 69
Legalism 33, 92, 106, 108, 112, 163; School of 179–80
Leviathan (Hobbes) 219; *versus Sanguo* 26–31
Li (rites), concept of 163, 169
Li Ji (Book of Rites) 63, 111n7
Liang, Qichao 7, 57; and global China 57–8, 66

Lin, Zexu 7
Liu, Bei 22–3
Lockean rivalry 21–2

MacArthur Foundation 148
Mandate of Heaven 205
manifest destiny 55
Mao, Zedong 59, 99–100, 104; and "three world" theory 69
Marshall, Alfred 49
Marxism 57, 59, 99–100, 116, 122–4, 146–8
Marxist humanism 195
Marxist-Leninist teachings 91
May 4th Movement 57
mean, the doctrine of 60, 79, 220
medicines, Chinese *versus* Western 40
"Melian Dialogue, The" 19
meta-relations, Chinese dialectics of 206
Ming dynasty 59, 106; maritime expeditions of 108
modern China 7, 57–8, 148
Morgenthau, Hans 73, 145, 154, 168, 207

nation state, concept of 60–2, 66, 71–2, 89–90, 93–4, 102, 147, 174, 177–8, 190–1
National Social Science Foundation (NSSF), China 119
NATO 166
New Development Bank, China 76
Newton, Isaac 43
Non-Western IR theories 2, 50, 52, 83, 91, no purposive engagement with 2;
Nü Wa 55
Nuclear Non-proliferation regime 127
Nye, Joseph S. 73, 93, 198; *Power and Interdependence* 145

Opium War 148; cultural consequences of 57; first (1840–1842) 7, 57, 202; second (1858–1860) 7, 57; "unequal treaties", abolition of 103

Pan Gu 55
peaceful rise: idea of 3–6, 11, 77, 94, 99, 101, 105, 109, 111n4, 130, 143, 147, 155, 160, 200, 213, 219
Pfaltzgraff, Robert 73
polytheism 55
Popper, Karl 131, 201
Pouliot, Vincent 69, 72
power politics, laws of 19–20, 22–3, 29, 58, 108, 122, 130, 219

Pye, Lucian 187

Qin, Yaqing 41, 44, 53, 69, 71–3, 76–7, 85, 87, 121, 123–4, 130, 198, 205–6, 214; diplomacy of Li Hongzhang 92; effort in constructing knowledge oriented theory 79; theorization of relationality in IR 88
Qing dynasty 57, 90, 137–8

raison de système 122–3, 138
relational governance 206
relationality 46, 79, 181, 205, 215; Chinese notion of 79, 206; inter- 25, 27; theorization of 88;
Ren (benevolence), concept of 163, 169
Rockefeller Foundation 118, 119

Said, Edward 161
Sanguo Yanyi (*Romance of the Three Kingdoms*) 21–4, 219; comparison with *Leviathan* 26–31; Confucian–Daoist legacy 26
Schmitt, Carl 61
Schumpeter, Joseph 11
science and research traditions, philosophy of 99–103
scientific behaviorialism 42
self-defence, right of 108
self-restraint, notion of 180, 182, 187
Shang dynasty 61
Shanghai Cooperation Organization 76
Shanghai School 50, 175
Silk Road 137
Sima, Yi 23, 26–7
Sino–Japanese War (1894–1895) 57
Sino–Soviet conflict 81
Sino–US relations 171, 172
Snyder, Jack 44, 149, 217
social norms: understanding of 206
social science 94, 195; 'colonial expenses' of 201
social symbiosis 49; *see also* "*gong sheng*"
soft power 75, 93, 110, 182, 185
Son of Heaven 25, 61, 189; *see also tian zi*
sovereign nation state: China's status as 103; Westphalian concept of 102
Spivak, Gayatri Chakravorty 216
Spring and Autumn period 86, 101, 132, 137, 149, 163, 171–5; and the golden age of Chinese philosophy 50; the international hierarchy of, 171; the "Zunwang" strategy of, 171; *see also* Warring States period

standard of civilization 136, 138, 140
Sun, Yat-Sen 7

tabula rasa 145
Taiwan, policies towards China: Balance of Relations Theory (BoR) 87; IRT scholars on 87; ROC's changing role and practice 92; scientific approach 81; traditional approach 81
Takashi, Inoguchi 77
Tang, Shiping 4, 54, 94, 125, 175
Theory of International Politics (1979) 5
Third World nation 91, 136
Thirty Years' War 18
"three world" theory 69
tian zi (the Son of Heaven) 61
tianxia 3, 7, 25–6, 61–2, 102, 107, 125, 133; Chinese cosmopolitanism and 62; concept of 61, 70, 77, 79, 207; dualism in 219; reinterpretation of 213; revival of 219; *Sanguo Yanyi* and 21–4; Zhao's explanation of 207–8, 219–20; *Tianxia Tixi* (The System of All-under-Heaven) 207
traditional China 57–8
trans-Atlantic IR: Chinese intellectual engagement with 192; diffusion of 199, 209; influence in China 194, 197–8; power of existing 203; theoretical hegemony of 199
tributary systems 78, 89–90, 92, 137, 148, 170, 218; as *tianxia* 61
Tsinghua Approach 50, 86, 93, 116, 124–5, 130, 133, 137, 141, 148, 175, 204, 219; characteristics of 162; outstanding problems and potential directions 172–4; strategy of 149; Yan Xuetong and; 162–76, 204–6; *see also* Chinese School of IR
tyranny (*qiangquan*) 101, 205

"unequal treaties", abolition of 103
United Nations 127; Security Council 166
United States: 9–11 terrorist attacks 188; bilateral relationship 186; rebalancing in Asia 186
US dollar, replacement of 110

Vietnam 21, 96, 108, 137, 177

Wæver, Ole 139, 198, 201
Waltz, Kenneth N. 5, 19–20, 55, 69, 73, 94, 149
Wang, Jisi 93–4, 104–5
Wang, Yangming 59
Wang, Yizhou 94, 121, 125, 145, 193, 200
wangdao (moral leadership), concept of 101, 109, 220
War of Resistance 92
Warring States period 50, 79, 101, 129, 132 136, 170; anarchic as post-Medieval Europe, 136; the "Zunwang" strategy of, 170;
Watson, Adam 117, 122, 134–5
weapons of massive destruction 177, 189
Wendt, Alexander 21–2, 72, 145
Western IR theories 4, 6, 11, 45, 52, 80, 83, 99–100, 121, 137, 159, 200, 202; application and adaptation of, 74; Chinese culture and 60–5; as culturally Western, 130; dominance of 74, 76; hypotheses of 59; intellectual hegemony of 6, 10, 128; introduction into China, 73, 74, 128; as theoretical resources for Chinese School of IR, 132; transplanting in China, 36; universality claim of 10, 66, 148; *see also* American IR theories; trans-Atlantic IR
Westphalia: conflict with Chinese *tianxia* 7; international society 134; patriarchy 30; system 86, 90, 93, 102, 219; Treaty of 18; visions for world order 20–1
Wight, Martin 38, 52, 117, 120, 131, 134, 151
World Bank 48, 127, 166, 194
world citizenship, rights of 61
world order, "Chinese" and "Western" views on 108
world politics: constructions of 106; rivalry in 22
World Trade Organization (WTO) 127, 166
World War II 37, 49, 128, 153
Wright, Quincy 8

Xi, Jinping 25, 88
'*xue yi zhi yong*' (learn to do), principle of 59

Yan, Xuetong 40–1, 43, 54, 79, 89, 101, 121, 124, 133, 162, 168–9, 173, 204–5, 214; research on pre-Qin interstate relations 162; Tsinghua Approach *see* Tsinghua Approach
Yi (justice), concept of 169
Yi Jing (Book of Change) 205
yin/yang dialectics 25–6

Zhang, Zhidong 57
Zhao, Tingyang 54, 61, 78–9, 90, 102, 133, 213–14; All-under-Heaven system 90, 92; reinterpretation of *tianxia* 207–8, 213, 219–20
Zheng, Bijian 111n4
Zheng, He 55
'*zhi xing he yi*' (unity of knowledge and practice), principle of 59

zhi zhonghe 60
Zhongguo (Middle Kingdom) 25
ZhongHe (moderation), concept of 64
Zhongyong culture 25, 72–3
Zhou dynasty 61–2, 79, 170
Zhou, Xiaochuan 110
Zhuge, Liang 23–4
"Zunwang Rangyi" strategy 171

Helping you to choose the right eBooks for your Library

Add Routledge titles to your library's digital collection today. Taylor and Francis ebooks contains over 50,000 titles in the Humanities, Social Sciences, Behavioural Sciences, Built Environment and Law.

Choose from a range of subject packages or create your own!

Benefits for you
- Free MARC records
- COUNTER-compliant usage statistics
- Flexible purchase and pricing options
- All titles DRM-free.

REQUEST YOUR FREE INSTITUTIONAL TRIAL TODAY

Free Trials Available
We offer free trials to qualifying academic, corporate and government customers.

Benefits for your user
- Off-site, anytime access via Athens or referring URL
- Print or copy pages or chapters
- Full content search
- Bookmark, highlight and annotate text
- Access to thousands of pages of quality research at the click of a button.

eCollections – Choose from over 30 subject eCollections, including:

Archaeology	Language Learning
Architecture	Law
Asian Studies	Literature
Business & Management	Media & Communication
Classical Studies	Middle East Studies
Construction	Music
Creative & Media Arts	Philosophy
Criminology & Criminal Justice	Planning
Economics	Politics
Education	Psychology & Mental Health
Energy	Religion
Engineering	Security
English Language & Linguistics	Social Work
Environment & Sustainability	Sociology
Geography	Sport
Health Studies	Theatre & Performance
History	Tourism, Hospitality & Events

For more information, pricing enquiries or to order a free trial, please contact your local sales team:
www.tandfebooks.com/page/sales

 | The home of Routledge books

www.tandfebooks.com